CATHOLICA

1987

CATHOLICA

THE WORLD
CATHOLIC
YEARBOOK
1987

Edited by
ELIO GUERRIERO

With a Preface by
JOSEPH CARDINAL RATZINGER

IGNATIUS PRESS   SAN FRANCISCO

Title of the Italian original:
Catholica: Annuario della Parola
e della Vita della Chiesa
© 1987 by Jaca Book, Milan

Cover by Roxanne Mei Lum

© 1988 Ignatius Press, San Francisco
All rights reserved
ISBN 0-89870-176-7 (SB)
ISBN 0-89870-179-1 (HB)
ISSN 0896-5994
Printed in the United States of America

CONTENTS

PREFACE

"Where Christ is, there is the Catholic Church." This conviction, witnessed to at the beginning of the second century by St. Ignatius of Antioch, has been restored to the consciousness of Christians with great clarity in the Second Vatican Council. The baptized, united with their bishop, constitute a particular church that is not only a part or section of the universal Church, but is the same universal Church in its local dimension. It is within the universal Church in its entirety. The particular church fully brings to realization the universal Church, but in a specific way. As the entire episcopate is within each bishop, in the same way, the entire Church is within each local church. Between these two there is a reciprocal interiority, best expressed in the term "catholic", which relates the idea of an organic whole. Whatever its spatial extension and its internal differentiation may be, the people of God is essentially oriented to one center which guarantees its unity: the presence of Christ.

The Church is raised up by Christ; that is, it is formed by the sacrament and therefore is itself a sacrament. The Eucharist, as the presence of Christ and as his sacrament, builds up the Church, which therefore is present wherever he is, wherever the Eucharist is celebrated adequately. Just as Christ is never only partially present but is present in all of his reality, so also the Church, where he is, is present in its totality. The local churches, therefore, are the Church in a complete sense, and are not merely limited portions cut out from the great body of the Church.

The discovery that Christ is present only in the totality of his reality leads to another insight: Christ is one and is present in the unity (oneness) of believers. The unity of the universal Church is, in this sense, an essential element of the local church, just as the multiplicity and the specific meaning of the local churches belong to the essence of this ecclesial unity.

The Church, in so far as it is local, is called to incarnate, in its own reality and according to its particular circumstances, the presence of Christ. It is in the particular circumstances of life that the mystery of the Word must be made flesh. Each bishop, by means of his

Translated from Italian by Mark Nemetz.

participation in the episcopal college, exercises a "widespread re-sponsibility" (H. de Lubac) regarding the universal Church. This responsibility is exercised in union with the successor of Peter, the bishop of Rome, whose singular prerogative consists in the unique task of bringing about, in space and time, the "form of unity" among those who are the successors of the apostles. In this way, the local church is constantly stimulated by the bishop to fully conciliate itself with the universal Church, the latter therefore becoming perceptible and efficacious in the former. In this double movement, which can be described as centrifugal and centripetal, the life of the Church is verified, and its catholicity is manifested.

The fact that the Holy Spirit is at the source of the self-realization of the Church is also manifested by a recurring phenomenon in the history of the Church, a phenomenon which is especially evident in this period after the Second Vatican Council: the spontaneous flowering of testimonies, of a multitude of initiatives and, above all, of renewal movements in the life of the Church. One of the great hopeful signs of the times in the universal Church—and this comes about in the heart of the crisis of the Church in the Western world—is the birth of movements. No one planned or projected their existence, but they flow spontaneously from the interior vitality of the faith itself. Some-thing like a season of Pentecost is manifested in them.

Certainly, these new associations are the occasion of some prob-lems; at times they bring about dangers and tensions within the already structured life of the local churches. This, however, comes about with every vital reality. What should be noted is that in every case the intense life of faith within these movements is fully catholic, and is therefore not an isolation from the life of the Church. In these movements the reference to the center, to Peter, guarantees an apos-tolic action which is capable of giving a new dynamic to the proclaim-ing of the gospel in this period of history, similar to ecclesial move-ments in former times, such as the great mendicant orders of the thirteenth century. Thus, even within the fruitful dialectic of "event" (charism) and "institution", the universal Church as such can become perceptible and efficacious in a new way; this occurs within the particular local churches and witnesses to their catholicity.

The term "catholic" appears to be very close to another concept coined by the early Church to express its understanding of that synthesis between unity and multiplicity which is realized within the ecclesial community: the concept of "symphony". This term desig-nates the unity of Christians among themselves, the form of unity proper to the Church. This unity is not a homophony, but is one which mirrors that formal structure of the expression of the truth on which unity is based. The foundation for unity cannot be an empirical fact, but is rather this symphony which is the Church, which is united by a non-empirical reality—the Holy Spirit. The goal of faith is not merely that unity of men living in society but is also a greater unity which is proper to man: his communion with the Divine. The unity of man with God, which actuates at the same time the unity among men, the unity with all of creation and, therefore, the unity of creation with the Creator: this is designated by the term "symphony".

If the interior unity of the particular church is a gift of the Spirit, then it does not consist in that mechanical or stereotyped uniformity which is used to guarantee the functioning of a monolithic organization or of a bureaucratic apparatus. This unity is, rather, a consonance in the Spirit of a multitude of gifts, given to the Church for its mission and for the life of the world.

Through the daring and interesting initiative of Elio Guerriero and of the publisher Jaca Book, *Catholica* has become today the name of a "Yearbook of the word and life of the Church": an echo of its "symphony". In this publication resounds, in a unique and varied melody, the voice of the Pope, bishop of the Church of Rome which presides in charity, as well as the voices of the particular churches, of their pastors, and of many witnesses who animate and stimulate the daily life of the Church. This is a year of "good" music, collected for the edification of the people of God. It is rich, multiform, yet, in some way also, incomplete. In fact, this publication is an invitation to the reader, to individuals, to families, to communities, in order that they might enter into the concert, to play their own pieces in the harmony. Thus, *Catholica* not only seeks to give the good music of ecclesiastical life, but is an invitation to compose good music, to help inspire others to participate in the great "symphony".

Joseph Cardinal Ratzinger
Rome
Feast of St. Bonaventure

INTRODUCTION

The Word operates in life, and life in its turn is illuminated by the Word. For the Christian, this fundamental experience is founded on the very life of the Trinity. Jesus says in one of the most solemn passages of the Gospel: "If anyone loves me he will follow my Word, and my Father will love him: and we will come to him and we will live with him. He who does not love me does not observe my Word, and the Word that he hears is not mine but that of the Father who sent me" (Jn 14:23ff). The inexhaustible richness of the words of Jesus may be partially formulated in the following propositions: (1) The Word of Jesus comes from God; (2) the disciple must receive the Word; (3) the Father and the Son will come to live with those who receive the Word of Jesus.

The key to these affirmations is Jesus himself: he is the Word of the Father, and together with the Father he will remain with whoever receives his Word. The communion of love between the Father and the Son is enunciated ("I am in the Father and the Father is in me", Jn 14:11) and a communion of grace is promised with the dwelling of the Father and the Son among the disciples. The participation in the Trinitarian communion is not reserved in any case to the disciples as individuals but to the communion of the faithful, "in order that the world will realize that it was you who sent me and that you have loved them as much as you loved me" (Jn 17:23). The Trinitarian communion and the communion of the Church are profoundly intertwined. The community of the Church must reproduce and testify to "the love with which you have loved me".

If we now turn our gaze from the heart of John's theology to Paul, we come upon another principle of enormous importance for the Christian faith: "The gospel is divine power for the salvation of those who believe: first the Jews and then the Greeks" (Rom 1:16). This is the universal dimension, the Catholic dimension of the Christian faith through which "there is neither Jew nor Greek, neither slave nor free, neither man nor woman" (Gal 3:28). The universality of the offering of grace has for Paul its ultimate basis in the mystery of God such that the apostle, having been overcome with so great

Translated from Italian by Robert and Veronica Royal.

a love, exclaims with a spirit of recognition: "Oh, unfathomable abyss of the wisdom and of the knowledge of God" (Rom 11:33).

The love of God is extended, therefore, to the universe: catholicity is an essential dimension of Christian reality. The Church, which is both the location and means of the communion and the salvific will of God, reproduces their characteristics. We confess, in fact, in our profession of faith: "I believe in the Catholic Church", catholic in its aspiration and its correspondence to the universal salvific will of the Father. The ancient Christian Church, which was characterized by the recognition of the office of the successors of Peter, has in our century even in its geography further accentuated its universality. The Ecumenical Council, the synods of bishops, the bishops' conferences testify to the catholicity of the Church more and more every day. Also, in this very century, liturgical ecclesiastical research has emphasized another dimension, certainly not a contradictory one, but definitely complementary in the Church. I am speaking of the local dimension, of the anchoring of the Church in the concrete community, which, united around its bishop, is a living center of Christian life: "As the body of our Lord Jesus Christ is one, and the chalice that unites us in his blood is one, and the altar is one, so is the bishop surrounded by the college of priests and deacons, companions of the ministry, one", according to the expression of Ignatius of Antioch (Phil 4). Ignatius was the most ancient and venerated exponent of this ecclesial concept. On the other hand, the quotation from Saint Ignatius permits us to pay attention to another equally distinctive attribute of the Church: unity. The universal Church and the individual churches cannot proceed in parallel, as if ignoring one another; rather, they are held in unity, "because you all are one thing only in Christ", as the second part of Galatians 3:28 puts it. The universal Church and the particular churches are, therefore, two expressions, two moving centers, of the unique communion of the body of Christ and the life of the Son in the Father. Universal communion is not achieved except by means of the concrete communities; communion is not achieved if one of the individual communities, closing itself up within itself, places obstacles in the way of universal communion.

The World Catholic Yearbook: Catholica, 1987 wishes to be of service to this dynamic community of the word and of life, to permit the Father and the Son to come to dwell in every single believer in the whole Church. In addition to this fundamental consideration, two practical reflections have been decisive for the birth of this initiative:

1. *The richness of the life of the Church.* We have become so accustomed to submitting to the weight of negative events that we completely lose sight of the experience of the faithful and their dedication,

even though, in the abstract, we know that they exist. *The World Catholic Yearbook*, instead, would like to give a voice to the works of the faithful, to Christ and the gospel, and to a sincere ecumenism and promotion of Christian and human life.

2. *The richness of the word of the Church.* As successors of Peter, the Roman popes have always recognized the need to sustain their brothers and sisters with their words, while the bishops, successors of the apostles, have "the responsibility to proclaim the gospel to every part of the earth" (LG, 23). In our day, the word of the magisterium has taken on dimensions never before known. The Pope has multiplied his word; the bishops have done likewise, and at times they make themselves heard as a group (Episcopal Conferences). The results of this are multiplicity and variety of contributions and perspectives, but also a difficulty for the faithful in orienting themselves amid these frequent pronouncements.

From this difficulty arises this project, a yearly anthology of the words of the Pope and the bishops, followed by the testimonies of response and fidelity in the Catholic world. Naturally, the selection is always somewhat arbitrary. Nevertheless, the great value of the present work is that it allows Christian families as well as individual Christians to follow the route of the Church toward new worlds and new horizons.

The World Catholic Yearbook is divided into three parts. The first part, "The Words of the Pope", is divided into four sections: "Catechesis", "Messages to the World", "Gospel Pilgrimage", and "Encyclical Letter". Parts Two and Three, "The Words of the Bishops" and "The Life of the Church" are organized geographically. The result is a polyphony of a number of voices, some of which come from nearby, while others express needs different from our own. In every case, the reception of the word permits us, above all else, to remain in communion with the Church, the one Church. The testimonies place the accent on service toward humanity. The title of this speech by John Paul II for the World Day of Prayer at Assisi, one of the most significant events of this past year, expresses in an excellent way the intention of *The World Catholic Yearbook*: "We will seek to be peacemakers in thought and deed."

Elio Guerriero

PART ONE

THE WORDS OF THE POPE

I

CATECHESIS

THE PRESENCE OF EVIL AND SUFFERING IN THE WORLD

1. Let us take up again the text of the First Letter of St. Peter to which we referred at the end of the previous catechesis:

> Praised be the God and Father of our Lord Jesus Christ, he who in his great mercy gave us new birth; a birth unto hope which draws its life from the resurrection of Jesus Christ from the dead; a birth to an imperishable inheritance, incapable of fading or defilement, which is kept in heaven for you (1 Pet 1:3–4).

Further on the same Apostle has an enlightening and consoling statement:

"In this *you rejoice, though now for a little while you may have to suffer various trials,* so that the genuineness of your faith, more precious than gold which though perishable is tested by fire . . ." (1 Pet 1:6–7).

From this text one can argue that the revealed truth about "predestination" in Christ of the created world and especially of man (*praedestinatio in Christo*), constitutes the principal and indispensable foundation of the reflections we intend to propose on the theme of the relation between Divine Providence and the reality of *evil* and *suffering* present under so many forms in human life.

2. For many this is the principal *difficulty in accepting the truth about Divine Providence.* In some cases this difficulty assumes a radical form when one even *accuses God* because of the evil and suffering in the world, even reaching the point of rejecting the truth itself about God and his existence (that is, atheism). In a less radical form, but nonetheless disturbing, this difficulty is expressed in the numerous *critical questions* that man asks about God. The doubt, the query or even the contestation arises from the difficulty of *reconciling* the truth about Divine Providence, of God's pastoral solicitude for the created world, with the reality of evil and suffering experienced by people in different ways.

We can say that the vision of the reality of evil and suffering is *present* in all its *fullness in the pages of Sacred Scripture.* It can be said that the Bible is, above all, a great book about *suffering.* This enters fully within the scope of the things which God wished to say to humanity, "in varied ways . . . through the prophets, but in these last days . . . through his Son" (cf. Heb 1:1). *It enters in the context*

The Bible: the great book on suffering

General Audience, June 4, 1986. Reprinted from *L'Osservatore Romano,* June 9, 1986.

of God's self-revelation *and in the context of the Gospel,* or the *Good News of salvation.* For this reason the only adequate method to find a response to the question about evil and suffering in the world is to seek it in the context of the revelation offered by the Word of God.

Evil Is Multiform

3. But first of all we must be quite clear about evil and suffering. *In itself it is multiform.* Generally one distinguishes evil in the *physical* sense from that in the *moral* sense. Moral evil is distinguished from physical evil, first of all by the fact that it implies guilt, because it depends on man's free will, and it is always an evil of a spiritual nature. It is distinguished from physical evil, because the latter does not necessarily and directly include *man's will,* even though this does not mean that it cannot be caused by man or result from his fault. Physical evil caused by man, at times through ignorance or lack of prudence, at times *by neglecting* the opportune precautions or even by inappropriate and harmful *actions,* appears in many forms. But it must be added that there are many cases of physical evil in the world which happen independently of man. Suffice it to mention, for example, natural disasters or calamities, and also all the forms of physical disability or of bodily or psychological diseases *for which man is not blameworthy.*

Man's suffering

4. *Suffering is engendered in man by the experience of these multiple forms of evil.* In some ways it can be found also in animals inasmuch as they are endowed with senses and the relative sensitivity, but in man suffering reaches the dimension proper to the spiritual faculties he possesses. It can be said that in man suffering is interiorized, intimately known, and experienced in the whole dimension of his being and of his capacities of action and reaction, of receptivity and rejection. It is a terrible experience, before which, especially when without guilt, *man* brings forward those difficult, tormenting, and at times dramatic *questions,* which constitute sometimes a complaint, sometimes a challenge, sometimes a cry of rejection of God and his providence. They are questions and problems which can be summed up thus: *how can evil and suffering be reconciled* with that *paternal solicitude,* full of love, which Jesus Christ attributes to God in the Gospel? How are they to be reconciled with the transcendent wisdom and omnipotence of the Creator? And in a still more dialectical form: in the presence of all the experience of evil in the world, especially when confronted with the suffering of the innocent, can we say that God does not will evil? And if he wills it, how can we believe that "God is love"? All the more so since this love cannot be but omnipotent?

5. Faced with these questions we too, like Job, feel how difficult

it is to give an answer. Let us seek it not in ourselves, but with humility and confidence in the Word of God. Already in the Old Testament we find the striking and significant statement: "against Wisdom evil does not prevail. She reaches mightily from one end of the earth to the other, and she orders all things well" (Wis 7:30; 8:1). In the presence of the multiform experience of evil and suffering in the world, the Old Testament already bears witness to the primacy of Wisdom and of the goodness of God, and to his Divine Providence. This attitude is outlined and developed in the Book of Job, which is completely dedicated to the theme of evil and suffering seen as a sometimes tremendous trial for the just man, but overcome by the certainty, laboriously acquired, that God is good.

From this text we become aware of the limit and transience of created things, so that *certain forms of physical "evil"* (due to the lack or limitation of the good) belong *to the very structure* of created beings, which by their nature are contingent and passing, and therefore *corruptible*. Besides we know that material beings are in a close relation of interdependence as expressed by the old saying: "the death of one is the life of another" (*corruptio unius est generatio alterius*). So then, in a certain sense death serves life. This law refers also to man inasmuch as he is at the same time an animal and spiritual being, mortal and immortal. In this regard, however, St. Paul's words open up much wider horizons: "Though *our outer nature is wasting away, our inner nature is being renewed* every day" (2 Cor 4:17). And again: "For this slight momentary affliction is preparing us for an eternal weight of glory beyond all comparison" (2 Cor 4:17).

Death as a service to life

6. The assurance of Sacred Scripture: "Against wisdom evil does not prevail" (Wis 7:30), strengthens our conviction that in the Creator's providential plan in regard to the world, *evil in the last analysis is subordinated to good*. Moreover, in the context of the integral truth about Divine Providence, one is helped to understand better the two statements: "God does not will evil as such" and "God permits evil." In regard to the first it is opportune to recall the words of the Book of Wisdom: ". . . God did not make death, and he does not delight in the death of the living. For he created all things that they may exist" (Wis 1:13–14). As regards the permission of evil *in the physical order,* e.g., in face of the fact that material beings (among them also the human body) are corruptible and undergo death, it must be said that that belongs to the very structure of the being of these creatures. On the other hand, in the present state of the material world, it would be difficult to think of the unlimited existence of every individual corporeal being. We can therefore understand that, if "God did not make death", as the Book of Wisdom states, he nonetheless permitted it in view of the *overall good of the material cosmos*.

7. In the case of moral evil, however, that is, of sin and guilt in their different forms and consequences also in the physical order, *this evil decisively and absolutely is not willed by God*. Moral evil is radically contrary to God's will. If in the history of man and of the world this evil is present and at times overwhelming, if in a certain sense it has its own history, it is *only permitted by Divine Providence* because God wills that there should be freedom in the created world. The existence of created freedom (and therefore the existence of man, the existence also of pure spirits such as the angels, of whom we shall speak later), is indispensable for that fullness of creation which corresponds to God's eternal plan (as we already said in a previous catechesis). By reason of that fullness of good which God wills to be realized in creation, the existence of free beings *is for him a more important and fundamental value* than the fact that those beings may abuse their freedom against the Creator, and that freedom can therefore lead to moral evil.

The presence of evil and man's freedom

Undoubtedly it is a great light we receive from *reason* and *revelation* in regard to the mystery of Divine Providence which, while not willing the evil, tolerates it in view of a greater good. However, the definitive light can come to us only from the victorious Cross of Christ. To that we shall devote our attention in the following catechesis.

CHRIST'S VICTORY CONQUERS EVIL

1. Our catecheses on God, the Creator of the things "that are unseen", have brought fresh light and strength to our faith concerning the truth about the evil one, or Satan; he is certainly not willed by God, who is supreme Love and Holiness, and whose wise and strong Providence knows how to guide our existence to victory over the prince of darkness. The Church's faith, in fact, teaches us that *the power of Satan is not infinite*. He is only a creature—powerful, in that he is pure spirit, but nevertheless always a creature, with the limits proper to creatures, subordinated to the will and dominion of God. If Satan is at work in the world because of his hatred of God and of his Kingdom, this is *permitted by Divine Providence* which directs the history of man and of the world with power and goodness (*fortiter et suaviter*). It is *certainly* true that Satan's action *causes much damage,* both of a spiritual kind and also indirectly of a material kind, to individuals and to society, but *he is not able* ultimately *to neutralize the definitive end* towards which man and all creation tend: the Good.

The truth about the Evil One, or Satan

General Audience, August 20, 1986. Reprinted from *L'Osservatore Romano*, August 25, 1986.

He cannot block the construction of the Kingdom of God, in which at the end there will be the full realization of the righteousness and the love of the Father for the creatures who are eternally "predestined" in Jesus Christ, his Son and Word. Indeed, we can say with St. Paul that the work of the evil one cooperates for the good (cf. Rom 8:28) and that it helps to build up the glory of the "chosen" ones (cf. 2 Tim 2:10).

Total Salvation

2. Thus, the whole history of humanity can be considered as serving total salvation which means *the victory of Christ over the "prince of this world"* (Jn 12:31; 14:30; 16:11). "You shall bow down only before the Lord your God, you shall adore him alone" (Lk 4:8), says Christ eternally to Satan. At a dramatic moment of his ministry, when he was openly accused of casting out demons because of his alliance with Beelzebub, the chief of the demons, Jesus replied with these *words* that are at once *severe and comforting:* "Every kingdom that is divided falls into ruins, and no city or family that is divided can stand upright. Now if Satan drives out Satan, than he is divided in himself. How then can his kingdom stand upright? . . . And if it is by the power of the Spirit of God that I cast out the demons, then it is certain that the Kingdom of God has come among you" (Mt 12:25–26, 28). "When a strong man, well armed, guards his palace, all his goods are secure. But if one stronger than he comes and overpowers him, he takes away the armor in which he trusted, and divides his spoils" (Lk 11:21–22). The words which Christ speaks about the tempter find their historical fulfillment *in the cross and resurrection of the Redeemer.* As we read in the Letter to the Hebrews, Christ became a sharer in human nature even to the cross *"in order to reduce to powerlessness, by means of death,* the one who has the power over death, that is, the devil . . . and thus to free those who . . . were held in slavery" (Heb 2:14–15). This is the great certainty of the Christian faith: "the prince of this world *has been judged"* (Jn 16:11); "the Son of God has appeared, *in order to destroy the works of the devil"* (1 Jn 3:8), as St. John bears witness. It is therefore the crucified and risen *Christ* who has revealed himself as that "stronger one" who has overpowered "the strong man", the devil, and has cast him down from his throne.

Jesus vanquishes Satan

The Church shares in Christ's victory over the devil, for Christ has given to his disciples the power to cast out demons (cf. Mt 10:1 and parallels; Mk 16:17). The Church uses this victorious power through faith in Christ and prayer (cf. Mk 9:29; Mt 17:19ff.), which in particular cases can take the form of exorcism.

3. It is to this historical phase of the victory of Christ that the announcement and the beginning of the final victory, *the Parousia*, belongs: this is the second and definitive coming of Christ at the close of history, and it is towards this that the life of the Christian is oriented. Even if it is true that earthly history continues to unfold under the influence of "that spirit who now is at work in rebellious men", as St. Paul says (Eph 2:2), believers know that they have been called to struggle for *the definitive triumph of the Good:* "for our battle is not against creatures made of blood and of flesh, but against the Principalities and Powers, against those who hold dominion over this world of darkness, against the spirits of evil that dwell in the heavenly places" (Eph 6:12).

Definitive Victory

4. As the end of the struggle gradually draws nearer, it becomes *in a certain sense ever more violent,* as Revelation, the last book of the New Testament, shows in a special emphasis (cf. Rev 12:7–9). But it is precisely this book that emphasizes the certainty that is given to us by all of divine Revelation, that the struggle *will finish* with the definitive *victory of the good.* In this victory, which is contained in anticipation in the paschal mystery of Christ, there will be the definitive fulfillment of the first *announcement in the Book of Genesis,* which is significantly called the *Proto-Evangelium,* when God admonishes the serpent: "I will put enmity between you and the woman" (Gen 3:15). In this definitive phase, God will complete the mystery of his fatherly Providence and "will set free from the powers of darkness" those whom he has eternally "predestined in Christ" and will "bring them over into the kingdom of his beloved Son" (cf. Col 1:13–14). Then the Son will subject even the whole universe to the Father, so that "God may be all in all" (1 Cor 15:28).

In the second coming there will be the definitive triumph of good

5. Here we finish the catecheses on God as the Creator of "the things that are visible and invisible", which are united, in our structuring of the catecheses, with the truth about Divine Providence. It is obvious to the eyes of the believer that *the mystery of the beginning* of the world and of history is joined indissolubly *to the mystery of the end,* in which the finality of all that has been created reaches its fulfillment. The creed, which unites so many truths in such an organic manner, is truly the harmonious cathedral of the faith.

In a progressive and organic way, we have been able to admire, struck dumb with wonder, the great mystery of the intelligence and love of God, in his *action of creation,* directed to the cosmos, to the human person, and to the world of pure spirits. We have considered the Trinitarian origin of this action and its wise orientation towards the life of man who is truly the "image of God", called in his turn to rediscover fully his own dignity in the contemplation of the glory of God. We have been enlightened about one of the greatest problems that perturb man and characterize his search for truth: *the problem of suffering and of evil*. At the root, there is no mistaken or wicked decision by God, but rather his choice—and in a certain manner the risk he has undertaken—of creating us free, in order to have us as friends. Evil too has been born of liberty. But God does not give up, and he predestines us with his transcendent wisdom to be his children in Christ, directing all with strength and sweetness, so that the good may not be overcome by evil.

We must now let ourselves be guided by Divine Revelation in our exploration of the other mysteries of our salvation. We have now received a truth which must be profoundly important for every Christian: that there are *pure spirits,* creatures of God, initially all good and then, through a choice of sin, irreducibly separated into angels of light and angels of darkness. And while the existence of the wicked angels requires of us that we be watchful so as not to yield to their empty promises, we are certain that the victorious power of Christ the Redeemer enfolds our lives, so that we ourselves may overcome these spirits. In this, we are powerfully helped by the good angels, *The good* messengers of God's love, to whom, *taught by the tradition of the* *angels* *Church,* we address our prayer: "Angel of God, who are my guardian, enlighten, guard, govern and guide me, who have been entrusted to you by the heavenly goodness. Amen."

ORIGINAL SIN CAUSES A FUNDAMENTAL CHANGE IN MANKIND

1. In the context of creation and of the bestowal of gifts by which God constitutes man in the state of holiness and of original justice *the description of the first sin,* which we find *in the third chapter of Genesis,* acquires a greater clarity. It is obvious that this description which hinges on the transgression of the divine command not to eat "of *The trans-* the fruit of the tree of the knowledge of good and evil", is to be *gression of the* interpreted by taking into account the character of the ancient text *divine command* and especially its literary form. However, while bearing in mind this scientific requirement in the study of the first book of Sacred Scripture, it cannot be denied that one sure element emerges from the detailed account of the sin: that it describes a primordial event, that is, *a fact,* which according to Revelation took place *at the beginning of*

General Audience, September 10, 1986. Reprinted from *L'Osservatore Romano,* September 15, 1986.

human history. For this very reason it presents as well another certain element, namely, the fundamental and decisive implication of that event for man's relationship with God, and consequently for the interior "situation" of man himself, for the reciprocal relationships between people, and in general for man's relationship with the world.

2. The fact underlying the descriptive forms that really matters is of a moral nature and is imprinted in the very roots of the human spirit. It gives rise to a fundamental change in the human condition. Man is driven forth from the state of original justice and finds himself in *a state of sinfulness (status naturae lapsae)*. It is a state in which sin exists and it is marked by an inclination to sin. From that moment the whole history of humanity will be burdened by this state. In fact the first human being (man and woman) received sanctifying grace from God *not only for himself,* but as founder of the human family, *for all his descendants.* Therefore through sin which set man in conflict with God, he forfeited grace (he fell into disgrace) even in regard to the inheritance for his descendants. According to the Church's teaching based on Revelation, the essence of original sin as the heritage of our progenitors consists in this privation of grace added to nature.

Essential Problems

3. We shall understand better the nature of this inheritance by analyzing the account of the first sin as contained in the third chapter of Genesis. It begins with the *conversation* between the tempter, presented under the form of a serpent, *and the woman.* This is something completely new. Until then the Book of Genesis had not spoken of the existence in the created world of other intelligent and free beings, apart from the man and the woman. The description of creation in chapters 1 and 2 of Genesis concerns, in fact, the world of "visible beings". The tempter belongs to the world of "*invisible* beings", purely spiritual, even though for the duration of this conversation he is presented by the Bible under a visible form. One must consider *The appearance of the evil spirit* this first appearance *of the evil spirit* in the Bible in the context of all that we find on this subject in the books of the Old and New Testaments. (We have already done so in the previous catecheses.) Particularly eloquent is the Book of Revelation (the last of Sacred Scripture) according to which "*the great dragon* was thrown down upon the earth, *that ancient serpent* (this is an explicit reference to Genesis 3), who is called the *Devil and Satan,* the deceiver of the whole world" (Rev 12:9). Because he "deceives the whole world" he is also called elsewhere "the father of lies" (Jn 8:44).

4. The human sin at the beginning of history, the primordial sin, of which we read in Genesis 3, occurred under the influence of this

being. The "ancient serpent" tempts the woman: "Did God say 'You shall not eat of any tree of the garden'?" She replies: "We may eat of the fruit of the trees of the garden; but God said, 'You shall not eat of the fruit of the tree which is in the midst of the garden, neither shall you touch it, lest you die'." But the serpent said to the woman: "You shall not die. For God knows that when you eat of it your eyes will be opened, and you will be like God, knowing good and evil" (Gen 3:1–5).

5. It is not difficult to discern in this text the essential problems of human life hidden under an apparently simple form. To eat or not to eat the fruit of a certain tree may itself seem irrelevant. However, the tree "of the knowledge of good and evil" denotes the first principle of human life to which is linked *a fundamental problem*. The tempter knows this very well, for he says: "When you eat of it . . . you will be like God, knowing good and evil." *The tree therefore signifies the insurmountable limit* for man and for any creature, however perfect. The creature, in fact, is always *merely a creature, and not God.* Certainly he cannot claim to be "like God", to "know good and evil" like God. God alone is the source of all being, God alone is absolute Truth and Goodness, according to which good and evil are measured and from which they receive their distinction. God alone is the eternal Legislator, from whom every law in the created world derives, and in particular the law of human nature (*lex naturae*). Man, as a *rational creature,* knows this law and should let himself be guided by it in his own conduct. He himself *cannot* pretend to establish the moral law, *to decide himself what is good and what is bad, independently of the Creator, even against the Creator.* Neither man nor any other creature can set himself in the place of God, claiming for himself the mastery of the moral order, contrary to creation's own ontological constitution which is reflected in the psychological–ethical sphere by the fundamental imperatives of conscience and therefore of human conduct.

6. In the account of Genesis, in the guise of an apparently irrelevant plot, we find man's fundamental problem linked to his very condition as a creature. Man as a rational being should let himself be guided by the "First Truth", which is moreover the truth of his very existence. Man cannot claim to substitute himself for this truth or to place himself on a par with it. If this principle is called into question, the foundation of the "justice" of the creature in regard to the Creator is shaken to the roots of human action. In fact the tempter, "the father of lies", by insinuating doubt on the truth of the relationship with God, calls in question the state of original justice. In yielding to the tempter, man commits a personal sin and causes in human nature the state of original sin.

Man must let himself be guided by the First Truth

7. As we see from the biblical account, human sin does not have its primary origin in the heart (and in the conscience) of man; it does not arise from his spontaneous initiative. It is *in a certain sense the reflection* and the consequence of the sin that had already occurred in the world of invisible beings. It is to this world that the tempter, "the ancient serpent", belongs. Already previously (*in antico*) these beings endowed with knowledge and freedom had been "put to the test" so that they could make their choice commensurate with their purely spiritual nature. In them arose the "doubt" which, as recounted in the third chapter of Genesis, the tempter insinuates in our first parents. Already they had placed in a state of suspicion and accusation God who as Creator, is the sole source of the good granted to all creatures and especially to spiritual creatures. They had contested the truth of existence, which demands the total subordination of the creature to the Creator. This truth was supplanted by an original pride, which led them to make their own spirit the principle and rule of freedom. They were the first who had claimed the power "to

Choose to be with God and not against him

know good and evil like God", and they had chosen themselves over God, instead of choosing themselves "in God", according to the demands of their existence as creatures: for "who is as God"? And man, by yielding to the suggestion of the tempter, became the slave and accomplice of the rebellious spirits!

8. The words which, according to Genesis 3, the first man hears beside the "tree of the knowledge of good and evil" contain *all the assault of evil* that can arise in the free will of the creature in regard to him who, as Creator, is the source of all being and of all good: he who, being absolutely disinterested and authentically paternal Love, is in his very essence the Will to give! This very gift of Love meets with objection, contradiction and *rejection*. The creature who wishes to be "like God" is a concrete realization of the attitude expressed very appositely by St. Augustine: "love of self to the point of contempt of God" (cf. *De civitate Dei*, XIV, 28; PL 41, 436). This is perhaps the most penetrating explanation possible of the concept of that sin at the beginning of history, which occurred through man's yielding to the devil's suggestion: *contemptus Dei*, the rejection of God, contempt of God, hatred of everything connected with God or that comes from God.

Unfortunately it is not an isolated event at the dawn of history. How often is one confronted with facts, deeds, words, conditions of life, in which the legacy of that first sin is evident!

Genesis places that sin in relation to Satan, and this truth about the "ancient serpent" is later confirmed in many other passages of the Bible.

9. *How is man's sin presented against this background?* We read also in

Genesis 3. "So when the woman saw that the tree was good for food, and that it was a delight to the eyes, and that the tree was to be desired to make one wise, she took of its fruit and ate; and she also gave some to her husband, and he ate" (Gen 3:6).

What does this description, in its own way very detailed, reveal? It attests that the first man acted *against the will of the Creator,* under the influence of the tempter's assurance that "the fruits of this tree serve to acquire knowledge". It does not seem that man had fully accepted the totality of negation and hatred of God contained in the words of the "father of lies". Instead, he accepted the suggestion to avail himself of a created thing *contrary to the prohibition of the Creator,* thinking that he also—man—could be "like God, knowing good and evil".

According to St. Paul, man's first sin consists *especially in disobedience* to God (cf. Rom 5:19). The analysis of Genesis 3 and the reflection on this marvelously profound text show how that "disobedience" can come about and in what direction it can develop in man's will. It can be said that the sin "at the beginning" described in Genesis 3, *in a certain sense* contains *the original "model" of every sin* of which man is capable.

THE STATE OF MAN IS FALLEN NATURE

1. The profession of faith proclaimed by Paul VI in 1968 at the conclusion of the "Year of Faith", reproposes in its entirety the teachings of Sacred Scripture and Sacred Tradition on original sin. Let us listen to it once again:

"We believe that in Adam all have sinned, which means that the original offence committed by him caused human nature, common to all men, to fall to a state in which it bears the consequences of that offence, *and which is not the state in which it was at first in our first parents,* established as they were in holiness and justice, and in which man knew neither evil nor death. It is *human nature so fallen,* stripped of the grace that clothed it, injured in its own natural powers and subjected to the dominion of death, that is transmitted to all men, and it is in this sense that *every man is born in sin.* We therefore hold, with the Council of Trent, that original sin is transmitted with human nature 'not by imitation, but by propagation' and that it is thus 'proper to everyone'."

"We believe that Our Lord *Jesus Christ, by the Sacrifice of the Cross, redeemed us* from original sin and all the personal sins committed by

General Audience, October 8, 1986. Reprinted from *L'Osservatore Romano,* October 13, 1986.

each one of us, so that, in accordance with the word of the Apostle, 'where sin abounded, grace did more abound'."

Following that, the profession of faith, also known as the *Credo of the People of God,* goes back, like the Decree of the Council of Trent, to holy Baptism, and first of all *to that of infants:* "in order that, though born deprived of supernatural grace, they may be reborn 'of water and the Holy Spirit' to the divine life in Christ Jesus".

Light of Redemption

The doctrine on sin in close reference to the mystery of redemption

2. As is evident, this text also of Paul VI confirms that the whole of revealed doctrine on sin and in particular on original sin is always *closely connected with the mystery of redemption.* Let us seek to present it also in this way in these catecheses. *Otherwise it would not be possible to understand fully the reality of sin* in human history. St. Paul sets that out clearly in the Letter to the Romans to which the Council of Trent especially refers in the Decree on original sin.

Paul VI in the *Credo of the People of God,* reproposed in the light of Christ the Redeemer all the elements of the doctrine on original sin contained in the Tridentine Decree.

3. In regard to the sin of our first parents the *Credo of the People of God* speaks of "fallen human nature". For the proper understanding of this expression it is well to return to the description of the fall contained in Genesis, chapter three. In it is contained also God's punishment of Adam and Eve, under the anthropomorphic presentation of the divine interventions described in the Book of Genesis. According to the biblical narrative, after the sin the Lord says to the woman: "I will greatly multiply your pain in childbearing; in pain you shall bring forth children, yet your desire shall be for your husband, and he shall rule over you" (Gen 3:16).

"To the man (God) said: 'Because you have listened to the voice of your wife, and have eaten of the tree of which I commanded you, "You shall not eat of it", cursed is the ground because of you; in toil shall you eat of it all the days of your life; thorns and thistles it shall bring forth to you; and you shall eat the plants of the field. In the sweat of your brow you shall eat bread till you return to the ground, for out of it you were taken; *you are dust, and to dust you shall return*'" (Gen 3:17–19).

4. These strong and severe words refer to man's situation in the world as it appears in history. The biblical author does not hesitate to attribute it to God as a sentence of condemnation. It implies the "cursing of the ground": *visible creation has become rebellious and hostile for man.* St. Paul says that as a result of man's sin "creation was subjected to futility", and for this reason also "the whole creation

has been *groaning in travail* together until now" until it will be "set free from its bondage to decay" (cf. Rom 8:19–22).

This lack of balance of creation has its influence on the destiny of man in the visible world. The labor by means of which man acquires the means of sustenance is carried out "in the sweat of his face" and is linked *with toil*. The whole of human existence is characterized by toil and *suffering* and this begins already from birth, accompanied by the sufferings of the woman in labor, and of the child itself, even though unconscious of them, who wails and whimpers.

Created by God for Immortality

5. Finally, the whole of human existence on earth is subject *to the fear of death*, which according to Revelation is clearly connected with original sin. Sin itself is synonymous with spiritual death, because through sin man has lost sanctifying grace, the source of supernatural life. *The sign and consequence of original sin* is *bodily death*, such as it has been experienced since that time by all mankind. Man was created by God for immortality; death, which appears as a tragic leap in the dark, is the consequence of sin, as if by an immanent logic, but especially as the punishment of God. Such is the teaching of Revelation and such is the faith of the Church: without sin, the end of the earthly trial would not have been so dramatic.

Man was created by God also *for happiness*, which, in the context of earthly existence, should have meant being *free from many sufferings*, at least in the sense of a possibility of exemption from them: *posse non pati*, as also the exemption from death, in the sense of *posse non mori*. As can be seen from the words attributed to God by Genesis (Gen 3:16–19), and from many other texts of the Bible and Tradition, with original sin this *exemption ceased to be man's privilege*. His life on earth was subjected to many sufferings and to the necessity of death.

6. The *Credo of the People of God* teaches that human nature after original sin is no longer in the "state at which it was at first in our first parents". It is "fallen" (*lapsa*), since it *is deprived of sanctifying grace*, and also of *other gifts*, which in the state of original justice constituted the perfection (*integritas*) of this nature. Here we are dealing not only with immortality and exemption from many sufferings, gifts lost because of sin, but also with *interior dispositions of the reason and will*, that is, with habitual energies of the reason and will. As a consequence of original sin the whole man, body and soul, has been thrown into confusion: *secundum animam et corpus*, as the Council of Orange expressed it in 529, and this was echoed by the Tridentine Decree when it noted that man had undergone a change for the worse: *in deterius commutatum fuisse*.

7. As regards man's spiritual faculties this deterioration consists in a *darkening* of the *intellect's* capacity to know the truth, and in a *weakening of free will,* which is weakened in the presence of the attractions of the goods perceived by the senses and is more exposed to the false images of good elaborated by reason under the influence of the passions. However, according to the Church's teaching, it is a case of a *relative and not an absolute* deterioration, not intrinsic to the human faculties. Man, therefore, even after original sin, can know by his intellect the fundamental natural and religious truths, and the moral principles. He can also perform good works. One should therefore speak rather of a darkening of the intellect and of a weakening of the will, of "wounds" of the spiritual and sensitive faculties, and not of a loss of their essential capacities even in relation to the knowledge and love of God.

The Tridentine Decree emphasizes this truth of the fundamental soundness of nature against the contrary thesis maintained by Luther (and taken up later by the Jansenists). The Council of Trent teaches that man, as a result of Adam's sin *has not lost free will* (Can. 5: *Liberum arbitrium . . . non amissum et extinctum*). He can therefore perform acts which have an authentic moral value: good or evil. This is possible only by the freedom of the human will. Fallen man, however, without Christ's help, is incapable of directing himslf to the supernatural goods which constitute his full fulfillment and salvation.

8. In the condition in which nature finds itself after sin, and especially because man is more inclined to evil than to good, one speaks of a "spark of sin" (*fomes peccati*), from which human nature was free in the state of original perfection (*integritas*). This "spark of sin" is also called "concupiscence" (*concupiscentia*) by the Council of Trent, which adds that it continues also in man justified by Christ, therefore even after holy Baptism. The Tridentine Decree clearly states that "*concupiscence*" *in itself is not yet sin,* but "*it derives from sin and inclines*

Concupiscence as a consequence of sin

to sin" (cf. DS, 1515). Concupiscence, as a consequence of original sin, is the source of the inclination to various personal sins committed by men through the evil use of their faculties (these sins are called *actual,* to distinguish them from *original* sin). This inclination remains in man even after holy Baptism. In this sense everyone bears in himself the "spark" of sin.

9. Catholic doctrine defines and describes the state of fallen human nature (*natura lapsa*) in terms which we have explained on the basis of the data of Sacred Scripture and Tradition. It is clearly proposed in the Council of Trent and in the "Credo" of Paul VI. However, once again we note that, according to this doctrine based on Revelation, human nature is *not only "fallen", but also "redeemed"* in Jesus

Christ: so that "where sin increased, grace abounded all the more" (Rom 5:20). This is the real context in which original sin and its consequences must be considered.

THE PROTOEVANGELIUM OF SALVATION

1. In the fourth Eucharistic Prayer (Canon IV) the Church addresses God in the following words: "Father, we acknowledge your greatness: all your actions show your wisdom and love. *You formed man* in your own likeness and set him over the whole world to serve you, his creator, and to rule over all creatures. *Even when he disobeyed you and lost your friendship you did not abandon him to the power of death. . . .*"

In harmony with the truth expressed in this prayer of the Church, we noted in the previous catechesis the complex content of the words of Genesis 3, which contain God's response to man's first sin. That text speaks of the combat against "the powers of evil" in which mankind has been involved from the very beginning of human history. At the same time, however, there is the assurance that *God does not abandon man* to himself, he does not leave him "in the power of death", reduced to a "slave of sin" (cf. Rom 6:17). Accordingly, God tells the serpent who has tempted the woman: "I will make you enemies of each other: you and the woman, your offspring and her offspring. He will crush your head and you will strike his heel" (Gen 3:15).

2. These words of Genesis are called the "Protoevangelium", or the first announcement of the Messiah Redeemer. They reveal God's salvific plan in regard to the human race which after original sin is found in the fallen state which we know (*status naturae lapsae*). They indicate especially *the central event* in God's plan of salvation. It is that same event referred to in the fourth Eucharistic Prayer, already quoted, when we turn to God with this profession of faith: "Father, you so loved the world that in the fullness of time you sent *your only Son* to be our Savior. He was conceived through the power of the Holy Spirit, and born of the Virgin Mary, a man like us in all things but *sin.*"

Messianic Goal

3. The statement of Genesis 3 is called the "Protoevangelium" because it has received its confirmation and fulfillment only in the Revelation of the New Covenant which is the Gospel of Christ. *In*

General Audience, December 17, 1986. Reprinted from *L'Osservatore Romano,* December 22–29, 1986.

the Old Covenant this announcement was *constantly re-evoked* in different ways in the rites, symbolisms, prayers, prophecies, and in the very history of Israel as the "people of God" reaching out towards a messianic goal, but always under the veils of the imperfect and provisional faith of the Old Testament. When the announcement will be fulfilled in Christ there will be the full revelation of the messianic and trinitarian content implicit in the monotheism of Israel.

The New Testament unveils the full meaning of the Old Testament

The New Testament will then lead to the discovery of the full meaning of the writings of the Old Testament, according to the famous aphorism of St. Augustine: "In the Old Testament the New lies hidden, and in the New the Old lies open" (cf. *Quaestiones in Heptateuchum,* II, 73).

4. The analysis of the "protoevangelium" informs us, by means of the announcement and promise contained in it, that God has not abandoned the human race to the power of sin and death. He wished to rescue and save it. He did so in his own way, *according to the measure of his transcendent holiness,* and at the same time according to a self-effacement such as only a God of Love could display.

The very words of the "protoevangelium" express this *saving self-effacement* when they announce the struggle ("I will put enmity!") between him who represents "the powers of evil" and the Other whom Genesis calls "the offspring of the woman". *It is a struggle which will end with the victory of Christ!* ("he shall bruise your head"). However, this will be *the victory bought at the price of the sacrifice of the Cross* ("and you shall bruise his heel"). The mystery of iniquity is dispelled by the "mystery of mercy". In fact it is precisely the sacrifice of the Cross that helps us to penetrate into the very essence of sin, enabling us to understand something of its dark mystery. In a particular way St. Paul is our guide when he writes in the Letter to the Romans: " . . . as by one man's disobedience many were made sinners, *so by one man's obedience many will be made righteous*" (Rom 5:18). "As one man's act of righteousness leads to acquittal and life for all men" (Rom 5:18).

The first announcement of Christ is in the proto-evangelium

5. In the "protoevangelium", in a certain sense, *the Christ is announced* for the first time as "the new Adam" (cf. I Cor 15:45). Indeed, his victory over sin obtained through "obedience unto the death of the cross" (cf. Phil 2:8), will imply such an *abundance* of pardon and of saving grace as to overcome immeasurably the evil of the first sin and of all the sins of the human race. St. Paul again writes: "If many died through one man's trespass, *much more* have the grace of God and the free gift in the grace of that one man Jesus Christ abounded for many" (Rom 5:15).

Moreover, solely on the basis of the "protoevangelium", it can be deduced that in regard to the destiny of *fallen man (status naturae lapsae)* there is already *introduced the prospect of future redemption (status naturae redemptae).*

6. The first response of the Lord God to man's sin, contained in Genesis 3, provides us therefore from the very beginning with a knowledge of God as *infinitely just* and at the same time *infinitely merciful.* From that very first announcement he is manifested as that God who "so loved the world that he gave his only Son" (Jn 3:16); who "sent his *Son to be the expiation* for our sins" (1 Jn 4:10); who "did not spare his own Son but gave him up for us all" (Rom 8:32).

Thus we have the certainty that *God,* who in his transcendent holiness, *abhors sin, justly punishes* the sinner, but at the same time in his ineffable mercy he embraces him in his *saving love. The "protoevangelium" already announces this saving victory of good over evil, which will be manifested in the Gospel through the paschal mystery of Christ crucified and risen.*

7. It is to be noted that in the words of Genesis 3:15, "I will put enmity", *the woman is placed in the first place in a certain sense:* "I will put enmity between you and the woman." Not: *between you and the man,* but precisely *between you and the woman.* Commentators from the earliest times emphasize that we have here an important parallelism. The tempter—"the ancient serpent"—according to Genesis 3:4, first addressed the woman, and through her obtained his victory. In his turn the Lord God, in announcing the Redeemer, makes the Woman the first "enemy" of the prince of darkness. *She* should be, in a certain sense, the *first beneficiary* of the definitive *Covenant,* in which the powers of evil will be overcome by the Messiah, her Son ("her offspring").

Woman, the first beneficiary of the definitive covenant

8. This—I repeat—is an extremely significant detail, if we bear in mind that in the history of the Covenant God first of all addresses men (Noah, Abraham, Moses). In this case *the precedence appears to belong to the Woman,* naturally *in consideration of her Descendant, Christ.* In fact, very many Fathers and Doctors of the Church see in the Woman announced in the "protoevangelium" the Mother of Christ, Mary. She is also the one who first shares in that victory over sin won by Christ: she is, in fact, *free from original sin and from every other sin,* as emphasized by the Council of Trent in line with tradition (cf. DS, 1516; 1573), and as regards original sin in particular, Pius IX solemnly defined it by proclaiming the dogma of the Immaculate Conception (cf. DS, 2803).

"Not a few ancient Fathers", as the Second Vatican Council says (Const. LG, 56), in their preaching present Mary, the Mother of Christ, as the new Eve (just as Christ is the new Adam, according to St. Paul). Mary takes the place and is the opposite of *Eve,* who is "the mother of all the living" (Gen 3:20), but also the cause, along with Adam, of the universal fall into sin, while Mary is for all the "cause of salvation" by her obedience in cooperating with Christ in our redemption (cf. Irenaeus, *Adv. haereses*, II, 22, 4).

9. The Council makes a magnificent synthesis of this doctrine, but we shall now limit ourselves to quoting a text which can serve as the best seal on the catecheses on sin, which we have developed in the light of the ancient faith and hope in the advent of the Redeemer:

"The Father of mercies willed that the Incarnation should be preceded by assent on the part of the predestined mother, *so that just as a woman had a share in bringing about death, so also a woman should contribute to life.* This is pre-eminently true of the Mother of Jesus, who gave to the world the Life that renews all things. . . . It is no wonder then that it was customary for the Father to refer to the Mother of God as all holy and free from every stain of sin, as though fashioned by the Holy Spirit and formed as a new creature. Enriched from the first instant of her conception with the splendor of an entirely unique holiness, the virgin of Nazareth is hailed by the heralding angel, by divine command, as 'full of grace' (cf. Lk 1:28) and to the heavenly messenger she replies: 'Behold the handmaid of the Lord, be it done unto me according to thy word' (Lk 1:38). Thus the daughter of Adam, Mary, consenting to the word of God, became the Mother of Jesus. Committing herself whole-heartedly and impeded by no sin to God's saving will, she devoted herself totally, as a handmaid of the Lord, to the person and work of her Son, under and with him, serving the mystery of redemption, by the grace of Almighty God" (LG, 56).

Mary the all holy

Thus in Mary and through Mary there has been reversed the situation of humanity and of the world, which in some way have re-entered into the splendor of the morning of creation.

THE MYSTERY OF THE INCARNATION

1. In the previous meeting our reflection was concentrated on the name "Jesus" which means "Savior". This same Jesus who lived for thirty years at Nazareth in Galilee, is the eternal Son of God "conceived by the power of the Holy Spirit and born of the Virgin Mary". That is proclaimed by the Creeds of the Faith, the Apostles' Creed and the Nicene-Constantinopolitan Creed. It was taught by the Fathers of the Church and the Councils, according to which Jesus Christ, eternal Son of God, is *"born in the world of his mother's substance"* (Creed *Quicumque*, DS, 76). The Church then professes and

General Audience, January 28, 1987. Reprinted from *L'Osservatore Romano*, February 2, 1987.

proclaims that Jesus Christ was conceived and born of a daughter of Adam, a descendant of Abraham and of David, the Virgin Mary.

St. Luke's Gospel states that *Mary conceived the Son of God through the power of the Holy Spirit,* "not knowing man" (cf. Lk 1:34 and Mt 1:18, 24–25). Mary was therefore a *virgin* before the birth of Jesus, and she remained a virgin in giving birth and after the birth. That is the truth presented by the New Testament texts, and which was expressed both by the Fifth Ecumenical Council at Constantinople in 553, which speaks of Mary as *"ever virgin"*, and also by the Lateran Council in 649, which teaches that "the mother of God . . . Mary . . . conceived (her Son) through the power of the Holy Spirit without human intervention, and in giving birth to him her virginity remained incorrupted, and even after the birth her viginity remained intact" (DS, 503).

Mary conceived through the work of the Holy Spirit

Mary's Consent

2. This faith is presented *in the teaching of the Apostles.* We read, for example, in the Letter of St. Paul to the Galatians: "When the time had fully come, *God sent forth his Son,* born of woman . . . so that we might receive adoption as sons" (Gal 4:4–5). The events linked to the conception and birth of Jesus are contained in the first chapters of Matthew and Luke, generally called "the Infancy Gospel", and it is to them that reference must be made.

3. Particularly well known is Luke's text, because it is frequently read in the eucharistic liturgy and used in the prayer of the Angelus. The passage of Luke's Gospel describes *the annunciation to Mary,* which took place six months after the announcement of the future birth of John the Baptist (cf. Lk 1:5–25).

". . . The angel Gabriel was sent from God to a city of Galilee named Nazareth, to a virgin betrothed to a man whose name was Joseph, of the house of David; and the virgin's name was Mary" (Lk 1:26). The angel greeted her with the words: "Hail, Mary", which became the Church's prayer (the "angelic salutation"). Mary was disturbed by the angel's greeting: "She was greatly troubled at the saying, and considered in her mind what sort of greeting this might be. And the angel said to her, 'Do not be afraid, Mary, for you have found favor with God. And behold, *you will conceive in your womb and bear a son, and you shall call his name Jesus.* He will be great, and will be called the Son of the Most High' . . . Then Mary said to the angel: 'How can this be, *since I have no husband?'* And the angel said to her: 'The Holy Spirit will come upon you and the power of the Most High will overshadow you'; therefore the child to be born will be called holy, the Son of God'" (Lk 1:29–35). The angel, in making

The salutation of the angel

the announcement, presents as a "sign" the unhoped-for maternity of Elizabeth, a relative of Mary, who had conceived a son in her old age, and adds: *"With God nothing is impossible."* Then Mary said: "Behold, I am the handmaid of the Lord; *let it be done to me according to your word"* (Lk 1:37–38).

4. This text of Luke's Gospel is the basis for the Church's teaching on the motherhood and virginity of Mary, from whom was born Christ, made man by the power of the Spirit. The first moment of the mystery of the Incarnation of the Son of God is identified with the miraculous conception which took place by the power of the Holy Spirit when Mary uttered her Yes: "Be it done to me according to your word" (Lk 1:38).

5. Matthew's Gospel completes Luke's narrative by describing certain circumstances which preceded the birth of Jesus. We read: "Now the birth of Jesus Christ took place in this way. When his mother Mary had been betrothed to Joseph, before they came to-gether she was found to be with child of the Holy Spirit; and her husband Joseph, being a just man and unwilling to put her to shame, resolved to send her away quietly. But as he considered this, behold, an angel of the Lord appeared to him in a dream, saying, 'Joseph, son of David, do not fear to take Mary your wife, for that which is conceived in her is of the Holy Spirit; she will bear a son, and you shall call his name Jesus, for he will save his people from their sins'" (Mt 1:18–21).

6. As is evident, both texts of the "infancy Gospel" are *in agreement on the fundamental facts:* Jesus was conceived by the power of the Holy Spirit and was born of the Virgin Mary; and they are *complementary* in clarifying the circumstances of this extraordinary happening: Luke in reference to Mary, Matthew in reference to Joseph.

Mary, source of information for Luke

To identify *the source of the infancy narrative* one must go back to St. Luke's remark: *"Mary kept all these things,* pondering them in her heart" (Lk 2:19). Luke states this twice: after the departure of the shepherds from Bethlehem and after the finding of Jesus in the temple (cf. Lk 2:51). The evangelist himself provides us with the elements to identify in the Mother of Jesus one of the sources of the information used by him in writing "the infancy Gospel". Mary, who "kept these things in her heart" (cf. Lk 2:19), could bear witness, after Christ's death and resurrection, in regard to what concerned herself and her role as Mother, precisely in the apostolic period when the New Testament texts were being written and when the early Christian tradition had its origin.

7. The Gospel witness to the *virginal conception of Jesus* on the part of Mary is of great theological importance. In fact, it constitutes a particular *sign of the divine origin of Mary's Son.* The fact that Jesus

did not have an earthly father because generated "without human intervention" sets out clearly the truth that he is the Son of God, so much so that even when he assumes human nature his Father remains exclusively God.

8. The revelation of the intervention of the Holy Spirit *in the conception of Jesus,* indicates *the beginning* of the history of the man of the new *"spiritual generation"* which has a strictly supernatural character (cf. 1 Cor 15:45–49). In this way the Triune God "is communicated" to the creature through the Holy Spirit. It is the mystery to which may be applied the words of the Psalmist: "Send forth thy Spirit, and *they are created,* and thou renewest the face of the earth" (Ps 103 [104]:30). In the economy of this self-communication of God to the creature, the virginal conception of Jesus through the power of the Holy Spirit is a *central and culminating event.* It *initiates the "new creation".* In this way God enters decisively into history to activate man's supernatural destiny, or the predestination of all things in Christ. It is the definitive *expression* of God's *salvific love* for man, about which we spoke in the reflections on Providence.

9. In the realization of the plan of salvation there is always a participation on the part of the creature. Thus in the conception of Jesus through the power of the Holy Spirit *Mary participates* in a *decisive* way. Enlightened interiorly by the angel's message about her vocation as Mother and the preservation of her virginity, Mary *expresses her will and her consent* and agrees to become the humble instrument of the "power of the Most High". The action of the Holy Spirit ensures that in Mary motherhood and virginity are simultaneously present in a way which, although incomprehensible to the human mind, enters fully within the scope of God's predilection and omnipotence. Isaiah's great prophecy is fulfilled in Mary: "a virgin shall conceive and bear a son" (7:14; cf. Mt 1:22–23). Her virginity, an Old Testament sign of poverty and availability to God's plan, becomes the sphere of the exceptional action of God who chooses Mary to be the Mother of the Messiah.

The creature's participation on the level of salvation

10. The exceptional character of Mary is seen also in the genealogies contained in Matthew and Luke. In accordance with Jewish custom *Matthew's* Gospel begins *with the genealogy of Jesus* (Mt 1:2–17) and, starting from Abraham, lists the generations in the male line. Matthew, in fact, is concerned to make evident, through the *legal* paternity of Joseph, the descent of Jesus from Abraham and David and, consequently, the legitimacy of his claim to Messiah. However, at the end of the list of ancestors we read: "Jacob was the father of Joseph, the husband of Mary, of whom Jesus was born, who is called Christ" (Mt 1:16). By emphasizing the motherhood of Mary, the

evangelist implicitly underlines the truth of the virginal birth: Jesus, as man, did not have a human father.

According to Luke's Gospel the genealogy of Jesus (Lk 3:23–28) is in ascending order; from Jesus through his ancestors it goes back *to Adam*. The evangelist wished to show the link between Jesus and *the whole human race*. Mary, as God's collaborator in giving human nature to his eternal Son, was the instrument that linked Jesus with the whole of humanity.

JESUS CHRIST, MESSIAH "KING"

1. As we have seen in the recent reflections, the Evangelist Matthew concludes his genealogy of Jesus, Son of Mary, at the beginning of his Gospel, with the words "*Jesus who is called Christ*" (Mt 1:16). The term "*Christ*" is the Greek equivalent of the Hebrew word "*Messiah*", which means "*Anointed*". Israel, God's chosen people, had lived for generations in the expectation of the fulfillment of the promise of the Messiah, whose coming was prepared by the history of the Covenant. The Messiah, that is, the "Anointed" sent by God, was to bring to *fulfillment* the *call* of the people of the Covenant, to whom was granted through Revelation the privilege of knowing the truth about God himself and about his plan of salvation.

2. The attribution of the name "Christ" to Jesus of Nazareth is the testimony that the Apostles and the primitive Church recognized that in him were *realized the plans of the God of the Covenant* and the expectations of Israel. That is what was proclaimed by Peter on the day of Pentecost when, inspired by the Holy Spirit, he spoke for the first time to the inhabitants of Jerusalem and to the pilgrims who had come up for the Feasts: "Let all the house of Israel therefore know assuredly that *God has made him both Lord and Christ, this Jesus whom you crucified*" (Acts 2:36).

The Anointed One

The meaning of Messiah-Christ

3. Peter's discourse and Matthew's genealogy propose once again the rich content of the term "Messiah-Christ" which is found in the Old Testament and which we shall treat of in the following reflections.

The word "Messiah", including the idea of *anointing,* can be understood only in connection with the anointing with oil, which was in use in Israel, and which—as we well know—passed from the Old

General Audience, February 11, 1987. Reprinted from *L'Osservatore Romano*, February 16, 1987.

Covenant to the New. *In the history of the Old Covenant this anointing was received by those called by God to the office and dignity of king, priest or prophet.*

The truth about the Christ-Messiah must therefore be understood in the biblical context of this threefold "office", which in the Old Covenant was conferred on those who were destined to guide or to represent the people of God. In the present reflection we intend to dwell on the office and dignity of Christ as *King.*

4. When the angel Gabriel announces to the Virgin Mary that she has been chosen to be the Mother of the Savior, he speaks to her of the kingship of her son ". . . the Lord God *will give to him the throne of his father David,* and he will reign over the house of Jacob forever; and of his kingdom there will be no end" (Lk 1:32–33).

These words seem to correspond *to the promise made to King David:* "When your days are fulfilled . . . I will raise up your offspring after you . . . and I will establish his kingdom. He shall build a house for my name, and I will *establish* the throne of his kingdom *forever.* I will be his father, and he shall be my son" (2 Sam 7:12–14). It can be said that this *promise was fulfilled* to a certain extent in Solomon, the son and immediate successor of David. But the full meaning of the promise goes well beyond the confines of an earthly kingdom and regard not only a *distant future,* but even a reality that goes *beyond history,* time and space: "I will establish the throne of his kingdom forever" (2 Sam 7:13).

5. In the annunciation *Jesus* is presented as *he in whom* the ancient promise is fulfilled. In this way the truth about Christ the King is *situated in the biblical tradition* of the "Messianic King" (of the Messiah-King). In this form it is frequently found in the Gospels which speak to us of the mission of Jesus of Nazareth and transmit to us his teaching.

In Jesus the ancient promise is fulfilled

In this regard the attitude of Jesus himself is significant, for example, when Bartimaeus, the blind beggar, cries out to him for help: "Jesus, Son of David, have mercy on me!" (Mk 10:47). Jesus, to whom this title had never been attributed, accepts as addressed to himself the words spoken by Bartimaeus. If necessary, he is concerned to clarify their significance. In fact, turning to the Pharisees he asks: "What do you think of the Christ? Whose son is he? They said to him, 'The son of David'. He said to them, *'How is it then that David,* inspired by the Spirit, calls him Lord, saying, "The Lord said to my Lord, Sit at my right hand, till I put thy enemies under thy feet"? (Ps 109 [110]:1). If David then calls him Lord, how is he his son?'" (Mt 22:42–45).

6. As can be seen, Jesus calls attention to the "limited" and insufficient manner of understanding the Messiah solely on the basis of

the tradition of Israel, linked to the royal inheritance of David. However, he does not reject this tradition, but he fulfills it in its full meaning, which appears already in the words spoken during the annunciation and will be manifested in his Pasch.

Fulfillment

7. Another significant fact is that, on entering Jerusalem on the eve of his Passion, Jesus *fulfills*—as mentioned by the Evangelists Matthew (21:5) and John (12:15)—the prophecy of Zechariah, in which the tradition of the "Messianic King" finds expression: "Rejoice greatly, O daughter of Zion! Shout aloud, O daughter of Jerusalem! Lo, your king comes to you; triumphant and victorious is he, humble and riding on an ass, on a colt the foal of an ass" (Zech 9:9). "Tell the daughter of Zion, behold, your king is coming to you, humble, and mounted on an ass, as on a colt, the foal of an ass" (Mt 21:5). Indeed, *riding on an ass Jesus makes his solemn entrance into Jerusalem,* accompanied by the enthusiastic cries: "Hosanna to the Son of David" (cf. Mt 21:1–10). Notwithstanding the indignation of the Pharisees, Jesus accepts the messianic acclamation of the "little ones" (cf. Mt 21:16; Lk 19:40), well knowing that every ambiguity about the title of Messiah would be dispelled by his glorification through the Passion.

"Exult, O daughter of Jerusalem, your king comes to you"

8. The understanding of the kingship as an earthly power will enter into crisis, but the tradition will emerge from it, not cancelled, but clarified. In the days following Jesus' entry into Jerusalem it will be seen *how the angel's words at the annunciation are to be understood:* "The Lord God will give to him the throne of his father David, and he will reign over the house of Jacob forever; and of his Kingdom there will be no end." Jesus himself will explain the nature of *his own kingship,* and therefore the messianic truth, and how it is to be understood.

9. The decisive moment of this clarification is in *Jesus' conversation with Pilate,* recorded in John's Gospel. Since Jesus was *accused* before the Roman governor *of claiming to be "King of the Jews",* Pilate questions him about this accusation which particularly interests the Roman authority because, if Jesus really claimed to be "King of the Jews" and his followers recognized him as such, this could be a threat to the empire.

Pilate therefore asks Jesus: "Are you the King of the Jews? Jesus answered, 'Do you say this of your own accord, or did others say it to you about me'"; and then he explains: *"My kingship is not of this world;* if my kingship were of this world, my servants would fight, that I might not be handed over to the Jews; but my kingship is not

"My kingdom is not of this world"

from this world. Pilate said to him, 'So you are a king?' Jesus answered, 'You say that *I am a king. For this I was born, and for this I have come into the world, to bear witness to the truth.* Every one who is of the truth hears my voice'" (cf. Jn 18:33–37). These unambiguous words of Jesus contain the clear statement that the kingly character or *office,* linked with the mission of the Christ-Messiah sent by God, *cannot be understood in a political sense as though it were treating of an earthly power,* not even in relation to the "Chosen People", Israel.

10. The sequel of Jesus' trial confirms the existence of the conflict between Christ's conception of himself as "Messiah-King" and the earthly and political one that was common among the people. Jesus is condemned to death on the charge that "he claimed to be king". The inscription placed on the cross, "Jesus of Nazareth, *the King of the Jews*" is a proof that for the Roman authority this was his crime. The very Jews who, paradoxically, aspired to the re-establishment of the "kingdom of David" in the earthly sense, at the sight of Jesus scourged and crowned with thorns, presented to them by Pilate with the words, "Behold your King!", cried out, "Crucify him . . . *we have no king* but Caesar" (Jn 19:15).

Against this background we can understand better the meaning of the inscription placed on Christ's cross, not without reference to the definition which Jesus gave of himself during the interrogation before the Roman procurator. Only in that sense is the Christ-Messiah "the King"; only in that sense does he fulfill the tradition of the "Messianic King", present in the Old Testament and inscribed in the history of the people of the Old Covenant.

11. Finally, on Calvary one last episode illumines the kingly messiahship of Jesus. One of the criminals crucified with Jesus manifests this truth in a penetrating way when he says, "Jesus, *remember me when you come in your kingly power*" (Lk 23:42). Jesus said to him, "Truly I say to you, today you will be with me in Paradise" (Lk 23:43). In this dialogue we find, as it were, a final confirmation of the words which the angel had addressed to Mary in the annunciation: Jesus "will reign . . . and of his kingdom there shall be no end" (Lk 1:33).

JESUS CHRIST, MESSIAH "PRIEST"

1. The name "Christ" is, as we know, the Greek equivalent of the word "Messiah" and means "Anointed". *Besides the "royal" character,* of which we treated in the previous reflection, it also includes,

General Audience, February 18, 1987. Reprinted from *L'Osservatore Romano,* February 23, 1987.

according to Old Testament tradition, the *"priestly"* character. As elements pertaining to the messianic mission, these two aspects, though differing among themselves, are nonetheless complementary. *The figure of the Messiah,* outlined in the Old Testament, embraces both elements by showing the profound unity of the royal and priestly mission.

Melchizedek, priest of the Most High God

2. This unity has its earliest expression, as it were a prototype and an anticipation, in Melchizidek, king of Salem, that mysterious figure in the Old Testament at the time of Abraham. We read of him in the Book of Genesis that in going out to meet Abraham, "he offered bread and wine; he was priest of God Most High. And he blessed him and said, 'Blessed be Abram by God Most High, maker of heaven and earth'" (Gen 14:18–19).

The figure of Melchizedek, king and priest, entered into the messianic tradition, as indicated especially by Psalm 109 (110)—the messianic psalm by antonomasia. In this psalm, in fact, God-Yahweh addresses "my Lord" (i.e., the Messiah) with the words: "'Sit at my right hand till I make your enemies your footstool.' The Lord sends forth from Zion your mighty scepter. Rule in the midst of your foes!" (Ps 109 [110]:1–2).

These expressions which leave no doubt about the royal character of the one addressed by Yahweh, are followed by the announcement: "The Lord has sworn and will not change his mind, *'You are a priest forever after the order of Melchizedek'"* (Ps 109 [110]:4). As is evident, the one whom God-Yahweh addresses by inviting him to sit "at his right hand", will be simultaneously *king and priest* "after the order of Melchizedek".

Sacrifices of Adoration and Atonement

3. In the history of Israel the institution of the Old Testament priesthood traces its origin to Aaron, the brother of Moses, and it was hereditary in the tribe of Levi, one of the twelve tribes of Israel.

In this regard, it is significant that we read in the Book of Sirach: "[God] exalted Aaron, the brother of Moses . . . of the tribe of Levi. He made an everlasting covenant with him *and gave him the priesthood of the people"* (Sir 45:6–7). "[The Lord] chose him out of all the living *to offer sacrifice to the Lord,* incense and a pleasing odor as a memorial portion, to make *atonement* for the people. In his commandments he gave him authority in statutes and judgments to teach Jacob the testimonies, and to enlighten Israel with his law" (Sir 45:16–17). From these texts we deduce that *selection as a priest* is for the purpose of worship, *for the offering of sacrifices of adoration and atonement,* and that worship in its turn is linked to teaching about God and his law.

4. In this same context the following words from the Book of Sirach are also significant: "For even (God's) covenant with David . . . was an individual heritage through one son alone; but *the heritage of Aaron is for all his descendants*" (Sir 45:25).

According to this tradition, *the priesthood* is placed "alongside" the royal dignity. *However, Jesus does not come from the priestly line,* from the tribe of Levi, but from that of Judah. Hence it would seem that the priestly character of the Messiah does not become him. His contemporaries discover in him, above all, the teacher, the prophet, some even their "king", the heir of David. It could therefore be said that *the tradition of Melchizedek,* the king-priest is *absent* in Jesus.

5. It is, however, only an apparent absence. The *paschal events* revealed the true meaning of the "Messiah-king" and of the "king-priest after the order of Melchizedek" which—present in the Old Testament—found its fulfillment in the mission of Jesus of Nazareth. It is significant that during his trial before the Sanhedrin, Jesus in reply to the high priest who asked him if he was "the Christ, the Son of God", said, "You have said so. But I tell you, hereafter *you will see the Son of man seated at the right hand of God* . . ." (Mt 26:63–64). It is a clear reference to the messianic Psalm (109 [110]) which expresses the tradition of the king-priest.

The Easter events unveil the true meaning of the Messiah-King

6. It must be said, however, that the full manifestation of this truth is found only in the Letter to the Hebrews which treats of the relationship between the levitical priesthood and that of Christ. The author of the Letter to the Hebrews touches the theme of Melchizedek's priesthood in order to say that *in Jesus Christ is fulfilled the messianic pre-announcement* linked to that figure who by a higher predestination already from the time of Abraham was inscribed in the mission of the people of God.

We read in fact of Christ who "being made perfect *became the source of eternal salvation to all* who obey him, being designated by God *a high priest after the order of Melchizedek*" (Heb 5:9–10). Then, after recalling what was said about Melchizedek in the Book of Genesis (Gen 14:18), the Letter to the Hebrews continues ". . . his name when translated means *king of righteousness,* and then he is also king of Salem, that is, *king of peace.* He is without father or mother or genealogy, and has neither beginning of days nor end of life, but resembling the Son of God he continues a priest forever" (Heb 7:2–3).

7. Using the analogies of the ritual of worship, of the ark and of the sacrifices of the Old Covenant, the author of the Letter to the Hebrews presents Jesus Christ as the *fulfillment* of all the figures and *promises* of the Old Testament, ordained "to serve a copy and shadow of the heavenly sanctuary" (Heb 8:5). Christ, however, a merciful and faithful high priest (Heb 2:17; cf. 3:2–5), bears in himself

Jesus, the fulfillment of the Old Testament

a *"priesthood that continues forever"* (Heb 7:24), *having offered "himself without blemish to God"* (Heb 9:14).

8. It is worthwhile quoting completely some particularly eloquent passages of this Letter. Coming into the world, Jesus Christ says to God his Father: "Sacrifices and offerings thou hast not desired, *but a body hast thou prepared for me:* in burnt offerings and sin offerings thou hast taken no pleasure. Then I said, 'Lo, I have come to do thy will, O God'" (Heb 10:5–7). "For it was fitting that we should have such a high priest" (Heb 7:26). "Therefore he had to be made like his brethren in every respect, so that he might become a merciful and faithful high priest in the service of God, to *make expiation for the sins of the people*" (Heb 2:17). We have, then, "a high priest . . . who in every respect has been tempted as we are, yet without sinning", a high priest who is able "to sympathize with our weaknesses" (cf. Heb 4:15).

9. Further on we read that such a high priest "has no need, like the other high priests, to offer sacrifices daily, first for his own sins and then for those of the people; he did this once for all when he offered up himself" (Heb 7:27). Again, "when Christ appeared as a *high priest of the good things that have come* . . . he entered once for all into the Holy Place . . . *taking his own blood,* thus securing an eternal redemption" (Heb 9:11–12). Hence our certainty that "the blood of Christ, who through the eternal Spirit, *offered himself without blemish to God,* will purify our conscience from dead works to serve the living God" (Heb 9:14).

This explains the attribution to *Christ's priesthood* of an everlasting saving power whereby ". . . he is able for all time to save those who draw near to God through him, since he always lives to make intercession for them" (Heb 7:25).

An Eternal Priesthood

10. Finally, we can note that in the Letter to the Hebrews there is stated clearly and convincingly that *Jesus Christ has fulfilled* with his whole life and especially with the sacrifice of the cross, *all that was written in the messianic tradition of divine Revelation. His priesthood* is situated in reference to the ritual service of the priests of the Old Covenant, which however he surpasses as *Priest and Victim*. In Christ then is fulfilled God's eternal design which provides for the institution of the priesthood in the history of the Covenant.

Jesus, priest and victim

11. According to the Letter to the Hebrews the messianic task is symbolized by the figure of *Melchizedek*. There we read that by God's will "another priest arises in the likeness of Melchizedek, not *according to a legal requirement* concerning bodily descent *but by the power of an*

indestructible life" (Heb 7:15). It is therefore an eternal priesthood (cf. Heb. 7:3–24).

The Church, faithful guardian and interpreter of these and other texts contained in the New testament, has reaffirmed over and over again the truth of the Messiah-Priest, as witnessed, for example, by the Ecumenical Council of Ephesus (431), that of Trent (1562) and in our own time, the Second Vatican Council (1962–1965).

An evident witness of this truth is found in the *eucharistic sacrifice* which by Christ's institution the Church offers every day *under the species of bread and wine,* "after the order of Melchizedek".

JESUS CHRIST, MESSIAH "PROPHET"

1. During the trial *before Pilate, Jesus,* on being questioned whether he was a king, at first denied that he was a king in the earthly and political sense. Then, on being asked a second time, he replied: "You say that I am a king. *For this I was born,* and for this I have come into the world, *to bear witness to the truth"* (Jn 18:37). This reply links the royal and priestly mission of the Messiah with the essential characteristic of the prophetic mission. *The prophet,* in fact, is called and sent to bear witness to the truth. As a witness to the truth *he speaks in God's name.* In a certain sense he is the voice of God. Such was the mission of the prophets sent by God to Israel throughout the course of the centuries.

It is particularly in the figure of David, king and prophet, that the *prophetic characteristic* is united to the *royal mission.*

Service to God and People

2. The history of the prophets of the Old Testament clearly indicates that the task of proclaiming the truth by speaking in God's name is above all a service, both in relation to God who gives the mandate, and to the people to whom the prophet presents himself as God's envoy. Consequently the *prophetic service is not only eminent and honorable,* but also *difficult and wearying.* The vicissitudes of Jeremiah are an obvious example; he met with resistance, rejection and even persecution, in the measure in which *the truth* he proclaimed was *unwelcome.* Jesus himself, who several times referred to the sufferings undergone by the prophets, had personal experience of them in full measure.

The suffering of the prophet Jeremiah

3. These preliminary references to the ministerial character of the prophetic mission introduce us *to the figure* of the Servant of God

General Audience, February 25, 1987. Reprinted from *L'Osservatore Romano,* March 2, 1987.

(*Ebed Yahweh*) which is found in Isaiah (precisely in the so-called "Deutero-Isaiah"). The messianic tradition of the Old Covenant finds in this figure a particularly rich and important expression if we consider that the Servant of Yahweh, in whom the characteristics of *prophet* stand out especially, unites in himself, in a certain way, the qualities of *priest* and *king* as well. The *Songs of the Servant* in Isaiah present an Old Testament synthesis on the Messiah, open to future developments. Although written so many centuries before Christ, they serve in a surprising manner *to identify his figure,* especially as regards the description of the Suffering Servant of Yahweh. The picture is so accurate and faithful that it would seem to be an account based on the events of Christ's Passion.

The servants of God in the Old Testament

4. One must observe that the term "Servant", "*Servant of God*", is widely used in the Old Testament. Many eminent personages are called or identified as "God's servants". For example, *Abraham* (Gen 26:26), *Jacob* (Gen 32:11), *Moses, David and Solomon, and the Prophets.* Sacred Scripture attributes this term even to certain pagan personages who played their part in the history of Israel; thus, for example, Nebuchadnezzar (Jer 25:8–9) and Cyrus (Is 44:26). Finally, *the whole of Israel* as a people is called "servant of God" (cf. Is 41:8–9; 42:19; 44:21; 48:20), according to a linguistic usage whose echo we find in the *Magnificat* where Mary praises God because "he has helped his servant Israel" (Lk 1:54).

5. As regards the *Songs of the Servant* in Isaiah we note especially thet they do not *regard* a collective entity, such as a people, but an *individual person,* whom the Prophet distinguishes in a certain way from Israel-sinner: "*Behold my servant whom I uphold*", we read in the first Song, "my chosen, in whom my soul delights; I have put my Spirit upon him, he will bring forth justice to the nations. He will not cry or lift up his voice, or make it heard in the street; a bruised reed he will not break, and a dimly burning wick he will not quench; . . . He will not fail or be discouraged till he has established justice in the

Covenant of the people and the light to the nations

earth . . ." (Is 42:1–4). "I am the Lord. . . . I have given you a covenant to the people, a light to the nations, *to open the eyes that are blind,* to bring out the prisoners from the dungeon, from the prison those who sit in darkness" (Is 42:6–7).

6. The second Song develops the same thought: "Listen to me, O coastlands, and hearken, you peoples from afar. *The Lord called me from the womb,* from the body of my mother he named my name. He made my mouth like a sharp sword, in the shadow of his hand he hid me; he made me a polished arrow, in his quiver he hid me away" (Is 49:1–2). "He says: '*It is too light a thing that you should be my servant* to raise up *the tribes of Jacob . . . I will give you as a light to the nations, that my salvation may reach to the end of the earth*'" (Is 49:6).

"The Lord God has given me the tongue of those who are taught, that I may know how to sustain with a word him that is weary" (Is 50:4). And again: "So shall he startle many nations, because of him kings shall stand speechless" (Is 52:15). "The righteous one, my servant, shall make many to be accounted righteous; and he shall bear their iniquities" (Is 53:11).

7. These last texts, from the third and fourth Songs, introduce us with striking realism to the *figure of the Suffering Servant,* to which we shall have to return later. All that Isaiah says seems to foretell in a surprising way all that was foretold by the holy old man *Simeon* at the very beginning of Jesus' life, when he greeted him as "*a light to enlighten the Gentiles*" and at the same time "*a sign of contradiction*" (cf. Lk 2:32, 34). Already from the Book of Isaiah the figure of the Messiah emerges as a *Prophet* who comes into the world to bear witness to the truth and, precisely *because of this truth he will be rejected by his people,* becoming by his death a cause of justification for "many".

Jesus, witness of the truth

8. The Songs of the Servant of Yahweh are fully echoed *in the New Testament* from the very beginning of Jesus' messianic activity. The description of the *baptism in the Jordan* allows one to establish a parallel with the texts of Isaiah. Matthew writes: "When Jesus was baptized . . . the heavens were opened and he saw the *Spirit of God* descending like a dove, and alighting on him" (Mt 3:16); in Isaiah it was said: "I put my spirit upon him" (Is 42:1). The evangelist adds, "And lo, a voice from heaven, saying, 'This *is my beloved son,* with whom I am well pleased'" (Mt 3:17), while in Isaiah God says to the Servant, "my chosen, in whom my soul delights" (Is 42:1). John the Baptist points out Jesus approaching the Jordan with the words, "Behold the Lamb of God, who takes away the sin of the world!" (Jn 1:29), an exclamation which summarizes, as it were, the third and fourth Songs of the *Suffering Servant of Yahweh.*

9. A similar relationship is found in the passage in which Luke records the first messianic words spoken by Jesus in the *synagogue of Nazareth* when Jesus reads the text of Isaiah: "The Spirit of the Lord is upon me, because he has anointed me to preach good news to the poor. He has sent me to proclaim release to the captives and recovery of sight to the blind, to set at liberty those who are oppressed, to proclaim the acceptable year of the Lord" (Lk 4:17–19). These are *the words of the first Song of the Servant of Yahweh* (Is 42:1–7; cf. also Is 61:1–2).

10. If then we look at the life and ministry of Jesus, he appears to us as the Servant of God, who brings *salvation to the people,* who *heals* them, who frees them from their iniquity, who wishes to win them to himself *not by force but by goodness.* The Gospel, especially

that of Matthew, refers frequently to the Book of Isaiah, whose prophetic announcement is fulfilled in Christ, as when he narrates that "when it was evening they brought to him many who were possessed with demons, and he cast out the spirits with a word, and healed all who were sick. *This was to fulfill what was spoken by the prophet Isaiah,* 'He took our infirmities and bore our diseases'" (Mt 8:16–17; cf. Is 53:4). And in another place: "Many followed him, and he healed them all. . . . *This was to fulfill* what was spoken by the prophet Isaiah: 'Behold my servant . . .'" (Mt 12:15–21), and at this point the Evangelist quotes a passage from the first Song of the Servant of Yahweh.

11. As in the case of the Gospels, so likewise the *Acts of the Apostles* show that the first generation of Christ's disciples, beginning with the Apostles, was profoundly convinced that in Jesus was fulfilled all that the prophet Isaiah had foretold in his inspired Songs: *that Jesus is the chosen Servant of God* (cf. Acts 3:13; 3:26; 4:27; 4:30; 1 Pet 2:22–25), *that he fulfills the mission of the Servant of Yahweh* and brings the new Law, he is the light of the covenant for all nations (cf. Acts 13:46–47). This same conviction is found later in the "Didache", in the "Martryrdom of St. Polycarp", and in the First Letter of St. Clement of Rome.

The first Christians considered Jesus the true servant of God

12. One must add an item of great importance: Jesus speaks of himself as a servant, clearly alluding to Isaiah 53, when he says: "The Son of man *came not to be served but to serve, and to give his life as a ransom for many*" (Mk 10:45; Mt 20:28). The same idea is expressed by the washing of the feet of the Apostles (Jn 13:3–4, 12–15).

Throughout the whole of the New Testament, beside the passages and allusions to the first Song of the Servant of Yahweh (Is 42:1–7), which underline the election of the Servant and his prophetic mission of liberation, of healing and of covenant for all people, the greater number of texts refers to the third and fourth Songs (Is 50:4–11; Is 52:13–53:12) on the Suffering Servant. It is the same idea which was summed up briefly by St. Paul in his Letter to the Philippians when he sings the praises of Christ "who, though he was in the form of God, did not count equality with God a thing to be grasped, but *emptied himself, taking the form of a servant,* being born in the likeness of men . . . he humbled himself and became *obedient unto death*" (Phil 2:6–8).

The hymn in the Letter to the Philippians

2

MESSAGES TO THE WORLD

WE WILL STAND SIDE BY SIDE
ASKING GOD TO GIVE US PEACE

1. As is known, next Monday, October 27, I shall be in Assisi together with numerous representatives of other Churches and Christian communities and of the other world religions for the purpose of praying for peace.

Undoubtedly it is an outstanding event of a religious character, exclusively religious. Thus it was planned, and it will take place in this perspective with the collaboration of all the participants. It will be a day of prayer, fasting and pilgrimage. I trust that, by the Lord's grace, it will really be a high point of that "movement of prayer and peace" that I hoped for on the threshold of 1986, proclaimed by the United Nations as the "International Year of Peace".

At Assisi all the representatives of the Christian Churches and communities and of the world religions will be engaged solely in invoking from God the great gift of peace.

2. I would like this fact, so important for the process of reconciliation of men among themselves and with God, to be seen and interpreted by all members of the Church in the light of the Second Vatican Council and of its teachings.

In the Council, in fact, the Church, under the inspiration of the Holy Spirit, reflected at length on her position in a world ever more marked by the encounter of cultures and religions. *The encounter of cultures and religions*

According to the Council, the Church is ever more aware of her mission and duty, indeed of her essential vocation to announce to the world the true salvation which is found only in Jesus Christ, God and man (cf. AG, 11–13).

Yes, it is only in Christ that all mankind can be saved. "There is no other name under heaven given among men by which we must be saved" (Acts 4:12). From the very beginning of history all who are truly faithful to God's call, as far as it is known to them, have been directed towards Christ (cf. LG, 16).

General Audience, October 22, 1986. Reprinted from *L'Osservatore Romano*, October 27, 1986.

Religious Values and Qualities

3. Conscious of the common vocation of humanity and of the unique plan of salvation, the Church feels herself linked to one and all, as Christ "is united in a certain way with everyone" (cf. GS, 22; RH, passim).

To one and all she proclaims that Christ is the center of the created world and of history.

Christ the center of the world and of history
Precisely because Christ is the center of the whole created world and of history, and because no one can come to the Father except through him (cf. Jn 14:6), we approach the other religions in an attitude of sincere respect and of fervent witness to Christ in whom we believe. In them there are, in fact, the "seeds of the Word", the "rays of the one truth", to quote the words of the early Fathers of the Church who lived and worked in the midst of paganism, and to which the Second Vatican Council refers both in the Declaration *Nostra Aetate* (no. 2), and in the Decree *Ad Gentes* (nos. 11, 18). We know what we believe to be the limits of these religions, but that does not at all take away from the fact that they possess even outstanding religious values and qualities (cf. NA, 2).

4. These are precisely the "traces" or the "seeds" of the Word and the "rays" of the truth. Among these there is undoubtedly prayer, often accompanied by fasting, by other penances and by pilgrimage to sacred places held in great veneration.

We respect this prayer even though we do not intend to make our own formulae that express other views of faith. Nor would the others, on their part, wish to adopt our prayers.

What will take place at Assisi will certainly not be religious syncretism but a sincere attitude of prayer to God in an atmosphere of mutual respect. For this reason the formula chosen for the gathering at Assisi is: being together in order to pray.

Certainly we cannot "pray together", namely, to make a common prayer, but we can be present while others pray. In this way we manifest our respect for the prayer of others and for the attitude of others before the Divinity; at the same time we offer them the humble and sincere witness of our faith in Christ, Lord of the Universe.

This is what will happen at Assisi where, at one time during the day, the separate prayers of the different religious representatives will be held in various places. Then, later, in the *Piazzale* of the Lower Basilica of St. Francis, there will follow, in succession, appropriately distinct, the prayers of the representatives of each religion, while all the others will assist with the respectful attitude, both interior and exterior, of one who is a witness of the supreme effort of other men and women to seek God.

5. This "being together to pray" takes on a particularly profound and eloquent significance inasmuch as they will be standing side by side to implore from God the gift of peace—the gift of which all humanity has so much need today for survival.

It is in fact my profound awareness of the necessity of this gift for all, of its urgency and of the fact that it depends solely on God, that moved me to address the other Christian Churches and the great world religions, who share the same concern for the fate of mankind and who manifest the same readiness to pledge themselves to seek peace through prayer.

The world religions, notwithstanding the fundamental differences that separate them, are all called to make their contribution to the birth of a world which is more human, more just and more fraternal. After having been frequently the cause of divisions, all would now like to play a decisive role in the building of world peace. This we wish to do together. As my predecessor Paul VI said in his Encyclical *Ecclesiam Suam:* ". . . with them we wish to promote and defend the ideals which we can have in common in the field of religious liberty, human brotherhood, culture and learning, social works of charity and civil order" (no. 112). *The religions of the world are called to a decisive role in the building of peace*

It is in this spirit that I invited the Churches and religions to come to Assisi. And it is in the same spirit that the invitation has been accepted. Everywhere the particular Churches, in their turn, have associated themselves with this initiative, frequently together with other Christian Churches and with representatives of other religions. Thus there is realized and extended that great "movement of prayer for peace" that I spoke of on January 25 this year.

The twenty-seventh of October will therefore be a day wholly devoted to prayer. This is its characteristic, since "prayer, which expresses in various ways man's relationship with the living God, is also the first task and almost the first announcement of the Pope, just as it is the first condition of his service in the Church and in the world" (John Paul II, *L'Osservatore Romano,* English edition, November 9, 1978, p. 1).

Prayer is the breath of the soul. Every adorer of the living and true God believes in the limitless value of prayer and feels welling up from his inmost being the need to pray. *Prayer, the breath of the soul*

6. At Assisi we shall be welcomed by the poor and humble Brother Francis. He will welcome us with the ardent and illuminating energy of his seraphic personality, by reason of which he has been likened to the sun, and his native land to a new East (Dante, *Paradise,* XI, 50).

He will welcome us with the irresistible charm of his unarmed and peace-making simplicity, which is capable of reaching the most secret parts of every heart.

He will welcome us with the tender and sublime accents of his Canticle, which alternates the strophes of created reality with the highest summit attainable by those who pray, when prayer becomes life and life becomes prayer: "Praised be you, my Lord."

And from the mystic hill the Franciscan greeting *Pax et Bonum* will again wend its way through the pathways of the world in the steps of new witnesses, to bring the conviction that peace is necessary, is possible, is a duty; and to prove that it alone can guarantee humanity of the second millennium a serene and industrious future.

I ask you to pray earnestly for these great intentions. If from all human hearts there arises to the one God the yearning for peace and universal brotherhood, fused as it were into one great prayer, then there is no doubt but that he will hear us: "Ask and you shall receive, seek and you shall find, knock and it shall be opened unto you" (Lk 11:9).

WE WILL SEEK TO BE PEACEMAKERS IN THOUGHT AND DEED!

My Brothers and Sisters,

Heads and Representatives of the Christian Churches and Ecclesial Communities and of the World Religions,

Dear Friends,

1. In concluding this World Day of Prayer for Peace, to which you have come from many parts of the world, kindly accepting my invitation, I would like now to express my feelings, as a brother and friend, but also as a believer in Jesus Christ, and, in the Catholic Church, the first witness of faith in him.

In relation to the last prayer, the Christian one, in the series we have all heard, I profess here anew my conviction, shared by all *True peace* Christians, that in Jesus Christ, as Savior of all, true peace is to be *is to be sought* found, "Peace to those who are far off and peace to those who are *in Christ,* near" (cf. Eph 2:17). His birth was greeted by the angels' song: *the Savior* "Glory to God in the highest and peace among men with whom he *of all* is pleased" (Lk 2:14). He preached love among all, even among foes, proclaimed blessed those who work for peace (cf. Mt 5:9) and through his Death and Resurrection he brought about reconciliation between heaven and earth (cf. Col 1:20). To use an expression of Paul the Apostle: "He is our peace" (Eph 2:14).

Concluding Address at Assisi, October 27, 1986. Reprinted from *L'Osservatore Romano,* November 3, 1986.

Many Shared Convictions

2. It is, in fact, my faith conviction which has made me turn to you, representatives of the Christian Churches and Ecclesial Communities and World Religions, in deep love and respect.

With the other Christians we share many convictions and, particularly, in what concerns peace.

With the World Religions we share a common respect of and obedience to conscience, which teaches all of us to seek the truth, to love and serve all individuals and peoples, and therefore to make peace among individuals and among nations.

Yes, we all hold conscience and obedience to the voice of conscience to be an essential element in the road towards a better and peaceful world.

Could it be otherwise, since all men and women in this world have a common nature, a common origin and a common destiny?

If there are many and important differences among us, there is also a common ground, whence to operate together in the solution of this dramatic challenge of our age: true peace or catastrophic war.

3. Yes, there is the dimension of prayer, which in the very real diversity of religions tries to express communication with a Power above all our human forces.

Peace depends basically on this Power, which we call God, and, as Christians, believe has revealed himself in Christ.

Peace depends on the Power whom we call God

This is the meaning of this World Day of Prayer.

For the first time in history, we have come together from everywhere, Christian Churches and Ecclesial Communities, and World Religions, in this sacred place dedicated to Saint Francis, to witness before the world, each according to his own conviction, about the transcendent quality of peace.

The form and content of our prayers are very different, as we have seen, and there can be no question of reducing them to a kind of common denominator.

4. Yet, in this very difference we have perhaps discovered anew that, regarding the problem of peace and its relation to religious commitment, there is something which binds us together.

The challenge of peace, as it is presently posed to every human conscience, is the problem of a reasonable quality of life for all, the problem of survival for humanity, the problem of life and death.

In the face of such a problem, two things seem to have supreme importance and both of them are common to us all.

The first is the inner imperative of the moral conscience, which enjoins us to respect, protect and promote human life, from the womb to the deathbed, for individuals and peoples, but especially for the weak, the destitute, the derelict: the imperative to overcome selfishness, greed and the spirit of vengeance.

The second common thing is the conviction that peace goes much beyond human efforts, particularly in the present plight of the world, and therefore that its source and realization is to be sought in that Reality beyond all of us.

Open Our Hearts to the Divine Reality beyond Us

This is why each of us prays for peace. Even if we think as we do, that the relation between that Reality and the gift of peace is a different one, according to our respective religious convictions, we all affirm that such a relation exists.

This is what we express by praying for it.

I humbly repeat here my own conviction: peace bears the name of Jesus Christ.

5. But, at the same time and in the same breath, I am ready to acknowledge that Catholics have not always been faithful to this affirmation of faith. We have not been always "peacemakers".

For ourselves, therefore, but also perhaps, in a sense, for all, this encounter at Assisi is an act of *penance*. We have prayed, each in his own way, we have fasted, we have marched together.

In this way we have tried to open our hearts to the divine reality beyond us and to our fellow men and women.

Yes, while we have *fasted,* we have kept in mind the sufferings which senseless wars have brought about and are still bringing about on humanity. Thereby we have tried to be spiritually close to the millions who are the victims of hunger throughout the world.

While we *have walked in silence,* we have reflected on the path our human family treads: either in hostility, if we fail to accept one another in love; or as a common journey to our lofty destiny, if we realize that other people are our brothers and sisters. The very fact that we have come to Assisi from various quarters of the world is in itself a sign of this common path which humanity is called to tread. Either we learn to walk together in peace and harmony, or we drift apart and ruin ourselves and others. We hope that this *The common origin and destiny of humanity* pilgrimage to Assisi has taught us anew to be aware of the common origin and common destiny of humanity. Let us see in it an anticipation of what God would like the developing history of humanity to be: a fraternal journey in which we accompany one another towards the transcendent goal which he sets for us.

6. Prayer, fasting, pilgrimage. This day at Assisi has helped us become more aware of our religious commitments. But it has also made the world, looking at us through the media, more aware of the

responsibility of each religion regarding problems of war and peace.

More perhaps than ever before in history, the intrinsic link between an authentic religious attitude and the great good of peace has become evident to all.

What a tremendous weight for human shoulders to carry! But at the same time what a marvelous, exhilarating call to follow.

Although prayer is in itself action, this does not excuse us from working for peace. Here we are acting as the heralds of the moral awareness of humanity as such, humanity that wants peace, needs peace.

7. There is no peace without a passionate love for peace. There is no peace without a relentless determination to achieve peace.

Peace awaits its prophets. Together we have filled our eyes with visions of peace: they release energies for a new language of peace, for new gestures of peace, gestures which will shatter the fatal chains of divisions inherited from history or spawned by modern ideologies.

Peace awaits its builders. Let us stretch our hands towards our brothers and sisters, to encourage them to build peace upon the four pillars of truth, justice, love and freedom (cf. *Pacem in Terris*).

Peace is a workshop, open to all and not just to specialists, savants and strategists. Peace is a universal responsibility: it comes about through a thousand little acts in daily life. By their daily way of living with others, people choose for or against peace. We entrust the cause of peace especially to the young. Many young people help to free history from the wrong paths along which humanity strays.

Peace in everyday life

Peace is in the hands not only of individuals but of nations. It is the nations that have the honor of basing their peacemaking activity upon the conviction of the sacredness of human dignity and the recognition of the unquestionable equality of people with one another. We earnestly invite the leaders of the nations and of the international organizations to be untiring in bringing in structures of dialogue wherever peace is under threat or already compromised. We offer our support to their often exhausting efforts to maintain or restore peace. We renew our encouragement to the United Nations Organization, that it may respond fully to the breadth and height of its universal mission of peace.

8. In answer to the appeal I made from Lyons in France, on the day which we Catholics celebrate as the feast of Saint Francis, we hope that arms have fallen silent, that attacks have ceased. This would be a first significant result of the spiritual efficacy of prayer. In fact, this appeal has been shared by many hearts and lips everywhere in the world, especially where people suffer from war and its consequences.

It is vital to choose peace and the means to obtain it. Peace, so frail in health, demands constant and intensive care. Along this path, we shall advance with sure and redoubled steps, for there is no doubt that people have never had so many means for building true peace as today. Humanity has entered an era of increased solidarity and hunger for social justice. This is our chance. It is also our task, which prayer helps us to face.

Praying and Witnessing

9. What we have done today at Assisi, praying and witnessing to our commitment to peace, we must continue to do every day of our life. For what we have done today is vital for the world. If the world is going to continue, and men and women are to survive in it, the world cannot do without prayer.

This is the permanent lesson of Assisi: it is the lesson of Saint Francis who embodies an attractive ideal for us; it is the lesson of Saint Clare, his first follower. It is an ideal composed of meekness, humility, a deep sense of God and a commitment to serve all. Saint Francis was *a man of peace*. We recall that he had abandoned the military career he had followed for a while in his youth, and discovered the value of poverty, the value of a simple and austere life, in imitation of Jesus Christ whom he intended to serve. Saint Clare was the *woman,* par excellence, *of prayer*. Her union with God in prayer sustained Francis and his followers, as it sustains us today.

St. Clare, a woman of prayer

Francis and Clare are examples of peace: with God, with oneself, with all men and women in this world. May this holy man and this holy woman inspire all people today to have the same strength of character and love of God and neighbor to continue on the path we must walk together.

10. Moved by the example of Saint Francis and Saint Clare, true disciples of Christ, and newly convinced by the experience of this day we have lived through together, we commit ourselves to re-examine our consciences, to hear its voice more faithfully, to purify our spirits from prejudice, anger, enmity, jealousy and envy. We will seek to be peacemakers in thought and deed, with mind and heart fixed on the unity of the human family. And we call on all our brothers and sisters who hear us to do the same.

Put into Action the Strategies of Peace with Courage and Vision

We do this with a sense of our own human limitations and with an awareness of the fact that by ourselves alone we will fail. We therefore reaffirm and acknowledge that our future life and peace depend always on God's gift to us.

In that spirit, we invite the leaders of the world to know that we humbly implore God for peace. But we also ask them to recognize their responsibilities and recommit themselves to the task of peace, to put into action the strategies of peace with courage and vision.

11. Let me now turn to each of you, representatives of Christian Churches and Ecclesial Communities and World Religions, who have come to Assisi for this day of prayer, fasting and pilgrimage.

I thank you again for having accepted my invitation to come here for this act of witness before the world.

I also extend my thanks to all those who have made possible our presence here, particularly our brothers and sisters in Assisi.

And above all I thank God, the God and Father of Jesus Christ, for this day of grace for the world, for each of you, and for myself. I do this in the words attributed to Saint Francis:

> Lord, make me an instrument of your peace: where there is hatred, let me sow love; where there is injury, pardon; where there is doubt, faith; where there is despair, hope; where there is darkness, light; and where there is sadness, joy.
>
> O Divine Master, grant that I may not so much seek to be consoled as to console; to be understood as to understand; to be loved as to love; for it is in giving that we receive, it is in pardoning that we are pardoned, and it is in dying that we are born to eternal life.

O Lord, make me an instrument of your peace

THE DEATH OF CHRIST IS A NEW BEGINNING

1. *Victimae paschali laudes immolent christiani.*
Praise and glory to the Paschal Victim!
Christians, let us join together in this hymn!
Christians of Rome and of the world!
Let us join together *in adoration of the Paschal Victim,* in adoration of the sacrificial Lamb, in adoration of the Risen Lord!

2. *Agnus redemit oves:* "The sheep are ransomed by the Lamb; and Christ, the undefiled, has sinners to his Father reconciled."
Behold Christ! Behold our Redeemer! The Redeemer of the World!
He has given his life for the sheep.
Let us join together *in adoration of that Death which brings us Life,* for Love is more powerful than death. See how the death accepted out of love conquers death!
See how the death accepted out of love reveals God, the lover of

Easter Message, 1987. Reprinted from *L'Osservatore Romano,* April 21, 1987.

life, who wishes us to have life, and to have it abundantly (cf. Jn 10:10)—to have *the same Life that is in him.*

To the Paschal Victim all glory and highest praise!

In his death there is *reconciliation with the Father.*

This is the reconciliation of sinners with God, the reconciliation of man, who because of sin dies to God, and no longer has in himself *the Life which is in God* and only in God.

In God alone.

The death of Christ is a new beginning.

The beginning of *Life which has no end.*

It is without end, because it is of God and in God.

Although the creature dies, God lives!

When Christ dies, all of creation is reborn.

Blessed are you, life-giving Death!

Blessed is the day given us by the Lord.

3. Blessed are you, O Christ, Son of the Living God!

Blessed are you, Son of Man, Son of Mary, blessed, because *you entered the history of man and of the world, even to the boundaries of death: Mors et vita duello conflixere mirando:* "Death with life contended: combat strangely ended!

Life's own Champion, slain, yet lives to reign."

Yes, the history of man and of the world is marked by the mystery of death, marked with the stamp of dying, from end to end.

You have taken this stamp upon yourself, eternally begotten Son, Son consubstantial with the Father: Life from Life, and you have carried it *through the boundaries of death,* the death which oppresses creation, through the boundaries of our human death, *in order to reveal in that death the Spirit who gives life.*

4. All of us who come into the world bearing death within us, we who are born of our earthly mothers marked by the inevitability of dying, *live by the power of the Spirit.*

And in the power of this Spirit, who is given to us by the Father, by the Power of your death, O Christ, we cross the boundaries of the death that is in us *and we rise from sin to the Life* revealed in your Resurrection!

You are the Lord of life, you who are consubstantial with the Father, who is Life itself, together with you, in the Holy Spirit who is Love itself—and truly Love is Life!

In your death, O Christ, *death appeared defenseless before love.*

And Life triumphed.

Mors et vita duello conflixere mirando Dux vitae mortuus, regnat vivus.

5. You who are the Risen One and "live to reign" forever, remain at the side of man, the man of today whom death, with its dark allure, in a thousand ways tempts and seeks to ensnare.

The death of Christ is the beginning of life

In your death, O Christ, death has appeared defenseless

Grant that man may rediscover *life as the gift* which in all its manifestations reveals the Father's love: when it is poured into those who
are reborn at the baptismal font, or courses through every fiber of
the body that moves, breathes and rejoices; when it reveals itself in
the vast variety of the animal world, or clothes the land with trees,
grass and flowers.

Every form of life has in your Father its inexhaustible source.

From him it flows without ceasing, and to him it inevitably returns:
to him, the generous giver of every perfect gift (cf. Jas 1:17).

6. In God the life of the human being has its eternal source in a
unique way, the human being whom *he* himself *fashions in his own
image* when he quickens in the mother's womb.

Life of the human being has its origin in God

May reverent wonder for the mystery of love that surrounds his
coming into the world not die out in contemporary man!

We beseech you, Lord of the living!

Grant that the man of the technological age *may not reduce himself
to a mere object,* but may respect, from its very beginning, the un-
renounceable dignity that is proper to him.

Grant that, in harmony with the divine plan, he may live according
to the only way worthy of him, *the way of giving,* from person to
person, in a context of love expressed through the flesh in an act
which from the very beginning God willed as a seal of the giving.

7. Grant, O Lord, that people may always respect the transcendent
dignity of all their fellow human beings, whether they be poor or
hungry, imprisoned, sick, dying, wounded in body or mind, beset
by doubt or tempted to despair.

They always remain children of God, for God's gift knows no
regrets.

Everyone is offered forgiveness and resurrection.

Each one deserves respect and support.

Deserves love.

8. *Dic nobis Maria, quid vidisti in via:* "Tell us, Mary: say what you
have seen upon the way."

Visiting the tomb at dawn on the third day, the place where he
was buried, tell us, Mary of Magdala, you who loved so much.

Behold, you found *the tomb empty: Sepulcrum Christi viventis, et
gloriam vidi Resurgentis.*

The Lord lives! I have seen the Risen One.

Angelicos testes, sudarium et vestes.

Who could testify to this? What human tongue?

Only the angels could explain the meaning of that empty tomb
and discarded shroud.

The Lord lives! *I have seen his glory,* full of grace and truth (cf.
Jn 1:14).

Christ,
my hope,
is risen

I have seen the glory! *Surrexit Christus spes mea:* "Christ, my hope, has risen: he goes before you into Galilee."

9. Yes, first of all there, in the land which gave him as Son of man.

In the land of his infancy and youth.

In the land of the hidden life.

First of all there, *in Galilee* to meet the Apostles.

And then . . . And then, through the testimony of the Apostles, in so many places, among so many nations, peoples and races!

Today *the voice of this Easter Message,* echoing in Jerusalem at the empty tomb, *seeks to reach everyone: Scimus Christum surrexisse a mortuis vere. Yes,* we are certain of it: Christ is truly risen.

"And you, victorious king, your salvation bring us."

Amen, alleluia!

3

GOSPEL PILGRIMAGE

"YOU ARE MY CO-WORKERS IN
SPREADING THE GOSPEL"

Beloved children of Colombia:
  —Do you love the Lord?
  —Do you love the Blessed Virgin, our Mother?
  —Do you love the Catholic Church?
  —Do you love your neighbor?

I am very happy to have this meeting with you, who represent so many thousands of Colombian children and especially those who belong to the missionary groups.

The joy which you have expressed in greeting me clearly shows with how much enthusiasm and desire you have awaited this moment. Isn't it true? I too have awaited and desired this moment to be with you.

In Rome, where I usually live, meeting the children on my visits to parishes is always a wonderful moment of joy for me.

Children of Colombia, your presence in the Church is important. How sad would be a Church composed only of older people! How empty would parishes and ecclesial communities feel without children to attend catechesis, to sing in the celebrations and to make it felt that the Church is a true family, in which all—great and small—are children of God!

The Church is a true family

Thus the Lord, as we know from the Gospel stories, wanted to have the children close: "Let the children come to me . . . for to such belongs the kingdom of heaven" (cf. Mt 19:14). Yes, you are certainly friends of Jesus and therefore you are also the friends of Pope John Paul II.

Beloved children of Colombia, you represent all the millions of children of your age, and especially those who belong to the Missionary Youth.

It is a joy for the Pope to know that you cooperate with him in that missionary work which Jesus has entrusted to him to bring the Gospel to the whole world. Yes, you are my associates; my great-small associates in spreading the Gospel.

You cooperate with me because you are united to the missionary intentions of the Pope; first of all with prayer; then with good

Meeting with Children, Colombia, July 4, 1986. Reprinted from *L'Osservatore Romano,* August 11, 1986.

behavior at home and with your companions; and also with alms for the missions, which are the result of self-denial and sacrifice. Where you cannot go with your word, you go with your prayer and your sacrifice.

Yes, this is what I expect of you and of all the children of Colombia. You will accompany me with your prayer, and I, for my part, will carry your greeting, your desires of peace and brotherhood to all the children that I constantly meet on my apostolic trips. Agreed? Thus we are going to form a chain of love and of brotherhood which unites all people and we are going to work for peace, that peace which is the aspiration of all.

You know that, unfortunately, many children like you experience the suffering of war, the need caused by hunger, the abandonment of orphanhood. And many, above all, do not know Jesus, nor know that they have in the Virgin Mary a Mother who watches over us as she watched over her Son Jesus when he was a Child. The Gospel message and the Church in which you feel at home is for them as well.

Dear children: You have said that you love Jesus, your Friend. Well, love him still more. Grow like him in age, in wisdom and in grace (cf. Lk 2:40). Say with your words, with your songs, with your life that he is alive, that he is present in the Church.

You have said that you love the Virgin Mary. Well, lovingly invoke her always, praying the holy Rosary to her.

You have said that you love the Church. Well, love her more every day and stay always united to her; ask the Lord to increase priestly and religious vocations. Pray every day for men and women missionaries.

The Pope loves you so much, dear children of Colombia, that he would like not to leave, so that he could remain always with you. But you already know that in Jesus and in the Church we are all united, that there are no distances which separate us. Pray for me and I will pray for you. Receive my apostolic blessing, which I extend from my heart to your families, to the Missionary Youth and to all the children of Colombia.

THE UNIVERSITY MUST SERVE THE COUNTRY IN THE CONSTRUCTION OF A NEW SOCIETY

Dear Cardinal,
Ladies and Gentlemen,
Rectors, Boards of Directors and Professors responsible for the university apostolate,

Meeting at Medellín, June 5, 1986. Reprinted from *L'Osservatore Romano*, August 25, 1986.

Patrons of culture and science,

Dear Students:

At the end of an intensive day and the conclusion of my visit to Medellín, I cannot leave this beloved city without a meeting with you, men and women of science and culture. It is to me a necessary tribute that the Pope and the Church owe you and, on your part, a natural and obvious gesture welcoming the presence of the Church and the Pope. Allow me to add another motive that is, so to speak, of a vital order: the chance to meet the young, the many young students of whom I can now meet only a representative number; last Wednesday, in "El Campin" of Bogotá, I had the joy of feeling you very close and seeing you in great numbers.

The Church has need of culture, just as culture has need of the Church. I have already said this on other occasions, and now I repeat it to you, adding that the Church, in the choice and exchange of goods between faith and culture, makes a preferential choice in the direction of the young (cf. *Puebla*, 1186), and expects from them, in turn, a preferential adherence.

The Church's preferential choice for the young

So I have come here to share some reflections with you on this fundamental reality in the life of men and peoples that is culture.

Ideal Center for Maturation of a New Culture

The university is an ideal center for the maturation of a new culture. Young people expend in this process the vital energies and solicitude necessary to bring about a qualitative transformation.

It is a fact that universities as such—both in relation to the body of students and professors and as centers where knowledge, considered in its totality, becomes the object of research, instruction and learning—constitute a suitable area for the effective orientation of the culture and society of a nation, a continent. For this reason the Church, too, with due respect for mutual autonomy, wishes to renew and strengthen the bonds that link her to Colombian universities from the moment of their foundation.

Your country counts fifty universities, not including institutes and centers of research, academies, museums, etc. This is an important patrimony of science and culture, which is cause for legitimate pride, but it is at the same time an instrument of serious responsibility before God and the people of Colombia for the future of this noble nation. Look to the future with hope, but also with a prudent sense of realism and integrity. Universities must serve the country in the common effort to build a society that is new, free, responsible, conscious of its cultural patrimony, just, fraternal, open to participation, where man, considered integrally, is always the one measure of progress.

In the journey towards this splendid goal it will be necessary to overcome grave difficulties of which you are well aware. The Church accompanies you by virtue of the supernatural mission entrusted to her by her Founder. In this sense she feels her ministry to be connatural with the university, and she considers it a "key and functional option of evangelization" (*Puebla,* 1055), out of a desire, not to dominate, but to serve man.

The culture must lead man to full realization

Culture, in fact, as I had occasion to point out several years ago in my visit to UNESCO, must lead man to full realization in his transcendence over created things. It must keep him from being dissolved in any kind of materialism and in consumerism, or from being destroyed by a science and technology at the service of greed and the violence of oppressive forces, enemies of man. It is necessary that men and women of culture possess not only proven competence, but also a clear and solid moral conscience, so that they will not have to subordinate their activities to the "apparent imperatives" prevailing today. Instead, they will serve man with love, "man and his moral authority, which come from the truth of his principles and the conformity of his actions with these principles" (Discourse to UNESCO, June 2, 1980, no. 11).

The university, which by vocation must be a disinterested and free institution, presents itself, as one of the institutions of modern society which is capable of defending, together with the Church, man as such; without subterfuge, without any other pretest, and for the sole reason that man has a unique dignity and deserves to be esteemed for himself. Dedicate, then, in fruitful dialogue with the local and universal Church, every legitimate means to this noble end: teaching, research, willingness to listen and collaborate, to begin anew with patience.

Service to the Deepening of Cultural Identity

In this noble endeavor to defend and promote the whole man, you serve the awareness and deepening of the cultural identity of your people. Cultural identity is a dynamic and critical concept: it is a process in which the patrimony of the past is re-created in the present moment and projected into the future, so that it may be assimilated by later generations. In this way the identity and progress of a social group is guaranteed.

Culture, a typically human requirement, is one of the fundamental elements constituting the identity of a people. It is here that the roots of its will to be what it is are sent down. Culture is the complete expression of its vital reality, and it embraces it in its totality: values, structures, persons. Hence the evangelization of its culture is the most radical, global and profound way of evangelizing a people. There are typical values that characterize the Latin American culture, such as, among others, the desire for change, the awareness of its own social and political dignity, the efforts of community organization, especially in the popular sectors, the growing interest in and respect for the originality of the indigenous cultures, the strengthening of the economy in order to face the situations of extreme poverty, the great qualities of humanity that are manifested especially in readiness to welcome others, to share what one has and to be united in the face of misfortunes (cf. *Puebla,* 1721). Using these secure values as a basis, the challenges of our time can be faced: the migration from rural areas to the cities, the influence of the means of social communication with their new cultural models, the legitimate aspiration to the advancement of women, the advent of the industrial society; materialistic ideologies, the problem of injustice and violence. . . . *Typical values of the Latin-American culture*

In this context of service to the cultural identity of your people, it is not out of place to remind you that "education is a human activity in the cultural order" (*Puebla,* 1024); not only because it is its "first and essential duty" (Discourse to UNESCO, no. 11), but also because education plays an active, critical and enriching role in forming the culture itself. The university, being the eminent place of education in all its components—persons, ideas, institutions— can make a contribution that goes beyond the mere awareness of the national and popular cultural identity. The education, as such, imparted by the university, can deepen and enrich that very culture.

Faith and Culture

In addressing you today, worthy representatives of the intellectual and cultural world in Colombia, and especially you committed lay persons, I wish to appeal to you to participate actively in the creation and defense of an authentic culture of truth, goodness and beauty, of freedom and progress, which will be able to contribute to the dialogue between science and faith, Christian culture, local culture and universal civilization.

Culture presupposes and requires an "integral vision of man understood in the totality of his moral and spiritual capacities, in the fullness of his vocation. It is here that the profound link—'the organic and constitutive relationship'—that unites Christian faith and human culture has its roots" (Discourse to UNESCO, no. 9). Faith offers the profound vision of man that culture requires; indeed, only faith can give culture its ultimate and radical foundation. Culture can find in the Christian faith nourishment and definitive inspiration.

But the link between faith and culture also works in the other direction. Faith is not a reality which is ethereal and extraneous to history, offering its light to culture in a purely gratuitous act but *Faith is lived* remaining indifferent to it. On the contrary, faith is lived in concrete *in concrete* reality, and is incarnated in and through it. "The synthesis between *reality* culture and faith is not a requirement only of culture, but also of faith. . . . A faith that does not become culture is a faith not fully embraced, not entirely thought out, not faithfully lived" (Discourse to UNESCO, no. 9). Faith involves man in the totality of his being and his aspirations. A faith that places itself on the margin of what is human, of what is therefore culture, would be a faith unfaithful to the fullness of what the word of God manifests and reveals, a decapitated faith, worse still, a faith in the process of self-annihilation. Faith, though it transcends culture—and by the very fact that it transcends it and reveals the divine and eternal destiny of man— creates and generates culture.

Function of Catholic Universities

In this dialogue between faith and culture, the Catholic universities of Colombia owe a particular service to the Church and society. The first obligation consists in reflecting, without masking it, their Catholic identity, finding their "ultimate and profound meaning in Christ, in his salvific message which embraces man in his totality" (Discourse to Catholic university students and staff, Mexico, January 31, 1979, no. 20) and seeking to build among all a "university family" (15).

In this context is situated—with the characteristics proper to it—the *The university* university apostolate. A difficult apostolate, but urgent and rich in *apostolate* possibilities. How well you know this, you who are leaders in this important activity of the local Church, generously dedicating time and energy to it. I ardently exhort you to continue in your efforts towards realizing, in a spirit of collaboration and with a sense of the Church, an effective pastoral presence in the universities, whether they be public or private.

May the Catholic universities work in a healthy and loyal spirit of emulation, with other universities, to strengthen the scientific and technical level of their faculties and departments, the competence and zeal of their professors, students and auxiliary personnel. May they actively collaborate with the other university centers, maintaining reciprocal exchange; and may they be active in the national inter-university and international organizations. May they maintain frequent contacts with the Congregation for Catholic Education and the Pontifical Council for Culture. In this way they will actively and efficaciously contribute to the promotion and renewal of your culture, transforming it with evangelical power and integrating in a harmonious unity the national, human and Christian elements.

Allow me on this occasion to address a congratulatory greeting to the illustrious Bolivariana Pontifical University of this city of Medellín, which is celebrating the fiftieth anniversary of its foundation. It enjoys solid prestige in Colombia for its cultural initiatives in the service of the region of Antiochia and of the whole country. I extend my cordial congratulations to all of you, to the Cardinal and Chancellor, the Rector, the Board of Directors, the group of Founders, the alumni, the Delegates and students here present. My fervent wish is that, as the vanguard of the particular church of Medellín, you may attain the goals I have proposed.

Conclusion

Now that the time has come to bid one another farewell, I cannot do so without first expressing to all present my gratitude for your efforts and contributions in favor of culture and science. I ask you to communicate to all your colleagues the gratitude of the Pope and the Church.

The Church has need of you! I will say even more: the Church has need of Latin America! Now that we stand at the threshold of the third Christian millennium and prepare ourselves for the imminent fifth centennial of the evangelization of America, I express, from Colombia, the wish that the gift of the various rich and original Latin American cultures, in which Christianity has been incarnated in a profound way, may reach the universal Church in beneficial exchange.

To my words of encouragement for your meritorious work, I unite my prayer to Almighty God, that he may assist you in your tasks, and I give my heartfelt blessing to all present, the institutions which you represent and your families.

THE CHURCH HAS A FUTURE: IT DEPENDS ON YOU!

On Sunday, October 5, in the Gerland Stadium in Lyons, Pope John Paul II met over fifty thousand young people. They staged a dramatic

Address to young people, Lyons, France, October 5, 1986. Reprinted from *L'Osservatore Romano,* November 3, 1986.

performance in three parts; after each part the Holy Father answered certain questions already submitted to him by the young people.

I

TO BEAR WITNESS, ONE MUST BE SURE OF ONE'S OWN FAITH.

After the first part of the dramatic representation of the martyrs of Lyons, the Holy Father was asked questions about faith:
  1. It is not easy to bear witness.
  2. How can we share our faith with others?
  3. Our friends laugh at us if we talk about God.
  4. By means of the sciences and its technology, the world unceasingly calls our faith into question.
  5. We have always a thirst for God: but what is the use of believing?
  6. It is a good fortune to know Christ.
  7. But how can one live God today?
  8. How can one rediscover this first fervor?
  9. Where then is this first Love?
  10. Tell us, Holy Father, if the young people of the other countries ask themselves the same questions as us.
  11. And you, Holy Father, do you ever have doubts?

The Holy Father replied as follows:
  1. *"Arise and walk!"* At Jerusalem, a few days after Pentecost, a sick man looked at Peter at the entrance to the Temple, to receive something from him. Peter said to him: "Silver and gold are not mine to give; but I give you what I have: in the name of Jesus Christ of Nazareth, *arise and walk*" (cf. Acts 3:6). He took up the word Jesus had spoken to the paralytic at Capernaum (cf. Lk 5:24).

Dear friends, the successor of Peter says to you today at Lyons likewise: "Arise and walk."

I do not have silver and gold. I do not have ready-made answers to the questions that you have just asked, and to the questions expressed in your fifteen thousand letters. I have paid careful attention to them. I recognize in them your seriousness, your will to make progress in the faith and to take your part in the Church and in society. You reflect on many of these questions in your groups, your movements, your associations, your parishes. You will continue to study them more deeply in the Church, with your friends, your priests, and those older than you. You will discover the elements of a response.

As for me, I shall seek to situate your problems in the light of Jesus Christ. I come as a *witness to Jesus Christ*. And I say to you, "Arise!" Do not lean back on your weaknesses and on the doubts that you feel, but live upright on your feet. With the faith that you have already placed in Jesus Christ, with the power of his Spirit, walk towards him to build a new world with him and with your brothers.

2. *Jesus Christ, "the Living one"* (cf. Rev 1:18)! For Peter and John, he was the one whom they had seen, touched, and heard after his resurrection. For Paul, he was the Lord who had taken hold of him on the Damascus road: "I am Jesus whom you are persecuting." Polycarp, the aged bishop of Smyrna, professed at the hour of his martyrdom in 155: "I have been a servant of Christ for eighty-six years; how could I curse the King to whom I owe my salvation?" Now, Polycarp had known John, the disciple of the Lord, and the bishop Irenaeus knew Polycarp. The martyrs of Lyons, at the end *The martyrs* of that second century, came in part from the country of Polycarp. *of Lyon* Their witness is linked almost directly to that of the Apostles who saw the Lord. It is the certainty of the resurrection of Jesus that sustains Blandina, and we all belong to the same apostolic Church.

Conscious and Mature Choice

3. *Jesus Christ!* Some adolescents or adults discover him, touched by a special grace of God, and change their life because of him: they are converted. Most, however, receive faith through the Church when they are very young, and it is later that they come to ask themselves questions about this faith, or even to doubt it; then they overcome these doubts. I understand this. I myself lived as a child and an adolescent in an atmosphere of faith, from which I have never really cut myself off. The fundamental problem for me, without there having been a question of doubt, was the passage from an inherited faith that was more emotional than intellectual, to a conscious and fully mature faith which had been deepened intellectually after a *personal choice*. On the basis of the basic conviction that God exists, I deepened my faith in Jesus with the Gospel and with the Church. As Peter's beautiful profession says, he is "the Christ, the Son of the living God" (cf. Mt 13:16), and Jesus Christ led me to know the Father, and to live with the Holy Spirit. Faith is God's gift, but it requires the total gift of self; it finds its fullness in love. "Peter, do you love me truly?" (Jn 20:15). Faith is this choice. It has *the certainty of the love of God*.

4. God does not cease to be *present to this world*. He is the source of all that exists, of all that lives, of all that is spirit and love. His presence *cannot be wiped out*. In 177, the pagans of Lyons believed that they had eliminated the faith in Jesus when they went to the length of throwing the ashes of the martyrs into the Rhone. The resurrection of Christ has a different power. The Holy Spirit does

not let himself be quenched. In point of fact, Lyons as a whole became Christian, and all of Gaul. In our time, some countries believed that they had destroyed the attraction of Jesus and wiped out the name of God. Much has been said about "the death of God", but he does not cease to rise up, astonishingly alive in consciences.

Dear friends, Christ looks intently on each one of you, whoever you may be, as he looked on the young man in the Gospel. Your letters speak of the good fortune of knowing Jesus Christ. I would define this more precisely: it is the good fortune of knowing that he is present, of becoming aware that one is joined to him like a member to the Head of the Body. This is what is effected by baptism, which configures us to Christ. For you who believe, it is Christ who lives in the Church, as in the time of the martyrs. You are the Church that bears witness that Jesus Christ is alive.

5. God is present, but it is true that *we can be absent*. It is not God who fails to turn up at the rendezvous: the risk is that *we* fail to meet him. We have just celebrated the anniversary of the conversion of St. Augustine in 386. After he had looked for happiness on many false paths, he confessed to God: "Late have I loved you, O Beauty ever ancient, ever new! . . . You were within me when I was outside myself, and it was outside that I sought you. . . . You were with me, and I was not with you." Many of our contemporaries too live in *religious indifference,* forgetful of God, organizing their lives without him; they try all the paths to happiness, without daring to believe that Christ is the Truth, the Way, the Life. May they have the strength to wake up, "to rekindle the gift of God that is in them", to pay attention to the One who is knocking at their door, who indeed is more intimate to their being than they themselves are! You are not indifferent. You recognize that in your depths there is the thirst for God, but you suffer from today's indifference.

"You were with me and I will not be with you"

6. You suffer even more from the objections, *the opposition,* the *mockery* of others, when you speak about God. The prophets experienced this suffering: "Who has believed our preaching?" (Is 53:1). Jesus warned us: "Blessed are you, when you are persecuted for my sake!" (Mt 5:11). We are all called to have the courage to bear witness to him without shame. St. Paul lived through these tribulations. Have you not heard in today's Mass how he warned his disciple Timothy: "It is not a spirit of fear that we have received, but a spirit of power, of love and of self-control. Do not be ashamed of bearing witness to our Lord, and do not be ashamed of me, who am in prison for his sake; but take your share of suffering for the proclamation of the Gospel, with the power of God" (2 Tim 1:7–9)? Your martyrs in Lyons suffered the most tremendous cruelties because they were faithful. This history continues today in other places.

Here, in your generation, the opportunity does not exist to resist even to the point of shedding your blood (cf. Heb 12:4). Yet you suffer because you cannot share your faith. God alone is the judge of the conscience of our brothers who believe differently or who do not believe; it belongs to him to bring his truth to fruition in minds and hearts who welcome it freely and without constraint. We will always act with respect, with patience, with love. Still, we desire with the whole of our being that all should know God in fullness; we pray that this gift of God may meet with openness in them; and we must work for this. We must bear clear witness to the faith which we have received, in a dialogue that is attentive to the slightest details and is careful to use language which strikes a chord; we must have confidence in the Holy Spirit who is at work in them. Jesus says to you too: "You shall be my witnesses." If you are not witnesses in the sphere of your family, at school, in the groups in which you spend your free time, in your groups at work, who will bear witness in your place?

7. However, in order to bear witness, one must be *sure of one's faith*. It happens that you doubt sometimes. The discoveries of science and the possibilities of technology dazzle you, so that you do not see the mysterious effectiveness of faith. You must tackle these problems. May you be able to discover that God is of another order than what can be observed and measured by the sciences; nor is he the unknowable figure whom many agnostic philosophers disregard; he is at the origin of existence, and he is of the order of love, as Pascal said! You are invited to *deepen unceasingly your reasons for believing,* and above all to come to know God as he has revealed himself in Jesus Christ. This is the object of your catecheses, of your meetings, of your reviews of life, of your reading, of your retreats, of your prayer. The testing through doubt can lead you to a purified faith, so that you will be ready, as the Apostle Peter said, "to justify the hope that is in you, before those who ask you the reason for it" (1 Pet 3:15).

The test of doubt can lead you to a purified faith

8. *"What is the use of believing?"*

This is the last agonizing question which occupies many of your friends. I would first say to you: what "usefulness" do you mean? If you try directly to utilize God and religion as something extra that will help you to achieve a happiness that can be felt, or to serve your own interests, or to ensure the effectiveness of undertakings that depend on the nature, the intelligence and the heart that God has given you so that you may dominate the world, or even as a means to perfect your moral stature, you risk disappointment. God is not an instrument to make up for our defects. He is Someone. He exists for himself, above everything. He deserves to be known, adored, served, and loved gratuitously, for his own sake. It is also true that he wills that we reach full realization of ourselves.

Irenaeus, the successor of Pothinus and second bishop of Lyons, said, "The glory of God is the living man, and the life of man is the vision of God." Some have asked me to speak about eternal life. Dear friends, *do you desire truly to see God?* Face to face in the next world, after having encountered him in faith in this world? Do you desire to share even now in his divine life, to be saved from what separates you from him, to be forgiven your sins? Such graces do not lie in your own power. God alone can grant you them. Starting from this point, he will do many other things too. You ask him to change things; better than this, he will change you. By looking at God, by giving him your faith, by praying, by nourishing your-selves on him, by "doing the truth" with him, and in particular by responding to the commandment of love, you will no longer be the same persons. In this sense, indeed, faith is very effective. These are the paths *to live God,* as you put it. God is greater than our heart.

9. This morning at Mass on the 27th Sunday of the Year, you heard the Apostles praying to Jesus: *"Increase our faith"* (Lk 17:5). This is indeed the prayer that we must address to the Lord, sustaining each other in this, for, with a little faith, so many things would be possible, as Jesus says.

"Increase our faith!"

I have in fact seen young people of many countries gathered to-gether like yourselves, in dialogue with myself, in almost every land that welcomes me. Many ask themselves the same questions that you ask about the faith. They would like to make a success of their human life, and they would also like to make a success of their life of faith and to renew the world. They are faced with serious problems, about which I shall speak to you. They do not fear to refer to Jesus Christ.

10. Can one rediscover *the first love,* that which the community of Lyons showed for its Lord at the beginning? The first fervor which you perhaps knew when you discovered the Lord?

It is good to find support in these testimonies of fervor: they show what can be produced by the encounter with Jesus Christ, when one sees with new eyes. Yet history never repeats itself exactly in its different situations. Feelings can vary. They are not what matters most. Sometimes one even passes through testing, in the night before the dawn, but the fidelity remains and the convinced attachment grows stronger. Rather than looking back with nostalgia, we must look ahead of us: Christ calls us to take a new step forward. The Holy Spirit is the same as in the first period. He makes the Gospel flourish anew for each generation. "Arise and walk!"

II

IT IS AN ILLUSION TO CLAIM THAT ONE CAN PRESERVE
FAITH IN CHRIST WITHOUT THE CHURCH.

*After the second part of the dramatic representation, dealing with St. Francis
de Sales and the Curé of Ars, the Holy Father was asked questions about
the Church:*

1. I do not ask for a Church with "keys in her hands", or a Church
   that dominates the world like a skyscraper. I would like a
   Church that we can build together.
2. The Church interests us. For us, it is a choice, a personal step.
3. Why do so many young people in France withdraw from the
   Church?
4. Why do we so often understand little of what she says?
5. I have such a great need of a priest who would listen to me;
   why are there so few of them?
6. The Church needs us; but one would not say that this is in fact
   the case!
7. Holy Father, talk to us about the Church; but not the Church
   that is in the books, or in the great ideas. Talk about a Church
   that helps us to live, in our daily life.

The Holy Father replied as follows:

11. "You are the royal priesthood, the holy nation, the people that
belongs to God . . . charged to proclaim the wonders of the one
who called you from the darkness to his marvelous light" (1 Pet 1:9).

Dear friends, this is how St. Peter addressed the new people of
the baptized, the Church. What a joy for me to hear you say: "The
Church needs us. For us, it is a choice, a personal step"! You situate
yourselves inside the Church. You know that it would be an illusion   *The Church
to claim that one can preserve faith in Christ without the Church.   is important
                                                                         to us*
12. This does not prevent you from suffering from the imperfec-
tions with which the Church appears to you to be afflicted, especially
when you see other young people leaving her and giving this as the
reason for their departure. You wish to see her always welcoming,
full of youth, transparent to the Gospel. I too should like to see the
Church like this, and I work unceasingly to this end, with the grace
of God. St. Paul said: "Husbands, love your wives as Christ loved
the Church: he gave himself up for her, in order to sanctify her. . . .
he wished to present her to himself all resplendent, without stain or
wrinkle or any such thing, but holy and immaculate" (Eph 5:25–27).

In fact, this is how the Church is in God's plan and in her actual,
invisible reality. The Second Vatican Council describes the mystery
of the Church before speaking of her structures, and says: the Holy

Spirit "dwells in her, giving her continual youth and renewal, leading her to the perfect union with her Spouse" (LG, no. 4). In this sense, one could speak of a perpetual Pentecost.

Reconciled Sinners

13. *Without stain or wrinkle . . .* but the Church does have wrinkles. She can certainly have them, because today she is no longer an adolescent—she is a Mother who has been confronted for two thousand years with the upheavals of history and the temptations of the world. In the course of the centuries, she has known persecutions that could have awakened a new fervor. However, some of her members too have known the seductions of the spirit of evil; they have become accustomed to riches, to routine; or they have simply known the temptation to make compromises in the necessary dialogue of salvation with the world. Jesus had prayed to his Father: "I do not ask you to take them out of the world, but to keep them from the evil one" (Jn 17:15). The Church is not a club of those who call themselves perfect, but a gathering of reconciled sinners, on the way towards Christ, with their human weaknesses.

The Church is not a club of perfect people

One of the great misfortunes of the Church has been the division of her children, and it is urgent to seek unity with all our separated brothers, just as St. Francis de Sales worked hard and so well to this end, using the methods of the Gospel: love and the search for truth. For infidelity to the truth would be another misfortune.

14. Thus, dear friends, the Church remains holy, because she has been made holy by Christ. Yet the concrete holiness of her members is never wholly realized, like the completed purchase of a house. There is always the duty to build, to rebuild, to purify. Besides, how shall we judge the sins of our elders, if we too are tainted by sin? Before the Lord, we are all poor and sinners. Yet the Church leads us to the sources of holiness, ever since our baptism. She is our Mother: a Mother who nourishes and reconciles. One cannot criticize one's mother as if she were a stranger, for one loves the person who gave one life!

The saints are the visible witnesses to the mysterious holiness of the Church. They remained the most human of people, but the light of Christ penetrated all of their humanity. The spirit that animated them knows no growing old. There are the saints that the Church beatifies and canonizes, but there are also all the hidden and anony-mous saints: they save the Church from mediocrity, they reform it from within—by contagion, one might say—and they draw it towards what it ought to be. The popes come to prostrate themselves before these servants of God, like the Curé of Ars or Father Chevrier.

Dear friends, God gives you a sign by means of the saints. You too are all called to sanctity!

15. With the saints, who are like lighthouse beacons, there is *the whole people of God* on the march. One of you writes: "We would like to have a Church like a house that is in evolution, with the Bible as its root, Christ as the cornerstone, and the Gospel as the chief girder." This is a beautiful image. St. Paul compared the Church to the Temple of God, but also to the human *body*. *"You are the body of Christ, and each one of you is his member"* (1 Cor 12:27). All the members do not have the same function. This is what constitutes the charm of the life of the body.

You young people, baptized and confirmed, are the basic cells, together with all *the Christian laity;* and without these cells there would be no body. An organism differentiated according to the various situations: child, young person, unmarried, married, man and woman, according to your professions, according to the capacities which you put at the service of others, according to the tasks of the apostolate or even the non-ordained ministries which you receive for the animation of your communities. There is no essential difference here between man and woman. On the hierarchical plane, only men are the successors of the Apostles; on the charismatic plane, women animate the Church just as much as men (cf. Discourse to the Youth, Parc des Princes, Paris 1980, no. 18). Yes, the Church truly counts on each one of you: first of all, so that you may develop in yourselves this divine life which has been given to you, and take your part in the service of the Church and in your mission as witnesses before your friends.

The Church is a differentiated organism

Superabundance of Love

16. In the Body of Christ, other members feel themselves called to leave all to follow Christ literally, in *the religious life* or the institutes of the consecrated life, remaining chaste, poor, ready, to signify better the Kingdom of God that is to come. This is a wonderful vocation, and likewise one that is essential to the Church. It can be explained only by a superabundance of love for Christ, like that of the fiancée for her betrothed. Blessed are those who hear this call, and who do not stifle it! Some people have admitted to me: "We are afraid of being called to a consecrated life." Do you not believe that Christ is capable of filling you with his joy and his strength?

17. *Priests* have a particular place within the Body of Christ. No one can enter the priesthood without being called to this by the Church, and being ordained. For the priest carries out a function different from that of the other baptized: in the name of Christ, Head

of the Body, he gathers together his brothers like the Pastor, and sees to it that his authentic Word is accessible to them; he forgives sins and makes the Body and Blood of Christ present to give them in nourishment to his brothers, and he remains at their service to support them and counsel them.

*I need
a priest*
How beautiful it is to hear one of you say: "I have such great need of a priest to listen to me!" Yes, the priest is close to you, while remaining in an intimate union with Christ, consecrated totally to the Gospel and available to all: his commitment to celibacy is necessary for him. Tomorrow, at Ars, I shall speak of this to all the seminarians of France, looking at the formidable ministry of the Curé of Ars. The priest does more than listen to you, of course: he can bring an answer to your doubts, and above all he can give God's answer to the admission of your weaknesses: this is the forgiveness of God, in the Sacrament of Reconciliation. Do you go to your priest to seek this forgiveness?

Why are there so few priests, when they are indispensable to the life of the Body? I put the question to you, dear friends. How could it be possible that no vocations to the priesthood and the religious life arise out of the group of young believers that you constitute, generous and eager to build up the Church? I am sure that many feel this call. What is it that discourages you? You must ponder this, dear friends. I have confidence. I see that in many countries of the world, there is a renewed increase in vocations to the priesthood.

18. In the construction that has Christ as its cornerstone, St. Paul tells us that the Apostles are the foundation (cf. Eph 2:20). You have asked me what is the role of *the bishops* and of the pope. They ensure the unbroken transmission of the life of Christ from the time of the Apostles onwards. They "have received the deposit of the Gospel" (cf. 2 Tim 1:14). They are responsible for the unity of the Christians in the diocese, for their fidelity in the faith and for their missionary drive; they are responsible for their access to the sacraments of Christ. They give "guidance" for your conduct, as you say; and more than guidance, for Christ has entrusted to them the demands made by the Kingdom of God, which are not superfluous counsels, but urgent appeals. Let us say that they are the *Shepherds* in your midst, whom Jesus has given to his Church. This is the reason why the hierarchy exists: they are those who go ahead of the flock as Shepherds. As you put it well, they help you to "keep going". Without a bishop, there is no Church, nor are there priests, for the priests share in the full priesthood of the bishop. St. Francis de Sales was a bishop without equal, a courageous Pastor.

I am the Bishop of Rome, successor of the Apostle Peter; the Lord asks me, as he did Peter, to watch in my turn over the whole of the flock—lambs and sheep—to serve the unity, the fidelity and the progress of all the local Churches, in union with my brothers the bishops. St. Peter is often shown with the keys in his hand! These are the keys designed to open the Kingdom of God and to facilitate access to it. Pray for me too. Let us pray for one another.

Build Together

19. *Let us carry out the precise role* which God has entrusted to each one in his Church. But do not let us erect partitions: let us build together, let us live in a spirit of brotherhood, in mutual esteem. Do not let us cause the gulf between adults and young people to grow. You too, *take your own place well.* Seek to understand the message of the Church—it is sometimes hard, because it is complex, nuanced, destined for all the members of the Body—and seek to explain it to others, and above all to live it humbly.

The life of the Body does not only have structures, a skeleton; it has smaller units, communities small enough to be human, where it is easier to share, to give and to receive. Your family, each of your movements, your associations are such units. The parish too is a *Parish life* necessary unit for it permits the members of the Body—however diverse they may be—to pray, to celebrate, to be reconciled to God and to act together, without divisions. Take part in it simply and act-ively, with respect for others; bring it your music, but harmonize it with the concert of your brothers and sisters who are different from you. The Sunday Eucharist is the high moment of the life in the parish. Do not join those who think that they can live their faith without taking part regularly in the fundamental gathering of the Church.

20. No matter how dynamic a local community may be, it cannot turn in upon itself; nor can a diocese do so. It is *the universal Church* which shows the dimensions of the Body of Christ.

One of you asks whether the Church has a future. She has a future, because she is founded on the living Christ. Has she a good future in one or other region? That depends also on Christians.

Will the Church evolve? She cannot change the foundations of the faith, of morality, of the sacraments, of the structure of the Body of Christ: The Church of Christ is not going to be invented afresh in the year 2000! But she can and must renew herself when confronted with new questions and new forms of unbelief. She has the capacity for this, with the Holy Spirit. Dechristianization is not fatal, but is an illness that passes, a challenge that must be taken up.

Church of France, let yourself be interrogated by the young Churches, those that your missionaries went to plant. Perhaps it is they who have a new impulse to give you! France was the elder daughter of the Church among the new nations, after what we call the barbarian invasions; the Church has other daughters who have grown up! Yet we still count greatly on you, young people of France, who have received so many graces in the course of your history.

With your bishops, in the name of Christ who gave the mandate for mission to the Apostles, I send you into the world!

III
DO NOT ACCEPT COMPROMISES ABOUT THE TRUTH, ABOUT THE GOOD, OR ABOUT RESPECT FOR HUMAN DIGNITY

After the third part of the dramatic representation, dealing with Blessed Antoine Chevrier and Pauline Jaricot, the Holy Father was asked questions about involvement in the world:

1. When the feast is finished, we young people will take up our daily life at once.
2. We are the future of the world.
3. The world is a world of discouragement and competition.
4. A world with its solitudes, its fears, its nuclear armaments, its crimes, its unemployment, its anguish, its drugs, its suicides, its racism, its tortures, its terrorism. . . .
5. A world with its Third World, and its Fourth World, cast on our shoulders like a fault.
6. Is unemployment our fault?
7. Are we guilty if we do not find work?
8. We are young, we want to live.
9. We are here with our projects to form families, our desires for peace and sharing, our dreams of seeing a change of mentalities, and our will to enter into communion.
10. Is the future before us not great?
11. Holy Father, what would you do in our place?
12. Please, Holy Father, do not give us prohibitions, but give us reasons to live.

The Holy Father replied as follows:

What should I do in your place?

21. What would I do in your place, dear friends? I should look at the world with you; I should look at my conscience; and at the same time I should look at the Gospel.

We read there that one day Jesus found himself in front of a great crowd, about five thousand persons eager to hear him, to be freed from their ills, to find in him reasons for living. But they had nothing to eat; it was evening; there was the desert. Jesus did not want to send them away without eating. The Apostles were helpless: "There is a boy here who has five barley loaves and two fishes, but *what are they for so many people?*" (Jn 6:9).

You, dear friends, seem to me to be full of sincerity and of generosity in the face of the multitudes of the world with their many needs. Yet you seem to be saying: "What is our good will for so many people?"

Begin by appreciating what you have, begin by discerning the beauties of the world, by discovering the good deeds of your brothers and sisters, and even by recognizing simply the good dispositions that God has put in your heart. I am happy to hear you say: "We want peace and a true communication among people. We want sharing. We are happy to be in a land of freedom, to have the support of a family that has made sacrifices for our studies. We have plans to form families. We want to live, to make a success of our lives, and also of the life of the world. Where it is necessary, we want to change mentalities." This is how Christ loves young people to be, *Christ loves* full of *ideals,* just as he loved the rich young man in the Gospel (cf. *youth full* my Letter to all the Youth of the world, March 31, 1985). I would *of ideals* add: do not compromise on truth, on goodness, on respect for human dignity. These are the principles of a new world.

22. However, this ideal is submitted to a *harsh testing.* Will it hold out against the hard reality of this world? Will it end up like the utopias? Will it be a flash in the pan? Will this evening's gathering be a feast with no follow-up?

The list of the evils of our society, which disturbs you sometimes even to the point of anguish, is long: so much human loneliness, the unemployment of so many young people, the miseries of every kind, the illusions of a false liberty, even the risks inherent in our nuclear progress, in the invasion of artificial gadgets, in a technology that increases anonymity, depersonalizes and goes as far as the sale of human embryos. Denounce without fear what is linked even more obviously to the sin of men, to their egotistic fears. There is no need to mention once more the intolerance, racism, torture, prostitution, drugs and the temptations to despair, crime, abortion, the trivializing of gestures of love, the blind and pitiless terrorism—to whatever motives it appeals. At Casablanca, before the young Muslims, I prayed to God as follows: "Do not allow us to invoke your name while justifying human disorders." For it is certain that God does not will evil. He has created men for love, for peace, for solidarity, for the reasonable dominion over the world. Continue to feel compassion, like Jesus, in the face of these sufferings. Continue to call evil evil.

Recognize the Dignity of the Poor

23. You will know how to look also with open heart at the miseries of the great crowds of the Third World, hungry for bread, for liberty,

for dignity, thirsty for God. In the quarter of La Guillotière, Father
Chevrier suffered when he saw the children exploited and illiterate,
the people exhausted by their work, badly nourished, badly housed,
old at thirty years of age. This, dear friends, is the lot of so many
peoples who struggle painfully for their development—it is also the
lot of your neighbors of the Fourth World.

Don't live
in anxiety
24. See things clearly, without however living in anguish. The
excessive diffusion of tragic news items and of insoluble problems
can put on your shoulders a burden too heavy to bear. Your anguish
would not bring anything to the poor. Must you feel yourselves
guilty, must you feel in yourselves the blame for all these evils? No,
you are not responsible in the strict sense for these great miseries,
but you will gradually come to have a responsibility to make a
contribution to remedy them. Do not be too quick to point the
accusing finger at the "great ones" of this world, at other categories
of persons and other countries. It is true that human responsibility does exist for many of these ills. But it is complex, and many
have their share in it in solidarity. God created the world in solidarity, and the world makes use of this solidarity, for better or
worse. Yet this solidarity gives us a chance; it will let us react together.

25. Things must change. First, *the heart of man must change*. It is
on the heart that the caring look of kindness depends; it is on the
heart that the helpful gesture depends. Father Chevrier began by
loving the poor of La Guillotière, he drew near, he lived in the midst
of them, he became poor like them. He looked at the Christ of the
crib, of the Cross, of the Eucharist, so poor and so close to us. Above
all, he recognized the dignity of the poor, and the good of which
they were capable. He saw Christ through them. And he could say,
with Jesus, "Blessed are the poor, and those who have the heart of
a poor man, because they are open to the Kingdom of God."

Dear friends, contemplate all your needy brothers with this look
of the Gospel, both those near to you and those far away.

Love Seeks to Help

Love is not content to look on: it tries to bring *its share* of relief, of
concrete and inventive *help*, of prayer. Pauline Jaricot, the laywoman
who was your compatriot, spent her life looking for solutions that
would permit her to come to the aid of the young weavers. She
helped them to form groups, she attempted to create employment
for them, she planned a fund of solidarity and ruined herself by so
doing. She began a movement of spiritual and financial support for
all the missionaries of the world. In her poverty, Pauline gave up

her soul to God without seeing the spread of her work of charity and of her missionary work. We benefit from it today.

26. Perhaps your question remains: "What is that for so many people?" The Second Vatican Council (GS) has explained well the relationship between our modest efforts today and the new world for which we hope. I will quote this text for you: "To the question of how this unhappy situation can be overcome, Christians reply that all these human activities, which are daily endangered by pride and inordinate self-love, must be purified and perfected by the cross and resurrection of Christ" (no. 37). "The fundamental law of human perfection, and consequently of the transformation of the world, is the new commandment of love. . . . Christ brings the certainty that the effort to establish a universal brotherhood will not be in vain. . . . This love is not something reserved for important matters, but must be exercised above all in the ordinary circumstances of daily life" (no. 38). "Certainly, the form of this world, distorted by sin, is passing away; but . . . charity and its works will remain" (no. 39). In other words, "although we must be careful to distinguish clearly between earthly progress and the growth of the kingdom of Christ, such progress is nevertheless of vital concern to the Kingdom of God" (ibid.).

"What is that for so many people?"

Thus, Christians cannot desert the tasks of this world, but must take them up with even more enthusiasm, in love and in hope.

27. You too, dear young people, take part now, at your present age, in raising up the world, where you are. First of all, prepare yourselves to play a role in this, a role of service, by means of all the human, scientific and technical skills that you are in the process of acquiring at school, at university, or in your apprenticeship. Above all, strengthen in yourselves the moral values of uprightness of heart, loyalty, purity, respect for others, the spirit of service and of the gift of self, perseverance in effort; without these, the material and technological change of the world would not lead to progress. One sees this in certain lands which have believed that they were making progress by changing the political or economic regime, but without raising the moral value of persons.

Apart from this important preparation, you must begin today to commit yourselves, not only by giving massive verbal support to the great causes of solidarity with men's efforts for a better world, but also in the thousand concrete gestures which you invent and carry out, personally and as a team, to better the lot of those around you and also of those far away, to help mentalities to change. Thus you will show that you are coming out of yourselves to take care of others. Do not despise these little things which count for much in the eyes of God, and which are never lost, because they are

Go out of yourselves in order to be concerned about others

accomplished in the charity of Christ. Jesus attached importance, and a reward in heaven, to the one who offered a simple "glass of cold water" to one of his disciples (cf. Mt 11:42) and to the one who courageously developed some few talents (cf. Mt 25:23). Why? Because Christ himself took into his hands the bread and the fish of the small boy. He multiplied them in his own way. You have made a small gesture of love, of justice, of forgiveness. Christ takes your offering along with his own, which led through the Passion to his Resurrection. It inaugurated the new world. Yes, *the* new world is born today, by means of your gestures of love and thanks to the breathing on you of the Holy Spirit!

Nuptial Love

28. There is one area in particular where a new world is born; I am speaking to those who are preparing to form a family, having just spoken about the religious and priests. This too was one of your questions, a very important question, and I should like to speak at greater length to you about it. I talk often about this subject, as I did in other circumstances this morning, at Paray-le-Monial. Too many of you suffer from the breakdown of your families. You say: "Is a true and lasting love still possible?" In the name of Christ, I say to you: yes, it is possible. This is the whole plan of God with regard to the family. If this is your vocation, the project of nuptial love that you cherish is very beautiful and corresponds to a call of the God who created the human being "man and woman". But one learns nuptial love day after day. Here too, you already have your responsibility today. As I explained in my Letter to the Youth (no. 10), there is an apprenticeship in the disinterested gift of self, in clarity and simplicity, which takes place in the whole of adolescence and youth, and without which marriage would be a failure, an egotism shared by two people. There is an apprenticeship in respect of the other, of his interior life and of all his person, of which the body is the expression. There is an apprenticeship in all the moral values necessary for life. There is a preparation for the responsibilities which you will carry together for the gift of life and for the education of the children, for the service of society. For marriage is an experience which fills the heart, but also a task to be accomplished. The time of getting to know each other, of being engaged, is this marvelous period of apprenticeship. Do not waste it. Take care to prepare yourself already now for such an engagement. Do not confuse the premature experience of pleasure with the gift of self in the love that arises out of a clear-headed consent for the whole of life. I wish that you may have this great happiness, to form before God, with the

grace of the sacrament of marriage, a couple in which each partner always seeks the happiness and the good of the other, and is not afraid of giving life, with the other, according to the plan of God. It is on the basis of such families that the tissue of society will be refashioned: this is the new world to which we aspire.

A couple who does not fear giving life

29. Here are reasons for living, dear friends. If they involve certain prohibitions, this is because moral evil remains always prohibited, not by the Pope in the first place but by the conscience of each one, which encounters the will of God. It is this evil, whatever form it has, that wounds the dignity of man, his honor, his humanity. Yet Christ never abandons us in evil. He says to the sinner, to the weak man who puts his confidence in him: *"Arise and walk!"*

30. I shall soon leave here to go to Notre Dame de Fourvière, where I am happy to pray to Our Lady with the religious. Pauline Jaricot invented the chain of prayer of the living Rosary. May Our Lady accompany you too on your journey! Like her, let yourselves be inhabited, invaded by the Holy Spirit. He will inspire you with the reasons for living. He will give you the strength to live for God and for others. And, in addition to this, he will give you joy!

THE SPIRITUAL TEMPLE IS BUILT OF THE LIVING STONES OF THE PRIESTHOOD COMMON TO ALL THE BAPTIZED

1. *"Jesus went through all the towns and all the villages"* (Mt 9:35).

This was how Jesus carried out his mission as Messiah in the Holy Land, without going beyond the borders of the land.

This is what still happens, when the disciples of Jesus carry the Gospel "to the ends of the earth". The Lord said to them: *"I am with you"* (Mt 28:20). Where they proclaim the Gospel, he too is present.

Sometimes, this presence—*the saving presence of Christ*— is felt in a particular manner. Then, a city or village takes on a particular radiance on the globe of evangelization.

This is indeed what happened last century *in this village of Ars,* in the years in which the parish priest *John Mary Vianney* carried out the priestly service here. Little by little, all of France and even other countries, other parts of the world, came to know the Curé of Ars. People came from everywhere to draw near to him, to hear him speak of the love of God, to be healed and set free from their sins. After his death, his example took on a new brilliance. Pius XI declared him the patron saint of the parish priests of the whole world. Today there are representatives here of the priests of very many countries.

Homily at Ars, France. Reprinted from *L'Osservatore Romano*, November 10, 1986.

Yes, through this priest it is Christ who has become especially present in this corner of France.

2. *John Mary Vianney came to Ars to exercise there the "holy priesthood"*, to "offer spiritual offerings acceptable to God through Jesus Christ" (1 Pet 2:5). He himself offered these sacrifices. He offered each day the Sacrifice of Christ, with great fervor. "All good works, taken together, do not have the value of the Sacrifice of the Mass, because . . . the holy Mass is the work of God" (*Jean-Marie Vianney, Curé d'Ars, sa pensée, son coeur*, by Fr Bernard Nodet, Le Puy, 1958, p. 107—hereafter cited as Nodet). He invited the faithful to unite their life to this "as a living sacrifice, holy and pleasing to God" (Rom 12:1). He offered himself: "A priest does well to offer himself in sacrifice every morning" (Nodet, p. 107). He offered all his life, constantly united to God in prayer, devoured by the spiritual service of his faithful, marked in secret by the personal penances which he undertook for their conversion and for his own salvation. He sought to imitate Christ, going to the limit of human possibilities, and he became *not only a priest, but a victim*, an offering, like Jesus.

He sought to imitate Christ all the way to the limits of human possibilities

Spiritual and Material

He knew and he proclaimed clearly that *Jesus Christ* is "the living stone" and that all men—through him, with him and in him—must become in their turn "living stones for the construction of the spiritual temple" (1 Pet 2:5).

In France, dear brothers and sisters, you have very many churches, *splendid temples* where the genius of artists has taken inert stones as its starting point and has sought to form in some way an exterior space for the presence of God.

John Mary Vianney benefited from all the splendid tradition of these temples in his own development. He himself undertook to beautify his little church, in accordance with the taste of his period, in order to give honor to God and to encourage the prayer of his people. Nevertheless, he knew *that no exterior space can be* that "construction" of which St. Peter speaks in his first Letter, because none of them is by itself a "spiritual temple".

The spiritual temple is to be built with the "living stones" of the holy priesthood which is common to all the baptized believers. The *root* of this priesthood is *one single* root; it has only one source: *Jesus Christ.*

3. Jesus Christ! John Mary Vianney came to Ars to announce this fundamental truth of our faith to his parishioners: *Jesus Christ, the cornerstone,* chosen by God so that on it there should rise up the temple of *the eternal salvation* of all humanity, the temple which unites

"the entire people whom the Son has gained for the Father" (cf. third eucharistic prayer), the people who are saved.

This temple is at the same time the temple *of the glory of God,* which man is called to contemplate and in which he will share, according to the magnificent words of St. Irenaeus of Lyons: "The splendor of God gives life; those who see God will therefore share in life. . . . The glory of God is the living man, and the life of man is the vision of God" (AH, IV, 20, 5–7). This faith led the Curé of Ars to say: "Our love will be the measure of the glory that we shall have in Paradise. The love of God will fill and inundate everything. . . . We shall see him. . . . Jesus is everything for us. . . . You all together make only one body with Jesus Christ" (Nodet, pp. 245, 246, 49).

It is true that this cornerstone—Jesus Christ—was *rejected by men,* rejected to the point of being condemned to death on the cross on Golgotha; but for God, he remains the stone that is "chosen and precious". For we read in Scripture: "See, I set in Sion a cornerstone, a stone that is chosen and precious. The one who believes in him shall not be put to shame" (1 Pet 2:6).

4. *John Mary Vianney came to Ars as a young man who had believed.* He had believed with all his soul and all his heart, with all the grace of his priesthood.

He had believed with his whole heart and soul

He had believed *in Christ as the cornerstone.* "The one who believes in him shall not be put to shame."

The Curé of Ars brought to his parishioners this fundamental *certainty of the salvation that is in Jesus Christ.*

"He is therefore glory for you who believe, but for those who refuse to believe . . . the stone rejected by the builders has become . . . *a stone on which one stumbles,* a rock that makes one fall. They stumble when they refuse to obey the Word" (1 Pet 2:7–8).

This is what *Peter* taught. This is what the *Curé of Ars* taught.

The word "salvation" is the word most frequently used by John Mary Vianney. He never ceased to warn his faithful, especially the lukewarm and indifferent souls, the sinners and the unbelieving, of the risk to their salvation which they were incurring by refusing to follow the path of faith and love traced by the Savior; he wanted to prevent them from falling, from being lost and separated from Light and Love forever. However, he added: "This Good Savior is so full of love that he seeks us everywhere" (Nodet, p. 50).

The words of Peter and of the Curé d'Ars are only an echo of the prophetic words which *Simeon* had earlier spoken about the newborn Jesus, forty days after his birth: "He will cause the fall and the rising of many . . . he will be a sign of contradiction" (Lk 2:34).

Dignity of the Laity

5. The Curé of Ars had the same faith in Jesus Christ as Simeon and the Apostle Peter: "Salvation is to be found in no one else" (Acts 4:12)

Strong in this faith, he came here, sent by the bishop *to make the work of salvation present and effective*.

His parishioners at that time were not perhaps very well acquainted with questions of faith: the Vicar General had warned him, "There is not much love of God in this parish, but you will put it there." Yet *he did not hesitate* to proclaim, by his words and by his life, to the people of Ars and to all those who came to join them, the message of Peter which rings out so forcefully in the teaching of the Second Vatican Council: "You are *a chosen race, a holy priesthood, a holy nation, the people that belongs to God*" (1 Pet 2:9).

Yes, this is what you are, dear brothers and sisters. This is your dignity, this is your vocation as laypeople who have been baptized and confirmed.

"You are therefore to proclaim the wonderful works of him who called you out of the darkness into his marvelous light" (ibid.).

The Curé of Ars himself walked in this light. He knew that it was destined for all: all are called to this "marvelous light".

The faithful share in the priesthood of Christ

Since his time, the Second Vatican Council has emphasized this dignity and this responsibility which belong to the baptized. They share in the priesthood of Christ in order to exercise the spiritual worship, in his prophetic function in order to bear witness, and in his kingly service: "they have received in the same way the faith that leads into the righteousness of God . . . ; the members have a common dignity because they have been reborn in Christ; the grace of filial adoption is common; the vocation to perfection . . . and to holiness is common" (cf. LG, no. 32). The Curé of Ars never ceased to remind his faithful of their dignity, as persons loved by God, sanctified by Christ and called to follow him.

6. Yes, all are called, and constantly *called* to come to the light, to come forth from the *darkness*. Sometimes from very deep darkness. From a darkness that obscures the spirit, *the darkness of sin*. From the obscurity of unbelief.

One hundred years later, the Second Vatican Council had the same reality before its eyes. It was to seek *the paths that led to an encounter*, to a dialogue with those who do not believe and with the believers of other religions. For it knew that this is always a case of the *"dialogue of salvation"*, as my predecessor Paul VI so well said.

The Curé of Ars knew only too well that what matters is the dialogue of salvation. He used all the means possible in his period to promote its progress. Could one reproach him because he carried out this dialogue of salvation in such simple places, worn-out places that still move us today: *this old pulpit, this confessional* which he occupied in a *tireless* manner?

The Priestly Ministry of Forgiveness Is a Gift from on High

7. What counts is first of all the fact that it was a *true dialogue of salvation,* an *astonishingly fruitful* dialogue that leaves us speechless even today.

The fruits which it produced were due to that *"marvelous light"* which comes, not from man, but from God. The priestly ministry of forgiveness is always a gift from on high; through the priest who has been ordained for this ministry, it is Christ who explains, who heals, who pardons. The Curé of Ars had a heart burning with love, which lent itself wonderfully to this action of Christ.

The priestly ministry of forgiveness

The fruits which it produced were fruits of *mercy,* that is to say of the merciful love of God, thanks to which "those who seemed to be deprived of mercy" came back from that state as "those who have obtained mercy" (cf. 1 Pet 2:10). They came back *converted.* They returned from Ars *absolved of their sins.*

The Curé of Ars put these words on the lips of Christ: "I will charge my ministers to announce to them that I am always ready to receive them, and that my mercy is infinite" (Nodet, p. 135).

Oh, dear brothers and sisters, do you measure sufficiently the unheard-of grace of being absolved from one's sins, of coming back to the love of God, to the state of friendship with him, of being indwelt by him, of being reborn to the life of God, of being reintegrated into those who are sanctified by God? Do you see the Cross where Christ gave his life for this redemption? Do you desire this pardon, this spiritual rebirth, which no one can give to himself, and without which there is no true communion with God and with our brothers? Do you prepare yourselves seriously for this? Do you go to ask your priests for the Sacrament of Reconciliation? Do you live it, and do you celebrate it worthily?

Thanks to the humble service of the Curé of Ars, those who were not "the people of God" became the true *"people of God",* the temple of living stones, built on the cornerstone, on Christ.

8. *To build up the Church!* That is what the Curé of Ars did in this village.

The conversion and forgiveness which were prepared by his direct and simple preaching were to permit his parishioners to make progress on the path of union with God, in Christian conduct, and in apostolic testimony and responsibility.

The Eucharist was the summit of the parochial assembly. He

celebrated it in such a way that each one was vividly aware of the presence of Christ. He invited those who were prepared, to receive Communion frequently.

He taught his parishioners to pray and to adore the Blessed Sacrament; or rather, they themselves felt drawn to come and pray in this church like him.

He saw to it that no work or business prevented the celebration of Sunday. He accepted the risk of opposition and calumnies when he preached against conduct or customs which seemed to him to be opposed to the spirit of truth, to honesty, purity, and charity according to the Gospel; but he promoted healthy popular feasts.

His parish quickly took on a new face. He himself did not fail to go to visit the sick and the families. He took special care of the poor, of the orphan girls of "La Providence", and of the children who did not receive schooling. He gathered the young girls together. He strengthened the fathers and mothers of families in their educative responsibilities. He organized the confraternities. He *brought about the cooperation of the parishioners,* who, in a sense, took charge of the work. He formed collaborators and associated them with himself. He organized parish missions. He gave education in prayer and in missionary help, at the time when another son of this diocese, St. Peter Chanel, set out for Oceania and died a martyr at Futuna.

Christ Stayed Here

Thus the Curé of Ars encouraged the various vocations to the service of the Church, with the means, in accordance with the methods, *Together with the laity he was building God's temple* and following the needs of his time. Together with the laity, he built here the temple of God; in communion with his priestly confrères, his bishop and the Pope.

Everyone knows how his *irreplaceable ministry as a priest,* carried out in the name of Jesus Christ, with the Holy Spirit, set this progress in being, gave life to it and nourished it.

9. Thus *Christ indeed came to stay here,* at Ars, in the period in which Jean Mary Vianney was the parish priest here.

Yes, he came to stay. *He saw* "the crowds" of men and women in the last century who were "weary and harassed, like *sheep without a shepherd"* (Mt 9:36).

Christ came to stay here as the Good Shepherd. "A good pastor, a pastor according to the heart of God", said John Mary Vianney, "is the greatest treasure that the good God can grant a parish, and one of the most precious gifts of the divine mercy" (Nodet, p. 104).

From this place, Christ has said to his disciples, as he had once said in Palestine, he has said to all the Church that is in France, and

to the Church, spread over all the earth: "*The harvest is plentiful, but*
the laborors are few. Pray therefore the Lord of the harvest to send
workers for his harvest" (Mt 9:37–38).

Today, he says this likewise, for the needs are immense and urgent.

The bishops, successors of the Apostles, and the successor of Peter
see more than others the great extent of the harvest, with the promises
of a renewal and also the wretchedness of the souls abandoned to
themselves, without apostolic workers.

The priests are well aware of this need, when they see how thinly
spread they are in many places, and they wait for the commitment
of more young people in the priesthood or the religious life.

The laity and the families are equally convinced of this, for they
count on the ministry of the priest to nourish their faith and stimulate
their apostolic life.

The children and the young people know it well, for they have
need of the priest to become disciples of Jesus, and perhaps to share
his joy in consecrating themselves entirely to the service of the Lord,
to his harvest.

All of us who are gathered together here, having meditated on the
life and the service of St. John Mary Vianney, Curé of Ars, this
exceptional "*worker*" of the harvest in which the salvation of men is
accomplished,

  we all raise an insistent supplication to the Lord of the harvest,
  we pray for France, for the Church throughout the whole world:
  Send workers into your harvest!
  Send workers!

A MORE SOLID EUROPEAN UNITY
BASED ON COMMON CHRISTIAN VALUES

1. "Before the mountains were born, and the earth and the world
came to birth, from all eternity you are God" (Ps 89 [90]:2).

Before the majestic spectacle of these almighty summits and this
spotless snow, our thought rises spontaneously to him who is the
Creator of these marvels: "From all eternity you are God."

In every age, humanity has considered the mountains to be the
place of a privileged experience of God and of his immeasurable
greatness. Man's existence is precarious and subject to change, while
that of the mountains is stable and lasts: an eloquent image of the
unchangeable eternity of God.

The chaotic din of the city falls silent on the mountains, the silence

Angelus address at Val D'Aosta. Reprinted from *L'Osservatore Romano*, September
22, 1986.

of the limitless spaces dominates: a silence in which man may hear more distinctly the echo of the voice of God within himself.

When we look at the peaks of the mountains, we have the impression that the earth juts out towards the height, as if it wished to touch heaven: man feels this to be a kind of representation of his own yearning for transcendence and for the infinite.

How evocative it is to look at the world from on high, and to contemplate this magnificent panorama, taking it all in with a single glance! The eye does not weary of admiring it, nor the heart of rising up higher still; the words of the liturgy, *Sursum corda,* re-echo in our mind, inviting us to go ever higher up, towards the realities that do not pass away, and even beyond time, towards the future life. *Sursum*

corda: each of us is invited to *go beyond himself,* to seek the "things that are above" (Col 3:1), as St. Paul puts it, to lift up his gaze to heaven, where Christ has ascended as "the first-born of all creation, because everything in heaven and on earth was created in him" (Col 1:16).

Contemporary man seems sometimes to follow the opposite principle, denounced by the same Apostle of the "knowledge of the things that are above the earth", that is, the principle of orientating himself exclusively towards the things of the earth, in a materialistic vision of life; he must learn afresh to look upwards, towards the peaks of grace and of glory, for which he has been created, and to which he is called by the goodness and greatness of God. *Agnosce, christiane, dignitatem tuam,* "Christian, recognize your dignity"; go beyond what is created, go beyond yourself, to find the traces of the living God that are impressed not only in these majestic beauties of nature, but above all in your own immortal spirit! Like your fathers, seek "the things that are above, not the things of the earth"!

Unity Rooted in Christian Patrimony

2. Drawn by the fascination of the mountains, man has sought in the course of the centuries to scale even the most difficult peaks, without ever giving up in the face of their harshness and his own failures.

Here too, man has continued to attempt to conquer the peak of Mont Blanc, the highest summit of Europe, although the difficulty of this undertaking slowed down for centuries the realization of the project. It was only two centuries ago, on the afternoon of August 8, 1786, that two brave mountaineers succeeded in setting foot for the first time on the summit of this mighty mountain covered in snow and ice.

We are here to celebrate this historic event, in which we admire the confirmation of the fundamental charge given to man by God at the dawn of time, to dominate the earth, the charge which the Bible has faithfully recorded on its first pages.

And we are here also to reflect on the meaning of the lively interest which that successful undertaking aroused then and continues to arouse even today in all of Europe. The interest is born of the fact that Europe has always seen a reason for pride, indeed almost a symbol of itself, in the high peak of Mont Blanc, set geographically at the center of the Continent. The celebration of the bicentenary of this courageous ascent offers us therefore in a certain sense the occasion to reflect on the profound unity that binds together the nations of Europe.

3. It is a unity that has its roots in the common patrimony of values from which the individual national cultures draw their life. The essential core of this patrimony consists of the truth of the Christian faith. A glance at the history of the formation of the European nations shows the decisive role played in each of them by the progressive inculturation of the Gospel.

It is, therefore, on the basis of such an essential core of human and Christian values that Europe can seek to reconstruct its renewed and more solid unity, and thus recover its significant role in the progress of humanity towards goals of authentic civilization.

Therefore, from the height of this Alpine peak, which permits us to look down on the territories of three different nations, I renew my appeal to Europe that anachronistic tensions and ancient prejudices be overcome, and the continent may recover the reasons for its unity, and find again the values that made it great in its history throughout the centuries.

4. I renew this appeal on the vigil of the day on which the Church celebrates the feast of the Nativity of the Most Holy Virgin. Mary is the mother of redeemed humanity, because she is the mother of Christ the Redeemer. No one has more power than the mother to promote the mutual understanding and the intimate unity of the members of the family. Europe is a family of peoples, united among themselves by the bonds of a common religious descent.

Mary promotes understanding and unity

I address my prayer to Mary, therefore, that she may deign to look with motherly benevolence on Europe, this continent that is covered with innumerable sanctuaries dedicated to her. May her intercession obtain for the Europeans of today the acute sensitivity towards those indestructible values which made all the world admire the Europe of yesterday, favoring the continent's progress towards prestigious goals of culture and well-being.

Europe has a role of its own to play in human affairs in the third millennium. It gave so much to human progress in past centuries, and will be able to be a bright beacon of civilization for the world tomorrow too, if it knows how to return and draw from its original sources, in harmony and concord: from the best classical humanism elevated and enriched by the Christian Revelation.

May Mary Most Holy, first fruits of redeemed humanity, help Europe to be worthy of its own historical tasks, and may she support it as it confronts the challenges that the future has in store for it.

[*The Holy Father continued in French:*]

I wish to address a very friendly greeting to all French-speaking persons who are listening to me here, in particular to the compatriots and successors of the first mountaineers who conquered Mont Blanc two centuries ago, setting out from Chamonix.

Be Enterprising and Faithful

Near this summit of Europe, where the boundaries meet in a majestic setting, I repeat my hopes to the men and women of the continent: may they preserve the enterprising spirit of those who went before them! It is my wish that the people of Europe may remain faithful to the values that made their history fruitful and that they may know how to tackle the challenges of the present epoch.

It is my wish that the Europeans may remain faithful to the values of their history

We call on the Creator of heaven and earth: may he grant you the power of hope and the ardor of charity!

May the Virgin Mary intercede for you!

The inhabitants of Courmayeur have put up her statue here on Mount Chetif to thank her for her protection, and they invoke her under the title of "Queen of Peace". May she preserve all the peoples of this region in peace! May she be the guide of the believers who take the steep path that leads to her Son, the Savior!

And may God fill you with his blessings!

CULTURE IS THE "REGAL WAY" OF TOTAL LIBERATION

Mr. Minister, Mr. Mayor and Authorities of Florence and the Region of Tuscany;

Distinguished Rector of the University of Florence and Mr. President of the European University Institute;

Italian and European Members of Parliament;

Address in Florence, Italy, October 18, 1986. Reprinted from *L'Osservatore Romano*, November 17, 1986.

Artists and Representatives of Florentine culture, and guests of this cultural capital of Europe;

Dear Brothers and Sisters:

1. You can understand the depth of my feeling as I stand in this palace and this hall, for centuries the heart of the civic, social, political and artistic life of Florence, whose ancient ties with the center of Catholicism are indelibly inscribed in history.

These ties were multiple and in many respects unique, born of both harmony and strife, sometimes even of fierce conflicts; but the Christian sense of life, so very strong here, prevailed in the end, without a doubt. Imperishable witness to this fact is borne by the famous masterpieces of religious art which, from the center of Christianity, point to this noble city, coming as they do from the hands of the greatest artists of Florentine origin or training.

I am grateful to you, illustrious and dear ladies and gentlemen, for your kindness in participating in this assembly, and I cordially greet you. You know what joy and what a sense of responsibility I feel when meeting men and women of the cultural world during my journeys. I feel close to them, especially because of the many opportunities I have had in my life to relate to universities and environments of study. Today I meet, along with other representatives of the political, cultural and artistic world, the Rector and the members of the academic body of the University Institute, whom I thank for their profound and noble welcome. Then there is a large group representing the European Parliament. This is an illustrious assembly, and the poet Mario Luzi has eloquently interpreted its sentiments and expectations. For all this I am grateful to you and to the world of culture which you so worthily represent.

Florence: This Year's European Capital of Culture

2. Perhaps there is no place more fitting than this hall to proclaim a message to people, summoning them to recognize once again in culture the "regal way" of liberation from the various forms of slavery which, today as yesterday—indeed, more than yesterday—suffocate and threaten the dignity of the human person in one way or another. It is true that in our time cities seem to be losing their physiognomy and, even more, the interior identity forged by their history. Yet we do not lack signs of a change of course. In reaction to the general leveling process, we are seeing a growing need—which, most importantly, is in direct proportion to the degree of technological progress—to seek in the past the principles of cohesion and of the recovery of values. Without these both individuals and social groups lose the

Culture, the "royal way" of liberation

conditions necessary for a harmonious growth integrating individual identity with openness to different identities.

3. In this context one sees the universal value of the European Community's inspiration to recognize, year after year, as its cultural capitals, the cities which have embellished the historical patrimony without which not only Europe but the whole world would feel impoverished. This year it was Florence's turn to be given the role of European capital of culture. Perhaps in this case as in no other it is possible to say that archeology can be converted into prophecy, that the future has an ancient heart. *Antiquitas saeculi, iuventus mundi.*

Truly, in this historic shrine of Florentine civilization, we seem to hear the many voices of those who have earned Florence the title of "the Athens of Italy". In this city we see the harmonious mingling of daring architectural lines, elegant movements sculpted in stone, the fine work of the chisel, evocative figures painted in beautiful gradations of color. The mystery of beauty—so luminous in its being, and so difficult to translate into words—shines brilliantly from Florence, bringing one to intuit the yearning for the divine that animates the expressions of art from within.

Here echoes the exalted Canto of "the sacred song to which both Heaven and Earth have set their hand" (*Paradiso* XXV, 1–2). The voice of Dante, with his sublime poetic rhythms and his human-divine vision of reality, seems to summarize Florence's title of greatness: city of writers, men of letters, poets, architects, painters and master sculptors, depository of the glories of Italy.

Yes. Together with you, I render fervent homage to Florence, worthily proclaimed the European capital of culture this year. I pay homage to her history, to her incomparable artistic patrimony, to her creative genius. I pay homage, in a special way, to the riches of intellect, heart and humanity contained in and expressed by this patrimony.

4. This, then, is one of the first tasks of culture: to reconstruct incessantly man's memory, in view of the ever new challenges that await him. A short while ago, the Florentine humanism from which modern Europe drew its identity was authoritatively recalled under its various aspects. It was and is a message destined for all times and peoples, not just for specialists in historical-literary research. The return to the Greeks and Romans was not a flight from the present into the past, but—within the continuity of the Christian tradition and profession—the recovery of an authentic human treasure for the sake of its higher confirmation within the horizons of faith.

Florentine humanism had given rise to modern Europe

Florentine humanism was thus a prophetic event, open to the future. In it there mingled the holiness of Antonino, the spirituality of Blessed Angelico, the vehemence of Savonarola and the wide-ranging learning of Leonardo and Michelangelo.

Florence's vocation as a "bridge" joining past and future characterizes her history from her origins to the present. Perhaps this is the real reason she manifests, even as the seasons pass, a sort of immutable essence. Already at the beginning of the fifteenth century the humanist Leonardo Bruni, who lived as a magistrate in this palace for many decades, had written: *"Nec ullus est in universa Italia qui non duplicem patriam se habere arbitretur privatim, propriam unusquisque suam, publice autem Florentinam urbem."* Florence had a particular opportunity to note this double citizenship not only of Italians, but of Europeans in general when she was submerged by floods twenty years ago: she was freed from the mud by young people who came from all parts of Italy and Europe, and even from America. A man's homeland is found not only where he is physically born and lives, but also where he can read, incarnate in the stones and traditions, the values that give meaning to his life.

5. From this perspective one grasps the profound meaning of Florence's cultural vocation as it appears throughout the successive periods of history, periods connected, in the last analysis, by the underlying thread of the *studia humanitatis,* which found their center and symbol in the *Studium Generale* founded, as the Rector recalled, in 1321.

"Florentinis ingeniis nil arduum est": This declaration, which consecrated the appearance of the first printed book in Florence around the year 1472, may be applied not only to the multiformity of the culture, but also, and perhaps above all, to its interior meaning as recognizing the value of man.

"To the clever Florentines nothing is difficult"

Here we find man's original dignity. The manifestations of human genius are a response to the Creator's initial command to "subdue the earth". This command is rich with meaning, not merely indicating dominion over the products of the soil, but including all that man can discover in the immensity of creation, and that he then elaborates with the resources of his intelligence (LE, no. 5). Strictly speaking, there can be no culture in the full sense without a conscious link with the transcendental dimension, which reflects the wellspring of culture and precisely in this does honor to man.

The Church looks sympathetically on the various expressions of culture. She is a friend to men and women of culture. She promotes the progress of culture. All this is with the aim of serving the great cause of the human person.

The Church favors the progress of the culture

I am extremely pleased to reaffirm the solid alliance of the Catholic Church with culture, today, in this city. As I have said, echoing the eminent speakers who preceded me, Florence is the home of an incomparably versatile culture open to the arts, poetry, literature and science. The common denominator is man. The horizon within which this vision is situated is the universality of the spiritual interests to which man is called by virtue of his intrinsic vocation as the living image of the living God.

6. This universality has impressed itself deeply upon the vocation characteristic of this city. In seeking the profound reasons for this, it is enough to let one's gaze fall upon the mysterious interplay between Arnolfo's tower of the City Hall and Brunelleschi's dome of the cathedral. It is the dialogue, embodied in visual beauty, between time and eternity, between the present kingdom which advances towards the future and the future Kingdom which approaches the present. It is no mere accident that the Florentines began their calendar year with the day of the Incarnation: that is, of the Angel's annunciation to Mary, to whom the most popular church in the city, the church of the Annunciation, is dedicated. So one cannot help but see the harmonious hierarchical articulation in Florence which joins the base to the summit, the artisan's shop to the Cathedral, work to contemplation. We must also recall that few cities in the world have produced such a wealth of saints as Florence.

Fatal Obscurity of the Truth and Dignity of Man

7. The glories inherited from the past must therefore act as a source of inspiration and commitment in seeking and developing universal values.

We have been called to live in an age which in many ways brings to mind the transformations which characterize the humanism of ages past. We are seeing once again today, in a certain way, a shift in the focus of attention from the Absolute of God to the relative of man, with the variations and nuances that are well known to you and that lead us to speak of diverse forms of humanism.

In reality, the true line of demarcation is univocal, having a precise identity. It is constituted by theoretical and practical atheism, which, in its various manifestations, promises a *regnum hominis* in opposition to, or in competition with, the *regnum Dei*. Today, therefore, many thinkers, even among those who do not travel along the path of Revelation, note with concern that the banishment of God carries with it a fatal obscurity of the truth and dignity of man, and thus an incessant decline in our civilization.

The Church made this situation the object of her loving concern, as you know, in her highest form of collegial expression in the Second Vatican Council. She examined it, first of all, in an analysis of herself, of the divine plan from which she arose, of the mission entrusted to her by her Founder and, in particular, of the way she is to carry out her mission relative to today's world; and so she concerned herself with man, always keeping her gaze fixed upon his two inseparable dimensions—transcendental and existential—in an objective and complete vision of created being. She also concerned herself with his culture: "It is specific to the human person that he cannot attain a truly and fully human level of life except through culture" (GS, no. 23). Thanks to a very broad concept of culture, understood as the complex of values and means by which man expresses the richness of his personality in all its dimensions, the Church draws upon her centuries-old experience, not bound to any particular form of culture, because she transcends and can adapt herself to all of them in a mutual exchange of authentic values.

The twofold dimension of man: the transcendent and the existential

These orientations can be seen in every dimension of culture that has at heart man and his genuine progress, his liberation from the nightmares and anguish that torment him, an increase of hope.

Balance between Spirit and Matter

8. Man! In the final analysis, he is the first architect and beneficiary of culture. Historical man! Man composed of soul and body! Man the saint and the sinner! Man called to collaborate with God in transmitting life and instilling in his works the rhythm of the harmony and beauty of the spirit.

As I said at the headquarters of UNESCO in Paris six years ago: "*Man is always the primary reality: man is the primordial and fundamental reality* of culture. Man is always this: *in the integral compound of his spiritual and material subjectivity.*"

It is from a distortion—conscious or otherwise—of this vision that the terrible problems which have been mentioned here were born; when man's primordial balance between spirit and matter is destroyed the way is opened wide to all forms of deception.

From this city of the spirit, then, it is necessary forcefully to proclaim that it is an urgent duty today to promote *the truth about man* in every way possible. It is a duty which cannot be postponed. "The truth that so elevates us" (*Paradiso* XXII, 42) is an incomparable value: in itself, as the light of the intellect; in historical situations that are inclined to lies, easily disposed to falsification, casually given to the cult of half-truths or pseudo-truths. These phenomena are fomented by cultural forms which reduce man to one dimension.

The truth of man and about man must be proclaimed from the integral perspective of his finite being and his infinite destiny. This truth is the specific goal of those who walk the paths of culture—"seekers of truth", as the Council defined them in its message to scholars and scientists, "explorers of man, pilgrims advancing towards the light".

Seekers of truth

Today, at the threshold of the year two thousand, humanity finds itself in the throes of unprecedented change, which can occur in a salvific way only through a new culture of global dimensions. The decisive vital energy needed for the passage from one form of culture to another with growing universality is the Faith, which—since it is never identified with any given culture—offers man the foundation upon which to climb above the horizon of what is being superseded.

Revealed truth, the object of faith, flows from God, the first and creative Being. The Son of God, who becoming man for man's salvation, presented himself as that same Truth: *Ego sum via, veritas et vita* (Jn 14:6). The way, outside of which one is lost in the labyrinth of contradictions and unanswered questions; the truth, which makes us free (cf. Jn 8:32); the life, which assures man of the dimension of eternity and even now situates him in it with the gift of grace.

Dante composed a vast synthesis of the human adventure, combining all the elements of biblical wisdom, Christian revelation and the Greco-Latin culture, along with the ferments of his disturbed age, in a quest for interior liberation leading from the "wild forest" of sin through higher and more intense purification, all the way to man's immersion in God himself—"which in his sight alone finds peace for aye" (*Paradiso* XXX, 102). This synthesis can only be understood in the light of the Gospel, of the word of Christ embraced as the only salvation, the salvation of medieval man and that of modern man as well.

Culture Is the Builder of Peace

9. In harmony with these presuppositions, which touch upon man's most intimate values, there derives the clear and convincing consequence that *culture is the builder of peace.* It is an invitation to overcome all conflicts, all wounds. An invitation which is all the more persuasive coming from Florence, which has been the bridge linking different cultures and civilizations. On the ecclesial plane, there comes to mind the Council of Ferrara-Florence, which saw the meeting here of the representatives of Rome and Byzantium and the most eminent personages of the Greek and Latin theological culture of the time. They met for a settlement between the two sister Churches, which culminated in the act of 1439. Though unfortunately it remained little more than formal relative to the goal initially set, still it provided the starting point for a fruitful encounter between the two cultures, from which benefits were reaped throughout the history of Europe and of the West as a whole. On the scientific plane, there was the work and example of Galileo: beyond the vicissitudes that dramatically accompanied his discoveries, the fact remains that he manifested an exemplary harmony between humanistic and scientific

knowledge, between human knowledge and divine revelation. The split between faith and science on the one hand, and scientific knowledge and humanistic culture on the other, was to come later.

With regard to Florence's role as mediator, one which has provided Italy with the unifying instrument of the national language—I recall the eloquent attitude of Allesandro Manzoni—it is particularly meaningful to recall here, as I have said, the value of the *culture of peace*. *Florence gave to Italy the unifying instrument of the language* It is with deep emotion that I repeat this word in your presence, as we are only a few days away from the gathering in Assisi to which I have invited representatives of the Christian confessions and of other religious denominations, with the aim of imploring from heaven the immense gift of peace. My faith, my hope, the most fervent wish of my heart, is that this initiative will signal a new impulse in the development of the attitude of peace. It is also to the creators of culture, to their genius and good will, that I would like to entrust, in a special way, this initiative. They will be able to discover in it stimuli for infusing into their endeavors love, fraternity, solidarity—in a word, all those goods of which the fabric of the supreme good of peace is woven. Peace, as the gift of Almighty. Peace, as an edifice constantly being constructed through the work of human minds, hearts and hands.

10. With reference to the words of Professor Scaramuzzi and to the overall framework of the projects, aims and problems of the Florentine university of which he is Rector, I want to express my satisfaction first of all for the vitality shown by the institution: in the remarkable number of its teachers, in its concern to communicate to young people coming from other regions of Italy, as well as from other countries, a truly complete formation, true learning.

I would like to assure those young people—as is my duty, and as I always do with them—that the Church shares their aspirations, their ideals and their anxieties, anxieties which are today often thorny because of the uncertainty aroused in many of them at the prospect of a future seemingly inaccessible to them. Still, I am confident that their academic efforts under the guidance of their professors, and the decisions and choices of the political world, will allow them to look more serenely to the tasks that await them, and to find suitable opportunities to assume full responsibility in the professional world.

From the perspective of a politics of culture that places today's most urgent needs in a privileged position, and which is thus deeply felt by the young, and in the light of the orientations which I have presented, I would like to express my hopes in certain areas which I consider of particular importance.

My first hope is that further study will be dedicated to man's

To examine carefully man's fundamental problems

fundamental problems, leading to a greater contribution in the following areas:

—defense of human rights, particularly those of the marginalized and of foreigners;

—the orientation of industry towards exclusively peaceful ends;

—the development of a technology suited to the needs and practices of developing countries.

It is also to be hoped that substantial efforts will be made to spread humanistic and scientific knowledge and to facilitate access to it, so that the right to learning and culture will be more broadly applied, in line with the United Nations Treaty on economic, social and cultural rights (articles 13–15).

11. Today's gathering is also an occasion for mentioning the participation of the Deputies of the European Parliament, in the context of the proclamation of Florence as the cultural capital of Europe.

I already referred to them at the beginning of this address; and the significance of their presence here has already been pointed out at various levels in this prestigious assembly, so I will not emphasize it further. Yet I cannot fail—before such an elect and numerous group of representatives of the highest body of the European Community—

The Christian roots of Europe

to recall once more the Christian roots of Europe. The Apostolic See has often referred to them in order to confirm the awareness of this common origin; she has also emphasized the need to conserve the physiognomy that has deeply impregnated the forms of public life, culture, art and literature of Europe.

It suffices to recall, as a symbol and a pledge of that spiritual continuity, the naming of Saint Benedict and the brothers Saints Cyril and Methodius as the Patrons of Europe. I once again entrust to those great geniuses of faith and culture, to those powerful intercessors in the Church of God, the future destiny of our ancient continent, which still has so much to say and to give to mankind today.

As from Santiago de Compostela in 1982, so today from Florence I cry to Europe: "Rediscover yourself. Be yourself. Rediscover your origins. Revive your roots. Live once again the authentic values that have made your history glorious and your presence on other continents fruitful. . . . You can still be a beacon of civilization and an incentive to progress for the world" (9-11-1982: *Insegnamenti*, V, 3, p. 1260).

12. Illustrious and dear gentlemen, on Christmas night of 1966, Pope Paul VI, pilgrim to a Florence still suffering from the wounds of floods, left the Florentines with this mandate: "Your vocation is in the spirit; your mission consists in spreading it" (*Insegnamenti*, IV, 1966, p. 637).

This is the mandate that Florence transmits to men and women of culture, and that they—I am sure—gladly embrace. The homage rendered to the cradle of humanism is not a purely symbolic act, but the expression of the will to contribute to the construction of that integral humanism which must impose itself on the conquests of technology as the solid basis of civilization in the remaining years of this century.

May this be the wide-ranging fruit of today's Florentine celebration, with the blessing of God, the Creator and Redeemer of man, which I heartily invoke upon you and upon the world of culture.

I APPEAL TO THE WORLD OF MEDICINE: LET NOTHING BE DONE AGAINST LIFE

Dear Friends,

1. I greet you in the love of our Lord and Savior Jesus Christ. I am delighted to have this opportunity to come to the Mercy Maternity Hospital, *to meet the sick and those engaged in health care.* In you I embrace all the sick and their helpers in every part of Australia. As a priest and a bishop, and now as Pope, I have always felt a special closeness to the sick. In Rome I try to be with the sick as often as possible. On my journeys to the local Churches throughout the world I look forward to the moment of meeting the sick and those who care for them; it is a very special moment. Today in the name of Christ and the Church, I greet the patients and I thank and encourage all those who work for them. May God be with you in all you do.

2. I have learned of the work of the Sisters of Mercy, begun in Ireland in 1831 by Catherine McAuley and carried on with great success in this country. You are a group of talented women committed to following Christ in the religious life, in the care of the sick, and in all the other spheres of your service, and I pray for the continued success of your Institute.

Talented women committed to following Christ

Nor can I forget that there are many other congregations of sisters and brothers working for the sick and the needy all over Australia. *Catholic hospitals are in fact an important and very obvious element of the life of the Church in this country.* If I cannot mention you all by name, be assured nevertheless that I hold you all in my heart. You have my deep gratitude and my prayerful support.

You, dear *religious sisters and brothers,* are *dedicated to bringing hope and healing,* in the name of Christ, to the sick and the poor, the aged and the uneducated; in fact to any of the suffering members of society,

Address in Melbourne, Australia, November 28, 1986. Reprinted from *L'Osservatore Romano,* December 9, 1986.

regardless of race, creed or social position. Through you the Church carries on the healing work of Christ. I pray that many young men and women will join your ranks and maintain undiminished in generations to come the charism of service to the sick. Your special place is in the Heart of Jesus and in the heart of the Church.

A Mysterious Vocation

3. We all recognize that the patients are the most important people in the hospital. Therefore I speak especially to them and to all the sick and infirm in Australia.

Sickness is one of the basic problems of life

Those who are ill know from experience that illness is one of the basic problems of human existence. Sometimes it strikes us when we least expect it, and when in human terms we least deserve it. When Jesus traveled from place to place during his earthly life, the sick flocked to him. In him they recognized a friend who understood them. They sensed that their suffering spoke deeply to his compassionate and loving heart. It was a constant appeal to his redeeming love.

Jesus certainly cured the bodies of many sick people, but more inportantly he cured their souls too. He purified their hearts, and turned their whole personalities from self-absorption towards God and other people.

4. Dear patients, I hope that medical care will be able to restore you to physical health. But I hope and pray too that your time of sickness, in spite of its burdens, and with the help you receive, will bring you *a profound peace of soul*.

For the person of faith, the path of suffering leads straight to Christ's redemptive Passion, Death and Resurrection: to the Paschal Mystery. Pain is not only an enigma and a trial. For some people it is *a mysterious vocation* which they live in close union with the sufferings of Jesus. The acceptance of pain in this way takes on extraordinary fruitfulness. Saint Paul explained that he was prepared to endure much for his people, and in fact rejoiced in this, because "through my sufferings in the flesh I complete what is still lacking for his body, which is the Church" (Col 1:24).

As Pastor of the Church I am close to you in *your sufferings*. Especially if your illness is chronic, or even incurable. I urge you to think about *the deep and hidden value of your pain and helplessness*. You must freely unite your sufferings to the Cross of Jesus Christ, and be one with him in his redemptive mission. Out of that union will come a new understanding, a new hope and peace. Dear sick people: you are my special friends. I entrust you to Jesus and to Mary. And I ask you to pray for me, and to offer your sufferings for the salvation of souls and the peace of the world.

5. Jesus tells us that those who care for the sick are caring for him.

Dear members of the medical and administrative staff here and in similar centers: your work is *a privileged form of human solidarity and Christian witness.* Your service is based on reverence for life, for all human life from the moment of conception until the moment of death. Through your expert and loving care of every patient, through your use and development of the best techniques available, through your research and education programs, you bear witness to the special dignity of the sick. Here in Mercy Maternity Hospital it is especially fitting to speak about the care of newborn life and to emphasize the special place children must have in any civilized community. Your work strengthens the family and supports mothers in a society where mothers and children are not always given the respect they deserve. May God bless you in this work.

6. Work in hospitals today is more difficult and complex than ever before. The spectacular *advances in medical science and technology,* a more complicated industrial and administrative situation, financial constraints, and a more demanding public—all of these call for an ever-increasing level of competence and dedication. Medical science has brought untold benefits to mankind. For this we must be supremely grateful. We see the cures you effect and the good you bring as signs of God's love continuing among us.

But medical science is *a servant science,* not an end in itself. It is meant to serve the total well-being of everyone. It is the work of people in the service of other people. Its methods and aims must always be judged in terms of human values and human rights and responsibilities. Like all powerful forces it can become destructive when used for wrong purposes. To speak of the autonomy of medical science as if it were independent of moral and ethical considerations is to unleash a force that cannot but cause grievous harm to man himself.

Medical science is a science of service

Catholic medical spokesmen must continue to emphasize that doctors and scientists are human beings, subject to the same moral law as other people, especially when dealing with human patients, human embryos or human tissue. You bring to your work a spirit of faith. This in no way hinders your collaboration with those who—perhaps with a different religious outlook, or with no certain opinion on religious questions—recognize the dignity and excellence of *the human person as the criterion of their activity.* In the delicate field of medicine and biotechnology the Catholic Church is in no way opposed to progress. Rather she rejoices at every victory over sickness and disability. Her concern is that nothing should be done *which is against life* in the reality of a *concrete individual existence,* no matter how weak or defenseless, no matter how undeveloped or how advanced. The

The Church rejoices in every victory over illness

Church therefore never ceases to proclaim the sacredness of all human life, a sacredness which no one has a right to subordinate to any other purpose, no matter how apparently lofty or beneficial.

I appeal to all of you in the world of medicine and health care to approach your science and your art with a respect and love for life as the first and sublime condition of all human rights and values.

7. May Almighty God grant his blessings of strength and courage to you all: *to those of you who are sick,* for the Lord sees into your hearts and knows your needs; *to those of you who serve the sick,* for the Lord's words are addressed to you: "I was sick and you came to me" (Mt 25:36).

The peace of Christ be with you today and always!

"THE HARDEST THING FOR THE POPE IS TO SEE THAT MANY DO NOT ACCEPT THE LOVE OF JESUS"

Answering children's questions:

Good morning, Children. As I fly above you on my way to Darwin, I am happy to speak with you and to all the young people of the outback. You are all very close to my heart. . . .*Over.*

Question 1: Very soon I will be making my first Holy Communion. Please, Holy Father, could you suggest something I could tell or ask Jesus on that day? [Jackie Doyle, age 8.] . . . *Over.*

1. On the day of your First Holy Communion, I suggest that you speak to Jesus *as to your best friend,* for that is what he really is. He is the greatest friend you will ever have, and he wishes to be your special companion every day of your life. So talk to him as a friend who knows your name and loves you dearly. Tell him your secrets. Tell him your joys and the things that make you sad. Tell him about the people whom you love, especially your parents and your brothers and sisters. Ask him to bless your families and all the families of the world. Above all tell him how much you love him. Speaking about her First Communion Day, Saint Teresa of the Child Jesus said that she felt loved by Jesus. It was then that she said to Jesus: "I love you, I give myself to you forever" (*The Story of a Soul,* chap. 4). You can tell Jesus that too. . . . *Over.*

A friend who knows your name

Question 2: Please, Holy Father, you know many children in the world. Which ones would you like us to pray for today? [Angus Elliott, age 10.] . . . *Over.*

Address given to students of the Katherine School of the Air, Australia, November 29, 1986. Reprinted from *L'Osservatore Romano,* December 9, 1986.

2. All children are special to me because *all children are special to Jesus*. Jesus told his disciples: "Let the little children come to me, and do not stop them; for it is to such as these that the Kingdom of God belongs" (Lk 18:16). Jesus welcomes all children into his Kingdom. But he has a particular concern for *children who suffer or who are lonely*, because they could more easily become discouraged and sad, and perhaps forget God's love. So I would suggest that, when you pray for others, you pray especially for children who are lonely and suffering. . . .*Over.*

Question 3: Holy Father, I would like to know what is the hardest thing about being a Pope? [Rebecca Underwood, age 9.] . . . *Over.*

3. The hardest thing about being Pope is to see that many people do not accept the love of Jesus, do not know who he really is and *how much he loves them*. Jesus came into the world and he offered his life on the Cross because he wanted everyone to be happy with him forever in heaven. He is the Savior of everyone in the whole world. But he does not force people to accept his love. He offers it to them and leaves them free to say *yes* or *no*. It fills me with joy to see how many people know and love our Lord, how many say *yes* to him. *It saddens me that some people say No* But it saddens me to see that some people say *no*. This is the hardest thing. . . . *Over.*

Question 4: Please, Holy Father, what would be the best prayer for children to say? [Jacky Doyle.] . . . *Over.*

4 Do you remember that the Apostles asked Jesus to teach them how to pray? And he told them to pray the "*Our Father*", the prayer that I am sure you already pray every day. This is the best prayer for children to pray; it is *the best prayer for any of us to pray*. And *The most beautiful prayer* remember when you say this prayer that God really *is* your loving Father. He knows each person by name and wants you to be happy with him forever. So now I invite all of you who are listening to join me as we say this prayer together:

Our Father who art in heaven, hallowed be thy name.
Thy kingdom come.
Thy will be done on earth as it is in heaven.
Give us this day our daily bread.
And forgive us our trespasses as we forgive those
    who trespass against us.
And lead us not into temptation, but deliver us from evil.
Amen.
. . . *Over.*

IT IS TIME FOR A JUST RECOGNITION
OF ABORIGINAL RIGHTS TO LAND

Dear Brothers and Sisters,

It is a great joy for me to be here today in Alice Springs and to meet so many of you, the Aborigines and Torres Strait Islanders of Australia. I want to tell you right away how much the Church esteems and loves you, and how much she wishes to assist you in your spiritual and material needs.

1. At the beginning of time, as God's Spirit moved over the waters, he began to communicate something of his goodness and beauty to all creation. When God then created man and woman, he gave them the good things of the earth for their use and benefit; and he put into their hearts abilities and powers which were his gifts. And to all human beings throughout the ages God has given a desire for himself, a desire *which different cultures have tried to express in their own ways.*

2. As the human family spread over the face of the earth, your people settled and lived in this big country that stood apart from all the others. Other people did not even know this land was here: they only knew that somewhere in the southern oceans of the world there was "The Great South Land of the Holy Spirit".

But for thousands of years you have lived in this land and fashioned a culture that endures to this day. And during all this time, the Spirit of God has been with you. Your "Dreaming", which influences your lives so strongly that, no matter what happens, you remain forever people of your culture, is *your own way of touching the mystery of God's Spirit* in you and in creation. You must keep your striving for God and hold on to it in your lives.

Age-old Culture

The rock paintings witness to a most ancient culture

3. The rock paintings and the discovered evidence of your ancient tools and implements indicate the presence of your age-old culture and prove *your ancient occupancy of this land.*

Your culture, which shows the lasting genius and dignity of your race, *must not be allowed to disappear.* Do not think that your gifts are worth so little that you should no longer bother to maintain them. Share them with each other and teach them to your children. Your songs, your stories, your paintings, your dances, your languages, must never be lost. Do you perhaps remember those words that Paul VI spoke to the aboriginal people during his visit to them in 1970?

Address to the Aborigines of Australia, November 29, 1986. Reprinted from *L'Osservatore Romano,* December 9, 1986.

On that occasion he said: "We know that you have a life style proper to your own ethnic genius or culture—a culture which the Church respects and which she does not in any way ask you to renounce. . . . Society itself is enriched by the presence of different cultural and ethnic elements. For us you and the values you represent are precious. We deeply respect your dignity and reiterate our deep affection for you" (Sydney, December 2, 1970).

4. For thousands of years this culture of yours was free to grow without interference by people from other places. You lived your lives in *spiritual closeness to the land,* with its animals, birds, fishes, waterholes, rivers, hills and mountains. Through your closeness to the land you touched the sacredness of man's relationship with God, for the land was the proof of a power in life greater than yourselves. You did not spoil the land, use it up, exhaust it, and then walk away from it. You realized that your land was related to the source of life.

A life in spiritual contact with the earth

The silence of the Bush taught you a quietness of soul that put you in touch with *another world, the world of God's Spirit.* Your careful attention to the details of kinship spoke of your reverence for birth, life and human generation. You knew that children need to be loved, to be full of joy. They need a time to grow in laughter and to play, secure in the knowledge that they belong to their people.

You had a great respect for the need which people have for *law, as a guide to living fairly with each other.* So you created a legal system— very strict it is true—but closely adapted to the country in which you lived your lives. It made your society orderly. It was one of the reasons why you survived in this land.

You marked the growth of your young men and women with ceremonies of discipline that taught them responsibility as they came to maturity.

These achievements are indications of human strivings. And in these strivings you showed a dignity *open to the message of God's revealed wisdom* to all men and women, which is the great truth of the Gospel of Jesus Christ.

Endurance, Patience and Courage

5. Some of the stories from your Dreamtime legends speak powerfully of the great mysteries of human life, its frailty, its need for help, its closeness to spiritual powers and the value of the human person. They are not unlike some of the great inspired lessons from the people among whom Jesus himself was born. It is wonderful to see how people, as they accept the Gospel of Jesus, find *points of agreement between their own traditions and those of Jesus and his people.*

Your legends speak of the great mysteries of human life

6. The culture which this long and careful growth produced was not prepared for the sudden meeting with another people, with different customs and traditions, who came to your country nearly two hundred years ago. They were different from Aboriginal people. Their traditions, the organization of their lives, and their attitudes to the land were quite strange to you. Their law too was quite different. These people had knowledge, money and power; and they brought with them some patterns of behavior from which the Aboriginal people were unable to protect themselves.

7. *The effects of some of those forces are still active among you today.* Many of you have been dispossessed of your traditional lands, and separated from your tribal ways, though some of you still have your traditional culture. Some of you are establishing Aboriginal communities in the towns and cities. For others there is still no real place for campfires and kinship observances except on the fringes of country towns. There, work is hard to find, and education in a different cultural background is difficult. The discrimination caused by racism is a daily experience.

You have learned how to survive, whether on your own lands, or scattered among the towns and cities. Though your difficulties are not yet over, you must learn to draw on the endurance which your ancient ceremonies have taught you. *Endurance* brings with it patience; *patience* helps you to find the way ahead, and gives you *courage* for your journey.

8. Take heart from the fact that many of your languages are still spoken and that *you still possess your ancient culture.* You have kept your sense of brotherhood. If you stay closely united, you are like a tree standing in the middle of a bush-fire sweeping through the timber. The leaves are scorched and the tough bark is scarred and burned; but inside the tree the sap is still flowing, and under the ground the roots are still strong. Like that tree you have endured the flames, and *you still have the power to be reborn.* The time for this rebirth is now!

You have preserved the sense of brotherhood

9. We know that during the last two hundred years certain people tried to understand you, to learn about you, to respect your ways and to honor you as persons. These men and women, as you soon realized, were different from others of their race. *They loved and cared for the indigenous people.* They began to share with you their stories of God, helped you cope with sickness, tried to protect you from ill-treatment. They were honest with you, and showed you by their lives how they tried to avoid the bad things in their own culture. These people were not always successful, and there were times when they did not fully understand you. But they showed you good will and friendship. They came from many different walks of life. Some

were teachers and doctors and other professional people; some were simple folk. History will remember the good example of their charity and fraternal solidarity.

Among those who have loved and cared for the indigenous people, we especially recall with profound gratitude all *the missionaries* of the Christian faith. With immense generosity they gave their lives in service to you and to your forebears. They helped to educate the Aboriginal people and offered health and social services. Whatever their human frailty, and whatever mistakes they may have made, nothing can ever minimize the depth of their charity. Nothing can ever cancel out their greatest contribution, which was *to proclaim to you Jesus Christ and to establish his Church in your midst.*

10. From the earliest times men like Archbishop Polding of Sydney opposed the legal fiction adopted by European settlers that this land was *terra nullius*—nobody's country. He strongly pleaded for *the rights of the Aboriginal inhabitants to keep the traditional lands* on which their whole society depended. The Church still supports you today. *The Church still supports you today*

Let it not be said that *the fair and equitable recognition of Aboriginal rights to land* is discrimination. To call for the acknowledgment of the land rights of people who have never surrendered those rights is not discrimination. Certainly, what has been done cannot be undone. But what can now be done to remedy the deeds of yesterday must not be put off till tomorrow.

Christian people of good will are saddened to realize—many of them only recently—*for how long a time Aboriginal people were transported from their homelands* into small areas or preserves where families were broken up, tribes split apart, children orphaned and people forced to live like exiles in a foreign country.

The reserves still exist today, and require *a just and proper settlement* that still lies unachieved. The urban problems resulting from the transportation and separation of people still have to be addressed, so that these people may make a new start in life with each other once again.

11. The establishment of *a new society for Aboriginal people* cannot go forward without just and mutually recognized agreements with regard to these human problems, even though their causes lie in the past. The greatest value to be achieved by such agreements, which must be implemented without causing new injustices, is respect for the dignity and growth of the human person. And you, the Aboriginal people of this country and its cities, must show that you are actively working for your own dignity of life. On your part, you must show that you too can walk tall and command the respect which every human being expects to receive from the rest of the human family.

12. The Gospel of our Lord Jesus Christ speaks all languages. *It*

esteems and embraces all cultures. It supports them in everything human and, when necessary, it purifies them. Always and everywhere the Gospel uplifts and enriches cultures with the revealed message of a loving and merciful God.

That Gospel now invites you to become, through and through, Aboriginal Christians. It meets your deepest desires. You do not have to be people divided into two parts, as though an Aboriginal had to borrow the faith and life of Christianity, like a hat or a pair of shoes, from someone who owns them. Jesus calls you to accept his words and his values into your own culture. To develop in this way will make you more than ever truly Aboriginal.

The message of Jesus Christ can elevate your life

The old ways can draw new life and strength from the Gospel. The message of Jesus Christ can lift up your lives to new heights, reinforce all your positive values and add many others, which only the Gospel in its originality proposes. Take this Gospel into your own language and way of speaking; let its spirit *penetrate your communities* and determine your behavior toward each other, let it bring new strength to your stories and your ceremonies. Let the Gospel come into your hearts and *renew your personal lives.* The Church invites you *to express the living word of Jesus in ways that speak to your Aboriginal minds and hearts.* All over the world people worship God and read his word in their own language, and color the great signs and symbols of religion with touches of their own traditions. Why should you be different from them in this regard, why should you not be allowed the happiness of being with God and each other in Aboriginal fashion?

13. As you listen to the Gospel of our Lord Jesus Christ, seek out the best things of your traditional ways. If you do, you will come to realize more and more *your great human and Christian dignity.* Let your minds and hearts be strengthened to begin a new life now. Past hurts cannot be healed by violence, nor are present injustices removed by resentment. Your Christian faith calls you to become the best kind of Aboriginal people you can be. This is possible only if reconciliation and forgiveness are part of your lives. Only then will you find happiness. Only then will you make your best contri-

You are part of Australia

bution to all your brothers and sisters in this great nation. You are part of Australia and Australia is part of you. And the Church herself in Australia will not be fully the Church that Jesus wants her to be until you have made your own contribution to her life and until that contribution has been joyfully received by others.

In the new world that is emerging for you, you are being called to live fully human and Christian lives, not to die of shame and sorrow. But you know that to fulfill your role *you need a new heart.*

You will already feel courage rise up inside you when you listen to God speaking to you in these words of the Prophets:

"Do not be afraid for I have redeemed you; I have called you by your name, you are mine. Do not be afraid, for I am with you" (Is 43:1–5).

And again:

"I am going to . . . gather you together . . . and bring you home to your own land. . . . I shall give you a new heart and put a new spirit in you. . . . *You shall be my people and I will be your God*" (Ezek 36:24, 26, 28).

14. With you I rejoice in the hope of *God's gift of salvation,* which has its beginnings here and now, and which also depends on how we behave towards each other, on what we put up with, on what we do, on how we honor God and love all people.

Dear Aboriginal people: *the hour has come* for you to take on new courage and new hope. You are called to remember the past, to be faithful to your worthy traditions, and to adapt your living culture whenever this is required by your own needs and those of your fellow-man. Above all you are called to *open your hearts ever more to the consoling, purifying and uplifting message of Jesus Christ,* the Son of God, who died so that we might all have life, and have it to the full (cf. Jn 10:10).

STRENGTHEN THE BASES OF
AN AUTHENTIC CHRISTIAN HUMANISM

1. "This is how it is with the reign of God. A man scatters seed on the ground" (Mk 4:26).

Enlightened by the Word of God proclaimed in today's liturgy, we want to celebrate, through Christ, with him and in him, this *holy Eucharistic sacrifice of the whole Church.*

As Pastor of the Universal Church it gives me great pleasure to exercise in this Sacrifice the priestly ministry on Argentinian soil, here in Bahia Blanca, together with my brother bishops and priests. My joy overflows at your presence and participation, knowing that you have come here from various parts of the Argentine *pampa.*

You have no idea how much I have longed for this meeting! I greet you all with the warmest affection, especially those who represent the rural world. The biblical readings in today's liturgy are really very appropriate, seeing that many of you, dear sisters and brothers, combine your Christian vocation with the cultivation of the land.

Address in Bahia Blanca, Argentina, April 7, 1986. Reprinted from *L'Osservatore Romano,* May 11, 1986.

However, my words are addressed to the hearts of all, because, as the Apostle tells us, we are all "God's cultivation" (1 Cor 3:9).

2. With one heart let us *bless the Lord with the Psalmist:*

"O Lord, my God, you are great indeed! You raise grass for the cattle, and vegetation for men's use, producing bread from the earth, and wine to gladden men's hearts, so that their faces gleam with oil and bread fortifies the hearts of men (Ps 104 [103]:2, 14–15).

Let us bless God the Creator who, from the beginning, has endowed the earth with varied and immeasurable wealth.

Man "scatters the seed on the ground" (Mk 4:26), then "the soil produces of itself first the blade, then the ear, finally the ripe wheat in the ear" (Mk 4:28).

"When the crop is ready he 'wields the sickle, for the time is ripe for harvest'" (Mk 4:28).

These words come from the lips of Christ who in his Gospel frequently refers to the work of farmers.

When it is "harvest time" what the Psalmist says is also accomplished: "They all look to you to give them their food in due time. When you give it to them they gather it; when you open your hand they are filled with good things" (Ps 104 [103]:27–28). The gift of God, that is the land, and the work of the farmer are intimately connected. It would be hard to find any other activity in which human beings feel so *strongly united with the divine work of the Creator*.

In agriculture man is closely united to the work of the Creator

The Gifts of the Creator

3. The liturgical readings in the Mass recall this for us. They refer, first of all, to the history of the people of Israel in the Old Covenant. This people wandered through the desert for forty years on their way to the land which God had promised to them, "a land of wheat and barley, of vines and fig trees and pomegranates, of olive trees and of honey, a land", Deuteronomy continues, "where you can eat bread without stint and where you will lack nothing, a land whose stones contain iron and in whose hills you can mine copper" (Dt 8:8–9).

There, the Sacred Book tells us, you will build comfortable houses in which to live, your sheep and cattle will increase and you will have gold and silver in abundance (cf. Dt 8:12–13).

Does this not seem like a description of your land? Dear people of Bahia Blanca: I know that you have a well-earned reputation of being hard workers. It is enough to see how work on the land, carried out with self-denial and sacrifice, is combined at the same time with other sources of production: fishing, commerce and industry. Like everything else, it is important, precisely because you enjoy the generous fruits of the earth, that you never forget the biblical exhortation: when "you have increased your wealth, do not become arrogant and forget the Lord. . . . Do not forget the Lord your God, but keep all his commandments and decrees and statutes" (Dt 8:14, 11).

4. As you see, the liturgical readings today cast light upon the *truth about God the creator and about man.* It is God who gives life to all creatures and keeps them in existence and constantly gives them the ability to work.

From the very beginning humanity has been called by God to "have dominion over the earth and subdue it" (Gen 1:28). He received the earth from the Lord as a *gift and a responsibility;* created in his image and likeness, men and women have a special dignity. They are lords and masters of the good things placed by the Creator in all his creatures; they are *co-workers with the Creator.*

For this same reason humanity should never forget that the good things of which the earth is full are the Creator's gifts. The Sacred Book reminds us: ". . .you might say to yourselves 'It is my own power and the strength of my own hand that has obtained for me this wealth.' Remember then, it is the Lord, your God, who *gives you the power to acquire wealth,* by fulfilling, as he has now done, the covenant which he swore to your fathers" (Dt 8:17–18).

How apt this reminder has been throughout the history of humanity! How appropriate it is now *especially* because of the *progress in science and technology!* Humanity indeed, seeing the results of its own ingenuity, of its mind and hands, seems to forget more and more the One who is the beginning of all those achievements and of all the good things that exist upon the earth and in all creation.

The *more he subdues and masters the earth* the more he seems to forget the One *who gave him the earth and all the good things* that it contains.

In unison with the Psalmist I would like to recall on this important day for Bahia Blanca that without the Creator the creature loses his meaning; when the human person tries to exalt himself and do without God he falls into the deepest abysses of inhumanity. On the other hand, fidelity to God, faith, charity . . . these are the treasure by which we reach true life (cf. 1 Tim 6:11–19). Humanity is at its greatest when it fully recognizes the sovereignty of God and works the land *in cooperation* with the Creator.

Without the Creator the creature loses his significance

Therefore, if you want your work and responsibility to take on a truly human and even transcendent dimension you must work with your gaze fixed on God and with a desire to contribute to the work of creation, as an act of adoration and thanksgiving to the Almighty. Is it not significant that the bread and wine, "fruits of the earth and the work of human hands", which we offer in the Eucharist, become the Body and Blood of the Lord?

May all your endeavors become through Christ "living hosts", and be made redemptive and sanctifying. Thus you too, tillers of the earth, will help to strengthen the foundations of an authentic Christian humanism and a liberating theology of work.

In this regard, remember the Lord's warning: "What profit does he show who gains the whole world and destroys himself in the process?" (Lk 9:25). This is why you must be careful that *your plans and purposes do not cause you to "forget the Lord"*. Think of the dignity which, as human beings and as Christians, your work has, and which *must mark all your progress*. Do not allow your work to degrade you as the price of achievement. Try, rather, to do it in a fully Christian way, following the word of God and the teachings of the Church.

Reject any kind of materialism which produces slavery: slavery to material goods, which takes away the true freedom by which we live as sons of God and brothers.

5. The human person is always more important than his work; his dignity is greater than his products, which are merely the fruit of his activity. As you will readily understand, it is more and more urgent to recognize, in the world of agriculture as well, that *the primacy of spiritual values* stands before everything else as the ferment of salvation and of authentic human progress. To this end it would be good if everyone, in the depths of his own consciousness, would make a commitment to ensure that the weight of material things will not quench the flame of the spirit.

Consequently, do not allow yourselves to be taken in by that modern image of greed which is *consumerism;* this would *lead only to the loss of your healthy human and family traditions* as well as that beautiful virtue of country people, *their solidarity*. I am thinking of all the difficulties, often unexpected, which people on the land have to face; I am thinking, above all, of the terrible floods which have destroyed your fields. Such disasters have no doubt provided ample opportunity for showing your solidarity with the most seriously affected, and your detachment and willingness to share.

Solidarity, a virtue of country people

6. Dear brothers and sisters of the Argentinian world of agriculture, you work the land with honesty and devotion; you must cultivate your spiritual lives with the same intensity. The soul, like the good soil, needs careful attention. First of all, the seed of the word of God must be received and then listened to and followed in order to produce a *harvest for eternal life*. Therefore I want to remind you today that precisely because you are the images of God you are also capable of loving him. Openness to the Creator, *a relationship with him, is engraved in the depth* of your being. May all those who work the land be conscious of that special vocation by which they are called to be God's closest collaborators in the work of creation. Do not lose

that traditional religious Christian feeling which is at the root of your culture.

Today more than ever, the Church needs members who personally experience and transmit to the whole community that message which comes from the life of Jesus: daily work *must be inserted in the divine plan of salvation;* work is a blessing from God and is part of the first vocation of each person.

With your gaze fixed on God, I repeat, you can and must become holy, *without leaving aside your daily occupations* on the land, in your home, among your friends, in your leisure time and at rest.

However, in order that human work really be a co-working with God, there is a need for you, dear friends, to be in constant union with God, to keep his commandments and precepts. You must leave some time for *divine worship,* going to Mass on Sundays and holy days, as an expression of your Christian life and of the sense of religion for which you are known. Receive the Sacrament of Reconciliation which will help you to keep your moral conduct pure and untainted. Frequently receive the Lord Jesus truly present in the Eucharist. Listen to the word of God and receive the sacraments instituted by Christ. They are means which no one can do without, man or woman, young or old.

You cannot be content just to have received Baptism and First Holy Communion and go to Church occasionally after that. You know very well that the land will never yield anything without proper attention; the earth must be tilled and fertilized and cared for if there is to be a good harvest. In the same way you must take care of the good soil of your souls; read and meditate upon the Sacred Scripture, pray often to the Blessed Virgin Mary, be actively involved in the life of the Church, follow the instructions given by your pastors, dedicate time and energy to acquiring a good Christian formation.

Cultivate the fertile land of your soul

Agricultural life is a limitless source of customs of immense human value: generous friendship, a willingness to share, solidarity with those in need, love for family and peace, a sense of the transcendence of life. These are human and Christian values which you must maintain and develop, because they are the chief supports of family and social life, today and for the future of Argentina.

Some Demands of Solidarity Underlined

7. Finally, I wish to underline some of the demands of the solidarity of which we spoke. It is the foundation of all living together in peace and thereby, an indispensable condition for true progress.

Certainly there is a great need to overcome, once and for all, all those conditions of inferiority which certain sections of the rural community have to suffer and which lead them to feel socially marginalized. At the same time there has to be an end to the discrimination and the imbalances which exist between the city and the country, which frequently cause a certain dislike for work on the land and produce massive migration to the cities where living conditions are very often much worse. Then, of course, as a matter of urgency, development in industry and commerce should not unjustly and adversely affect rural life. There is an urgent need to educate youth in the country areas, to give them adequate professional, human and Christian formation so that they can give a valid response to the demands of modern Argentinian society.

Take up the challenge of our time of organizing *an effective technical and cultural assistance* for agriculture: let the farmer's professional capacity give him back his love for the land; let him be able to avail of proper legal assistance, both for himself and his family, wherever illness, old age or unemployment occur; let salaries be set in accordance with human dignity and the personal and family needs of the worker rather than what are sometimes the cold and inhuman *laws of the market*. In a word, let the conditions of rural life be truly human and worthy of the children of God.

Let the conditions of rural life be authentically humane

The land is a gift of the Creator to *all men and women*. Its wealth—produce, animals, minerals—cannot be shared by a limited number of sectors or categories of people while the rest are excluded from its benefits.

I am reminded, dear people of Argentina, of so many men and women, born in other parts of the world, who in recent times have come to work among you and who already consider themselves children of this noble land. As I pointed out in my encyclical *Laborem Exercens:* "Emigration in search of work must in no way become an opportunity for financial or social exploitation. As regards the work relationship, the same criteria should be applied to immigrant workers as to all other workers in the society concerned" (no. 23).

Of course, in certain circumstances this way of behavior may demand heroic efforts, but we should not forget the words of the Apostle: "Tell those who are rich . . . to do good, to be rich in good works and generous, sharing what they have" (1 Tim 6:17–18).

Dear friends, men and women who work upon the land, *you have the right* to be treated as your dignity as human beings and children of God deserves! At the same time, *you have the duty* to treat others in the same way!

8. "The Kingdom of God is like the man who scatters seeds upon the earth" (Mk 4:26).

If the Kingdom of God in Jesus Christ *is given* to all men and women *as both gift and duty,* it is given in a special way to you, sons and daughters of the land which you cultivate "with the sweat of your brow" and with work of every kind.

Be conscious of this truth about the Kingdom of God! Be conscious of your vocation, which is both human and Christian!

You are called in a particular way to *fulfill the covenant* which God, Creator and Father, has made with humanity in the beginning, when he told them to master and subdue the earth.

Sons and daughters of this land: "It has pleased your Father to give you the Kingdom" (Lk 12:32).

Never forget it! Amen.

IN EDITH STEIN WE FIND A DRAMATIC SYNTHESIS OF THE TRUTH WHICH TRANSCENDS MAN

"These are the ones who have survived the great period of trial; they have washed their robes and made them white in the blood of the lamb" (Rev 7:14).

1. Today we greet in profound honor and holy joy a daughter of the Jewish people, rich in wisdom and courage, among these blessed men and women. Having grown up in the strict traditions of Israel, and having lived a life of virtue and self-denial in a religious order, she demonstrated her heroic character on the way to the extermination camp. Unified with our crucified Lord, she gave her life "for genuine peace" and "for the people" (see *Edith Stein, Jüdin, Philosophin, Ordensfrau, Märtyrin*).

Cardinal, dear Brothers and Sisters,

Today's beatification marks the realization of a long-outstanding wish on the part of the Archdiocese of Cologne as well as on the part of many individuals and groups within the Church. Seven years ago the members of the German Bishops' Conference sent a unanimous request for this beatification to the Holy See. Numerous bishops from other countries joined them in making this request. As such, we are all greatly gratified that I am able to fulfill this wish today and can present *Sister Teresa Benedicta of the Cross* to the faithful on behalf of the Church as *blessed in the glory of God.* From this moment on we can honor her as a martyr and ask her intercession at the throne of God. In this I would like to express congratulations to all, most of all to her fellow sisters in the order of Our Lady of Mount Carmel here in Cologne and in Echt as well as in the entire order. The fact that Jewish brothers and sisters, relatives of Edith

Address in Cologne, Germany, May 1, 1987. Reprinted from *L'Osservatore Romano,* May 18, 1987.

Stein's in particular, are present at this liturgical ceremony today fills us with great joy and gratitude.

A Call for Help

2. "O Lord, manifest yourself in the time of our distress and give us courage" (Esther 4:17).

The words of this call for help from the first reading of today's liturgy were spoken by Esther, a daughter of Israel, at the time of the Babylonian captivity. Her prayer, which she directs to the Lord God at a time when her people were exposed to a deadly threat, is profoundly moving.

O my Lord, come to my aid for I am alone

"My Lord, our King, you alone are God. Help me, who am alone and have no help but you, for I am taking my life in my hand . . . you, O Lord, chose Israel from among all peoples . . . and our fathers from among all their ancestors as a lasting heritage. . . . Be mindful of us, O Lord. . . . Save us by your power" (Esther 4:17).

Esther's deathly fear arose when, under the influence of the mighty Haman, an archenemy of the Jews, the order for their destruction was given out in all of the Persian Empire. With God's help and by her sacrificing her own life Esther rendered a key contribution towards saving her people.

3. Today's liturgy places this more than two-thousand-year-old prayer for help in the mouth of *Edith Stein,* a servant of God and a daughter of Israel in our century. This prayer became relevant again when here, in the heart of Europe, a new *plan for the destruction of the Jews* was laid out. An insane ideology decided on this plan in the name of a wretched form of racism and carried it out mercilessly.

Extermination camps and *crematoriums* were rapidly built, parallel to the dramatic events of the Second World War. Several million sons and daughters of Israel were killed at these places of horror—from children to the elderly. The enormously powerful machinery of the totalitarian state spared no one and undertook extremely cruel measures against those who had the courage to defend the Jews.

She died as a daughter of her martyred people

4. Edith Stein died at the Auschwitz extermination camp, the daughter of a martyred people. Despite the fact that she moved from Cologne to the Dutch Carmelite community in Echt, her protection against the growing persecution of the Jews was only temporary. The Nazi policy of exterminating the Jews was rapidly implemented in Holland, too, after the country had been occupied. Jews who had converted to Christianity were initially left alone. However, when the Catholic bishops in the Netherlands issued a *pastoral letter* in which they sharply protested against the deportation of the Jews, the Nazi rulers reacted by ordering the extermination of Catholic

Jews as well. This was the cause of the martyrdom suffered by Sister Teresa Benedicta a Cruce together with her sister, Rosa, who had also sought refuge with the Carmelites in Echt.

On leaving their convent Edith took her sister by the hand and said: "Come, we will go for our people." On the strength of Christ's willingness to sacrifice himself for others she saw in her seeming impotence a way to render a final service to her people. A few years previously she had compared herself with Queen Esther in exile at the Persian court. In one of her letters we read: "I am confident that the Lord has taken my life for all [Jews]. I always have to think of Queen Esther who was taken away from her people for the express purpose of standing before the king for her people. I am the very poor, weak and small Esther, but the King who selected me is infinitely great and merciful."

Incessant Search for Truth

5. Dear brothers and sisters, the second reading in this special Mass is from Saint Paul's letter to the Galatians. He wrote there: "May I never boast of anything but the cross of our Lord, Jesus Christ. Through it, the world has been crucified to me and I to the world" (Gal 6:14).

During her lifetime, Edith Stein too encountered the secret of the cross that Saint Paul announces to the Christians in this letter.

Edith encountered Christ and this encounter led her step by step into the Carmelite community. In the extermination camp she died as a daughter of Israel "for the glory of the Most Holy Name" and at the same time, as *Sister Teresa Benedicta of the Cross,* literally, "blessed by the Cross".

Edith Stein's entire life is characterized by an incessant search for truth and is illuminated by the blessing of the cross of Christ. She encountered the cross for the first time in the strongly religious widow of a university friend. Instead of despairing, this woman took strength and hope from the cross of Christ. Later she wrote about this: "It was my first encounter with the cross and the divine strength it gives those who bear it. . . . It was the moment in which my atheism collapsed . . . and Christ shone brightly: Christ in the mystery of the cross." *Her own life and the cross she had to bear were intimately connected with the destiny of the Jewish people.* In a prayer she confessed to the Savior that she knew that it was his cross that was now being laid on the Jewish people and that those who realized this would have to accept it willingly on behalf of all the others. "I wanted to do it—all he has to do is show me how." At the same time she attains the inner certainty that God has heard her prayer. The more often

Her life was characterized by her untiring search for truth

swastikas were seen on the streets, the higher the cross of Jesus Christ rose up in her life. When she entered the Carmelite order of nuns in Cologne as Sister Teresa Benedicta a Cruce in order to experience the cross of Christ even more profoundly, she knew that she was "married to the Lord in the sign of the cross". On the day of her first vows she felt, in her own words, "*like the bride of the lamb*". She was convinced that her heavenly Groom would introduce her to the profound mysteries of the cross.

Ethical Idealism

6. *Teresa, Blessed by the Cross* was the name given in a religious order to a woman who began her spiritual life with the conviction that *God does not exist*. At that time, in her schoolgirl years and when she was at university, her life was not yet filled with the redeeming cross of Christ. However, it was already the object of constant searching on the part of her sharp intellect. As a fifteen-year-old schoolgirl in her home town of Breslau, Edith who had been raised in a Jewish household suddenly decided, as she herself put it, "not to pray any-more". Despite the fact that she was deeply impressed by the strict devotion of her mother, during her school and university years Edith slips into the intellectual world of atheism. She considers the existence of a personal God to be unworthy of belief.

In the years when she studied psychology, philosophy, history and German at the Universities of Breslau, Göttingen and Freiburg, God didn't play an important role, at least initially. Her thinking was based on a demanding ethical idealism. In keeping with her intellectual abilities, she did not want to accept anything without careful examination, not even the faith of her fathers. She wanted to get to the bottom of things herself. As such, she was engaged in a constant search for the truth. Looking back on this period of intel-lectual unrest in her life she saw in it an important phase in a process of spiritual maturation. She said: "My search for the truth was a constant prayer." This is a comforting bit of testimony for those who have a hard time believing in God. The search for truth is, itself, in a very profound sense a search for God.

My search for truth has been a true prayer

Under the influence of Edmund Husserl and his phenomenological school of thought the student Edith Stein became increasingly dedi-cated to the study of philosophy. She gradually learned to "view things free of prejudice and to throw off 'blinkers'". She *came into contact for the first time with Catholic ideas* through a meeting with *Max Scheler* in Göttingen. She described her reaction to this meeting as follows: "The barriers of rationalistic prejudice, something I grew up with without being aware of it, fell and suddenly I was confronted with the world of faith. People I dealt with on a daily basis, people I looked up to in admiration, lived in that world."

Her long struggle for a personal decision to believe in Jesus Christ was not to come to an end until 1921, when she began to read the autobiographical *Life of Saint Teresa of Avila*. She was immediately taken with the book and could not put it down until she had finished it. Edith Stein commented: "When I closed the book I said to myself: 'That is the truth!'" She had read through the night until sunrise. In that night she found truth—not the truth of philosophy, but rather the truth in person, the loving person of God. Edith Stein had sought the truth and found God. She was baptized soon after that and entered the Catholic Church.

Continuing Heritage

7. For Edith Stein baptism as a Christian was *by no means a break with her Jewish heritage*. Quite on the contrary she said: "I had given up my practice of the Jewish religion as a girl of fourteen. My return to God made me feel Jewish again." She was always mindful of the fact that she was related to Christ "not only in a spiritual sense, but also in blood terms". She suffered profoundly from the pain she caused her mother through her conversion to Catholicism. She continued to accompany her to service in the synagogue and to pray the psalms with her. In reaction to her mother's observation that it was possible for her to be pious in a Jewish sense as well, she answered: "Of course, seeing as it is something I grew up with."

Although becoming a member of the Carmelite Order was Edith Stein's objective from the time of her encounter with the writings of Saint Teresa of Avila, she had to wait more than a decade before Christ showed her the way. In her activity as a teacher and lecturer at schools and in adult education, mostly in Speyer, but also in Münster, she made a continuous effort to combine *science and religion* and to convey them together. In this she only wanted to be a "tool of the Lord". "Those who come to me I would like to lead to him", she said. During this period of her life she already lived like a nun. She took the vows privately and became a great and gifted woman of prayer. From her intensive study of the writings of Saint Thomas Aquinas she learned that it is possible "to approach science from a religious standpoint". She said that it was only thus that she was able to decide to return seriously (after her conversion) to academic work. Despite her respect for scholarship, Edith Stein became increasingly aware that the *essence of being a Christian is not scholarship, but rather love.*

Love is the essence of Christian being

When Edith Stein finally entered the Carmelite Order in 1933,

this step did not represent an escape from the world or from responsibility for her, but rather a *resolved commitment to the heritage of Christ
on the cross*. She said in her first conversation with the prioress there:
"It is not human activity that helps us—it is the suffering of Christ.
To share in this is my desire." On being registered in the order she
expressed the wish to be named "Blessed by the Cross". She had
the words of Saint John of the Cross printed on the devotional picture
presented to her on taking her final vows: *"My only vocation is that
of loving more."*

8. Dear brothers and sisters: We bow today with the entire Church
before this great woman whom we from now on may call upon as
one of the blessed in God's glory, before this great daughter of Israel,
who found the fulfillment of her faith and her vocation for the people
of God in Christ the Savior. In her conviction those who enter the
Carmelite Order are not lost to their own—on the contrary they are
won for them. It is our *vocation to stand before God for everyone*. After
she began seeing the destiny of Israel from the standpoint of the
cross, our newly beatified sister let Christ lead her more and more
deeply into the mystery of his salvation to be able to bear the multiple
pains of mankind in spiritual union with him and to help atone for
the outrageous injustices in the world. As "Benedicta a Cruce"—
Blessed by the Cross—she wanted to bear the cross with Christ for
the salvation of her people, her Church and the world as a whole.
She offered herself to God as a "sacrifice for genuine peace" and
above all for her threatened and humiliated Jewish people. After she
recognized that God had once again laid a heavy hand on his people,
she was convinced *"that the destiny of this people is also my destiny"*.

*The destiny of
this people is
also mine*

His Suffering

When Sister Teresa Benedicta a Cruce began her last theological
work, "The Science of the Cross", at the Carmelite convent in Echt
(the work remained incomplete since it was interrupted by her own
encounter with the cross) she noted: "When we speak of the *science
of the cross* this is not . . . mere theory . . . but rather *vibrant, genuine
and effective truth*." When the deadly threat to the Jewish people
gathered like a dark cloud over her as well she was willing to realize
with her own life what she had recognized earlier: "There is a vocation
for suffering with Christ and by that means for involvement in his
salvation . . . Christ continues to live and to suffer in his members.
The suffering gone through in union with the Lord is *his* suffering,
and is a fruitful part of the great plan of salvation."

With her people and "for" her people Sister Teresa Benedicta a

Cruce traveled the road to death with her sister Rosa. She did not accept *suffering and death* passively, but instead combined these consciously with the *atoning sacrifice of our Savior Jesus Christ.* A few years earlier she had written in her will: "I will gladly accept the death God chooses for me, in full submission to his holy will. I ask the Lord to accept my suffering and death for his honor and glory, and for all interests. . . . of the holy Church." The Lord heard her prayer.

An Example

The Church now presents Sister Teresa Benedicta a Cruce to us as a blessed martyr, as an example of a heroic follower of Christ, for us to honor and to emulate. Let us open ourselves up for her message to us as a woman of the spirit and of the mind, who saw in the science of the cross the acme of all wisdom, as a great daughter of the Jewish people, and as a believing Christian in the midst of millions of innocent fellow men made martyrs. She saw the inexorable approach of the cross. She did not flee in fear. Instead, she embraced it in Christian hope with final love and sacrifice and in the mystery of Easter even welcomed it with the salutation *"Ave crux spes unica."* As Cardinal Höffner said in his recent pastoral letter, "Edith Stein is a gift, an invocation and a promise for our time. May she be an intercessor with God for us and for our people and for all people."

9. Dear brothers and sisters, today the Church of the twentieth century is experiencing a great day. *We bow in profound respect before the testimony of the life and death of Edith Stein,* an outstanding daughter of Israel and, at the same time, a daughter of Carmel, Sister Teresa Benedicta a Cruce, a person who embodied a dramatic synthesis of our century in her rich life. Hers was a synthesis of a history full of deep wounds, wounds that still hurt, and for the healing of which responsible men and women have continued to work up to the present day. At the same time, it was a synthesis of the full truth on man, in a heart that remained restless and unsatisfied "until it finally found peace in God".

Edith Stein is a gift, a warning, a promise for our time

Spirit and Truth

When we pay a spiritual visit to the place where this great Jewish woman and Christian experienced martyrdom, the place of horrible events today referred to as "Shoah", we hear the voice of Christ the Messiah and Son of Man, our Lord and Savior.

As the bearer of the message of God's unfathomable mystery of salvation he said to the woman from Samaria at Jacob's well:

"After all, salvation is from the Jews. Yet an hour is coming, and is already here when authentic worshipers will worship the Father in spirit and truth. Indeed, it is just such worshipers the Father seeks. God is Spirit, and those who worship him must worship in spirit and truth" (Jn 4:22–24).

Blessed be Edith Stein, Sister Teresa Benedicta a Cruce, a true worshiper of God—in spirit and in truth.

She is among the blessed. Amen.

4

ENCYCLICAL LETTER

MATERNAL MEDIATION
Part III of the Encyclical *Redemptoris Mater*, March 25, 1987

1. *Mary, the Handmaid of the Lord*

38. The Church knows and teaches with Saint Paul that *there is only one mediator:* "For there is one God, and there is one mediator between God and men, the man Christ Jesus, who gave himself as a ransom for all" (1 Tim 2:5–6). "The maternal role of Mary towards people in no way obscures or diminishes the unique mediation of Christ, but rather shows its power":[94] it is mediation in Christ.

The Church knows and teaches that "all *the saving influences of the Blessed Virgin* on mankind originate . . . from the divine pleasure. They flow forth *from the superabundance of the merits of Christ,* rest on his mediation, depend entirely on it, and draw all their power from it. In no way do they impede the immediate union of the faithful with Christ. Rather, they foster this union."[95] This saving influence is sustained by the Holy Spirit, who, just as he overshadowed the Virgin Mary when he began in her the divine motherhood, in a similar way constantly sustains her solicitude for the brothers and sisters of her Son.

In effect, Mary's mediation *is intimately linked with her motherhood.* It possesses a specifically maternal character, which distinguishes it from the mediation of the other creatures who in various and always subordinate ways share in the one mediation of Christ, although her own mediation is also a shared mediation.[96] In fact, while it is true that "no creature could ever be classed with the Incarnate Word and Redeemer", at the same time "the unique mediation of the Redeemer does not exclude but rather gives rise among creatures to *a manifold cooperation* which is but a sharing in this unique source." And thus

---

Reprinted from *Mother of the Redeemer,* with the permission of the Daughters of Saint Paul.

[94] Second Vatican Ecumenical Council, LG, 60.

[95] Ibid., 60.

[96] Cf. the formula of mediatrix "ad Mediatorem" of Saint Bernard, *In Dominica infra oct. Assumptionis Sermo,* 2: *S. Bernardi Opera,* V, 1968, 263. Mary as a pure mirror sends back to her Son all the glory and honor which she receives: Id., *In Nativitate B. Mariae Sermo—De Aquaeductu,* 12: ed. cit., 283.

"the one goodness of God is in reality communicated diversely to his creatures."[97]

The teaching of the Second Vatican Council presents the truth of Mary's mediation as *"a sharing in the one unique source that is the mediation of Christ himself"*. Thus we read: "The Church does not hesitate to profess this subordinate role of Mary. She experiences it continuously and commends it to the hearts of the faithful, so that, encouraged by this maternal help, they may more closely adhere to the Mediator and Redeemer."[98] This role is at the same time *special and extraordinary*. It flows from her divine motherhood and can be understood and lived in faith only on the basis of the full truth of this motherhood. Since by virtue of divine election Mary is the earthly Mother of the Father's consubstantial Son and his "generous companion" in the work of redemption "she is a mother to us in the order of grace."[99] This role constitutes a real dimension of her presence in the saving mystery of Christ and the Church.

39. From this point of view we must consider once more the fundamental event in the economy of salvation, namely the Incarnation of the Word at the moment of the Annunciation. It is significant that Mary, recognizing in the words of the divine messenger the will of the Most High and submitting to his power, says: *"Behold, I am the handmaid of the Lord; let it be to me according to your word"* (Lk 1:38). The first moment of submission to the one mediation "between God and Man"—the mediation of Jesus Christ—is the Virgin of Nazareth's acceptance of motherhood. Mary consents to God's choice, in order to become through the power of the Holy Spirit the Mother of the Son of God. It can be said that this *consent to motherhood* is above all *a result of her total self-giving to God in virginity*. Mary accepted her election as Mother of the Son of God, guided by spousal love, the love which totally "consecrates" a human being to God. By virtue of this love, Mary wished to be always and in all things "given to God", living in virginity. The words "Behold, I am the handmaid of the Lord" express the fact that from the outset she accepted and understood her own motherhood as a total *gift of self*, a gift of her person to the service of the saving plans of the Most High. And to the very end she lived her entire maternal sharing in the life of Jesus Christ, her Son, in a way that matched her vocation to virginity.

Mary's motherhood, completely pervaded by her spousal attitude as the "handmaid of the Lord", constitutes the first and fundamental dimension of that mediation which the Church confesses and

Acceptance of motherhood in total gift to God

---

[97]Second Vatican Ecumenical Council, LG, 62.
[98]Ibid., 62.
[99]Ibid., 61.

proclaims in her regard[100] and continually "commends to the hearts
of the faithful", since the Church has great trust in her. For it must
be recognized that before anyone else it was God himself, the Eternal
Father, who *entrusted himself to the Virgin of Nazareth,* giving her his
own Son in the mystery of the Incarnation. Her election to the
supreme office and dignity of Mother of the Son of God refers, on
the ontological level, to the very reality of the union of the two
natures in the person of the Word (*hypostatic union*). This basic fact
of being the Mother of the Son of God is from the very beginning
a complete openness to the person of Christ, to his whole work,
to his whole mission. The words "Behold, I am the handmaid of
the Lord" testify to Mary's openness of spirit: she perfectly
unites in herself the love proper to virginity and the love characteristic of motherhood, which are joined and, as it were, fused
together.

"Behold, I am the handmaid of the Lord"

For this reason Mary became not only the "nursing mother" of
the Son of Man but also the "associate of unique nobility"[101] of the
Messiah and Redeemer. As I have already said, she advanced in her
pilgrimage of faith, and in this *pilgrimage* to the foot of the Cross
there was simultaneously accomplished her maternal *cooperation* with
the Savior's whole mission through her actions and sufferings. Along
the path of this collaboration with the work of her Son, the Redeemer,
Mary's motherhood itself underwent a singular transformation, becoming ever more imbued with "burning charity" towards all those
to whom Christ's mission was directed. Through this "burning charity", which sought to achieve, in union with Christ, the restoration
of "supernatural life to souls",[102] Mary *entered, in a way all her own,
into the one mediation* "between God and men" *which is the mediation
of the man Christ Jesus.* If she was the first to experience within herself
the supernatural consequences of this one mediation—in the Annunciation she had been greeted as "full of grace"—then we must say
that through this fullness of grace and supernatural life she was especially predisposed to cooperation with Christ, the one Mediator of
human salvation. *And such cooperation is precisely this mediation subordinated* to the mediation of Christ.

In Mary's case we have a special and exceptional mediation, based
upon her "fullness of grace", which was expressed in the complete
willingness of the "handmaid of the Lord". In response to this interior
willingness of his Mother, *Jesus Christ prepared her* ever more
completely to become for all people their "mother in the order of
grace". This is indicated, at least indirectly, by certain details noted

[100]LG, 62.
[101]Ibid., 61.
[102]Ibid., 61.

by the Synoptics (cf. Lk 11:28; 8:20–21; Mk 3:32–35; Mt 12:47–50) and still more so by the Gospel of John (cf. 2:1–12; 19:25–27), which I have already mentioned. Particularly eloquent in this regard are the words spoken by Jesus on the Cross to Mary and John.

40. After the events of the Resurrection and Ascension, Mary entered the Upper Room together with the Apostles to await Pentecost, and was present there as the Mother of the glorified Lord. She was not only the one who "advanced in her pilgrimage of faith" and loyally persevered in her union with her Son "unto the Cross", *but she was also the "handmaid of the Lord", left by her Son as Mother in the midst of the infant Church:* "Behold your mother." Thus there began to develop a special bond between this Mother and the Church. For the infant Church was the fruit of the Cross and Resurrection of her Son. Mary, who from the beginning had given herself without reserve to the person and work of her Son, could not but pour out upon the Church, from the very beginning, her maternal self-giving. After her Son's departure, her motherhood remains in the Church as maternal mediation: interceding for all her children, the Mother cooperates in the saving work of her Son, the Redeemer of the world. In fact the Council teaches that the "motherhood of Mary in the order of grace . . . *will last without interruption* until the eternal fulfillment of all the elect."[103] With the redeeming death of her Son, the maternal mediation of the handmaid of the Lord took on a universal dimension, for the work of redemption embraces the whole of humanity. Thus there is manifested in a singular way the efficacy of the one and universal mediation of Christ "between God and men". Mary's cooperation shares, in its subordinate character, *in the universality of the mediation of the Redeemer,* the one Mediator. This is clearly indicated by the Council in the words quoted above.

"For," the text goes on to say, "taken up to heaven, she did not lay aside this saving role, but by her manifold acts of intercession continues to win for us gifts of eternal salvation."[104] With this character of "intercession", first manifested at Cana in Galilee, Mary's mediation continues in the history of the Church and the world. We read that Mary "by her maternal charity, cares for the brethren of her Son who still journey on earth surrounded by dangers and difficulties, until they are led to their happy homeland".[105] In this way Mary's motherhood continues unceasingly in the Church as the mediation which intercedes, and the Church expresses her faith in

(margin note) Mary, mother of the infant Church

---

[103] LG, 62.

[104] Ibid., 62.

[105] Ibid., 62; in her prayer too the Church recognizes and celebrates Mary's "maternal role"; it is a role "of intercession and forgiveness, petition and grace, reconciliation

this truth by invoking Mary "under the titles of Advocate, Auxilia-trix, Adjutrix and Mediatrix".[106]

41. Through her mediation, subordinate to that of the Redeemer, Mary contributes *in a special way to the union of the pilgrim Church* on earth with the eschatological and heavenly *reality* of the Communion of Saints, since she has already been "assumed into heaven".[107] The truth of the Assumption, defined by Pius XII, is reaffirmed by the Second Vatican Council, which thus expresses the Church's faith: "Preserved free from all guilt of original sin, the Immaculate Virgin *was taken up body and soul into heavenly glory* upon the completion of her earthly sojourn. She was *exalted* by the Lord *as Queen of the Universe,* in order that she might be the more thoroughly conformed to her Son, the Lord of lords (cf. Rev 19:16) and the conqueror of sin and death."[108] In this teaching Pius XII was in continuity with Tradition, which has found many different expressions in the history of the Church, both in the East and in the West.

The Assumption as an anticipation of glory

By the mystery of the Assumption into heaven there were defini-tively accomplished in Mary all the effects of the one mediation of *Christ the Redeemer of the world* and *Risen Lord:* "In Christ shall all be made alive. But each in his own order: Christ the first fruits, then at his coming those who belong to Christ" (1 Cor 15:22–23). In the mystery of the Assumption is expressed the faith of the Church, according to which Mary is "united by a close and indissoluble bond" to Christ, for, if as Virgin and Mother she was singularly united with him *in his first coming,* so through her continued collaboration with him she will also be united with him in expectation of the second; "redeemed in an especially sublime manner by reason of the merits of her Son",[109] she also has that specifically maternal role of mediatrix of mercy *at his final coming,* when all those who belong to Christ "shall be made alive", when "the last enemy to be destroyed is death" (1 Cor 15:26).[110]

---

and peace" (cf. Preface of the Mass of the Blessed Virgin Mary, Mother and Mediatrix of Grace, in *Collectio Missarum de Beata Maria Virgine, ed. typ.* 1987, 1, 120).

[106] LG, 62.

[107] Ibid., 62; cf. Saint John Damascene, *Hom. in Dormitionem,* I, 11; II, 2, 14; III, 2: S. Ch. 80, 111f.; 127–131; 157–161; 181–185; Saint Bernard, *In Assumptione Beatae Mariae Sermo,* 1–2; S. Bernardi Opera, V, 1968, 228–238.

[108] LG, 59; cf. Pope Pius XII, Apostolic Constitution, *Munificentissimus Deus* (1 November 1950): AAS 42 (1950) 769–771; Saint Bernard presents Mary immersed in the splendor of the Son's glory: *In Dominica infra oct. Assumptionis Sermo,* 3; S. Bernardi Opera, V, 1968, 263f.

[109] LG, 53.

[110] On this particular aspect of Mary's mediation as *implorer of clemency* from the "Son as Judge", cf. Saint Bernard, *In Domenica infra oct. Assumptionis Sermo,* 1–2: S. Bernardi Opera, V, 1968, 262f.; Pope Leo XIII, Encyclical Epistle *Octobri Mense* (22 September 1891): Acta Leonis, XI, 299–315.

Connected with this exaltation of the noble "Daughter of Sion"[111] through her Assumption into heaven is the mystery of her eternal glory. For the Mother of Christ is glorified as "Queen of the Universe".[112] She who at the Annunciation called herself the "handmaid of the Lord" remained throughout her earthly life faithful to what this name expresses. In this she confirmed that she was a true "disciple" of Christ, who strongly emphasized that his mission was one of service: the Son of Man "came not to be served but to serve, and to give his life as a ransom for many" (Mt 20:28). In this way Mary became the first of those who, "serving Christ also in others, with humility and patience lead their brothers and sisters to that King whom to serve is to reign",[113] and she fully obtained that "state of royal freedom" proper to Christ's disciples: to serve means to reign!

"Christ obeyed even at the cost of death, and was therefore raised up by the Father (cf. Phil 2:8–9). Thus he entered into the glory of his kingdom. To him all things are made subject until he subjects himself and all created things to the Father, that God may be all in all (cf. 1 Cor 15:27–28)."[114] Mary, the handmaid of the Lord, has a share in this Kingdom of the Son.[115] The *glory of serving* does not cease to be her royal exaltation: assumed into heaven, she does not cease her saving service, which expresses her maternal mediation "until the external fulfillment of all the elect".[116] Thus, she who here on earth "loyally persevered in her union with her Son unto the Cross", continues to remain united with him, while now *"all things are subjected to him, until he subjects to the Father himself and all things"*. Thus in her Assumption into heaven, Mary is as it were clothed by the whole reality of the Communion of Saints, and her very union with the Son in glory is wholly oriented towards the definitive fullness of the Kingdom, when *"God will be all in all"*.

In this phase too Mary's maternal mediation does not cease to be subordinate to him who is the one Mediator, *until the final realization of "the fullness of time"*, that is to say until "all things are united in Christ" (cf. Eph 1:10).

---

[111] LG, 55.
[112] Ibid., 59.
[113] Ibid., 36.
[114] Ibid., 36.
[115] With regard to Mary as Queen, cf. Saint John Damascene, *Hom. in Nativitatem*, 6; 12; *Hom. in Dormitionem*, I, 2, 14; II, 11; III, 4; S. Ch. 80, 59f.; 77f.; 83f.; 113f.; 117; 151f.; 189–193.
[116] LG, 62.

2. *Mary in the Life of the Church and of Every Christian*

42. Linking itself with Tradition, the Second Vatican Council brought new light to bear on the role of the Mother of Christ in the life of the Church. "Through the gift . . . of divine motherhood, Mary is united with her Son, the Redeemer, and with his singular graces and offices. By these, the Blessed Virgin is also intimately united with the Church: *the Mother of God is a figure of the Church* in the matter of faith, charity and perfect union with Christ."[117] We have already noted how, from the beginning, Mary remains with the Apostles in expectation of Pentecost and how, as "the blessed one who believed", she is present in the midst of the pilgrim Church from generation to generation through faith and as the model of the hope which does not disappoint (cf. Rom 5:5).

Mother of God, figure of the Church

Mary believed in the fulfillment of what had been said to her by the Lord. As Virgin, she believed that she would conceive and bear a son: the "Holy One", who bears the name of "Son of God", the name "Jesus" (= God who saves). As handmaid of the Lord, she remained in perfect fidelity to the person and mission of this Son. As Mother, *"believing and obeying* . . . she brought forth on earth the *Father's Son*. This she did, knowing not man but overshadowed by the Holy Spirit."[118]

For these reasons Mary is honored in the Church "with special reverence. Indeed, from most ancient times the Blessed Virgin Mary has been venerated under the title of 'God-bearer'. In all perils and needs, the faithful have fled prayerfully to her protection."[119] This cult is altogether special: it bears in itself and *expresses* the profound link which exists *between the Mother of Christ and the Church.*[120] As Virgin and Mother, Mary remains for the Church a "permanent model". It can therefore be said that especially under this aspect, namely as a model, or rather as a "figure", Mary, present in the mystery of Christ, remains constantly present also in the mystery of the Church. For the Church too is "called mother and virgin", and these names have a profound biblical and theological justification.[121]

43. The Church *"becomes herself a mother* by accepting God's word with fidelity."[122] Like Mary, who first believed by accepting the

[117] LG, 63.
[118] Ibid., 63.
[119] Ibid., 66.
[120] Cf. Saint Ambrose, *De Institutione Virginis,* XIV, 88–89: PL, 16, 341; Saint Augustine, *Sermo* 215, 4: PL 38, 1074; *De Sancta Virginitate,* II, 2; V, 5; VI, 6: PL 40, 397; 398f.; 399; *Sermo* 191, II, 3: PL 38, 1010f.
[121] LG, 63.
[122] Ibid., 64.

word of God revealed to her at the Annunciation and by remaining faithful to that word in all her trials even unto the Cross, so too the Church becomes a mother when, *accepting with fidelity the word of God,* "by her preaching and by baptism *she brings forth to a new and immortal life children* who are conceived *of the Holy Spirit* and born of God".[123] This "maternal" characteristic of the Church was expressed in a particularly vivid way by the Apostle to the Gentiles when he wrote: "My little children, with whom I am again in travail until Christ be formed in you!" (Gal 4:19). These words of Saint Paul contain an interesting sign of the early Church's awareness of her own motherhood, linked to her apostolic service to mankind. This awareness enabled and still enables the Church to see the mystery of her life and mission modeled *upon the example of the Mother of the Son,* who is "the first-born among many brethren" (Rom 8:29).

The Church learns true motherhood from Mary

It can be said that from Mary the Church also learns her own motherhood: she recognizes the maternal dimension of her vocation, which is essentially bound to her sacramental nature, in "contemplating Mary's mysterious sanctity, imitating her charity and faithfully fulfilling the Father's will".[124] If the Church is the sign and instrument of intimate union with God, she is so by reason of her motherhood, because, receiving life from the Spirit, she "generates" sons and daughters of the human race to a new life in Christ. For, just as *Mary is at the service of the mystery of the Incarnation,* so *the Church* is always *at the service of the mystery of adoption to sonship* through grace.

Likewise, following the example of Mary, the Church remains the virgin faithful to her spouse: "The Church herself is a virgin, who keeps whole and pure the fidelity she has pledged to her Spouse."[125] For the Church is the spouse of Christ, as is clear from the Pauline Letters (cf. Eph 5:21–33; 2 Cor 11:2), and from the title found in John: "bride of the Lamb" (Rev 21:9). If *the Church* as spouse "keeps the fidelity she *has pledged* to Christ", this fidelity, even though in the Apostle's teaching it has become an image of marriage (cf. Eph 5:23–33), also has value as a model of total self-giving to God in celibacy "for the kingdom of heaven", *in virginity consecrated to God* (cf. Mt 19:11–12; 2 Cor 11:2). Precisely such virginity, after the example of the Virgin of Nazareth, is the source of a special spiritual fruitfulness: *it is the source of motherhood in the Holy Spirit.*

But *the Church* also preserves the faith *received from* Christ. Following the example of Mary, who kept and pondered in her heart everything relating to her divine Son (cf. Lk 2:19, 51), the Church is

[123] LG, 64.
[124] Ibid., 64.
[125] Ibid., 64.

committed to preserving the word of God and investigating its riches with discernment and prudence, in order to bear faithful witness to it before all mankind in every age.[126]

44. Given Mary's relationship to the Church as an exemplar, the Church is close to her and seeks to become like her: "Imitating the Mother of her Lord, and by the power of the Holy Spirit, she preserves with virginal purity an integral faith, a firm hope, and a sincere charity."[127] Mary is thus present in the mystery of the Church as a *model*. But the Church's mystery also consists in generating people to a new and immortal life: this is her motherhood in the Holy Spirit. And here Mary is not only the model and figure of the Church; she is much more. For, *"with maternal love she cooperates in the birth and development"* of the sons and daughters of Mother Church. The Church's motherhood is accomplished not only according to the model and figure of the Mother of God but also with her "cooperation". The Church *draws* abundantly from this cooperation, that is to say from the maternal mediation which is characteristic of Mary, insofar as already on earth she cooperated in the rebirth and development of the Church's sons and daughters, as the Mother of that Son whom the Father "placed as the first-born among many brethren".[128]

She cooperated, as the Second Vatican Council teaches, with a maternal love.[129] Here we perceive the real value of the words spoken by Jesus to his Mother at the hour of the Cross: "Woman, behold your son" and to the disciple: "Behold your mother" (Jn 19:26–27). They are words which determine *Mary's place in the life of Christ's disciples* and they express—as I have already said—the new motherhood of the Mother of the Redeemer: a spiritual motherhood, born from the heart of the Paschal Mystery of the Redeemer of the world. It is a motherhood in the order of grace, for it implores the gift of the Spirit, who raises up the new children of God, redeemed through the sacrifice of Christ: that Spirit whom Mary too, together with the Church, received on the day of Pentecost.

Her motherhood is particularly noted and experienced by the Christian people at the *Sacred Banquet*—the liturgical celebration of the mystery of the Redemption—at which Christ, his *true body born of the Virgin Mary*, becomes present.

The piety of the Christian people has always very rightly sensed a *profound link* between devotion to the Blessed Virgin and worship of the Eucharist: this is a fact that can be seen in the liturgy of both

[126] Cf. DV, 8; Saint Bonaventure, *Comment. in Evang. Lucae,* Ad Claras Aquas, VII, 53, no. 40; 68, no. 109.
[127] LG, 64.
[128] Ibid., 63.
[129] Cf. ibid., 63.

the West and the East, in the traditions of the Religious Families, in the modern movements of spirituality, including those for youth, and in the pastoral practice of the Marian Shrines. *Mary guides the faithful to the Eucharist.*

45. Of the essence of motherhood is the fact that it concerns the person. Motherhood always establishes a *unique and unrepeatable relationship* between two people: *between mother and child* and *between child and mother.* Even when the same woman is the mother of many children, her personal relationship with each one of them is of the very essence of motherhood. For each child is generated in a unique and unrepeatable way, and this is true both for the mother and for the child. Each child is surrounded in the same way by that maternal love on which are based the child's development and coming to maturity as a human being.

It can be said that motherhood "in the order of grace" preserves the analogy with what "in the order of nature" characterizes the union between mother and child. In the light of this fact it becomes easier to understand why in Christ's testament on Golgotha his Mother's new motherhood is expressed in the singular, in reference to one man: "Behold your son."

It can also be said that these same words fully show the reason *for the Marian dimension of the life of Christ's disciples.* This is true not only of John, who at that hour stood at the foot of the Cross together with his Master's Mother, but it is also true of every disciple of Christ, of every Christian. The Redeemer entrusts his mother to the disciple, and at the same time he gives her to him as his mother. Mary's motherhood, which becomes man's inheritance, is a gift: *a gift which Christ himself makes* personally to every individual. The Redeemer entrusts Mary to John because he entrusts John to Mary. At the foot of the Cross there begins that special *entrusting of humanity to the Mother of Christ,* which in the history of the Church has been practiced and expressed in different ways. The same Apostle and Evangelist, after reporting the words addressed by Jesus on the Cross to his Mother and to himself, adds: "And from that hour the disciple took her to his own home" (Jn 19:27). This statement certainly means that the role of son was attributed to the disciple and that he assumed responsibility for the Mother of his beloved Master. And since Mary was given as a mother to him personally, the statement indicates, even though indirectly, everything expressed by the intimate relationship of a child with its mother. And all of this can be included in the word "entrusting". Such entrusting is *the response* to a person's love, and in particular *to the love of a mother.*

The Marian dimension of the life of a disciple of Christ is expressed in a special way precisely through this filial entrusting to the Mother

The Marian dimension of Christ's disciples

of Christ, which began with the testament of the Redeemer on Golgotha. Entrusting himself to Mary in a filial manner, the Christian, like the Apostle John, "welcomes" the Mother of Christ "into his own home"[130] and brings her into everything that makes up his inner life, that is to say into his human and Christian "I"; he "*took her to his own home*". Thus the Christian seeks to be taken into that "maternal charity" with which the Redeemer's Mother "cares for the brethren of her Son",[131] "in whose birth and development she cooperates"[132] in the measure of the gift proper to each one through the power of Christ's Spirit. Thus also is exercised that motherhood in the Spirit which became Mary's role at the foot of the Cross and in the Upper Room.

46. This filial relationship, this self-entrusting of a child to its mother, not only has its *beginning in Christ* but can also be said to be *definitively directed towards him*. Mary can be said to continue to say to each individual the words which she spoke at Cana in Galilee: "Do whatever he tells you." For he, Christ, is the one Mediator between God and mankind; he is "the way, and the truth, and the life" (Jn 14:6); it is he whom the Father has given to the world, so that man "should not perish but have eternal life" (Jn 3:16). The Virgin of Nazareth became the first "witness" of this saving love of the Father, and she also wishes *to remain* its *humble handmaid always and everywhere*. For every Christian, for every human being, Mary is the one who first "believed", and precisely with her faith as Spouse and Mother she wishes to act upon all those who entrust themselves to her as her children. And it is well known that the more her children persevere and progress in this attitude, the nearer Mary leads them to the "unsearchable riches of Christ" (Eph 3:8). And to the same degree they recognize more and more clearly the dignity of man in all its fullness and the definitive meaning of his vocation, for "Christ . . . fully reveals man to man himself."[133]

This Marian dimension of Christian life takes on special importance in relation to women and their status. In fact, femininity has a *unique relationship* with the Mother of the Redeemer, a subject which can be studied in greater depth elsewhere. Here I simply wish to note that the figure of Mary of Nazareth sheds light on *womanhood as such*

[130] Clearly, in the Greek text the expression "*eis tà ídia*" goes beyond the mere acceptance of Mary by the disciple in the sense of material lodging and hospitality in his house; it indicates rather a *communion of life* established between the two as a result of the words of the dying Christ: cf. Saint Augustine, *In Ioan. Evang. tract.* 119, 3: CCL 36, 659: "He took her to himself, not into his own property, for he possessed nothing of his own, but among his own duties, which he attended to with dedication."

[131] LG, 62.

[132] Ibid., 63.

[133] GS, 22.

*Looking at
Mary, women
find the secret
for living their
femininity*
by the very fact that God, in the sublime event of the Incarnation
of his Son, entrusted himself to the ministry, the free and active
ministry of a woman. It can thus be said that women, by looking
to Mary, find in her the secret of living their femininity with dignity
and of achieving their own true advancement. In the light of Mary,
the Church sees in the face of women the reflection of a beauty which
mirrors the loftiest sentiments of which the human heart is capable:
the self-offering totality of love; the strength that is capable of bearing
the greatest sorrows; limitless fidelity and tireless devotion to work;
the ability to combine penetrating intuition with words of support
and encouragement.

47. At the Council Paul VI solemnly proclaimed that *Mary is the
Mother of the Church,* "that is, Mother of the entire Christian people,
both faithful and pastors".[134] Later, in 1968, in the Profession of
Faith known as the "Credo of the People of God", he restated this
truth in an even more forceful way in these words: "We believe that
the Most Holy Mother of God, the new Eve, the Mother of the
Church, carries on in heaven her maternal role with regard to the
members of Christ, cooperating in the birth and development of
divine life in the souls of the redeemed."[135]

The Council's teaching emphasized that the truth concerning the
Blessed Virgin, Mother of Christ, is an effective aid in exploring
more deeply the truth concerning the Church. When speaking of the
Constitution *Lumen Gentium,* which had just been approved by the
Council, Paul VI said: "Knowledge of the true Catholic doctrine
regarding the Blessed Virgin Mary will always be a key to *the exact
understanding of the mystery of Christ and of the Church.*"[136] Mary is
present in the Church as the Mother of Christ, and at the same time
as that Mother whom Christ, in the mystery of the Redemption,
gave to humanity in the person of the Apostle John. Thus, in her
new motherhood in the Spirit, Mary embraces each and every one
in the Church, and embraces each and every one *through* the Church.
In this sense Mary, Mother of the Church, is also the Church's
model. Indeed, as Paul VI hopes and asks, the Church must draw
"from the Virgin Mother of God the most authentic form of perfect
imitation of Christ".[137]

Thanks to this special bond linking the Mother of Christ with the
Church, there is further *clarified the mystery of that "woman"* who,
from the first chapters of the Book of *Genesis* until the Book of
Revelation, accompanies the revelation of God's salvific plan for

[134] Cf. Pope Paul VI, *Discourse of 21 November 1964:* AAS 56 (1964) 1015.
[135] Pope Paul VI, *Solemn Profession of Faith* (30 June 1968), 15: AAS 60 (1968) 438f.
[136] Pope Paul VI, *Discourse of 21 November 1964:* AAS 56 (1964) 1015.
[137] Ibid., 1016.

humanity. For Mary, present in the Church as the Mother of the Redeemer, takes part, as a mother, in that "monumental struggle against the powers of darkness"[138] which continues throughout human history. And by her ecclesial identification as the "woman clothed with the sun" (Rev 12:1),[139] it can be said that "in the Most Holy Virgin the Church has already reached that perfection whereby she exists without spot or wrinkle". Hence, as Christians raise their eyes with faith to Mary in the course of their earthly pilgrimage, they "strive to increase in holiness".[140] Mary, the exalted Daughter of Sion, helps all her children, wherever they may be and whatever their condition, *to find in Christ the path to the Father's house.*

Thus, throughout her life, the Church maintains with the Mother of God a link which embraces, in the saving mystery, the past, the present and the future, and venerates her as the spiritual mother of humanity and the advocate of grace.

3. *The Meaning of the Marian Year*

48. It is precisely the special bond between humanity and this Mother which has led me to proclaim a Marian Year in the Church, in this period before the end of the Second Millennium since Christ's birth. A similar initiative was taken in the past, when Pius XII proclaimed 1954 as a Marian Year, in order to highlight the exceptional holiness of the Mother of Christ as expressed in the mysteries of her Immaculate Conception (defined exactly a century before) and of her Assumption into heaven.[141]

Now, following the line of the Second Vatican Council, I wish to emphasize the *special presence* of the Mother of God in the mystery of Christ and his Church. For this is a fundamental dimension emerging from the Mariology of the Council, the end of which is now more than twenty years behind us. The Extraordinary Synod of Bishops held in 1985 exhorted everyone to follow faithfully the teaching and guidelines of the Council. We can say that these two events— the Council and the Synod—embody what the Holy Spirit himself wishes "to say to the Church" in the present phase of history.

In this context, the Marian Year is meant to promote a new and

The special presence of the Mother of God in the mystery of Christ and of his Church

---

[138]GS, 37.

[139]Cf. Saint Bernard, *In Dominica infra oct. Assumptionis Sermo: S. Bernardi Opera,* V, 1968, 262–274.

[140]LG, 65.

[141]Cf. Encyclical Letter *Fulgens Corona* (8 September 1953): AAS 45 (1953) 577–592. Pius X with his Encyclical Letter *Ad Diem Illum* (2 February 1904), on the occasion of the 50th anniversary of the dogmatic definition of the Immaculate Conception of the Blessed Virgin Mary, had proclaimed an Extraordinary Jubilee of a few months; *Pii X P. M. Acta,* I, 147–166.

more careful reading of what the Council said about the Blessed Virgin Mary, Mother of God, in the mystery of Christ and of the Church, the topic to which the contents of this Encyclical are devoted. Here we speak not only of *the doctrine of faith* but also of *the life of faith,* and thus of authentic "Marian spirituality", seen in the light of Tradition, and especially the spirituality to which the Council exhorts us.[142] Furthermore, Marian *spirituality,* like its corresponding *devotion,* finds a very rich source in the historical experience of individuals and of the various Christian communities present among the different peoples and nations of the world. In this regard, I would like to recall, among the many witnesses and teachers of this spirituality, the figure of Saint Louis Marie Grignion de Montfort,[143] who proposes consecration to Christ through the hands of Mary, as an effective means for Christians to live faithfully their baptismal commitments. I am pleased to note that in our own time too new manifestations of this spirituality and devotion are not lacking.

There thus exist solid points of reference to look to and follow in the context of this Marian Year.

49. This Marian Year *will begin on the Solemnity of Pentecost, on June 7 next.* For it is a question not only of recalling that Mary "preceded" the entry of Christ the Lord into the history of the human family, but also of emphasizing, in the light of Mary, that from the moment when the mystery of the Incarnation was accomplished, human history entered "the fullness of time", and that the Church is the sign of this fullness. As the People of God, the Church makes her pilgrim way towards eternity through faith, in the midst of all the peoples and nations, beginning from the day of Pentecost. *Christ's Mother*—who was present at the beginning of "the time of the Church", when in expectation of the coming of the Holy Spirit she devoted herself to prayer in the midst of the Apostles and her Son's disciples—constantly "precedes" *the Church* in her *journey* through human history. She is also the one who, precisely as the "handmaid of the Lord", cooperates unceasingly with the work of salvation accomplished by Christ, her Son.

Thus by means of this Marian Year *the Church is called* not only to remember everything in her past that testifies to the special maternal cooperation of the Mother of God in the work of salvation in Christ the Lord, but also, on her own part, *to prepare* for the future

---

[142] LG, 66–67.

[143] Saint Louis Marie Grignion de Montfort, *Traité de la varie dévotion à la sainte Vièrge.* This saint can rightly be linked with the figure of Saint Alfonso Maria de' Liguori, the second centenary of whose death occurs this year; cf. among his works *Le glorie di Maria.*

the paths of this cooperation. For the end of the Second Christian Millennium opens up as a new prospect.

50. As has already been mentioned, also among our divided brethren many honor and celebrate the Mother of the Lord, especially among the Orientals. It is a Marian light cast upon ecumenism. In particular, I wish to mention once more that during the Marian Year there will occur the *Millennium of the Baptism* of Saint Vladimir, Grand Duke of Kiev (988). This marked the beginning of Christianity in the territories of what was then called Rus', and subsequently in other territories of Eastern Europe. In this way, through the work of evangelization, Christianity spread beyond Europe, as far as the northern territories of the Asian continent. We would therefore like, especially during this Year, to join in prayer with all those who are celebrating the Millennium of this Baptism, both Orthodox and Catholics, repeating and confirming with the Council those sentiments of joy and comfort that "the Easterners . . . with ardent emotion and devout mind concur in reverencing the Mother of God, ever Virgin."[144] Even though we are still experiencing the painful effects of the separation which took place some decades later (1054), we can say that *in the presence of the Mother of Christ we feel that we are true brothers and sisters* within that messianic People, which is called to be the one family of God on earth. As I announced at the beginning of the New Year: "We desire to reconfirm this universal inheritance of all the sons and daughters of this earth."[145]

Before the Mother of Christ, Orthodox and Catholics feel like true brothers

In announcing the Year of Mary, I also indicated that it will end next year on *the Solemnity of the Assumption of the Blessed Virgin into heaven,* in order to emphasize the "great sign in heaven" spoken of by the *Apocalypse.* In this way we also wish to respond to the exhortation of the Council, which looks to Mary as "a sign of sure hope and solace for the pilgrim People of God". And the Council expresses this exhortation in the following words: "Let the entire body of the faithful pour forth persevering prayer to the Mother of God and Mother of mankind. Let them implore that she who aided the beginning of the Church by her prayers may now, exalted as she is in heaven above all the saints and angels, intercede with her Son in the fellowship of all the saints. May she do so until all the people of the human family, whether they are honored with the name of Christian or whether they still do not know their Savior, are happily gathered together in peace and harmony into the one People of God, for the glory of the Most Holy and Undivided Trinity."[146]

[144]LG, 69.
[145]Homily on January 1, 1987.
[146]LG, 69.

Conclusion

51. At the end of the daily Liturgy of the Hours, among the invocations addressed to Mary by the Church is the following:

"Loving Mother of the Redeemer,
gate of heaven, star of the sea,
assist your people who have fallen yet strive to rise again.
To the wonderment of nature you bore your Creator!"

The wonderment of all creation

"To the wonderment of nature"! These words of the antiphon express that *wonderment of faith* which accompanies the mystery of Mary's divine motherhood. In a sense, it does so in the heart of the whole of creation, and, directly, in the heart of the whole People of God, in the heart of the Church. How wonderfully far God has gone, the Creator and Lord of all things, in the "revelation of himself" to man![147] How clearly he has bridged all the spaces of that infinite "distance" which separates the Creator from the creature! If in himself he remains *ineffable and unsearchable,* still more *ineffable and unsearchable is he in the reality of the Incarnation* of the Word, who became man through the Virgin of Nazareth.

If he has eternally willed to call man to share in the divine nature (cf. 2 Pet 1:4), it can be said that he has matched the "divinization" of man to humanity's historical conditions, so that even after sin he is ready to restore at a great price the eternal plan of his love through the "humanization" of his Son, who is the same being as himself. The whole of creation, and more directly man himself, cannot fail to be amazed at this gift in which he has become a sharer, in the Holy Spirit: "God so loved the world that he gave his only Son" (Jn 3:16).

At the center of this mystery, in the midst of this wonderment of faith, stands Mary. As the loving Mother of the Redeemer, she was the first to experience it: "To the wonderment of nature you bore your Creator"!

52. The words of this liturgical antiphon also express *the truth of the "great transformation"* which the mystery of the Incarnation establishes for man. It is a transformation which belongs to his entire history, from that beginning which is revealed to us in the first chapters of *Genesis* until the final end, in the perspective of the end of the world, of which Jesus has revealed to us "neither the day nor the hour" (Mt 25:13). It is an unending and continuous transformation between falling and rising again, between the man of sin and the

[147] DV, 2: "Through this revelation . . . the invisible God . . . out of the abundance of his love speaks to men as friends . . . and lives among them . . . , so that he may invite and take them into fellowship with himself."

man of grace and justice. The Advent liturgy in particular is at the very heart of this transformation and captures its unceasing "here and now" when it exclaims: "Assist your people who have fallen yet strive to rise again"!

"Help the people who fall, but long to rise again"

These words apply to every individual, every community, to nations and peoples, and to the generations and epochs of human history, to our own epoch, to these years of the Millennium which is drawing to a close: "Assist, yes assist, your people who have fallen"!

This is the invocation addressed to Mary, the "loving Mother of the Redeemer", the invocation addressed to Christ, who through Mary entered human history. Year after year the antiphon rises to Mary, evoking that moment which saw the accomplishment of this essential historical transformation, which irreversibly continues: the transformation from "falling" to "rising".

Mankind has made wonderful discoveries and achieved extraordinary results in the fields of science and technology. It has made great advances along the path of progress and civilization, and in recent times one could say that it has succeeded in speeding up the pace of history. But the fundamental transformation, the one which can be called "original", constantly accompanies man's journey, and through all the events of history accompanies each and every individual. It is the transformation from "falling" to "rising", from death to life. It is also *a constant challenge* to people's consciences, a challenge to man's whole historical awareness: the challenge to follow the path of "not falling" in ways that are ever old and ever new, and of "rising again" if a fall has occurred.

As she goes forward with the whole of humanity towards the frontier between the two Millennia, the Church, for her part, with the whole community of believers and in union with all men and women of good will, takes up the great challenge contained in these words of the Marian antiphon: "the people who have fallen yet strive to rise again", and she addresses both the Redeemer and his Mother with the plea: "Assist us." For, as this prayer attests, the Church sees the Blessed Mother of God in the saving mystery of Christ and in her own mystery. She sees Mary deeply rooted in humanity's history, in man's eternal vocation according to the providential plan which God has made for him from eternity. She sees Mary maternally present and sharing in the many complicated problems which *today* beset the lives of individuals, families and nations; she sees her helping the Christian people in the constant struggle between good and evil, to ensure that it "does not fall", or, if it has fallen, that it "rises again".

I hope with all my heart that the reflections contained in the present Encyclical will also serve to renew this vision in the hearts of all believers.

As Bishop of Rome, I send to all those to whom these thoughts are addressed the kiss of peace, my greeting and my blessing in our Lord Jesus Christ. Amen.

Given in Rome, at Saint Peter's, on March 25, the Solemnity of the Annunciation of the Lord, in the year 1987, the ninth of my Pontificate.

PART TWO

THE WORDS OF THE BISHOPS

I

AFRICA

"WITH A NEW HEART AND NEW SPIRIT"

Pastoral Letter of the Bishops of Uganda

Introduction

a. Responding to the new changes

"Keep watch over yourselves and over all the flock which the Holy Spirit has placed in your care. Be shepherds of the Church of God, which he made his own through the sacrificial death of his Son" (Acts 20:28).

1. Dear brothers and sisters, these striking words of farewell spoken by the Apostle Paul to the elders of the Christian community at Ephesus express very well the responsibility which we, your bishops, have towards you. We have been set apart by the Lord within the Church precisely for this service: to watch over you, to build up your faith, to guide you to a true understanding of the events that took place and are still taking place here in Uganda, to stimulate and encourage you to throw yourselves with enthusiasm and courage into your apostolic and social responsibilities. It is because of this pastoral duty that we send you this letter, a message that has been made urgent by the important changes that have affected our country and which are a new challenge for all of us.

2. As pastors who feel for you with the heart of Jesus himself (Mt 9:36), we cannot but begin by expressing our sympathetic solidarity with all of you who have suffered in a special way during this time. Many of you have lost members of your family and close friends. Many of you have been refugees or exiles with all the uncertainty and sadness this involves. Many of you have suffered physically and

Solidarity with those who suffer

Uganda has held the one-hundredth anniversary celebration in honor of the Martyrs of Uganda (twenty-two young blacks who underwent martyrdom between November 15, 1886 and January 27, 1887), and Uganda's sufferings are still going on. However, the long letter of that country's bishops, whose first two parts we publish here, offers a glimmer of hope for peace for Catholics and everyone else in Uganda. The two concluding chapters of the document, that for reasons of space had to be omitted, were entitled, respectively, "Evangelization: a sound method for moral reform" and "Church and politics". The letter was published in English in *L'Osservatore Romano,* September 1, 1986.

have been seriously injured in one way or another. Many of you bear the emotional and psychological scars of terror and persecution. All of us, in one way or another, have experienced what terrible things violations of human rights and war are and how they bring misery especially to the most innocent and defenseless.

3. It was indeed a great sadness to us that the differences and tensions within our nation were not in the end resolved by peaceful means, for we know that the use of violence always runs the great risk of generating more violence. We particularly regret the fact that once again significant numbers of Ugandans find themselves in exile, with all the hurt and disruption that this obviously causes.

4. However, it is only right that we should express our appreciation of the way in which the National Resistance Army has generally behaved. The evil effects of military action were kept to a minimum; respect was shown for human life and property; prisoners of war were usually treated with propriety. In the period following the war, we have seen that in general there has been an attempt to use political power as a means of service and through negotiation. We have also been favorably impressed by the attempt on the part of the government to overcome tribal divisions and prejudices. Certainly, all these ways of acting have been a most welcome breath of fresh air for us in Uganda, and an example to the rest of the world.

5. As pastors who represent Christ in your midst, we have a word also for those of you who have emerged from recent events with a *The Lord is* heavy conscience. Perhaps you know yourselves guilty of some seri-*quick to forgive* ous wrong: murder, perhaps, or extortion or robbery or violence or false accusation, or any of the other ills which have blighted our country. To you we have this to say: the Lord is ready to forgive you and re-create you if you would only honestly admit your sin, repent of it and make serious amends. In the Lord's eyes there is no such thing as "a gone case"; in every one of us he sees the potential of something new. We appeal to you to open yourselves to him because Uganda also needs you and your contribution in building a peaceful future (cf. Joel 2:12–13).

6. At the outset of the new Government a famous statement was publicly made that the new changes were not to be understood as a simple change of guards, but rather as a fundamental change. As the religious leaders of a large part of the citizens of this country, we want to say this: a fundamental change is urgent and necessary in our country. Indeed, we have been calling for such a change for many years especially through our various Pastoral Letters. Indeed it is an essential part of the Church's mission to promote such a change for the good of our country. As a recent instruction of the Holy See says, ". . . the love which impels the Church to communi-

cate to all the people a sharing in the grace of divine life also causes her, through the effective action of her members, to pursue people's true temporal good, help them in their needs, provide and promote an integral liberation from everything that hinders the development of individuals . . ." (CFL, no. 65).

7. We want the Church, then, to be actively involved in this change. Also, as we shall explain more fully later in this letter, the Church's proclamation of the saving Gospel of Jesus Christ is the most effective instrument for a fundamental change of the human person and human society, because it reaches the inner side of man: "I shall give you a new heart and put a new spirit in you" (Ezek 36:25).

The Gospel, an efficacious instrument of change

8. This Pastoral Letter, then, is meant to be much more than a statement of Christian principles. Indeed, much of what is said here we have already spoken of in our previous Pastoral Letters. This present message however is, above all, a call to action. To all Ugandan Christians we make this pressing invitation: understand what the Lord is saying to you in this present moment; view Ugandan society in the light of the Gospel message; place at the disposal of all your brothers and sisters, believers and non-believers, the vision and energy that come from your belonging to Jesus Christ. The basic Christian attitude in this moment of Uganda's history is not and must not be: "Let us wait and see", but rather: "Let us be the light of the world and the salt of the earth *now*" (cf. Mt 3:13–14).

b. Interpreting the true meaning of our history

9. Christians through their baptism are called to carry out a prophetic task in the world. Like the prophets of old they live in solidarity with the rest of mankind but are chosen by God to judge the events of history in the light of the Covenant between God and man.

10. In interpreting the history of our nation it is important to take into account all the events and to see them in the light of faith. God is the Lord of history and is leading mankind towards its destiny. His plan for the salvation of mankind, and of Uganda in particular, cannot be frustrated. "We know that God cooperates with all those who love him by turning everything to their good" (Rom 8:28).

11. We received the Word of God from the early missionaries and embraced the faith of Jesus Christ with great enthusiasm. The great witnesses to this are our Holy Martyrs. We saw in this faith a true prosperity through the efforts the Church made for human development in the fields of health, education and agriculture. We understood that God had blessed us with many gifts, both spiritual and material, particularly our fertile soil.

12. When Uganda attained political independence we were filled

with hope of a widespread growth of peace and prosperity. We have to admit that in the years since independence many of our dreams and hopes have not been fulfilled. Rather we have witnessed a growth of exploitation, corruption, robbery, violence, tribal strife and hatred which has led to the loss of moral conscience, a collapse of the economy and a life of indescribable suffering for a large number of our population.

13. Particularly in view of the events of recent years it would be shortsighted to ascribe all the blame for the present plight of our country to external factors. As we said in our Pastoral Letter "Be Converted and Live" of 1981: "We blame everybody but ourselves. It is time for Ugandans to grow out of this attitude and face the future with honesty. We are reaping what we have sown. Evils from the outside have prospered in Uganda because they have found fertile and receptive soil. This is what we mean by conversion and reconciliation: Let us recognize what is lacking within us, accept the blame for our choices and vow never to go back to them again" (no. 18).

14. Like the people of Israel in the promised land, all too often the good things that God has given us have become idols that have taken the place of God in our lives. We have pursued wealth, pleasure and power, ignoring God and his commands, and these idols have destroyed us: "Vanity they pursued, and vanity they became" (Jer 2:5).

15. The greatest idolatry for us, as for Israel, lies in the fact that while recognizing God as Creator we have not looked to his presence among us in Christ and the Church as the *way,* the method in working for prosperity in our life and in building a nation that is one: "I am the Way, the Truth and the Life" (Jn 14:6). We have put more faith in our own efforts, and in things like "magendo", bribery, economic strategies, personalities in public life, the overthrow of different regimes, than in the power of Christ who changes our hearts and brings about a new unity which is the source of fundamental change in our society. This is why we have failed in bringing peace, stability and prosperity to our country.

16. Through the events of history God is not simply punishing us. Rather it is through such events that we grow in life, in faith and love.

These painful years have given us many examples of people who gave brave witness to their faith in God, often by the sacrifice of their lives, for the sake of the faith, for justice or in defense of the oppressed. Their blood and the blood of all the innocent has not been shed in vain, and we call on all parishes to recall those who gave witness to the faith in these years, and to record their testimony as an essential part of our history, for edification of our Christians and of future generations.

17. Furthermore we call on all Ugandans to remember all who died as victims of violence since independence.

In the Holy Eucharist and in other prayers on the second of November we shall pray for the repose of their souls. We shall offer the Holy Sacrifice for the purification of all living Ugandans and ask the Lord to help all of us to drive out sin from our lives and to follow Christ who is calling us through his Church to true happiness, peace and national prosperity.

We will offer the Holy Sacrifice for the purification of all the people of Uganda

18. God has made us understand that these cannot be simply the fruit of human effort, however intelligent, but come to us as his gift. God has already made us his children in Christ, and it is only in recognizing this and by facing up to our problems as one family according to his law that we can hope to build our nation. "If the Lord does not build the house, in vain do its builders labor; if the Lord does not watch over the city, in vain does the watchman keep vigil" (Ps 126).

1. *Urgent Needs*

a. Reconciliation

19. In our previous Pastoral Letters we have on several occasions called for sincere reconciliation among the citizens of Uganda. In the present situation we find ourselves once again having to repeat this appeal. We do so against the background of the recent sad conflict in our country which has led to a new flare-up of divisions and the desire for revenge.

20. The teaching of the Gospel on this point is very clear and we have to thank Jesus for his message, so abundantly explained in the Gospel. It suffices to quote these words from the Sermon on the Mount: "You have learned how it was said, 'You must love your neighbor and hate your enemy'. But I say this to you: Love your enemies and pray for those who persecute you. In this way you will be sons of your Father in heaven, for he causes his sun to rise on bad men as well as good and his rain to fall on honest and dishonest men alike" (Mt 5:45–46).

21. The history of our country as an independent nation has been marred by the totally unchristian phenomenon of revenge. It is urgent that all men and women of good will should uproot the desire for revenge from their hearts, especially since we have all had abundant proof that the taking of revenge simply leads to a spiral of violence that nobody can in the end control. Indeed, revenge has caused many Ugandans to lose their lives or their jobs or their property, and it has also caused the harassment of innocent people, simply because

Banish from your heart the desire for vengeance

they belong to the same tribe as some evil-doers. As the pastors of the Catholic Church here in Uganda we want unequivocally to declare that those who take revenge are separating themselves from Christ and his grace.

22. Christ calls for the eradication of revenge by means of reconciliation, forgiveness and works of charity. Such reconciliation is vital in order that peace should be established in our society.

The good of this society must prevail over our personal feelings and interests. Of course, we well know that reconciliation is very difficult but, with God's help, it is not beyond our moral capacity. It is only Jesus Christ the Savior who can help us uproot from our hearts the spirit of revenge and in its place communicate to us a spirit of reconciliation and the moral strength to practice it. When God asks us to do something, he always gives us the strength to do it.

23. It is important that reconciliation among us should not be superficial, because if it is, it will not produce lasting results. It must be a true conversion of mind and heart, inspired by the Christian vision that all men and women are children of God. Reconciliation with brothers is a condition for reconciliation with God. Remember the Lord's clear teaching: "If you are bringing your offering to the altar and there you remember that your brother has something against you, leave your offering there before the altar, go and be reconciled with your brother first and then come back and present your offering" (Mt 5:23–24).

24. It is easy enough to find former enemies working together but often their hearts are far from true reconciliation. It is simply a matter of wanting to share power at all costs and being ready in this pursuit to turn against their fellow citizens. In this regard we need to remember that in the end it is only men and women of principle who are respected and the principle behind reconciliation is not the mere struggle for political survival but rather the inner need of following the teaching of Christ.

25. In the past Catholics from the different dioceses of Uganda used to meet often at national level to get to know each other and to overcome the barriers that distance and ethnic differences tended to erect. These meetings served for an exchange of experiences in living the Gospel and for drawing up plans of apostolic action. In recent years such meetings have become more and more infrequent.

To promote meetings on the national level

We exhort the various national Catholic organizations once again to favor such encounters as they are a great help in building up a spirit of reconciliation and forgiveness.

26. Another field where the task of reconciliation calls us to renewed commitment is that of ecumenism. We need to increase the

number of our fraternal contacts with members of the other denominations and religions for we are sure that this would open up new areas for the exercise of our Christian love.

We encourage also other initiatives which may help us in the struggle for reconciliation.

b. Moral rehabilitation

27. In the past years our country has undergone many disasters as we all know. The greatest tragedy of all, however, has been the collapse in the moral standards of our people and a loss of moral conscience. Many people no longer feel guilty when they carry out some evil actions; and they are no longer aware that what they are doing is evil. When we think that the vast majority of those who have committed crimes are baptized Christians we feel very uneasy.

28. If we list the crimes and other evils that have been done we see they are clearly forbidden by the commandments of God that we have been teaching since the origin of Christianity in our country: killing, wounding and torturing are all forbidden by the fifth commandment; rape, adultery and other wrong use of sex are all forbidden by the sixth commandment; all kinds of stealing are forbidden by the seventh commandment; false witness, that has deepened divisions and caused imprisonment, death, torture and loss of property is forbidden by the eighth commandment.

29. We should like to say more about the seventh commandment at this point because offenses against this have involved not only soldiers and their accomplices, but also many ordinary people. We give here some examples of sins against this commandment that many people have forgotten are truly wrong, offenses against God and our fellow men: *looting;* this has become a habit for some. They think that situations of insecurity give them the right to help themselves to the property of other people, especially the property of government institutions. The fact that property is not defended does not mean it has no owner. Looting, then, is a clear case of stealing, and it requires restitution to be made. It is a personal sin, but also a social sin as it disrupts the supply of goods necessary for the life of the community.

Pillage is both a personal and a social sin

30. The making of maximum profit in economic dealing with the minimum effort, without reference to the true value of goods, is wrong. Also wrong is the creation of an artificial shortage of goods in order to increase the demand and consequently the prices. All this is done at the expense of the poor who depend on the traders for goods essential to their life. Instead they are exploited by unscrupu-

lous business men. All these are sinful deeds. These practices contribute to the inflation that reduces the purchasing power of the currency and are thus a grave sin against the community, a social sin.

31. A person who accepts employment is bound in conscience to carry out his duty well. One who receives a full salary without doing his job responsibly is guilty of stealing. This has been forgotten by many, particularly in government service.

Other forms of corruption

32. Other forms of corruption that we have to denounce are the following: embezzlement of public funds, demanding money from the public in order to perform the very duties that one is salaried to perform (bribery), exacting an undue percentage on public contracts, careless or irresponsible administration of public funds, even when there is no outright theft, as it often leads to a breakdown in the national economy; disorganization of administrative services that have been drained of the spirit that should animate them, namely, professional conscience and dedication (cf. JEA).

We have become so used to seeing this kind of behavior that it no longer seems sinful, but it is.

After having considered these facts we realize that the moral standards of the nation have declined because both leaders and citizens have lost sight of certain *key values* which lie at the foundation of social and political life.

2. Key Values for the Rebuilding of Our Nation

33. The human tragedy of the recent years in Uganda has left its scars on many citizens. Any program for moral rehabilitation in the country must start from some principles common to all citizens that may guide their everyday life. Any education for democracy or for justice, any political education must keep in mind certain good and true values for the life of society.

a. The dignity of the human person

Man is the image of God

34. The dignity of the human person is given by God in the moment of creation: "Let us make man in our own image . . . In the image of God he created him, male and female he created them. God blessed them, saying to them, 'Be fruitful, multiply, fill the earth and conquer it'" (Gen 1:26–28).

35. Man is the presence of God on earth and makes him known and loved; he is the image of God the Creator, cooperating with him in generating more human persons and loving them; he is the image of God in his infinite power, subjecting the earth to himself. He is the image of God because his immortal soul will never die. He has

an eternal destiny. For this reason the psalmist says, "You have made him little less than a god, with glory and honor you crowned him, gave him power over the works of your hand, put all things under his feet" (Ps 8:5–7).

36. Because of his origin and his call man is superior to anything on the earth. Any offense to his dignity, any violence against his rights is an offense against God himself. This is clear from the greatest commandment of love of God and neighbor, as well as from the Ten Commandments, seven of which refer to our relationship with our fellow men. Man is so important for God that when he sinned, God did not abandon him, but sent his Son into the world to suffer and to die for him.

37. Thus Christ restored the dignity that human beings had received at their creation. In Christ we discover the image of the "new human being" that is the ultimate foundation of our dignity (cf. Eph 2:15; Rom 8:14–17). For this Jesus identifies himself with the human person and affirms that anything done to the least of them is done to him, and that he will welcome into his kingdom those who have done good to others (cf. Mt 25).

38. This human dignity is proper to everyone, man or woman, born or unborn, rich and poor, sane or insane, healthy or sick, young or old, literate or illiterate, good or bad. Christ himself has a particular concern for the poor, the sinners, the weak, the despised, the sick.

39. This is why we have been horrified by the frequent violations of basic human rights over the past years in our country. Several times we raised our voice on this question through our Pastoral Letters. In 1980 we wrote: "In Uganda today the scale of values seems to be lopsided and indeed to a certain extent upside down. In some cases human life seems to have less value than the acquisition of money" (*Reshaping Our Nation*, cf. "I have heard the cry of my people", 1980).

Those who are indignant at the frequent violation of human rights

And in the following year: "Since independence many Ugandans have died as a consequence of unjust arrest, detention, torture, persecution and murder" ("Be Converted and Live", cf. our message, June 1985). We know how things became even worse later. In more recent times our spokesman His Eminence E. Cardinal K. Nsubuga again has intervened against such violations.

We do not want to see the repetition of these sad events and we encourage the Government, many of whose members have been victims of such violations, to fulfill their commitment to safeguard human rights in all areas of our nation as well as in the international community.

40. In this effort to safeguard human rights we would like to add here that also the criminals need to be treated as human persons. We

dislike the incapacity of condemning them, but also we intensely detest popular revenge, execution without proper trial, torture, punishment in contrast with the moral law and the just laws of the country. "Even the worst criminal does not lose his inborn human rights" (our pastoral letter "In God We Trust", 1982).

Education in social justice

41. On our part we commit ourselves to a program of education in social justice. Social justice is the attitude by virtue of which the rights of every man are recognized with strong and constant determination.

We entrust to our *National Commission for Justice and Peace:*

—the responsibility of giving wide publicity to the International Declarations on Human Rights, and the African Charter on Human and Peoples' Rights and of organizing, either directly or, through the diocesan commissions, study groups in national institutions, including major seminaries and training centers for religious;

—the responsibility of scrupulously identifying violations of human rights and intervening in these cases after consultation with the relevant Episcopal Commission;

—the responsibility of proposing to the Episcopal Conference or its Executive Committee lawful means of combating violations of human rights.

The Commission will keep regular contact with the Pontifical Commission for Justice and Peace in Rome and other national and international organizations which work for justice and peace. We entrust to our diocesan Commissions the responsibility of organizing the regular study of the Declarations of Human Rights in schools, in youth movements, in associations of lay apostolate, parishes, Christian communities and other Church centers in the diocese.

42. We propose and encourage a concerted effort by government institutions, by all religious groups and other humanitarian organizations present in Uganda to create in the nation a mentality that understands and respects the dignity of the human person, his freedom and his rights.

Such an education would lead all citizens to a conscientious respect of these rights, a task entrusted by God and the Church.

b. Promoting the common good

43. Moral rehabilitation is a task that must begin with individuals, with each person taking up his own responsibility. However the community too, needs to be rehabilitated, as the human person is bound to a community in his daily life for good or for bad. Every citizen must be aware of this and harmonize the struggle for his own prosperity and that of his clan with the interests of the nation as a whole.

44. Since independence, Uganda has become a State but it has still a long way to go in order to be one nation. The people are divided because of loyalty to ethnic, religious and political groupings, and these divisions have given rise to hatred, fear and suspicion. It is necessary that every Ugandan should grow in the sense of belonging to one nation. We need to promote in each citizen a determined will to live and work in sincere solidarity and unity.

Uganda has a long way to go before becoming one nation

At the same time we have to recognize the differences between the various ethnic groups in our country, with different cultures and traditions. We have to recognize also the different religious traditions amongst our citizens. These differences become evil only when used to divide one group of people against the other.

45. If we look at the history of our country we see that this has happened when sections of the population have been granted privileges on religious or tribal grounds, and given too great a share in political or economic power, discriminating against the other groups. This is what gave rise to sectarianism, an evil which must be eliminated. But sectarianism cannot be eliminated by seeking to destroy the different cultures, religions and traditions. Such a policy would violate man's fundamental freedom and would produce discontent, more strife and new divisions.

46. The solution lies in avoiding all kinds of discrimination either for or against different groups, against individuals on the grounds of race, religion or political affiliation. All the different groups must be made to feel at home in Uganda, enjoying equal rights and having equal duties in the life of the nation.

47. In this context we welcome the policy of a broad-based Government. However we would like to see such broadness not only in the top-level structures, but also in the numerous posts of responsibility in government and government-controlled bodies, in the army, the civil service, the police, the schools, and other posts where the appointments are made by public authorities.

48. The love of one's nation and all its members is called patriotism and a patriot is one who loves his nation and defends its freedoms and rights. This love is to be lived as a Christian virtue: Christian as it is a consequence of the great commandment of love of one's neighbor, virtue as it avoids exaggerations in practical behavior.

49. One exaggeration is in despising or hating the citizens of other countries; this happened in the past with the expulsion or harassment of non-citizens, or migrants, or foreigners, or refugees who were law-abiding people who did no harm, but were even a help to the country. We pray that this will not happen in the future as it is against our African tradition of hospitality and against all standards of Christian love, fairness and human rights.

To cultivate a generous and loyal patriotic spirit

Citizens should cultivate a generous and loyal spirit of patriotism, but avoid a narrow-minded nationalism, keeping in mind that Uganda is part and parcel of the whole human family which is formed into one by links of various kinds between races, peoples and nations (cf. GS, 75, and our pastoral letter "Shaping Our Nation", 1962).

50. Love of the nation is first of all to be shown by those in public office in both the political and economic fields. They are to accept their office with a deep sense of responsibility, of service to the nation and its people, as a way of living personally and expressing publicly their love for neighbor. Their office is not merely a means of earning a living, of granting privileges to their favorites or enriching themselves, or of winning popularity or of making people fear them. When they are irresponsible, careless, disorganized or simply lazy, public officers cause damage to the lives of millions of people and to the whole country. We have seen in the past how one man or a small group of people can throw the whole country into disarray and ruin for many years, causing many citizens to flee the country and bringing them untold misery.

51. A person in public office is accountable not only to the nation but also to God, and God will be his final judge (cf. GS, 75).

A public office is a real burden and those who feel unable or unfit for an office should not accept it, or should resign, not stay there for their personal benefit or that of their clan or party at the expense of the common good. This is true patriotism, as indeed it would be patriotic to refuse to cooperate in a government that does not promote the common good, even though one may be competent to hold an office.

52. Patriotism is required of all citizens. Their love for the nation should be shown not only by enthusiastic demonstrations on public feasts, but by a real concern for the common good. They are expected to participate in the affairs of the country by exercising their right to vote when requested and by giving their support to honest well-intentioned leaders who will serve the community and not only the personal interest of the voter.

Citizens must participate in the life of the country

Citizens are also expected to pay their taxes, to abide by the fiscal and financial laws of the country. "Give back to Caesar the things that belong to Caesar" (Lk 19:25) and all the other just laws legitimately approved by the competent authorities (cf. Rom 13:1–7).

To work for the common welfare, after all, is to work for one's own good, as we are all together in one nation for bad or for good.

53. To encourage the citizens in their responsibility and in fulfilling their duties, the authorities at all levels should give true and adequate information about their work, national planning and investments.

We hope that the days are gone when we had to turn to foreign news-media in order to know the truth about our own country.

Access to true information is a basic right of all citizens, and public authorities are expected not only to respect the freedom of a responsible press, but also to use their own means of social communication like radio, television, newspapers, to keep the public informed of their activities, even if these include their setbacks or shortcomings. Any responsible citizen knows that not everything can be perfect and successful in public administration, but the concealing of the truth may destroy the people's confidence in public authorities and so lead to mistrust, apathy and disregard for the common good, whereas the publication of the true state of affairs may obtain a sympathetic understanding of the population. It very much depends on the kind of relationship public authorities are able to establish with the common people.

54. Patriotism may also lead to the challenging of public authorities without fear whenever required by justice. Fear has been one of the main factors that has damaged the relationship between public authorities and the people. We hope that this state of affairs will not continue. In situations of grave injustices courage and strength are needed to defend the common good. "When citizens are being oppressed by a public authority that acts beyond its competence, they must not refuse to give or to do what is objectively demanded by the common good, but it is legitimate for them to defend their own rights and those of their fellow citizens against abuses by the authority within the limits of natural law and of the Gospel" (GS, 74).

The present Government has asked for this kind of cooperation and we appreciate the guarantee of protection it has given to those who, in all honesty and sincerity, have recourse to higher authorities and to the judiciary for the protection of their rights.

c. The presence and action of God in Uganda

55. "Ever since God created the world his everlasting power and deity, however invisible, have been there for the mind to see in the things he has made" (Rom 1:19–20).

The different cultural traditions of Africa and of Uganda in particular bear out the truth of this statement of St. Paul. Belief in the presence and action of God is widely present, though it may be expressed in forms that differ from each other.

In creating man in his own image God has given him intelligence and love, and an infinite desire that can only be satisfied by the knowledge and love of his Creator. No person, whether good or bad, can ignore God or run away from him. Adam and Eve, and their son Cain failed to hide from him (Gen 3:4). The psalmist sings, "O where can I go from your spirit, or where can I flee from your face? If I climb the heavens, you are there. If I lie in the grave, you are there" (Ps 139:7ff.).

God has endowed man with a moral sense of right and wrong or conscience. Through this, man can come to a certain knowledge of God and his law which guides him in life. In this way man feels more and more the need of the full truth, of love, justice and peace.

The community must recognize God and respect his law

56. Since the human person has been created as a social being, the religious dimension of his life is awakened and developed in the human community. It is God who has created the community through the cooperation of man and woman. So the community must acknowledge God and keep his laws. These are the basic foundation for the life and activities of human persons and for all the laws of human society. Religion leads the human person to the fullness of life through his daily activities, private and social. Right or wrong, good or bad, just or unjust, these actions are seen by God who will be their final Judge (cf. Mt 25).

The community then is to show gratitude to God. Participation in gatherings of prayer is not only an individual religious duty, but also a duty of the community. It is the public worship of God the Creator of the society.

57. God is the eternal loving Father of the community and the nation, through his assistance and providence: "From one single stock he not only created the whole human race so that they could occupy the entire earth, but he decreed how long each nation should flourish and what the boundaries of its territory should be. And he did so that all nations might see the deity and, by feeling their way towards him, succeed in finding him. Yet in fact he is not far from any one of us, since it is in him that we live and move and exist" (St. Paul to the Athenians, Acts 17:26–28).

58. God is a mystery and man could not, unassisted, find out much about his Creator. It is only through *revelation* that we can truly know and talk about him: "No one has ever seen God; it is the only Son who is nearest to the Father's heart, who has made him known" (Jn 1:18). Christ Son of God is the Revelation of the Father, and his Law to us, here in our nation. We have seen how God has been good to us in spite of the sufferings of all these years. As we set ourselves to work on personal renewal and the rebuilding of our nation, God must be our inspiration and guide, the yardstick by which we measure our successes and failures, our teacher as we plan for the future.

59. Only the laws of God and his help can renew and restore private and public life, redress the true balance of rights and duties,

checking unbridled self-interest, controlling passion, implementing
and perfecting the course of strict justice with his overflowing charity. *Only the law of*
"He who could once give his commands to wind and sea can turn *God can balance*
man's heart to peace and brotherly love" (cf. Pope Pius XI: *Foundations* *public and private*
of Peace). *life*

60. Activities of human persons in the political and economic fields
cannot be to the full advantage of man without the presence and
action of God. In fact man is so made that he has an infinite desire
for personal fulfillment and if this desire is not guided by the laws
of God it will turn into an endless desire for power, money and
pleasure that can never be satisfied. Theories based on materialism,
that hold that man's needs can be met purely by economic and
political strategy are doomed to produce lust for power and money
and thus lead to dissension, strife, crime and war.

61. In Uganda we enjoy several freedoms. These should be upheld
so that we continue to enjoy them even in the future. At this point
we wish to emphasize freedom of religion as a means of making
God's presence felt in the world. According to the present Ugandan
Constitution that echoes the international Declarations of Human
Rights (art. 18), freedom of religion is wider than simply freedom *Freedom of*
of worship. "Except with his own consent, no person shall be hin- *thought and*
dered in the enjoyment of his freedom of conscience, and for the *religion*
purposes of this article the said freedom includes freedom of thought
and of religion, freedom to change his religion or belief, and freedom
either alone or in community with others and both in public and in
private to manifest and propagate his religion or belief in worship,
teaching, practice and observance" (no. 16, 1).

Besides the freedom of worship in private and public, both on
Sundays and on weekdays, we are also free to teach our religion in
private and in public, in churches and schools, by preaching and
through the means of social communication like radio, TV, books
and newspapers, and the distribution of literature.

62. We have also organizations and associations for different purposes and social services; since religion is not a private affair we are
free also for that within the limits of just laws. Moreover freedom
of assembly and of association is guaranteed by the Ugandan Constitution, too (no. 18).

We are also free to ask for the help of personnel from other countries
if we feel it necessary for our work (Uganda Const. no. 19).

63. We appeal to all believers in God to make the presence of God,
his action and his word meaningful and relevant in Uganda now.
All those who acknowledge God "preserve precious religious and
human elements in their traditions" (GS, 92), and are all to be used
for the well-being of the nation, and this is assured if the presence

of God is felt in the minds and hearts of all Ugandans and through them penetrates our culture.

On our part we are going to intensify the efforts of evangelization as the contribution of the Catholic Church towards this goal.

AN URGENT MESSAGE
TO THE STATE PRESIDENT

The Southern African Bishops' Conference

Mr. State President,

1. We members of the Southern African Catholic Bishops' Conference find ourselves compelled to express our views on the present situation in South Africa. It is a situation of conflict, of violence, of bloodshed. The State Bureau for Information maintains that there has been a lessening of conflict since the imposition of the state of emergency. Be that as it may, the state of emergency cannot last indefinitely and when it is lifted or becomes inoperative it will be found not to have effected a cure. While apartheid remains in force, its consequences will be with us. As long ago as 1975 our Conference wrote:

"To all White South Africans we direct an earnest plea to consider carefully what apartheid means: its evil and anti-Christian character, the injustice that flows from it, the resentment and bitterness it arouses, the harvest of disaster that it must produce in the country we all love so much" (*Statement on Apartheid,* July 1975).

The word of God is a word of peace

2. The word of God is concerned with peace between people. As hearers and ministers of that word peace is our great concern too and so we express our views in an endeavor to make a contribution to promoting peace in South Africa in the context of the great prayer of Jesus for his disciples: "May they all be one, Father, may they be

1986 was a year of unusually severe tension in South Africa. The Catholic bishops there have many times made their voices heard against apartheid and social injustice. In this present document published in August 1986 the bishops addressed the president of the Republic of South Africa, inviting him to suspend the state of emergency that was the cause of violence and bloodshed. Reprinted from the English edition of *L'Osservatore Romano,* November 17, 1986.

one in us, as you are in me and I am in you" (Jn 17:21); in the context too of his special legacy: "Peace I leave with you: my peace I give you" (Jn 14:27).

3. Peace in any human society exists only if there is general observance in that society of the values that ensure good relations between its members. These values are truth, justice, love and freedom. We see these values as goals to be pursued by the whole human family in terms of God's will in creating us. We find them proclaimed in his word in the Bible, most especially in the preaching of the kingdom by Jesus. We recognize that sinfulness has disfigured human conduct but thank God for the gift of redemption in Jesus by which the disfigurement is healed and people are given the grace to struggle bravely and vigorously to express those values in their personal and social life.

4. Social life embraces four important dimensions: the religious, the political, the economic and the cultural. In all these dimensions human society should seek to emphasize the values of truth, justice, love and freedom and so achieve peace; peace between the religious and political dimensions, peace between members of society, peace between government and citizens, peace between the societies that make up the human family.

5. Since this is our interpretation of God's will for his people in terms of the mysteries of creation and redemption we must obviously be concerned to play our part in bringing this vision of peace into the society in which we live and in which we exercise our ministry.

6. South African society is being torn apart by the consequences of apartheid. A fierce confrontation has arisen between the structures of apartheid and the forces of liberation. We recognize that the government has committed itself to the dismantling of apartheid and has taken some measures towards this end. But much more needs to be done. We urge that the total dismantling of apartheid be pursued without further delay and as a matter of priority.

7. The present tempo and scope of the dismantling process does not appear to take into account the needs of this time in our history. A piecemeal abolition of unjust and discriminatory structures of the past is not enough to meet the critical situation in our country. A firm undertaking to dismantle apartheid totally will not only give credence to the government's stated desire for justice and peace for all but it should in some measure alleviate the suffering, anger and injustices experienced by the majority of our people and open the way for meaningful negotiations.

8. We are perturbed at this suffering and anxiety. We deplore the escalation of all forms of violence on the part of the state, the security forces, those who experience oppression and even among the people

themselves. We are saddened by the deterioration of the quality of life of all, and especially the Blacks.

We are concerned about the youth of our country

9. We are especially concerned for the youth of our country. They are caught up in this spiral of violence. Black youth are trapped in situations obstructing their normal development to adulthood. If the development of their personality is damaged, what hope remains for the South Africa of tomorrrow? Youth serving in the security forces are faced with ever-increasing crises of conscience.

10. We all know that a spirit of liberation cannot be quenched, it cannot be suppressed forever. The history of South Africa provides a vivid example of the eventual triumph in the Afrikaner people of their spirit of national liberation. They, as well as their English-speaking counterparts, should be able to recognize the spirit of liberation when they see it in their Black compatriots. The longer the present struggle takes, the worse the final condition will be.

11. The state of emergency has been declared to control the striving for liberation. Our assessment of the state of emergency is born of personal knowledge and experience of its effects, of exchanges with church personnel, or reports from various parts of the country, especially those areas where the repression and reaction to it have been most intense. We are conscious too of the practical implications of the regulations proclaimed for the state of emergency. They are hampering us and our co-workers in the communication of information and of moral guidance to our people, for instance, in the matter of public pronouncements and pastoral letters which may be declared "subversive".

12. The picture that emerges from personal or reported knowledge of the effects of the state of emergency is very disturbing: increased, even extreme repression is its major feature.

The behavior of the security police is deplorable

13. Especially deplorable are the actions of the security forces in general against persons who are opposed to government policy and in particular against Church personnel. For example, the suspension of civil liberties such as the right of assembly and the right to information; also physical assaults, destruction of property, detentions, deportations, unjustified arrests and intimidatory raids. The detention net has been cast very wide, enveloping countless persons far removed from political activism and has imposed on them long periods of imprisonment frequently in most uncomfortable and humiliating conditions with very poor diet and all too often subjected to the psychological torture of solitary confinement. We are dismayed too by instances of the violation of religious freedom, such as interference with Church services, disregard for the sacred character of church buildings and the detention of whole congregations.

14. A second major consequence of the present state of emergency

is the people's reaction to the primary violence on the part of the state. Inspired and impelled by the unquenchable spirit of liberation the people and especially the youth, are unyielding in the face of increased repression and respond with counterviolence against state institutions and personnel and against persons, both Black and White, seen to be active in this latest form of repression. We deplore in the strongest possible terms the summary trial and "execution" of those suspected of collaborating with the state. Sadly, the unspeakable cruelty of the "necklace" continues. These tragic developments emphasize how mistrust grows and polarization intensifies.

15. A third effect of the state of emergency is the suppression of information and the blocking of communication. As a result of the restrictions on the free flow of information there is a proliferation of rumors often grossly exaggerated. Confusion intensifies in a public already confused and uncertain. The result of ignorance or misinformation is at the root of growing fear and suspicion which in turn is fueling already strong feelings of insecurity and hopelessness among a nervous and frightened people.

16. The state of emergency is at best a misguided concept to crush the urge for liberation which has irreversibly taken hold of the Black, oppressed people of South Africa. The state of emergency is not a solution. It constitutes rather a formidable obstacle to the search for a true and lasting peace because:

— it heightens the impression that the government's intention is to hold on to power no matter what the consequences;

— it exposes more and more people to the repressive might of the state;

— it aggravates the feelings of frustration, anger and bitterness;

— it makes it impossible for the leadership to emerge that in due course must represent the people at the conference table.

17. In short, we see the state of emergency as being one of the principal obstacles to the process of rapprochement and negotiation between the contending parties. As an interim measure it may suppress conflict to some extent. But essentially it is treating the symptoms, not the disease.

18. Since the beginning of this year, the government has admitted the need to negotiate with representatives of the Black opposition. No progress can be made as long as those who have a major claim to leadership are excluded from meaningful participation in the political process. We see the problem in the criteria the government applies to these negotiations: only representatives of groups who renounce violence are to be considered as partners in negotiation, and a number of vital issues—such as the introduction of the universal suffrage—are non-negotiables.

The necessity to negotiate with the representatives of the Black opposition

19. As regards the first criterion, the call for a renunciation of violence, under normal circumstances this would be a valid point. However, it cannot be denied that the long-standing repression of the majority of South Africa's people under the system of apartheid has provoked the oppressed to adopt violence as a last resort to express their total rejection of this unjust system. The declaration of a state of emergency twice within a year has only compounded the impasse: massive repression on the part of the security forces is seen by the Black majority as state-sanctioned violence, and finds its response in widespread outbursts of counterviolence against any symbols of power vested in the state.

20. As regards the non-negotiables, the government itself based to a large extent the 1983 Constitution of the Republic of South Africa on the process of negotiation, preferring consensus wherever possible to the imposition of majority rule. We believe in the creative momentum that negotiation can unleash for the good of all the people in our country. Through it, the non-negotiables of both parties to the conflict can give way to mutual trust and understanding. This negotiation process must not exclude any of the accepted leaders of the oppressed majority in our country, whether they are residing in it at the moment or living in exile abroad.

21. We take the liberty of quoting here from a letter sent to us in April 1986 by the Cardinal President of the Justice and Peace Commission of the Holy See:

"May I bring to the fore some aspects of the problematic that concerns your country:

"*a.* The complete elimination of apartheid and a new social fabric that guarantees the participation, on an equal footing, of every citizen for the development of South Africa, must be sought after without resorting to further acts of violence which could fatally compromise the very results that it is seeking to obtain.

"*b.* The various ethnic groups that make up the South African society must be able to negotiate this new fabric and, to that end, their leaders who are banned or in prison must be given back their freedom of movement.

"*c.* During the process of negotiation, all the above mentioned groups must seek to understand one another's positions and be open to a fruitful collaboration by eliminating prejudices and gradually overcoming the obstacles that interfere with the formation of a South African community proud of the rich variety that exists among its different components."

22. Many have urged the release of political prisoners and the unbanning of their organization as a prerequisite for meaningful negotiations about the future of our country between the government and

its extra-parliamentary opposition. We strongly support this proposal. We are convinced that the longer such unconditional negotiations are delayed the greater will be the danger that these persons and their organizations will, in despair, increasingly turn to Moscow and other communist centers of power for ideological and material support. Repression is more a stimulus than an antidote to communism.

Repression is more a stimulus than an antidote to communism

23. As we join our voice to other voices calling for negotiations about the future of South Africa we come back again to the question of Namibia. We made a strong appeal in our *Report on Namibia* of 1982 "for a creative, humane and Christian effort on the part of South Africa to conclude a just and peaceful settlement, and for sustained and fervent prayer that, with the help of God, this will be achieved". Unfortunately, peace has not yet come to Namibia. If South Africa had the will the way would surely be found. While continuing to maintain its armed occupation of Namibia, South Africa remains responsible for the death and disruption that plague that unhappy country. Once again, we urge the acceptance of Resolution 435 of the United Nations Security Council.

24. Both in the case of South Africa and of Namibia we realize the obstacles to negotiation. We realize that in terms of human politics it will be extremely difficult to open negotiations. So in concluding this expression of our views we return once again to the vision given to us by the word of God and our Christian faith. The will to negotiate must be inspired by the Christian values that we cherish and that we accept as normative for our personal and domestic life and consequently should accept as normative too for our social life. There must be a compelling desire for peace. There must be a willingness to make sacrifices in the cause of peace, including sacrifices that involve a too exclusive view of one's own nation or people. From the Bible we learn that Israel received its special calling as God's chosen people and was granted liberation from slavery in order ultimately to be at the service of other nations in the mystery of redemption. "I have given you as a covenant to the people, a light to the nations" (Is 42:6).

To make sacrifices for the cause of peace

25. The life and teaching of Christ impress upon us that the cross is part of every human life and of all dimensions of human life, including the political. This has special significance in the pursuit of peace. Jesus has taught us that it must be the mark of the Christian, no matter how painful, to take the first step in seeking peace. "So if you are offering your gift at the altar, and there remember that your brother has something against you, leave your gift there before the altar and go; first be reconciled to your brother, and then come and offer your gift" (Mt 5:23–24). This may be painful indeed. It may seem humiliating in political life but even in regard to political

life the words of Jesus are relevant: "Truly, truly, I say to you, unless a grain of wheat falls into the earth and dies, it remains alone; but if it dies, it bears much fruit. He who loves his life loses it, and he who hates his life in this world will keep it for eternal life" (Jn 12:24–25).

26. The will to negotiate must be characterized by hope, another of the great values taught by Christ. In the matter of negotiation there must be Christian hope for a sufficient degree of trust and communication between the contending parties to produce a result conducive to peace.

27. The assurance can be given that a great volume of prayer will rise up to God that the will to negotiate may triumph over the whole unfortunate heritage of the past with its fears and suspicions, divisions and hatreds and so that it may open the way to a peaceful resolution of the present conflict and the birth of a new South Africa.

2

AMERICA

ECONOMIC JUSTICE FOR ALL: CATHOLIC SOCIAL TEACHING AND THE U.S. ECONOMY

Pastoral Letter of the Bishops of the United States

Brothers and sisters in Christ:

1. We are believers called to follow our Lord Jesus Christ and proclaim his Gospel in the midst of a complex and powerful economy. This reality poses both opportunities and responsibilities for Catholics in the United States. Our faith calls us to measure this economy not only by what it produces, but also by how it touches human life and whether it protects or undermines the dignity of the human person. Economic decisions have human consequences and moral content; they help or hurt people, strengthen or weaken family life, advance or diminish the quality of justice in our land.

2. This is why we have written "Economic Justice for All", a pastoral letter on Catholic social teaching and the U.S. economy. This letter is a personal invitation to Catholics in the United States to use the resources of our faith, the strength of our economy and the opportunities of our democracy to shape a society which better protects the dignity and basic rights of our sisters and brothers both in this land and around the world.

This letter is a personal invitation to Catholics

3. The pastoral letter has been a work of careful inquiry, wide consultation and prayerful discernment. The letter has been greatly enriched by this process of listening and refinement. We offer this introductory pastoral message to Catholics in the United States seeking to live their Faith in the marketplace—in homes, offices, factories and schools, on farms and ranches, in board rooms and union halls, in service agencies and legislative chambers. We seek to explain why

After lengthy preparations, the plenary session of the United States' Conference of Catholic Bishops approved, on November 13, 1986, their long-awaited statement on the economy. Because of the text's great length, the United States bishops distributed, on November 27, 1986, a message summarizing the criteria and contents of their pastoral letter. Reprinted from *Origins*, November 27, 1986.

153

we wrote this pastoral letter, to introduce its major themes and to share our hopes for the dialogue and action it might generate.

Why We Write

The challenge to live our Faith in the world

4. We write to share our teaching, to raise questions, to challenge one another to live our Faith in the world. We write as heirs of the biblical prophets who summon us "to do justice, to love kindness and to walk humbly with our God" (Micah 6:8); and we write as followers of Jesus, who told us in the Sermon on the Mount: "Blessed are the poor in spirit. . . . Blessed are the lowly. . . . Blessed are those who hunger and thirst for justice. . . . You are the salt of the earth. . . . You are the light of the world" (Mt 5:1–6, 13–14). These words challenge us not only as believers, but also as consumers, citizens, workers and owners. In the parable of the Last Judgment, Jesus said, "I was hungry and you gave me to eat, thirsty and you gave me to drink. . . . As often as you did it for one of these the least of my brothers, you did it for me" (Mt 25:35–40). The challenge for us is to discover in our own place and time what it means to be "poor in spirit" and "the salt of the earth" and what it means to serve "the least among us" and to "hunger and thirst for justice".

5. Followers of Christ must avoid a tragic separation between faith and everyday life. They can neither shirk their earthly duties nor, as the Second Vatican Council declared, "immerse ourselves in earthly activities as if these latter were utterly foreign to religion and religion were nothing more than the fulfillment of acts of worship; and the observance of a few moral obligations" (GS, 43).

6. Economic life raises important social and moral questions for each of us and for society as a whole. Like family life, economic life is one of the chief areas where we live out our faith, love our neighbor, confront temptation, fulfill God's creative design and achieve our holiness. Our economic activity in factory, field, office or shop feeds our families—or feeds our anxieties. It exercises our talents—or wastes them. It raises our hopes—or crushes them. It brings us into cooperation with others—or sets us at odds. The Second Vatican Council instructs us "to preach the message of Christ in such a way that the light of the Gospel will shine on all activities of the faithful". In this case we are trying to look at economic life through the eyes of faith, applying traditional Church teaching to the U.S. economy (GS, 43).

7. In our letter we write as pastors, not public officials. We speak as moral teachers, not economic technicians. We seek not to make some political or ideological point, but to lift up the human and

ethical dimensions of economic life, aspects too often neglected in public discussion. We bring to this task a dual heritage of a Catholic social teaching and traditional American values.

8. As *Catholics* we are heirs of a long tradition of thought and action on the moral dimensions of economic activity. The life and words of Jesus and the teaching of his Church call us to serve those in need and to work actively for social and economic justice. As a community of believers, we know that our faith is tested by the quality of justice among us, that we can best measure our life together by how the poor and the vulnerable are treated. This is not a new concern for us. It is as old as the Hebrew prophets, as compelling as the Sermon on the Mount and as current as the powerful voice of Pope John Paul II defending the dignity of the human person. *The Catholic inheritance in the economic field*

9. As *Americans,* we are grateful for the gift of freedom and committed to the dream of "liberty and justice for all". This nation, blessed with extraordinary resources, has provided an unprecedented standard of living for millions of people. We are proud of the strength, productivity and creativity of our economy, but we also remember those who have been left behind in our progress. We believe that we honor our history best by working for the day when all our sisters and brothers share adequately in the American dream.

10. As bishops, in proclaiming the Gospel for these present times, we also manage institutions, balance budgets and meet payrolls. In this we see the human face of our economy. We feel the hurts and hopes of our people. We feel the pain of our sisters and brothers who are poor, unemployed, homeless, living on the edge. The poor and vulnerable are on our doorsteps, in our parishes, our service agencies and our shelters. We see too much hunger and injustice, too much suffering and despair, both in our own country and around the world. *The human face of the economy*

11. As pastors, we also see the decency, generosity and vulnerability of our people. We see the struggles of ordinary families to make ends meet and provide a better future for their children. We know the desire of managers, professionals and business people to shape what they do by what they believe. It is the faith, good will and generosity of our people that gives us hope as we write this letter.

Principal Themes of the Pastoral Letter

12. The pastoral letter is not a blueprint for the American economy. It does not embrace any particular theory of how the economy works nor does it attempt to resolve the disputes between different schools of economic thought. Instead our letter turns to Scripture and to the

social teachings of the Church. There we discover what our economic life must serve, what standards it must meet. Let us examine some of these basic moral principles.

13. *Every economic decision and institution must be judged in light of whether it protects or undermines the dignity of the human person.* The pastoral letter begins with the human person. We believe the person is sacred—the clearest reflection of God among us. Human dignity comes from God, not from nationality, race, sex, economic status or any human accomplishment. We judge any economic system by what it does *for* and *to* people and by how it permits all to *participate* in it. The economy should serve people, and not the other way around.

14. *Human dignity can be realized and protected only in community.* In our teaching, the human person is not only sacred but also social. How we organize our society—in economics and politics, in law and policy—directly affects human dignity and the capacity of individuals to grow in community. The obligation to "love our neighbor" has an individual dimension, but it also requires a broader social commitment to the common good. We have many partial ways to measure and debate the health of our economy—gross national product, per capita income, stock market prices. The Christian vision of economic life looks beyond them all and asks, Does economic life enhance or threaten our life together as a community?

15. *All people have a right to participate in the economic life of society.* Basic justice demands that people be assured a minimum level of participation in the economy. It is wrong for a person or group to be unfairly excluded or unable to participate or not contribute to the economy. For example, people who are both able and willing to work, but cannot get a job, are deprived of the participation that is so vital to human development. For it is through employment that most individuals and families meet their material needs, exercise their talents and have an opportunity to contribute to the larger community. Such participation has special significance in our tradition because we believe that it is a means by which we join in carrying forward God's creative activity.

16. *All members of society have a special obligation to the poor and vulnerable.* From the Scriptures and Church teaching we learn that the justice of a society is tested by the treatment of the poor. The justice that was the sign of God's covenant with Israel was measured by how the poor and unprotected—the widow, the orphan and the stranger—were treated. The kingdom that Jesus proclaimed in his word and ministry excludes no one. Throughout Israel's history and in early Christianity the poor are agents of God's transforming power. "The Spirit of the Lord is upon me, because he has anointed me to preach the good news to the poor." This was Jesus' first public

The Pastoral Letter begins with the human person

A society's justice is measured by its treatment of the poor

utterance. Jesus takes the side of those most in need. In the Last Judgment so dramatically described in St. Matthew's Gospel, we are told that we will be judged according to how we respond to the hungry, the thirsty, the naked, the stranger. As followers of Christ, we are challenged to make a fundamental "option for the poor"—to speak for the voiceless, to defend the defenseless, to assess lifestyles, policies and social institutions in terms of their impact on the poor. This "option for the poor" does not mean pitting one group against another, but rather, strengthening the whole community by assisting those who are most vulnerable. As Christians we are called to respond to the needs of *all* our brothers and sisters, but those with the greatest needs require the greatest response.

17. *Human rights are the minimum conditions for life in community.* In Catholic teaching, human rights include not only civil and political rights, but also economic rights. As Pope John XXIII declared, all people have a right to life, food, clothing, shelter, rest, medical care, education and employment. This means that when people are without a chance to earn a living and must go hungry and homeless, they are being denied basic rights. Society must ensure that these rights are protected. In this way we will ensure that the minimum conditions of economic justice are met for all our sisters and brothers.

18. *Society as a whole, acting through public and private institutions, has the moral responsibility to enhance human dignity and protect human rights.* In addition to the clear responsibility of private institutions, government has an essential responsibility in this area. This does not mean that government has the primary or exclusive role, but it does have a positive moral responsibility in safeguarding human rights and ensuring that the minimum conditions of human dignity are met for all. In a democracy, government is a means by which we can act together to protect what is important to us and to promote our common values.

The government has a concrete moral responsibility to safeguard man's rights

19. These six moral principles are not the only ones presented in the pastoral letter, but they give an overview of the moral vision that we are trying to share. This vision of economic life cannot exist in a vacuum; it must be translated into concrete measures. Our pastoral letter spells out some specific applications of Catholic moral principles. We call for a new national commitment to full employment. We say it is a social and moral scandal that one of every seven Americans is poor, and we call for concerted efforts to eradicate poverty. The fulfillment of the basic needs of the poor is of the highest priority. We urge that all economic policies be evaluated in light of their impact on the life and stability of the family. We support measures to halt the loss of family farms and to resist the growing concentration in the ownership of agricultural resources. We specify

ways in which the United States can do far more to relieve the plight of poor nations and assist in their development. We also reaffirm Church teaching on the rights of workers, collective bargaining, private property, subsidiarity and equal opportunity.

20. We believe that the recommendations in our letter are reasonable and balanced. In analyzing the economy, we reject ideological extremes and start from the fact that ours is a "mixed" economy, the product of a long history of reform and adjustment. We know that some of our specific recommendations are controversial. As bishops we do not claim to make these prudential judgments with the same kind of authority that marks our declarations of principle. But we feel obliged to teach by example how Christians can undertake concrete analysis and make specific judgments on economic issues. The Church's teachings cannot be left at the level of appealing generalities.

A "new American experiment"

21. In the pastoral letter we suggest that the time has come for a "new American experiment"—to implement economic rights, to broaden the sharing of economic power and to make economic decisions more accountable to the common good. This new experiment can create new structures of economic partnership and participation within firms, at the regional level, for the whole nation and across borders.

22. Of course, there are many aspects of the economy the letter does not touch, and there are basic questions it leaves to further exploration. There are also many specific points on which men and women of good will may disagree. We look for a fruitful exchange among differing viewpoints. We pray only that all will take to heart the urgency of our concerns, that together we will test our views by the Gospel and the Church's teaching, and that we will listen to other voices in a spirit of mutual respect and open dialogue.

A Call to Conversion and Action

23. We should not be surprised if we find Catholic social teaching to be demanding. The Gospel is demanding. We are always in need of conversion, of a change of heart. We are richly blessed, and as St. Paul assures us, we are destined for glory. Yet it is also true that we are sinners, that we are not always wise or loving or just, that for all our amazing possibilities we are incompletely born, wary of life and hemmed in by fears and empty routines. We are unable to entrust ourselves fully to the living God, and so we seek substitute forms of security: in material things, in power, in indifference, in popularity, in pleasure. The Scriptures warn us that these things can become forms of idolatry. We know that, at times, in order to remain

truly a community of Jesus' disciples, we will have to say no to
certain aspects in our culture, to certain trends and ways of acting
that are opposed to a life of faith, love and justice. Changes in our
hearts lead naturally to a desire to change how we act. With what
care, human kindness and justice do I conduct myself at work? How
will my economic decisions to buy, sell, invest, divest, hire or fire
serve human dignity and the common good? In what career can I
best exercise my talents so as to fill the world with the Spirit of
Christ? How do my economic choices contribute to the strength of
my family and community, to the values of my children, to a sensitivity to those in need? In this consumer society, how can I develop a
healthy detachment from things and avoid the temptation to assess
who I am by what I have? How do I strike a balance between labor
and leisure that enlarges my capacity for friendships, for family life,
for community? What government policies should I support to attain
the well-being of all, especially the poor and vulnerable?

24. The answers to such questions are not always clear—or easy
to live out. But conversion is a lifelong process. And it is not undertaken alone. It occurs with the support of the whole believing community, through baptism, common prayer and our daily efforts,
large and small, on behalf of justice. As a Church we must be people
after God's own heart, bonded by the Spirit, sustaining one another
in love, setting our hearts on God's kingdom, committing ourselves
to solidarity with those who suffer, working for peace and justice,
acting as a sign of Christ's love and justice in the world. The Church
cannot redeem the world from the deadening effects of sin and injustice unless it is working to remove sin and injustice in its own life
and institutions. All of us must help the Church to practice in its
own life what it preaches to others about economic justice and cooperation.

Conversion occurs with the support of the whole community

25. The challenge of this pastoral letter is not merely to think
differently, but also to act differently. A renewal of economic life
depends on the conscious choices and commitments of individual
believers who practice their faith in the world. The road to holiness
for most of us lies in our secular vocations. We need a spirituality
which calls forth and supports lay initiative and witness not just in
our churches but also in business, in the labor movement, in the
professions, in education and in public life. Our faith is not just a
weekend obligation, a mystery to be celebrated around the altar on
Sunday. It is a pervasive reality to be practiced every day in homes,
offices, factories, schools and businesses across our land. We cannot
separate what we believe from how we act in the marketplace and
the broader community, for this is where we make our primary
contribution to the pursuit of economic justice.

26. We ask each of you to read the pastoral letter, to study it, to pray about it and match it with your own experience. We ask you to join with us in service to those in need. Let us reach out personally to the hungry and the homeless, to the poor and the powerless, and to the troubled and vulnerable. In serving them, we serve Christ. Our service efforts cannot substitute for just and compassionate public policies, but they can help us practice what we preach about human life and human dignity.

27. The pursuit of economic justice takes believers into the public arena, testing the policies of government by the principles of our teaching. We ask you to become more informed and active citizens, using your voices and votes to speak for the voiceless, to defend the poor and vulnerable, and to advance the common good. We are called to shape a constituency of conscience, measuring every policy by how it touches the least, the lost and the left out among us. This letter calls us to conversion and common action, to new forms of stewardship, service and citizenship.

The letter calls to conversion and to action in common

28. The completion of a letter such as this is but the beginning of a long process of education, discussion and action. By faith and baptism, we are fashioned into new creatures, filled with the Holy Spirit and with a love that compels us to seek out a new profound relationship with God, with the human family and with all created things. Jesus has entered our history as God's anointed son who announces the coming of God's kingdom, a kingdom of justice and peace and freedom. And what Jesus proclaims he embodies in his actions. His ministry reveals that the reign of God is something more powerful than evil, injustice and the hardness of hearts. Through his crucifixion and resurrection, he reveals that God's love is ultimately victorious over all suffering, all horror, all meaninglessness and even over the mystery of death. Thus we proclaim words of hope and assurance to all who suffer and are in need.

29. We believe that the Christian view of life, including economic life, can transform the lives of individuals, families, schools and our whole culture. We believe that with your prayers, reflection, service and action our economy can be shaped so that human dignity prospers and the human person is served. This is the unfinished work of our nation. This is the challenge of our faith.

UNITY IN TRUTH

Instruction of the Bishops' Conference of Paraguay on the Position of Catholics before Non-Catholic Christians

Part One
ANALYSIS OF OUR RELIGIOUS SITUATION

1. The Catholic tradition of Paraguay

Since our country's beginnings, the Paraguayan people, like all our fellow Latin Americans, have found the unity of Catholics to be a precious heritage from colonial times. According to Puebla, this fact constitutes "a fundamental characteristic of identity and unity on the continent and, at the same time, a lasting concern" (Puebla document [PD], no. 1099).

After the miserable wars with the Triple Alliance and Bolivia, an open and hospitable Paraguay accepted groups from all over the world into its decreased population, which increased its human numbers, generated wealth, and introduced new religious beliefs. Thus the small group of non-catholics we spoke of, which existed at the beginning of the century, began growing considerably.

2. The spirit of Vatican Council II

Through the Holy Spirit, who is always active in his Church, we have had wonderful experiences on an international, continental and national level. Many are aware of the events of the Ecumenical Council of Vatican II (1962–1965), the General Conferences of the Latin American Bishops of Medillín (1968), and Puebla (1979), and the launching of the Pastoral Growth Plan for our Church in Paraguay (1976–1978 and 1981 . . .).

The proliferation of sects in Latin America presents a challenge to the Catholic Church. Without summarily condemning the new religious groups, the bishops of Paraguay have reiterated the value of Catholic identity. Their letter was published at Asunción on December 8, 1986. This translation from the Spanish is by Lydia Collins. Given the length of the letter, the introduction and the final section of the document have been omitted.

As we said in our Pastoral Letter of June 12, 1976, we are aware that our ecclesial progress is realized "among the persecutions of the world and the consolations of God". Nonetheless, we are certain that "the Lord has been with us" (Ps 124:1) and our efforts to "guarantee the morality of the nation" have not been futile. "He who plants nor he who waters is of any special account", we repeat with Saint Paul, "only God, who gives the growth" (1 Cor 3:7).

3. The proliferation of religious sects

In the last few years, our urban and rural centers have become covered with revival tents and preachers urgently calling upon the faith of believers, like our own Catholics. One of the sects, *Pueblo de Dios*, has proclaimed itself in daily notices running over two long periods of time in one of the capital city's morning papers. The lack of immigration control in the northern and eastern zones of our country also helps sectarian proselytism deal rather effective blows.

Sectarian proselytism

In addition to the daily efforts, these sects work on well-organized waves of periodic, widely publicized, discussion campaigns. They also work with health-care workers who offer excellent treatment to the poor. These poor people lack any other means of attaining medical attention, so they turn to the help offered by the religious sects.

There are also religious missionaries who go from door to door asking Catholics for a few moments of their time. Besides these, there are others who invade the homes of Catholics without giving them the opportunity to decide whether to accept or reject their visitors: radio announcers and television programs reach into all homes.

Within each sect there are psychologically confusing elements, each of which is made to fit in with that particular faith but which are so shrewdly presented that these sects appear to be superior religions. In fact, we see that they have won over numerous Catholics ignorant of their own faith.

This invasion of sects is supported by appeals for huge sums of money and the use of communication methods and technology to try to sway the consciences of Catholics in urban as well as rural communities.

4. Our religious situation in the light of the gospel

Many of the preachers in these sects act in good faith and are examples of commitment to their respective beliefs. We would be unjust not to admit that, according to the teaching of our Lord (Lk 16:8). But

we are also wise enough to realize that the purpose of these proselytizing activities is to weaken the unity of the Catholic Church. We are
especially aware of this when we see evidence of the analysis made
in Puebla: "Many sects have not only been clearly and persistently
anti-Catholic, but also unjust in criticizing the Church and have tried
to undermine the faith of the least-educated members of our Church"
(PD, no. 80).

This situation has caused anxiety among Catholics. They have
heard talk about opening up the Church in order to cast out old,
antagonistic positions. They have been truly sensitive to all that
implies loving our neighbor, understanding and communication, so
they have joyfully welcomed the ideas of "religious freedom",
"mutual collaboration", "co-existing with pluralism", which they
have heard presented as the universal message of Vatican II. Some
have also heard the word "ecumenism". A number of imprecise
feelings arose which especially agitated Catholics of good will and
confused their thinking. Sometimes they have formulated their questions for us; at other times they lack even the clarity needed to
formulate the question. We would like our message to be a precise
response to this ambivalent and confusing situation.

Uneasiness among Catholics

Part Two
CATHOLIC IDENTITY

I. *The Revelation of God*

1. God reveals himself

Religion is the relationship that occurs between God and human
beings. It is the bond that unites man with God; it is at the same
time a gift from God that elevates the spiritual faculties of man. The
foundation of religion is in God. Anyone can see how God has
revealed himself in the marvelous work of creation, which requires
a Creator. When we find ourselves with the dilemma of a universal
moral law, we must realize, deep within our conscience, that there
is a supreme Lawmaker above the laws that men make and break.

But God also wanted to reveal himself through the Scriptures,
"addressing men as his friends in order to invite and receive them
into his own company" (DV, no. 2). There came a time in history
when God called Abraham to be the father of a great nation. Through
Moses and the prophets God taught this nation to recognize him as
the only living and true God, as a provident Father and just judge,
and to look for the promised Savior. "And so, throughout the ages,

he prepared the way for the gospel" (DV, no. 3). This is what we call the Old Testament, found in the first part of the Holy Bible.

2. Jesus Christ as the fullness of revelation

It is in Christ, his person, his actions, and his words, that this revelation is fulfilled. All of the Old Testament is a preparation for this final revelation. "God spoke in fragmentary and varied ways to our fathers through the prophets; in this final age, he has spoken to us *Jesus tells us* through his Son" (Heb 1:1–2). In effect, Jesus Christ, the eternal *about God's* Word made flesh, tells us of the intimacy of God. He carries out the *intimacy* work of salvation which the Father has entrusted to him. All of revelation is brought to fulfillment by his death and resurrection and by the sending of the Holy Spirit: "That God is with us to deliver us from the darkness of sin and death, and to raise us up to eternal life" (DV, no. 4). This revelation is now the definitive covenant: "and no new public revelation is to be expected before the glorious manifestation of our Lord, Jesus Christ" (DV, no. 4).

3. Transmission of divine revelation

The communication of these truths to men, in different historical periods and finally through Jesus, could not have been accomplished if God had not made sure that they would arrive as unadulterated truths to all men of all time.

"God graciously arranged that the things he had once revealed for the salvation of all peoples should remain in their entirety, throughout the ages, and be transmitted to all generations. Therefore, Christ the Lord, in whom the entire Revelation of the most high God is summed up, commanded the apostles to preach the Gospel, which had been promised beforehand by the prophets and which he fulfilled in his own person and promulgated with his own lips. This Gospel was to be the source of all saving truth and moral discipline. In addition, those apostles and other men associated with the apostles, under the inspiration of the Holy Spirit, committed the message of salvation to writing" (DV, no. 7).

Tradition, Scripture, and the magisterium, therefore were present from the first moment. "In order that the full and living gospel might always be preserved in the Church, the apostles left bishops as their successors. They gave them 'their own position of teaching authority'. This sacred tradition then, and the sacred Scripture of both Testaments, are like a mirror in which the Church, during its pilgrim journey here on earth, contemplates God, from whom she receives everything, until such time as she is brought to see him face to face as he really is" (DV, no. 7).

4. The revealed deposit of the Faith: sacred Scripture and tradition

Part of what was revealed was immediately, or later, collected into books inspired by the Holy Spirit. For this reason they are called holy Scripture.

That part of revelation not recorded in writing also continues to live in the heart of the Christian people and is passed on from one generation to the next; that is why it is called tradition (from *traditio*: to pass on, deliver). *From generation to generation*

Sacred Scripture and tradition contain, as one treasure, the entirety of what has been revealed to men. We repeat these concepts in order to clarify the dialogues, and sometimes polemics, that frequently appear between Christian brethren in our daily papers. According to Vatican Council II: "The Church has always regarded the Scriptures together with sacred tradition as the supreme rule of her faith. For, since they are inspired by God and committed to writing once and for all time, they present God's own Word in an unalterable form, and they make the voice of the Holy Spirit sound in the words of the prophets and apostles. It follows that all the preaching of the Church, as indeed the entire Christian religion, should be nourished and ruled by sacred Scripture" (DV, no. 21).

We venerate the Scriptures as we have always venerated them. If at one time they were not given the attention they deserve, it is due to pastoral reasons in certain historical circumstances. Today the Church is in the forefront in the study and use of the Bible. At the same time, we affirm the value of tradition. Because "tradition and Scripture are bound closely together and communicate with one another, flowing out from the same divine well-spring, they come together in some fashion to form one thing, and move toward the same goal" (DV, no. 9) and never contradict each other.

Jesus Christ did not leave any written works. Only some of the apostles and disciples, who established the principles of the Church with their lives and teachings, left in writing the life and words of their Master and teacher. The inspired books of the Bible were accepted as such, not because of written testimonies within these books, but through an authority exterior to them in accordance with the faith of the Christian communities. No one will find a catalogue of inspired books in the Bible. St. Augustine profoundly said: "I would not have believed in the Gospels if the authority of the Catholic Church had not moved me to accept it" (*Against Manichaeism,* 5, 6: RJ 1581).

Before the New Testament was written, Jesus Christ founded and established his Church. According to St. Paul, the same Bible asks us to remain true to tradition: "Brothers, stand firm. Hold fast to the traditions you received from us either by our word or by letter" (2 Thes 2:15).

5. The relationship between sacred Scripture and tradition

"Tradition transmits in its entirety the word of God, which has been entrusted to the apostles by Christ the Lord and the Holy Spirit. It transmits it to the successors of the apostles so that, enlightened by the Spirit of truth, they may faithfully preserve, expound, and spread it abroad by their preaching. Thus . . . the Church does not draw her certainty about all revealed truths from the holy Scriptures alone" (DV, no. 9).

Hence, tradition is fundamentally important. It is true that the first Protestants cast aside tradition because of the moments of confusion that existed in their minds between "human" and "divine" traditions. They also intended to base themselves only on the Scriptures. But today among our separated brethren there is another sentiment concerning legitimate tradition. For our part, we are happy to see among Catholics the growing practice of constantly nourishing their faith with the sacred Scriptures. We are pleased to see these promising lines of convergence.

Convergence of Scripture and tradition

6. The deposit of the Faith and the magisterium

As Catholics, universal, we do not follow a free, individualistic interpretation of the doctrine revealed in the Bible and tradition, which we call "the deposit of the Faith". If everyone interpreted this deposit of revelation in his own manner, each would begin his own Church that naturally would not be one and even less the Church of Jesus Christ. Saint Peter has already warned us that "there is no prophecy contained in Scripture which is a personal interpretation" (2 Pet 1:20). In the same way that Christ "opened the mind" of the disciples of Emmaus "to the understanding of the Scriptures" (Lk 24:45), Philip guides the eunuch in the reading and interpretation of Isaiah (Acts 8:31). The follow-up to what St. Peter announced at the beginning of the aforementioned letter, is a later reference to the epistles of Paul which have "certain passages in them hard to understand. The ignorant and the unstable distort them (just as they do the rest of Scripture) to their own ruin" (2 Pet 3:15–16). The Catholic Church has an authentic magisterium which preserves us from wrong interpretations.

We understand the function of the magisterium to be the official teaching body of the Church. This function is entrusted to the hierarchy, which Christ established, and to which was promised the special aid of the Holy Spirit in order to preserve it from mistakes in the exercise of its magisterial function (Mt 28:19–20). But the Church can only teach as revealed truths that which is contained in the deposit of revelation, that is to say, in sacred Scripture and tradition. Because "the magisterium is not superior to the word of God, but is its servant, it teaches only what has been handed on to it. At the divine command and with the help of the Holy Spirit, it listens to this devotedly, guards it with dedication, and expounds it faithfully. All that it proposes for belief as being divinely revealed is drawn from this single deposit of the faith (DV, no. 10).

7. The importance of integrating Scripture, tradition and the magisterium

We are firmly convinced that the principle of "free examination" proclaimed by some of our separated brethren is what justifiably explains the multitide of separate churches. They distanced themselves by beginning with individual interpretations of the same content of faith. On the other hand, we do not believe that those who speak of "free interpretation" of the Scriptures are that coherent either. They want to impose their interpretations on us and deny Catholics the power to interpret in another manner.

We, rather, with Vatican II, affirm that "tradition, Scripture and the magisterium of the Church are so connected and associated that one of them cannot stand without the others. Working together, each in its own way, under the action of the one Holy Spirit, they all contribute effectively to the salvation of souls" (DV, no. 10).

II. *Jesus Christ Founded One Church*

1. Jesus Christ wanted one Church

Jesus Christ, who is, as we said earlier, the fullness of the revelation of the Father, extended his human-divine mystery in the community of the faithful that we call the Church. He described it as *one* sheepfold (Jn 10:1–5), that must bring together all its sheep; as *one* vine (Jn 15:1–5), that must be vitally bound to all of its shoots; as *one* family, where "there are no strangers nor aliens, but fellow citizens of the saints and members of the household of God" (Eph 2:19); as *one* temple of the one God (Jn 2:19–21); as *one* body (Rom 12:5); as *one* bride (Mt 9:15). Each one of these images, and others that we can find in sacred Scripture (LG, no. 6), speak to us of *one* Church. There are two such expressions that most fully emphasize this sense of unity: the Body of Christ and the Bride of Christ.

The Church as the Body of Christ

If the Church is the Body of Christ, then in the face of any division we could ask with St. Paul: "Has Christ, then, been divided into parts?" (1 Cor 1:13). We cannot imagine a divided body as being alive. It would only be a chimera. The same apostle emphasizes this: "Because the loaf of bread is one, we, though many, are *one* body, for we all partake of the *one* loaf" (1 Cor 10:17).

If the Church is the Bride of Christ, it must be *one* and remain indissolubly united to Christ. The theology of marriage of St. Paul, based on Genesis (Gen 2:22–23) and on the gospels (Mt 19:5), attempts to show the indissoluble *unity* of Christ with his Church, as is the unity between husband and wife; one groom with one bride.

Christ, in speaking of his Church, did not use images but its own name (Mt 16:18); he did not say my churches, but clearly my Church, in the singular, as is shown in the authentic translations of the original text.

2. Jesus Christ founded the Church on the rock of Peter

We have the rock of Peter as the guarantee of our membership in the one church of Christ. "Our Saviour, after his resurrection, entrusted to Peter's pastoral care this sole Church of Christ (Jn 21:17), commissioning him and the other apostles to extend and rule it (Mt 28:18ff), and which he raised up for all ages as the pillar and mainstay of the truth (1 Tim 3:15). This Church, constituted and organized as a society in the present world, subsists in the Catholic Church, which is governed by the successor of Peter and by the bishops in communion with him. Nevertheless, many elements of sanctification and truth are found outside its visible confines. Since these are gifts belonging to the Church of Christ, they are forces impelling towards Catholic unity" (LG, no. 8).

The bishops of Paraguay are in communion with the Bishop of Rome, as the apostles were with St. Peter. In addition, we consider him to be the principle and foundation of our unity as head of our episcopal college. He is a visible sign of union with the whole, universal ('catholic') Church, which is seen as one in him, just as Christ wanted. Always present in our hearts are those clear and final words of our Lord: "You are Peter, and on this rock I will build my Church" (Mt 16:16).

Our people have always joyfully viewed this unity with the Pope as a clear sign of their Catholic identity. At this historical point in time we enthusiastically await his coming. He is seen as the Vicar of Christ and a Universal Father, especially to the dispossessed. And today, by the grace of God, the Pope is known as John Paul II.

Unity with the Pope, an evident sign of Catholic identity

3. Jesus Christ builds the Church in the Eucharist

Incorporated into the Church as children of God through baptism, and reconciled with her through the sacrament of reconciliation (if we do not betray her), we participate in the Eucharistic celebration, "the source and summit of the Christian life" (LG, no. 11). In the Eucharist we offer to God the true sacrifice of the Body and Blood of Jesus Christ, which he himself gave to us (Mt 26:26ff). At the same time we participate with Christ in the community of the Church. Each day, the Church continues to grow in this communion with the Son of God until the Eternal Passover which each celebration of the Eucharist anticipates.

As the Church celebrates the Eucharist, the Eucharist builds up the Church. We will take some time here to reflect on this sacrament.

But the Church is not brought into being only through the union of people, through the experience of brotherhood to which the Eucharistic banquet gives rise. The Church is brought into being when, in that fraternal union and communion, we celebrate the Sacrifice of the Cross of Christ, when we proclaim "the Lord's death until he comes" (1 Cor 11:26), and later, when, being deeply compenetrated with the mystery of our salvation, we approach as a community the table of the Lord, in order to be nourished there, in a sacramental manner, by the fruits of the Holy Sacrifice of propitiation. Therefore in Eucharistic Communion we receive Christ, Christ himself; and our union with him, which is a gift and grace for each individual, brings it about that in him we are also associated in the unity of his Body, which is the Church (John Paul II, Letter to all the Bishops of the Church on the mystery and worship of the Holy Eucharist, February 24, 1980, no. 4).

This is why our people traditionally consider participation (at least weekly) of the faithful in the Mass as a sign of true membership in the Church (even though this sign is sometimes distorted). For this reason, we, the bishops, also feel the more visible signs of the unity of the Church when we celebrate on the altar, surrounded by our diocesan communities; "the mystery of the Lord's Supper is celebrated so that, by means of the flesh and blood of the Lord, the whole brotherhood of the Body may be welded together" (LG, no. 26). This same unity is felt when we celebrate the Eucharist as an episcopal conference in the great national events that unite all of the

Church of Paraguay—events such as the annual feast day of the
Virgin of the Miracles of Caacupé.

The Eucharist, a sign and motive of Catholic unity

With the certainty that the Eucharist is the fount of spiritual life
and fraternal dialogue, the sign of and motive for unity, and that it
is nourishment for the individual and community in religious life,
we the bishops of Paraguay decided in a recent assembly that we
would like to convocate a National Eucharistic Congress. It will be
the second such Congress, since next year will mark fifty years since
the one which our predecessor, Mons. Juan Sinforiano Bogarín,
celebrated, with much benefit to our Church, during the height of
his term. Because the Eucharist is proof of our Catholic identity, we
see this event as providing our pastoral agents and the faithful in
general with the opportunity to prepare for a celebration of the fifth
centenary of the evangelization of our continent.

4. The Holy Spirit guides the Church

Nourished by the Eucharist, all of us as Christians form one body
with Christ as the Head. Just as the soul directs the whole body and
gives it unity, so have the Fathers of the Church seen the Holy Spirit
as the principle of life that gives unity to the Church (LG, no. 7).
Sent by Christ on Pentecost, the Holy Spirit "lives in the Church
and in each of the faithful as in a temple" (1 Cor 3:16; 6:19). "The
Spirit himself gives witness with our spirit that we are children of
God (Gal 4:6; Rom 8:15–16, 26). He guides the Church to all truth
(Jn 16:13), he unifies her in communion and ministry, he provides
for and governs her with various hierarchical and charismatic gifts,
and he embellishes her with his fruits (Eph 4:11–12; 1 Cor 12:4; Gal
5:22). With the power of the gospel he rejuvenates the Church,
constantly renewing her and guiding her to the consummated union
with her Groom.

Hence the universal Church is seen to be "a people brought into
unity from the unity of the Father, the Son and the Holy Spirit: (LG,
no. 4). With the coming of the Holy Spirit, John Paul II tells us in
his last encyclical, the era of the Church began, an era that lasts
through the centuries and generations of people.

5. Mary, Mother of the Church

If we say that the Church is an extension of the human–divine mystery
of Jesus, then his Mother, Mary, is also the Church's mother. She
is above all those whom Jesus adopted as brothers and members of
his own Body.

Mary plays an extremely important role in the mystery of the

Incarnation of the Word of God. According to the unanimous testimony of the Gospels, the Acts of the Apostles (Acts 1:14) and St. Paul (Gal 4:4), the Incarnation of Jesus depended on her Yes (Lk 11:38) to God, on the cooperation of the one who was truly his Mother. Mary stands firmly at the foot of the Cross (Jn 19:25) when Jesus, dying on the Cross, gives up his Spirit (Jn 19:30), which is to be the soul of the Church. She is with the apostles on the day of Pentecost when the Spirit of God comes in his fullness to give the gifts to begin the Church as an organized body. With reason, through the centuries the Catholic Church has seen Mary as her own Mother as well as her model.

"This motherhood of Mary in the order of grace continues uninterruptedly from the consent which she loyally gave at the Annunciation and which she sustained without wavering beneath the Cross, until the eternal fulfillment of all the elect. Taken up to heaven, she did not lay aside this saving office, but by her manifold intercession continues to bring us the gifts of eternal salvation" (LG, no. 62).

The church of Paraguay, which will be four-and-a-half centuries old on the Feast of the Assumption next year, through the cooperation of the people throughout the centuries, continues to complete the prophecy of Mary in the Gospel: "All ages to come shall call me blessed, for God who is mighty has done great things for me" (Lk 1:48–49)). The root and cause of all the glory of Mary—according to Mary herself—is always in Almighty God.

The Church of Paraguay proclaims the Virgin Mary blessed

Therefore, entrusting all cares "to Christ through Mary" (MC, no. 25), in various parts of our country and in different manners, but especially in Caacupé, she has been and is joyfully venerated by all Christians. All those faithful to the gospel consider themselves Mary's children because of her individual collaboration, then and now, in the work of our salvation.

6. Devotion to Mary and Christian unity

Mary's part in the work of our salvation is also a strong point in the simple faith of our people. Recognizing that Christ is our only Mediator (1 Tim 2:5), they have associated the figure of his mother with him and his triumph over evil, just as God designed. These designs of God concerning Mary's role can be found from the first pages of Genesis (Gen 3:15) through the last pages of Revelation (Rev 12:1–11) with the fullness of revelation and redemption in Bethlehem (Lk 2:7) and on Calvary (Jn 19:26–27). Without Mary, one cannot conceive of an incarnated Christ or of a Christ dying for our sins. Therefore, veneration of the Virgin Mary is an indispensable part of Catholic belief.

"Because of its ecclesial character, devotion to the Blessed Virgin reflects the preoccupations of the Church herself. Among these, especially in our day, is her anxiety for the reestablishment of Christian unity. Thus devotion to the Mother of the Lord is in accord with the deep desires and aims of the ecumenical movement. . . . In venerating with particular love the glorious Theotokos and in acclaiming her as the "Hope of Christians", Catholics unite themselves with their brethren of the Orthodox churches, in which devotion to the Blessed Virgin finds its expression in a beautiful lyricism and in solid doctrine. Catholics are also united with Anglicans, whose classical theologians have already drawn attention to the sound scriptural basis for devotion to the Mother of our Lord, while those of the present day increasingly underline the importance of Mary's place in the Christian life. Praising God with the very words of the Virgin, they are united, too, with their brethren in the churches of the Reform, where love for the sacred Scriptures flourishes (MC, no. 32).

"We realize that there exist important differences between the thought of many of our brethren in other churches and ecclesial communities and the Catholic doctrine on 'Mary's role in the work of salvation'. In consequence, there are likewise differences of opinion on the devotion that should be shown to her. Nevertheless, since it is the same power of the Most High that overshadowed the Virgin of Nazareth and that today is at work within the ecumenical movement and making it fruitful, we wish to express our confidence that devotion to the humble handmaid of the Lord, in whom the Almighty has done great things, will become, even if only slowly, not an *Mary, the* obstacle but a path and a rallying point for the union of all who *meeting point* believe in Christ. We are glad to see that, in fact, a better understand- *of the faithful* ing of Mary's place in the mystery of Christ and of the Church on *in Christ* the part also of our separated brethren is smoothing the path to union. Just as at Cana the Blessed Virgin's intervention resulted in Christ's performing his first miracle (Jn 2:1–12), so today her intercession can help to bring to realization the time when the disciples of Christ will again find full communion in faith" (MC, no. 33).

Part Three
THE PROBLEM OF RELIGIOUS SECTS

I. *The Religious Sects*

1. Introduction

Catholics frequently encounter people eager to speak with others who are not of their faith. Among them are people sincerely interested in finding the truth. It is necessary to pay attention to them. We owe them our cordial consideration. It is our duty to give them all the time and sacrifice required. But in other cases, there are people who try to convince Catholics to adopt their own religious beliefs. This is the case with religious sects.

The phenomenon of sects, which appear to be more or less Christian, causes concern among the hierarchy of many Latin American Churches. What attitude should one take toward these sects? What pastoral problems does their presence cause on our continent and, in particular, in our country? We will try to show, on one hand, a better explanation of their characteristics and how to deal with this phenomenon, and on the other hand, the attutude of faithful Catholics toward the sects, where, on many occasions, they are confused and unable to respond to "the reason for this hope of yours" (1 Pet 3:15).

Pastoral problems caused by sects

2. The difference between sects and churches

This differentiation poses a difficult problem. None of the religious groups now wants to be called a "sect", because with that name they would be automatically rejected. We do not find the word *sect* in any of the titles taken by these religious groups. They name and describe themselves as "religious movements". Some include within the sects, as an oversimplification, churches and ecclesial communities that are not in perfect accordance with the Roman Catholic Church. We even look upon our beloved Orthodox brethren, heirs of the great eastern patriarchs, as sects. They are venerable churches. We also consider the churches of the Reformation to be sects, arising from the historical conditions of the sixteenth century: Lutherans, Anglicans, Calvinists.

What criteria could we use to distinguish the "sects" from the "churches" within the Christian religious movements?

3. Some distinctive criteria of sects

We will base the distinction on the *source* of instruction in these groups. The sects would be those groups that, besides the Bible, have other "revealed" books—the Book of Mormon or Testimonies of Jehovah, for example—or "prophetic messages", such as "Pueblo de Dios" and "Saint Luke" in Paraguay. They would also be those groups that exclude some canonical books from the Bible or radically alter their content.

In its document about sects dated May 3, 1986, the Vatican Secretariat on Christian Unity has described sects as "religious groups with a specific view of the world derived—although without complete fidelity—from the teachings of the great world religions. They are characterized by a determined authoritarian structure which, as a type of brainwashing, forms groups that foment a determined feeling of guilt or fear" (1.1.1).

Difference between proselytism and missionary spirit

The World Council of Churches, in collaboration with our Roman Catholic Church in the document of Zagorsk (1969), named "proselytism" as an identifying sign of the sects, as a distinct factor in the "missionary spirit" of such an ecclesial community. Proselytism, contrary to the gospel, uses dishonest means to acquire religious followers: states of misery or ignorance, advantageous positions in the political order, half-truths, blackmail, psychological pressure, manipulation in the midst of group gatherings. According to the document, "it includes all that violates the rights of all human beings, Christian or not, all that is external coercion in religious matters, and all manners of proclaiming the gospel that do not conform to the ways of God, who calls man to freely respond to his vocation and serve him in spirit and truth" (Document of Zagorsk, no. 4).

4. Pastoral problems posed by sects

a) *Diffusion*

One of the causes of the diffusion of sects in our midst is the pastoral abandonment of large, popularly Catholic areas. Parishes with thousands of faithful spread over a huge territory, and with only one priest to attend to them, are areas ripe for the proselytizing action of religious groups. These groups rely on powerful means of propaganda through books, pamphlets, radio, and television programs. These pastoral vacuums are a seed bed for the proliferation of the sects.

This situation is combined with the spiritual and religious dissatisfaction of the people who feel "like sheep without a shepherd". The free religious movements then come to offer something attractive. It does not matter whether they are Jehovah's Witnesses or spiritualists. What matters is that here is someone to talk to, who understands and comforts them, who treats them as brothers and sisters, who gives them advice about their personal problems, who invites them to community meetings where they actively participate, and where they hear the word of God.

b) *Popular religious needs*

The adherence of a multitude of people to the different sects is proof that great religious anxiety exists among our people. It indicates a dissatisfaction with what they receive or not longer receive from the Catholic Church.

It is urgent to establish what the religious needs of the people are, and whether the Church has the means to satisfy them. We must ask ourselves if we should present a pastoral plan of action to our people, like the one proposed in the plan of Pastoral Organica. *Planning of Pastoral Organica*

One could say that the needs, among others, that the people expect to be met by turning to religion belong to three categories:

—problems of sickness and possible cures
—problems of enough food and work
—problems of loneliness and love

For many people, religion exists to solve these types of problems. This does not mean that they do not have other needs as well. They also see in religion a sense of their existence and life before God, the desire to reach the fullness of happiness, the possibility of interior peace in the midst of suffering, the hope of reward or the fear of punishment after death, the search for a kind God who sees and loves them. . . . But one does not specifically hear of these higher values of religion. Or perhaps they have not succeeded in discovering them. Their religious requirements remain a part of the search for solutions to their more immediate problems.

Often the Church is not in a position to solve these problems, even though her social works help many of the poor. But in one sense, she finds herself inferior to movements of the spirit and pentecostals who promise the cure of all infirmities. The Church cannot fall into those types of immediate remedies. She would betray her evangelical mission and show little faith in the power of the Good News Jesus taught his apostles.

II. *Attitude toward the Sects*

1. Vision of faith

The first thing we should do in dealing with the problem is to strengthen our faith in the Holy Spirit and learn to be instruments of his power. It is not we who actually evangelize. It is the Holy Spirit working through us. It is therefore important to act as good instruments in his hands, united with him and obedient to his almighty power. We should have greater confidence in the prayer that asks the Holy Spirit to be effective in our lives. *Submission to the powerful action of the Holy Spirit*

One should take into account the fact that some pastoral agents act with a certain permissiveness. They are afraid to speak of sin and obligation in the life of a Christian. They do not consider the personal and social disintegration as a consequence of sin, sin which wears away the boundaries of the Law of God. They fall into a certain "secularism" with respect to what they call "sacramentalization", which is in reality a life of grace.

We must not forget that the Church's principal work is to provide the means by which each person can find God, form a relationship with him, and arrive at possession of eternal life. The excessive—at time, exclusive—preoccupation with resolving social problems, as if this were the only or principal mission of the Church, weakens her pastoral mission and causes her to lose effectiveness by overlooking the heart of the gospel message.

2. The pastoral plan of action: a preventative attitude

The order of pastoral action will be first to examine carefully whether the pastoral methods we use are adequate. We are frequently unaware of the spiritual needs of the people. Our words are abstract, without concrete, practical applications and do not give enough attention to perceived emotional and affective factors.

In planning, we must also determine which areas have been invaded by religious sects, and even if they have been, whether they have been affected by the sects.

A high priority in this pastoral action should be the rescuing of abandoned sheep through catechesis that offers them the complete Catholic doctrine and its biblical-ecclesial foundation in a simple and systematic form. Hence, before the eventual arrival of false shepherds, they will have arguments with which they can respond. We must personify the parable of the Good Shepherd who goes to look for the lost sheep and does not abandon those in danger. For this we need more workers. It is necessary "to ask the harvest-master to send workers to his harvest" (Lk 10:2).

3. Pastoral action in affected areas

The pastoral attitude toward the religious sects cannot be without charity, even if it is known that charity will not be reciprocated and despite how much some of them present the Catholic Church as an invention of Satan. This must be treated as a pastoral problem which must be faced with concern, with seriousness, with prudence, with the marks of charity.

Many of the faithful, because of their poor religious formation, are easily involved in arguments with members of the sects. It would be better to advise them to refuse, with firmness and charity, to engage in a long conversation or accept pamphlets. A simple recourse would be to invite the visitor to pray together to the Lord and his holy Mother. This would serve, at the same time, as a way of strengthening the religious formation of the faithful.

Other Christians with more background in their Faith can engage in a dialogue, but always without intending to offend anyone. In any case, it would be wise to remain alert since at times a person engages in dialogue, not actually to find the truth, but rather to maintain a firm, pre-established position.

4. Attitude of the parishes

When a parish becomes aware of the presence of the sects and they have only affected some families, the parish must pay close, personal attention to those families. If the phenomenon is more widespread, a public statement of the truth should be made to the faithful. At the same time, it would be wise to revise the pastoral action among the more vulnerable groups: the youth, the sick and the marginalized. It is important to examine the catechetical and general teaching methods: Are they simple, do they have the capacity to give certainty, or do they generate doubts and a lack of confidence? We must not forget that the great attraction of the sects is the certainty and conviction with which they present their beliefs. If some priests appear not to be convinced themselves by what they preach, the people will turn to look for the "believers". We also need to examine the catechesis that the priests present. Is it catechesis with precise statements, or does it have vague formulations and generic statements that neither educate nor help the growth of faith? Also, it woud not be bad to look at the progress of biblical formation in our communities.

A test of the biblical formation of the community

One of the strongest forces of the sects is their ability to welcome people, to establish a personal, one-on-one relationship with new people. Their followers no longer feel like a number, and acquire continual responsibilities. This is a good example of how we must try carefully to cultivate personal relationships in a parish. We must give greater importance to spiritual direction, to listening, and to receiving people in order to give more responsibilities to the faithful, being careful not to exceed their capabilities.

5. Attitude of catechists and pastoral workers

At this point we can mention some specific recommendations for the catechists, those responsible for the education in the faith of children, youth, and adults. We would insist that they frequently and accurately use the word of God with reference to tradition and the Church and her magisterium.

We ask the pastoral workers, united with their parish priest, to be living images of Jesus in the midst of the people: men and women with peaceful minds, generous hearts, and a spirit of sacrifice; builders of unity in communion and participation.

In conclusion, we suggest trying not to remain inactive, afraid, or limited to useless lamentations. As one pastoral vicar said, "I do not complain about the sects. I see a sign from God in them, a call to a greater challenge, to a greater deepening of the faith, to a greater surrender to my ministry, and to a greater commitment on the part of the parish" (P. Crery, *L'Offensive des sectes*, p. 437).

6. Attitude of the faithful toward sectarian proselytism

Christ came to save mankind

The Catholic must always begin with the supposition that Christ came to save all men and to enable them to come to know the truth (1 Tim 2:4). For this reason, Catholics must love all without regard for race, language, nationality, political party, or religion. In dealing with non-Catholics, we could find people who are sincerely searching for the truth. Do not be afraid to manifest the truth that we live. On the contrary, if we did not do so we would be hypocrites. Because we respect the beliefs of others, we will not speak of religion if they do not want to. We should be ready to defend their freedom of conscience, since God does not desire that violence be done to another's conscience.

But do not confuse freedom of conscience with religious indifference. Our sincerity and our respect will allow us to be friends. Sincerity attracts without necessarily giving way in our faith or morals.

Finally, the presence of the sects should encourage faithful Catholics better to understand and live out their Faith. This will produce a more noticeable unity in their Catholic community and strengthen their own identity, which is gauranteed in the living hierarchy of the Church, just as her founder, Jesus Christ, wanted.

Conclusion

In this instruction, we have expressed what we believe to be suitable for strengthening our Catholic identity and our unity in faith and love. We also wanted to note the proper attitude toward the problem of religious sects, which is causing noticeable anxiety among our faithful

We would like to open our hearts and voices to all men of good will, of whatever religion or having doubts of faith, to manifest our personal and communal esteem and to say that all have a place in this marvelous Church of Christ.

We would like to share with all a place in the work of building a civilization of love, guaranteeing the morality of a nation, defending peace with sincere dialogue, promoting justice, giving preference to the weak, making each community an example of peaceful coexistence "where they succeed in combining liberty with solidarity, where authority is exercised with the spirit of the Good Shepherd, where a different attitude toward riches exists, where forms of organization and structured participation are tried, capable of opening the way toward a more humane society. And where, above all, it is made unmistakably clear that without a radical communion with God in Jesus Christ, any other form of purely human communion afterward results in an inability to sustain itself, and fatally ends by turning against man himself" (PD, no. 273).

May all receive our blessing in the name of the Father, the Son, and the Holy Spirit and invoking the protection of the Holy Virgin Mary, Mother of Jesus Christ and Mother of the Church.

MAN: HIS PLACE IN NATURE

Pastoral Letter of the Conference of Bishops of the Dominican Republic

Introduction

1. On August 10, 1982, we made a very clear statement on the eve of the inauguration of a new government: "We cannot keep on deceiving ourselves about preserving and improving the environment in which we live. Disturbing the balance of ecology is something we simply cannot get away with. Man's sins against nature will

In the Dominican Republic, failure to protect the environment has reached a point where recovery is all but impossible. In the interests of awakening national responsibility, the bishops have raised their voices in concern. Our whole country would do well to heed this courageous stand. This pastoral letter was published in Santo Domingo on January 21, 1987, and was translated from the Spanish by Mary E. Hamilton. One part, which describes in detail the specific ecological problems of the Dominican Republic, has been omitted here.

always be visited upon him sooner or later. Our destruction of our forests, to give only one example, without prompt and efficient reforestation, is already causing severe damage to our rivers, our farmlands, and our climate. It is urgent, then, that we take a firm and well thought out political position on this very serious national problem" (Pastoral Letter, August 10, 1982, no. 3). This situation has not improved since 1982; in fact, it has steadily deteriorated.

2. Pope John Paul II, in his first encyclical *Redemptor Hominis* (1979), affirms: "Sometimes man seems to care only about those aspects of his natural environment that serve his immediate purposes and needs as a producer and consumer. However, it was the Creator's will that man in his relationship to nature be a noble, intelligent steward and caretaker, not an exploiter and destroyer, who wantonly disregards his obligation to replace what he has taken" (RH, no. 15).

3. In the Dominican Republic at present, environmental problems are not just a danger we need to ward off, but a tragic reality that must be confronted; they will require drastic action to be corrected. This situation forces us to cease today putting off the fulfillment of a promise we made some time ago, to write about the place of the human being in nature, that is, in modern parlance, about national ecological problems.

4. It is encouraging that, finally, many voices have been raised to call attention to this very grave problem and to elicit a sense of responsibility and concerted action from all the people. These voices included those of experts in the field, of serious and concerned persons, of terrified and indignant people who had daily witnessed, with their own eyes, flagrant crimes against nature on the very sites where those crimes had been perpetrated.

Offences against nature

5. Among these voices, a consensus was reached on five points that we would like to emphasize:

—Ecological problems, instead of getting nearer to a solution, have continued to get worse.

—The determining factor in this situation is the way those who aggressively abuse the environment have gone scot free.

—Another determining factor of primary importance is the grinding poverty that forces many citizens of the Dominican Republic to destroy the environment in order to make enough money to survive.

—What we need is top-level guidance that executes policies with authority, coordinates, and gives clear direction.

—And, above all, we need a national political thrust that channels funds, human resources, legal and educational actions, and judgments right down to the grass roots level, the deep conviction that this is our homeland and we must take good care of it.

6. It fills us with satisfaction and hope to observe the increasing

sensitivity to ecological problems, the sincere concern of many people, and certain concrete initiatives that have been set in motion and promoted, despite all kinds of difficulties, in some of which people of the Church have taken a personal interest.

7. It is indisputable that, in this matter, the scientific and technical aspect is most important, and that this aspect, although outside our province as bishops, still should interest us vitally and ought to be kept urgently in mind. But in addition to these two items, there is the ethical and moral dimension of the problem, aspects that have a direct bearing on our mission and our function. And it is this dimension that we find proper to explore at this point. . . .

II. *God's Marvelous Plan for Nature*

God's Plan

30. God, in his wisdom and power, created—brought into existence from nothing things that had never before existed—the whole universe and within that universe, the planet earth, in accordance with his admirable laws, and he endowed that cosmos he had created for himself with those same laws.

31. It is recorded for us that God created the world, both inanimate matter and living creatures: vegetable and animal life, and finally, human life. He endowed man with intelligence, the capability for love, various talents, and accountability for his own freedom, and God made for man both the center and the crown of his creation, the earth.

32. He turned over to this "man"—all of humanity present and to come—as a *common inheritance*, the earth and all that is in it.

33. Having endowed this inheritance with marvelous and frequently mysterious laws, including enormous potential for maintaining and improving the quality of human life by combining those laws to good effect, God imposed on man the task and the duty of "subduing" and "replenishing" the earth by means of science and technology, and in this way, God enabled man to succeed in making the earth ever more useful and apt for perfecting human beings and society (see Gen 1:26–28 and Ps 8:5–9).

34. So, to use human intelligence and ability (science and technology) to destroy the earth or to threaten it—or not to use those abilities when difficulties or new challenges arise—is to make nonsense of our humanity, to ride roughshod over the divine plan, and to be disrespectful toward the will of the Creator who is absolute Lord of the earth and of man.

Principles

35. Out of this framework come certain basic principles, from which are derived fundamental moral requirements that we want to emphasize:

The earth is man's patrimony

a. The earth with all its benefits is humanity's birthright. It is the inheritance that we have received, that we are to administer and share with others justly and equitably, and that we must pass on to those who come after us in good condition, undamaged—indeed, on the contrary, in an improved condition.

b. The earth with all its benefits is a challenge to the industry, talent, and intelligence of the human being, both as an individual and as a society.

c. The earth with all its benefits is intended for everyone's use. Appropriation of part of this inheritance for the use of one person or of one group is legitimate only when it is restricted to that minimum amount that will fulfill the needs of the individual or group, or when it is directed toward enhancing and rendering more effective the reality of its fundamental end, namely, to be of use to all mankind.

d. Science and technology are the fruit and the legacy of our humanity. What each scientist achieves—however eminent he may be—is but a part inseparable from the whole of human science and technology, and always owes something to what others have previously or simultaneously achieved. This social debt must be paid by respecting and giving greater scope to the social function of science, technology, and all human endeavor.

e. Human beings are to take advantage of the common inheritance of the earth and all its benefits only as administrators, perfectors, and stewards—functions that ought to be fulfilled nobly and intelligently.

f. This is why we read, in the inspired book of Wisdom: "God of my fathers, Lord of mercy, you who have made all things by your word and in your wisdom have established man to rule the creatures produced by you, to govern the world in holiness and justice, and to render judgment in integrity of heart: give me Wisdom, the attendant at your throne" (Wis 9:1–4).

Thus, in his relationship with nature, the human being is required to act with wisdom, integrity, justice, and holiness; and he is consequently forbidden to act with disregard, ignorance, irrationality, avarice, exploitiveness, aggressiveness, perversity, and impiety.

g. God created earth as a paradise for man. Man's sin is what transformed this paradise into "cursed ground". "Cursed be the ground because of you! In toil shall you eat its yield all the days of your life. Thorns and thistles shall it bring forth to you . . ." (Gen 3:17–18).

Morals and ecology

36. As we have already shown, the duties of the human being toward God and toward his neighbors include very serious obligations toward nature, because we all depend on the environment and owe to the environment both our relationship with nature and nature's relationship to us; these obligations have not been left to our free will; rather, they have been made clear to us by God. What God wills has been manifested to us both in the natural law itself and in revelation. Of course, our relationship to nature includes our dealings with our neighbors and our relationship with God as well.

37. From the principles that have been set forth comes a series of moral criteria that we wish to explain, to reflect upon, and to use as a guide for our actions:

Exploitation of natural resources should never be undertaken by those seeking the rapid accumulation of riches, according to what we might call "mining" standards, caring nothing for correct forest management and reforestation, but rather, should be undertaken as a function of the needs of the whole human family, present and future. Our woodlands, with very rare exceptions, have been, sadly, a typical case of this depletion and abuse.

Our forests have been the center of abuse and raids

38. We cannot allow so many peasants, just because they do not have better access to land, to see themselves as irremediably condemned to extreme poverty. This situation obliges them, occasionally, to an insidious over-exploitation of that land, causing deterioration and real destruction of the soil. Such destruction, for lack of cultivable land and, above all, because of failure to contour-plow hillsides in mountainous areas, is as damaging as deforestation.

39. It is not fair for those who have higher incomes (countries, cities, groups, and individuals) to indulge in wasteful, conspicuous consumerism that, besides being an insult and a provocation to the poor, is a sinful misuse of the natural resources so desperately needed by the deprived among the population.

40. Those members of society who have enough influence over the use of natural resources cannot be governed in their decisions by motives of economic profit or political gain, without being held accountable for what happens in the future to coming generations.

41. Proper regulation and emphasis on the common good should help us to establish and accept priorities concerning the limited re-

sources the government has at its disposal right now. Therefore,

since reforestation is a desperately urgent project to which the government has committed itself, it is unfair and indeed foolish to insist on and keep calling for public projects that are of secondary importance, in spite of this national emergency.

42. In the case of non-renewable resources, highly industrialized, developed nations cannot keep exercising a monopoly in the exploitation and use of those resources without being held accountable for the present and future needs of countries that supply those resources. Nor can these suppliers, in their turn, exhaust and misuse their present and future national treasure to alleviate immediate economic demands.

43. Since nature possesses resources that have taken millions of years to form, extraction of these resources demands reflection and prudence, taking into account that millions of years will be needed to restore them, if indeed they can ever again be replenished.

44. Income generated from exploiting non-renewable resources should be put to work toward finding permanent solutions for the people who currently suffer dehumanizing and unjust poverty and toward generating income to help future generations, who will not have the advantage of being able to exploit those resources.

45. A substantial part of the benefits obtained from operations that upset the ecological balance ought to be used to recover that balance, to the extent this is possible.

46. Renewable resources, such as woodlands, soil, and water, so necessary for life, ought to be used in a way that respects the fact that these resources have to be given a chance to renew themselves, so that they may be of use to future generations, to whom they also belong.

47. We must be watchful and use the best remedies we can find so that neither greed for money nor the pressing necessities of the poor have a negative impact on the conservation of natural resources.

48. Where privileged groups exist that have enjoyed great and undeserved benefits from taking advantage of renewable resources, it is not fair that the whole burden of renewing those resources should be dumped on the shoulders of the poor.

49. It is as contrary to the plan of the Creator to treat natural resources carelessly and unreasonably as it is to prohibit their controlled use to satisfy the needs of the whole populace.

50. To maintain and to defend the necessary ecological balance is a moral obligation incumbent on all, and not an exclusive function of the government. To abuse natural resources (e.g., trees, water, minerals) is to commit an offense against nature, against the human

beings who need those resources, and against God, the Creator of nature and of human beings.

51. The most extraordinary scientific progress, the most spectacular technical successes, and the most stupendous economic growth can turn to man's disadvantage if there is not a parallel and genuine moral and social progress on the part of individuals and society.

52. The ideology of work as the mastery and unlimited exploitation of matter is false. It is incorrect to seek the maximum return or profit from production as an end in itself. The quest for unlimited efficiency and hedonistic consumerism is a trap that leads to ruin like that of the prodigal son. It is risky and dangerous for us to be fascinated with or make idols of science and technology; although they can lead to the increase and transformation of reserves of resources, they have not the power to create them.

Spirituality and ecology

53. Christ, to whom all things are subject (1 Cor 15), who freed all things from the bondage of corruption (Rom 8:21), taught us during his life on earth to admire and respect nature; to make use of it and to enjoy it without soiling it or tearing it up; to be inspired by it, and to love it.

54. To explain various aspects and conditions of the kingdom of God, the kingdom he came to inaugurate upon the earth, he continually referred, like a teacher, to realities such as sowing, reaping, wheat and tares, the grain of mustard seed, the fig tree, the vine, the sun, the rain, the lilies of the field, the birds . . . (Mt 13:18–23; Mk 4:13–20; Lk 8:11–15; Mk 4:26–29; Mt 13:24–30; Mk 4:30–32; Lk 13:18–19; Mt 5:45; Lk 12:27; Mt 6:28; Lk 12:4–7). He always liked to go up into the mountains to withdraw from the crowds and pray (Mt 17:1; Mk 6:45), and, from the lower slope of a mountain, with only the blue sky above for a roof, he proclaimed the Beatitudes to the world (Mt 5:3–13; Lk 6:17–20). After having called the first disciples from its shores (Lk 5:1–11; Mk 1:19–20), he returned time and again to the Sea of Galilee, or the Sea of Tiberias, or the Lake of Gennesaret, to preach, to perform miracles, and to rest (Mk 1:21–28; Mt 13:1–52; Mk 4:35–41; Jn 21:1–14).

Jesus loved the earth, the mountains

55. The progressive bringing of humanity to perfection includes the steady perfecting of the natural environment, whose intelligent and faithful master, caretaker, and steward, as we have already said, is the human being.

56. The inspiring and enthralling Francis of Assisi, patron of

ecologists, always called nature "Sister". And he treated nature like a sister. Thus, in his Canticle he sings of his Brother, the Sun:

> Praised be Thou, my Lord,
> For our Sister, Mother Earth
> Who sustains and cares for us,
> And brings forth diverse fruits
> With flowers and plants in all their colors.

Francis of Assisi is a living, clear voice, calling not just for the reconciliation of all men with one another, but for the reconciliation of all mankind with all of nature. On that account, he is an extraordinarily modern and forceful figure.

57. St. Ignatius Loyola, loyal servant of the Church, always loved to see God in nature: Behold—he says—how God dwells in his creatures: in the elements, giving them being; in the plants, giving them life; in the animals, giving them sensation; in men, giving them understanding. So he dwells in me, giving me being, life, sensation, and intelligence, and making a temple of me, since he created me to the likeness and image of his Divine Majesty. Then I will reflect upon myself in the manner stated in the first point, or in any other way that may seem more beneficial (*Spiritual Exercises,* no. 235). In this very profound manner, he illustrates the interrelatedness of everyone with all of nature.

III. *Why We Must Act Now*

58. All that we have said so far will be mere words blown away in the wind, if little or nothing is done as a result. Efficient, coordinated action is imperative.

59. Nevertheless, the means we choose ought to be twofold: technical and ethical. Both are necessary. Neither of the two, by itself, can do the job.

60. We understand that reforestation and planning for the proper use of our soil entail difficulties, owing to the present state of depletion, and owing to the chaotic atmosphere that characterizes this aspect of our material existence, springing from root causes of a social nature that have landed us in this predicament.

The measures to be adopted

61. We think that the efforts to bring deforestation to a complete halt have been well planned, as a first step in a series of approaches to ward off the grave problem of national ecological ruin.

62. We understand, nonetheless, that it has always been, and always will be, necessary to take into account the diversity of groups that

have a deleterious impact on renewable resources. It would not be fair to deal with all of them in exactly the same way. Each case requires individual attention. Among these groups we wish to name are:

a. Those who have grown rich from destroying the environment.

b. Those who have taken advantage of their position and influence to seek profit from the environment, no matter what the cost.

c. Those who destroy the environment from necessity, without having any other immediate choice, since they have no share of land of their own.

d. Those who, although they themselves have no direct contact with natural resources, still depend on these resources to a large extent for their living, such as the poor who cook with charcoal and kindling-wood.

e. Groups who in good faith want to institute what they believe is a still better use for the soil than the reforestation and related agricultural activities that would benefit the country.

63. It would be unfair, in the name of ensuring the physical survival of our nation, to treat all these groups the same. Of these groups, the peasants and the urban poor, who depend on charcoal, deserve special attention.

64. Marginalization of peasants and their consequent poverty, that in turn brings on many of our ecological problems, must be remedied in context as being not a secondary, but a central part of the ecological problem. The defense of the environment is not an end in itself, unless it tends toward a balance in the relationship between environment and man to attain a more humane world for everyone by means of improving the quality of the environment.

65. Just as it is unacceptable to allow the wood merchants to continue their destructive activity in the woods, it would also be unacceptable to plunge deeper into misery those poor peasants from the mountains or the drought-stricken areas that our society has deprived of all but nomadic agriculture, for lack of a tiny sack of charcoal to burn. Likewise, it would be unacceptable for us to cut off distribution to the poor of the only fuel they know how to use to cook their food, without having first found them a workable alternative.

66. We consider it opportune, as immediate steps to complement the means of combatting deforestation, to mention the following:

a. To continue strictly and deliberately our vigilance over critical areas in our national territory.

b. To organize, at a grass-roots level, the production of charcoal so as to alleviate the penury of so many citizens of the Dominican

To organize the production of charcoal

Republic, who cannot even find anything to cook with; this will then improve the situation of so many charcoal-makers, who are numbered among the poorest people in the country.

This organization should be accomplished while doing the least possible harm to the ecosystem, and while actively seeking other solutions: easier, viable, and economical alternatives.

c. To levy a tax to benefit peasants who live in the mountains and are substantially affected by the necessary prohibitions against cutting down trees in endangered areas. In this way many of these families can begin to relocate to other places or other work where they can earn enough to live on.

d. To confront the opinions of foreign and domestic technologists, together with the opinions of the mountain peasants, so as to clear up the misunderstandings that we think have arisen concerning the reality of the problem and the real possibilities of solving it.

e. To begin again the agricultural and tourist-oriented projects that will do the country good and not affect the ecosystem significantly.

f. To take, every year, an active part in supporting the National Reforestation project.

g. Not to forget fruit trees in the plan for reforestation.

67. In the long run, we must deal with reforestation of endangered areas. All the experts agree that we would have to replant at least 600,000 hectares of the most important watersheds and take conservation measures for, among others, the two national parks in the Cordillera Central, in order to secure the water supply the country must have. To get this done in a reasonable amount of time could compel us to spend yearly a sum equivalent to one-tenth of our national budget.

68. To prepare for this undeferable large-scale project, we would be pleased to see a number of approaches that would take a moderate amount of time to accomplish, among which we suggest the following:

a. To determine, with the help of foreign and native technologists, exactly how every bit of soil in the Dominican Republic can be put to its best possible use and to revise the laws to establish a legal system regulating the proper use of the soil, regardless of who owns the land.

A national strategy for the restoration of the country's woodland

b. To devise a national strategy to restore our country's woodlands. As we see it, this strategy would not do any good if it did not include the previously mentioned approach. It could also include special training for groups of peasants and for the armed forces and park police in this area. In addition, it could require reforestation work as a prerequisite for high-school and college graduation.

c. To design programs to guarantee an adequate living standard for those whom misery presently forces to plunder resources.

d. To educate the citizenry of the Dominican Republic generally about environmental matters, using educational mass-media and formal education, and requiring adequate schooling in conservation for technologists and peasants who are planning to earn a living from forestry.

e. To reinforce and take advantage of the experimental work the country is completing in tree-culture education for the peasants.

69. As for non-renewable resources, we are also concerned with the use of the commodities produced by our mining industries.

70. These mineral resources have been here for millions of years and belong to all citizens of the Dominican Republic, those living and those yet unborn.

71. Consequently, it is immoral for the benefits coming from mineral resources to go mainly to international corporations, or for those in power to feel pressured into using up these profits for immediate, non-priority expenditures. Extraction of mineral resources is fully justified only when the benefits derived are used for permanent programs that will allow the Dominican Republic to be a place where citizens can live and work as befits human beings.

72. Benefits that accrue from mining of non-renewable natural resources can be well spent, when we have risen above immediate pressures, to cover the costs of the nation's ecological recovery.

73. We are aware that the proper care and recovery of our renewable natural resources is everybody's job. However, the government, as administrator of the state, has the obligation to direct and coordinate this most important task, and all citizens ought to understand that.

The government has the obligation of safeguarding the natural resources

74. The state, as representative of both present and coming generations, must guarantee the use of natural resources to satisfy immediate needs while also holding itself accountable to future generations.

75. It is imperative that we form a leadership organization with real authority that can inspire, coordinate, account for, and regulate everything relative to natural resources in their ecological aspect.

76. There is much that the Church can do in the area of morality and in cooperating with the experts in technical fields in their task of promoting and assisting development. Faithful to a centuries-long tradition in this respect, the Church is committed to this work.

77. We direct that parish clergy, presidents of parish councils, lay ministers, and all pastoral workers pay close attention to the obligations of human beings toward nature. Let them teach special catechetical lessons on this subject. Let them organize days of study and reflection. Let them adapt the old customs and feasts of an agricultural

era, giving particular attention to recurring events like Arbor Day or the planting or harvest of some specific fruit of the earth (e.g., coffee, cocoa, olive oil, tobacco). In their counseling, let them advise people to be conscious of sins against the environment and against nature. Let them respond enthusiastically to every initiative that points toward the protection or betterment of nature. Let them not be afraid to propose toward this end whatever kind of "lay ministry" they see as helpful. . . . There are, certainly, places where, for example, the parish and the worshipping community could be the ideal agency to take the responsibility of being the "tree nursery" or the "seed bed", and so on, for their region.

To sensitize the consciences to sins against the environment and nature

78. We congratulate those parish priests who have already begun to develop among their faithful initiatives and action toward reforestation.

79. There are five Catholic radio stations in this country. These stations have strong influence over the peasants because they have earned and deserve the confidence and respect of the country-folk. They are "Radio Santa María" in La Vega; "Radio Seibo" in Seibo; "Radio Enriquillo" in Tamayo; "Radio Marien" in Dajabón; and "Radio ABC" in the capital. We ask them to make this project very much their own. We hope they will come together and make plans for various community programs. Let them exhort, inspire, inform, instruct, denounce all negative practices, propose other positive and necessary actions, support all constructive initiatives, cooperate, and be ever alert. They can do a lot in the area of ecology. Let them do it enthusiastically and creatively.

80. We direct that the national Catholic weekly, *Camino*, keep up this campaign. We shall make the same suggestion to all other Catholic publications.

81. We shall also make a public request to Caritas Dominicana, an information, publicity, and assistance agency of the Church on a national level, and to the various diocesan and parish human resource centers, to integrate into their plans and programs the ecological problem in all its ramifications. They can always count on our support and encouragement in this regard. It should be feasible to carry out many of these ecological programs in coordination with parish clergy.

Ecological education in schools

82. Finally, we ask the Catholic institutions of higher learning and the schools in general to give an ecological education from the primary grades on. Let them implant in future generations a deep love and respect for nature, and let them teach those future generations to be aware that morality extends to the environment.

83. Let us now conclude with some inspired reflections from the Book of Sirach:

The works of God are all of them good; in its own time every need is supplied. At his word the waters become still as in a flask; he had but to speak and the reservoirs were made. He has but to command and his will is done; nothing can limit his achievement. The works of all mankind are present to him; not a thing escapes his eye. His gaze spans all the ages; to him there is nothing unexpected. No cause then to say: "What is the purpose of this?" Everything is chosen to satisfy a need (Sir 39:16–21).

84. In conclusion: we planned to write this pastoral letter on a subject that affects all citizens of the Dominican Republic, on the Feast of Our Lady of Divine Grace, Protectress of our country. She has always interceded efficaciously in our favor before God. She has done so especially at critical times and in difficult undertakings. Once again, we beg her maternal protection, and place our task under her sheltering mantle, that she may watch over this work that is of such urgency for the people of the Dominican Republic: the reforestation of our country.

Santo Domingo
Feast of Our Lady
of Divine Grace
January 21, 1987

THE CHALLENGE OF MORAL LIVING

Pastoral Reflections by the
Canadian Conference of Catholic Bishops,
for the Use of Priests, Catechists, and
Other Pastoral Workers

Prepared by the Episcopal Commission for Theology

Introduction

1. In our Pastoral Reflections on Jesus Christ[1] we have tried to renew and strengthen people's faith in Jesus as the centre of the universe and of history. We answered some of the questions and concerns about Jesus which they have shared with us as bishops, with their parish priests, or with religious educators. In this present message on the challenge of moral living, we wish to continue these efforts of helping and supporting through our teaching the work of all those who have a special place in the proclamation of the gospel.

These reflections are addressed in a particular way to priests, catechists, and other pastoral workers. We share these thoughts as elements of reflection for our pastoral collaborators. What we say here is not all that can be said about this vast and crucial question. It is our hope that, encouraged and enlightened by our reflections, these pastoral leaders, in turn, will help all Catholics understand and appreciate better the call of moral goodness. In this way, all people of God will reach fullness of life with greater clarity and commitment.

2. In a time of widespread indifference about right and wrong, we must recall clearly and reaffirm forcefully the need for moral values and their central role for true happiness in life. In a time of deep moral confusion, we wish to point out once again how to find and follow the path of goodness and truth. As the Holy Father said during his 1984 visit to Ottawa:

[1] *Jesus Christ, Centre of the Christian Life*, Canadian Conference of Catholic Bishops, 1981.

If the world no longer dares to speak about God, it expects from the Church, and especially from the bishops and from the priests, a word which witnesses to God with strength and conviction, in a persuasive and adapted language, without ever reducing the greatness of the message to the expectation of the listeners.[2]

3. Our reflections will first show how the norms for moral living are given for our own good. Our God is a living God who gives life and guides his children to glory.

Norms for moral living given for our good

As human persons we walk this road toward life in freedom. It is a difficult and sometimes unforeseen road to follow. We must search for it with care and sincerity.

However, as we will see in Part III, we are guided on our journey by the wisdom of past generations. They have left with us universal values and norms that enlighten our conscience and urge us on to do right.

All people can learn from the lessons of history, but as Christians we receive added strength and guidance through the work of the Holy Spirit. Strengthened by his light, we become able to follow Jesus with greater love and in more complete truth.

I

Moral Living: The Path toward Fullness of Life

Humanity's quest for happiness

4. The desire for happiness and fulfillment is a basic thrust in the life of all people. This longing for ultimate self-realization and success drives us on, even if we experience failure and frustration. Indeed, many psychologists today base their theories of personality development on this desire for self-fulfillment, and many philosophers see self-realization as the criterion that determines the goodness of our actions.

Such an analysis of morality is not a new phenomenon for the Church. Christian tradition has always looked at personal fulfillment as a central goal of moral living. No doubt, there is a need to recall this basic insight of our own tradition, but it must be done in a way that spells out the true meaning of this principle. The Christian notion of fulfillment is very different from any egoistic pursuit of individual happiness. Christian self-realization calls us to grow in self-discipline and to reach out to others, especially to God, creator of heaven and earth and father of Jesus Christ.

Christian self-realization requires self-discipline

[2] Published in the *Canadian Catholic Review* 2 (1984) 76.

A call to fullness of life

5. At times, moral discourse, especially Catholic moral teaching, has been perceived as contrary to our deep-felt desire for happiness. This false impression may have been reinforced by certain presentations of morality that were overly concerned with laws and duties. In reality, however, and in the eyes of faith, it is clear that this inner force and desire for fulfillment and happiness is something beautiful and basic. God himself has placed it in our hearts. Sin often tempts us to pursue false and misleading aspirations, but God's original design remains unchanged. He wants all of us to be happy, free from every bondage, and perfect according to our own highest abilities. Many years ago, St. Irenaeus of Lyon expressed this very teaching in his magnificent phrase: "It is the living human being who is God's glory",[3] i.e., the glory of people who shine forth wholeness and who reach "the fullness of their being".[4]

A reality taught by the Bible

6. The very first pages of the Scriptures speak of this divine plan in the splendid account of humanity's creation. Having called Adam and Eve into being, God blessed them and said: "Be fruitful, multiply, fill the earth and conquer it. Be masters of the fish of the sea, the birds of heaven and all living animals on the earth." And the text concludes: "God saw all he had made, and indeed it was very good" (Gen 1:26–28).

At the heart of the Gospel, Jesus' own message is one of good news, a "good news" of salvation and wholeness. His promise is happiness and fulfillment: "How happy are the poor in spirit, theirs is the kingdom of heaven. . . . Happy those who mourn: they shall be comforted . . ." (Mt 5:3–11).

Nor should we forget the Book of Revelation and its great vision of the new Jerusalem where God's original design will come to completion. Here God lives among humanity.

> He will make his home among them, they shall be his people, and he will be their God, his name is God-with-them. He will wipe away all tears from their eyes, there will be no more death, and no more mourning or sadness. The world of the past has gone (Rev 21:1–4).

---

[3] *Adversus Haereses*, IV, 20:7.
[4] Cf. John Paul II, General Audience, July 27, 1983. In: *Osservatore Romano*, August 1, 1983, 3.

Fullness of life and life's shortcomings

7. Each of these texts in its own way confirms the Bible as a message of salvation, a truly real and concrete salvation that is intimately linked with our aspirations and that affects every dimension of our innermost lives.[5] True, perfect happiness cannot be reached in this world. At times, the trials of life slow our path and suffering threatens to overwhelm our hopes. Yet, we are always sustained by our faith in the Creator's unfailing desire for our fulfillment and joy. Indeed, God's intervention in history by entering a covenant with his people, the sacrifice of his own son on the Cross and his triumph over death in the Resurrection, and the sending forth of the Church through the outpouring of the Spirit at Pentecost, all of these saving actions are meant to answer our deepest yearnings and bring us true and ever-lasting joy and happiness through communion with God himself.

II
Finding the Path toward Life

We take the road toward life in freedom

8. As human beings, we are free to follow or reject the path of goodness. Animals are guided by instinct rather than reason, but humans are left free to make their own decisions (cf. Sir 15, 14). As St. Paul says, we must strive "to discover the will of God and know what is good, what it is that God wants, what is the perfect thing to do" (Rom 12:2).[6]

We are free to follow or reject goodness

In other words, we must accept the grave challenge of finding the meaning of true happiness and discover the path toward it. God offers himself to us in freedom, a call that we can accept joyfully or refuse at our peril. We may draw closer to the fountain of life that will quench our thirst for happiness, or we may neglect it and move away from the true fulfillment of our deepest desires. In sum, we are called to take charge of our lives and to answer for our actions.

[5] In our message on sickness and healing we spoke at length of the health and life-giving power of God our Father. Cf. *A Pastoral Message on Sickness and Healing*, Canadian Conference of Catholic Bishops, 1983, Part I.

[6] See also the *Pastoral Constitution on the Church in the Modern World of Vatican II*, No. 17.

A difficult and sometimes unforeseen road to follow

9. No doubt, self-realization and self-fulfillment, "achieving the fullness of one's personal being",[7] are noble but also eminently difficult tasks. There are many roads we can follow, some leading to life but others to corruption. There are many choices we can make, but not all are equally valid. From our own life experience we know that some decisions bring immediate satisfaction and yet, in the long run, they endanger our well-being because, at root, they attack family life, promote injustice, or spread ill-health. Other examples would be the actions of people who use narcotics, of people who deliberately break their promises, or of those who use others for their own profit.

Other decisions seem to negate our desires at first, but, in the end, they bring a more authentic fulfillment to our lives. Such is the case, for example, with people who spend much of their leisure time on community work or with couples who give up many comforts to welcome a new child in their midst.

Some decisions are morally right in themselves and others wrong

Some decisions are morally right or wrong in themselves

10. All through our lives, and often in difficult and complex circumstances, we must strive to discover that which leads to real growth and that which leads to destruction. In other words, we must discover what is morally good and what is morally evil. However, this search is not an arbitrary one. As Vatican II teaches:

> In the depths of our consciences, we detect a law which we do not impose on ourselves, but which holds us to obedience. . . . For human persons have in their hearts a law written by God. To obey it is the very dignity of people; according to it they will be judged".[8]

Some choices, by their very nature, help people and society grow. Others are negative and destructive forces in themselves, even though the people who take these decisions do so in good faith and with the best of intentions.

Moral good promotes growth. Moral evil destroys

11. This is the very point moral philosophers affirm when they speak of objective moral good and evil. The moral good is what preserves life and leads to its fullness. It allows people as individuals and as a society to grow and to find true fulfillment. Moral evil, on the other

---

[7] John Paul II, General Audience, July 27, 1983. In: *Osservatore Romano*, August 1, 1983, 3.

[8] *Pastoral Constitution on the Church in the Modern World*, No. 16.

hand, hinders people's authentic development and of the world around them.

As human persons we have a clear and special destiny in God's plan. Our growth as people depends, therefore, on specific forces and structures that can be discovered. As Pope John Paul II said recently:

> Human persons are gifted with a truth of their own, with an intrinsic order of their own, with a make-up of their own. When their deeds are in harmony with this order, with the make-up proper to a human person created by God, they are good deeds "which God prepared for us in advance".

And the Holy Father continued:

> The goodness of our acting springs from a deep harmony between our personal being and our acts, while on the contrary, moral evil signals a break, a profound division between the person who is acting and his or her actions. The order inscribed in our being, that order which is our proper good, is no longer respected in and by our actions. The human person is no longer in his or her truth. Moral evil is precisely the evil of the person as such; moral good is the good of the person as such.[9]

The need for careful and critical reflection

12. Reflecting on these affirmations, we realize with even greater clarity how important our decisions are and how grave is the responsibility that flows from this reality.

These affirmations also highlight our basic and vital duty to question our own first-hand aspirations and to ask in truth: Is the action I am about to take morally good? Will it help me grow as a person and advance the growth of people around me? Does this action lead to greater service of others? Will it really respond to the depth of my being, or am I giving in to fleeting and superficial desires? Does it make life more human? Will my decision reflect God's plan for my life? All of these considerations are moral questions of the highest order. The answers we give will influence profoundly our own existence and happiness and, indeed, the future of all people around us.

The danger of "doing what others do"

13. To follow through with this critical analysis of our actions is not an easy task. Often enough, we would like to remain shallow in our

---

[9] John Paul II, General Audience, July 20, 1983. In: *Osservatore Romano*, July 25, 1983, 3.

scrutiny and simply follow the behaviour of others. In recent years, traditional attitudes and norms have disappeared or come under heavy attack, and formerly all-powerful authorities have been weakened. This may make us feel more liberated, more autonomous and adult than before. However, reality is different. Our moral decisions are under enormous pressures from social trends and the media. Sports figures, entertainers, and TV stars all exercise a subtle or not so subtle influence on our conscience. Consider the hidden but pervasive impact of slogans, of stereotypes, and of the standard "that everyone does it". An especially powerful example is the myth that only the young, athletic, beautiful, and rich are worthy of our attention and esteem. Lack of commitment and responsibility is presented as desirable. No doubt, if we would seriously study the influence of this stereotype on our lives, we would find a surprising impact on our attitudes and decisions.

Social trends and the media exert pressure

Our desire for immediate satisfaction

14. A second threat to our freedom is the unbridled desire for immediate gratification. Often the prospect of instant pleasure makes us avoid serious moral reflection and analysis. This danger is especially prevalent in our consumer society, a society of impatience where our wishes must be realized as quickly as possible. It almost seems as though we were caught up in a race to have everything at once. "Wait no more", we are told. Buying on credit, catching up with fast-changing fashions, racing against the clock are all symptoms of our haste to have.

The need to form and renew our conscience daily

15. Faced with these pressures from within ourselves and from without, we need to reflect and meditate constantly on our actions. We must learn how to fight and become free of trends and forces that promote instant pleasure and partial fulfillment. "Becoming free" means probing our heart and listening quietly to its message so as to discover our deepest goals in life and how to achieve them. It means being open to all aspects of life, becoming aware of the real powers active in society and within ourselves. It means forming and renewing our conscience daily, discovering what makes us grow as individuals and what humanizes the world around us. This is our first moral duty if we wish to follow the Lord's call.

Daily need to form and renew our conscience

III
The Light of Moral Values and Norms

Values express the wisdom of history

16. As we have seen, the challenge of moral living is central for our fulfillment as human persons. It is a difficult task, but we need not face it alone. We can benefit from the experience of history, which has identified for us the moral values that are essential for integral human development and happiness. Dignity of the person, respect for life, justice, goodness, unselfishness, honesty, sincerity, loyalty, fidelity, truthfulness, moderation, courage, participation, solidarity, forgiveness: these are some of the values that we must strive for and be guided by if we want to be faithful to ourselves and achieve wholeness. These values serve as guide-posts for our actions and, at the same time, they challenge us to grow in goodness.

Whoever disregards these values recommended by the wisdom of generations—and confirmed by the word of God—will become a slave to his or her environment and instincts. Disrespect for these basic principles of human living can only lead in the end to failure and despair. The same principle holds true for communities and nations. As soon as a society loses its sense of justice, its respect for human dignity, or its sincerity, decadence and corruption take hold. We cannot be truly positive and constructive in our lives and at the same time fail to honour these fundamental guidelines. Moral values sharpen the call of our conscience to do good.

Norms translate values into practical terms of action

17. Several times in history, these values have been set down in clear charters of rights and duties to signify their vital importance for personal and community living. For example, if we read the Ten Commandments in this light, we realize how much these norms serve to protect and promote our humanity. Most of the interdictions they express signify in negative form some very central and positive values:

The Ten Commandments

> Honour your father and your mother . . . You shall not kill . . . You shall not commit adultery . . . You shall not steal . . . You shall not bear false witness against your neighbour . . . You shall not covet your neighbour's house (Ex 20:12–17).

Committing such acts means destroying one's community and thus destroying one's own being. Humanity has had this unfortunate experience all too often in the destructive horror of wars and of other social diseases.

Some values and norms are universally valid

18. Thus it is easy to see why, after the dark years of World War II, we felt the need to enshrine these values in the *Universal Declaration of Human Rights*. The forceful preamble of this declaration affirms the need to base all our collective and individual decisions on a deep respect for the dignity of each person. As the text says:

> Recognition of the inherent dignity and of the equal and inalienable rights of all members of the human family is the foundation of freedom, justice and peace in the world. Disregard and contempt for human rights have resulted in barbarian acts which have outraged the conscience of mankind, and the advent of a world in which human beings shall enjoy freedom of speech and belief and freedom from fear and want, has been proclaimed as the highest aspiration of the common people.

Hence, beginning with Article One, there is a claim of universally valid rights and duties: "All human beings are born free and equal in dignity and rights. They are endowed with reason and conscience and should act toward one another in a spirit of brotherhood."[10]

Values and norms protect and promote humanity

19. Our search for happiness will be in vain unless we accept these universal norms and the values they promote. Moral values protect humanity in people and help us discover our true inner destiny. They help protect against violence, pride, distrust, selfishness, and hate. They prevent us from destroying people by using them as simple means.

IV
Walking the Path of Life Guided by the Holy Spirit

Only communion with God brings true fulfillment

20. Moral values and norms help our search for happiness. However, there is another dynamic at work in our world that stirs our hearts and leads us toward true self-realization. This is the dynamic of salvation and grace which joins our deepest aspirations and brings

---

[10] *Universal Declaration of Human Rights*. United Nations, Preamble and Article One.

fulfillment that goes beyond the inherent powers of nature. St. Irenaeus not only links God's glory and humanity. He goes on to say human life is the vision of God. In this way we come to know what reason alone could not have discovered: only in communion with the living God do we find true fulfillment and real happiness. Life's meaning and the road toward it have thus been revealed more clearly. We realize with certainty that concern for our own fulfillment means following our deepest desire for communion with God, but through the way of the cross.

The Holy Spirit guides us and God's love surrounds us

21. This path of life was charted for us by Jesus Christ himself. Renewed and reborn as Christians by the waters of baptism, we can rely on the presence of the Holy Spirit in us. He is our light and strength. He helps us find the right path as if by instinct and gives us courage to walk on this road. The Holy Spirit introduces us into the mysteries of God and helps us discover this extraordinary message that changes our whole outlook on life: God is truly Father for us all and we are his children. The proof that you are children is that God has sent the Spirit of his Son into our hearts: the Spirit that cries, 'Abba, Father' (see Gal 4:6). And elsewhere St. Paul writes: "This hope is not deceptive, because the love of God has been poured into our hearts by the Holy Spirit which has been given to us" (Rom 5:5).

Our whole life has been transformed by God's love, which has been revealed to us, and our desire for happiness has been strengthened by it. Joyfully we realize: we are not left alone in an absurd and meaningless universe but preceded and held by God's love, whatever our sin, weakness, or limitation. Thus we learn how to wonder at our own life, how to receive it with gratitude and become trustful.

Our life transformed by God's love

We respond in love

22. And then, from the depth of our being and supported by the action of the Holy Spirit, that fundamental attitude arises which enlivens our actions and transforms our judgment, namely love. We begin to realize and appreciate the central message and deepest call of the gospel:

> You must love the Lord and God with all your heart, with all your soul, and with all your mind. This is the greatest and the first command-ment. The second resembles it: You must love your neighbour as

yourself. On these two commandments hang the whole Law, and the Prophets also (Mt 22:37–40).

From now on, love will be at the heart of all our actions.

A self-giving love

23. Christian love means following God on a path that is often unforeseen. We know there will be suffering and the cross. The demands on us will be radical. They will require self-denial, the gift of self, and forgiveness, on the example of Jesus himself, who, on the Cross, gave up his own life for our salvation. Love of God and of neighbour is the basis of moral life and of human fulfillment, but a love that is true and total, that welcomes others and is truly open to them. Such love seeks out and accepts peace and reconciliation. At this very point where we give our life to welcome others, we will find, to our surprise, the self-realization and wholeness we desire. As the Gospel says: "Anyone who wants to save his or her life will lose it; but all who lose their lives for my sake, they will save it" (Lk 9:24).

True, total love of God and neighbor is required

In a culture marked by desperate striving for the pleasures of money, comfort, and power, we must recall clearly the challenge of the gospel, a challenge whose truth is confirmed by our own deepest experiences. In the bond of true love and lasting commitment, we find our very freedom. In active solidarity and sharing with others, we find that joy which led Mary to exult in the work of the Spirit.

A path of daily renewal and growth

24. The challenge is clear, but we all know the experience of weakness, of being lax in our commitment, and of selfishness. As St. Paul reminds us, evil continues to pursue us, even though we have received the Spirit's pledge and have been marked by his seal (2 Cor 1:22). Thus, we need to distinguish carefully between the work of the Spirit and that of sin. "When self-indulgence is at work", says St. Paul, "the results are obvious: fornication, gross indecency and sexual irresponsibility, idolatry and sorcery; feuds and wranglings, jealousy, bad temper and quarrels; disagreements, factions, envy, drunkenness, orgies, and similar things." And St. Paul adds the terrible admonition: "I warn you now, as I warned you before: those who behave like this will not inherit the kingdom of God."

On the other hand, the shining fruits of the Spirit are: "Love, joy, peace, patience, kindness, goodness, trustfulness, gentleness and self-control. There can be no law against things like that, of course" (Gal 5:19–23).

If we reflect carefully on our actions and the fruits they bring forth, we will realize evermore where change is needed and that without it, true love cannot grow.

Listening to the Word of God

25. In this journey of moral growth, we need to rely heavily on the word of God, especially the gospel. The gospel is foremost a message of hope, but also of radical challenge. Prodding the depth and quality of our innermost thoughts, it forces us to drop our illusions and face reality. It makes us look at people and events in a new light, and work for justice. For example, reading the Sermon on the Mount, we will realize the need for our own conversion. How will we respond to the words of Jesus who exhorts us:

> But I say this to you: anyone who is angry with his brother will answer for it before the court. . . . But I say this to you: if a man looks at a woman lustfully, he has already committed adultery with her in his heart. . . . If any one hits you on the right cheek, offer the other as well. . . . But I say this to you: love your enemies and pray for those who persecute you, in this way you will be children of your Father in heaven, for he causes his sun to rise on the bad as well as the good, and his rain to fall on honest and dishonest people alike (Mt 5:22, 27, 39, 44–45).

These words do not tell us exactly what to do in every situation, but they point the way. They disturb our complacency and in this way open the way to conversion and growth. Only if we reflect deeply and prayerfully on the challenge of the gospel will we transform our hearts and follow the right path.

Guided by the teachings of the Church and the example of the saints

26. The Bible text is not the only guide for our conscience in the complex and ever-changing circumstances of our lives. God's word lives on throughout the ages in the community of those who believe in Jesus Christ. As his Church, they are together guided by the Holy Spirit. Catholics can rely on the teachings of the Holy Father and the bishops—Council documents, encyclicals, messages of the Bishops' Conference or of individual bishops—as they exercise their ministry of proclaiming "the truth which is Christ" and "the principles of the moral order which spring from human nature itself". [11]

The Bible, the Church, and the saints are our guides

[11] Vatican II, *Declaration on Religious Liberty*, No. 14.

These messages—just as the example of the saints who lived before us and the witness of Christians today who base their whole lives in Christ—probe the specific call of the gospel for each generation and help us follow the road toward Christ. The whole Church, as the community of believers, must listen to the Spirit of God and in this way discern that which is good and worthy of praise.

Conclusion

27. Let us conclude and affirm once again: the final glory of our lives cannot be left to chance, to our fleeting desires, or to the vacillations of social trends. We must take charge of our own lives and exercise freely the responsibilities we have received.

28. This central challenge of moral living implies the need always to renew our conscience. For this we must learn how to pause in silence and reflect critically on our actions. For this we must free ourselves from fascination with public opinion, and learn how to withstand the tempting desire for easy and instant pleasure. In tranquility and openness to the values and norms offered by the wisdom of history, we must search for what is best in us and for us. In prayer we must open our hearts to the call of God's word as it frees us from sin and enables us to love in all truth. We must search together as a community of believers, especially with those who suffer, and welcome the guidance of the Church's pastors. In the final analysis: we must welcome Jesus in our lives.

29. "Fear not: open your doors wide for Christ Jesus".[12] These words of our Holy Father are central because God's design is fulfilled in Jesus Christ. He reveals for us the true meaning of life. Through the gift of his Spirit he frees us from ourselves, widens our hearts, and opens us to the fullness of life.

Then the way toward happiness and the glory of God will become clearer. Then we will build on a firm and everlasting foundation, just as Christ's own deeds remain with us forever, he who died on the cross but rose again in the light of Easter morning: "I have told you this so that my own joy may be in you and your joy be complete" (Jn 15:11).

---

[12]John Paul II, Homily during the Mass of Inauguration, 1978.

3

ASIA

"GIVE THANKS TO THE LORD.
I AM GOING TO PRISON."

A Letter to the Faithful of Huê

Dear brothers and sisters,

In 1971, during the meetings of the world synod, I made the following statement: "In the past, many bishops have died to safeguard the interests of the Church. But today does there exist a bishop who is ready to die for the defense of the rights of man?" Therefore I am happy today: the Lord is calling me to suffer prison and death for the defense of the rights of man and for justice.

The Decree on Religion, signed at Hanoi on June 14, 1955, by the president of the Democratic Republic of Vietnam, Ho Chi Minh, and by the President of the National Assembly, Pham Van Dông, in chapter 4, article 13, affirms: "The civil authority does not intervene in the internal affairs of religions. The relations between the Vietnamese Catholic Church and the Holy See of Rome constitute an internal affair." Article 14 adds: "Religious organizations must respect the legislation of the Democratic Republic of Vietnam, just like other organizations of the people."

But when this legislation goes against the divine will, it violates the rights of man, the most fundamental of which is freedom of religion, just as I have maintained also in the deposition given to the police of the province of Binh Tri Thien, on October 15, 1984: "Like the apostles of old and the martyrs of each generation, I must obey the law of God rather than the law of men." Without doubt, the consequences will be prison and death. Your pastor is ready today to suffer these consequences. Rather, he accepts them willingly, as

Since the unification of Vietnam, we know very little about the situation of the Church in that country. So it has seemed important to us to report the letter of Mons. Nguyên-Kim-Diên, archbishop of Huê, an important port city of Vietnam. This letter is evidence of a state of suffering, but also of courageous witnessing on the part of believers. Written in October of 1985, the letter was published by France-Asie and translated into English by Lawrence Romani.

the reward that the Lord is granting him after twenty-five years as bishop, twenty-two of which were in the service of the diocese of Huê.

When I am arrested, I ask you not to believe any statement, even if it bears a signature produced as if it were mine.

In this hour, dear brothers and sisters, I ask of you one thing alone: give thanks with me to the Lord, and intensify your prayers so that I may remain absolutely faithful to the Lord and to the Church until my last breath.

I entrust you all, brothers and sisters, to the Lord, to our Lady of Lavang. I give you my loving benediction.

Praise to Christ Jesus.

Huê, October 19, 1985

Ph. Nguyên-Kim-Diên
Archbishop of Huê

VOCATION AND MISSION OF THE LAITY IN THE CHURCH AND SOCIETY OF ASIA

Fourth Plenary Assembly of the Asian Bishops' Conference

1.0 Preamble

1.1 May your kingdom come! (Lk 11:2). This prayer of Jesus is a cry from the heart of Asia—Asia, an arena of conflict and division, the world's exploited marketplace, the continent of suffering humanity; Asia, cradle of culture, birthplace of great religions, a continent awakening to new and gigantic responsibilities.

1.2 May your kingdom come! The plea is both a vocation and a challenge to the Church.

The Fourth Assembly of the Asian Bishops' Conference (FABC) was held in Tokyo, Japan, September 16–25, 1986. The purpose of this assembly was to reflect upon the themes of the bishops' synod of 1987. At its conclusion, the Asian bishops composed this statement (published in Asia Focus on September 12, 1986, here reprinted).

1.3 The battered condition of Asia is before us. Its poverty, wretchedness, and misery bear in themselves the contradictions of humanity. Asia "groans with pain, like the pain of childbirth" (Rom 8:22). It "waits for God" to set its "whole being free" (Rom 8:23).

1.4 Deep in the heart of Asia, the paschal mystery of Jesus is being remembered, becomes present, and is relived. The immersion into the darkness of suffering, pain, death, and despair brings the light of the Resurrection—its hope, justice, love, and peace, integral liberation. This we believe because of the promise of the Father.

1.5 We believe that he is calling us to be instruments of his work of liberation. The Spirit of Jesus enables us to discern his call, and we want to listen to his voice today. Our hope based on the paschal mystery of Jesus urges us to discover how we can be the instruments of God, the harbingers of the good news of integral liberation for Asia.

2.0 *FABC Background*

2.1 Therefore, we bishops of Asia have come together in Tokyo, Japan, with laity, Religious, and priests, for the Fourth Plenary Assembly of the Federation of Asian Bishops' Conferences (FABC).

2.2 This gathering of ours with the laity marks a very important moment in our common journey that began in Manila in 1970. In that meeting, as well as in Taipei in 1974, we directed our gaze to the task of the Church in the world of Asia. Our gathering in Calcutta in 1978 brought us to the realization that prayer and interiority are indispensable ingredients in facing the tremendous challenges in this continent. When we met in Bangkok in 1982 for the Third Plenary Assembly, it became clear to us that we had to respond to the call of the Lord together, as a community of faith.

2.3 This Fourth Assembly has brought us a deeper and renewed awareness of the urgency of the call, and the need to accelerate the pace of our involvement, since we experience a deep crisis in every sector and a threat to human life and dignity. In the face of the manifold challenges of Asia, we have reflected prayerfully on the theme: "The Vocation and Mission of the Laity in the Church and in the World of Asia". These reflections are made in deep communion with the universal Church. The presence in our plenary assembly of representatives from the Holy See and from other episcopal conferences and federations has helped us to deepen this communion.

2.4 The contribution by countless numbers of the laity to the life of faith among the people of God in Asia cannot be measured. The saga of the laity themselves, preserving their faith through long centuries of their history in countries such as Korea and Japan, stirs

The heroic story of the Asian laity

our imagination and inspires our hearts. Under changed circumstances, today the laity of Asia continue to share zealously in the mission of the Church as a leaven in the world and a sign of the reign of God. Many laymen and laywomen are also serving as missionaries in countries other than their own, in various continents. We are grateful to the Lord and to our coworkers, the laity, for this ineffable grace.

3.0 Challenges of Asia

3.0.1 We need to confront the dark realities in the heart of Asia—not in order to moan and wail in despair, but in order that we may be challenged by the magnitude of the task and thus place our hope in the Lord, who remains, despite our valiant efforts, the ultimate builder of the kingdom (see Ps 127).

3.0.2 A basic presupposition. We are keenly aware that the struggle for a full human life is not confined to the Christian community. We acknowledge that there are many great religious traditions in Asia which form the basis of the establishment, growth, and development of the many cultures and nations in this great continent. In solidarity with them, we seek the full flowering of the human person and the transformation of the world of Asia into that which pleases the Creator (see Gen 1).

3.1 Politics and the community of believers

3.1.1 The impact of misguided and selfish power politics on the reality of Asia today in the form of the massive poverty and degradation is beyond imagining. Today's Asia has spawned structures and relationships in the political and economic community that are widening the scandalous gap between the rich and poor, denying to the latter a just and fair access to the resources of the earth. Repression, oppression, and exploitation are realities that result from the greed of vested economic interests and political power. Ethnic, cultural, and linguistic conflicts which unleash violence, death, and destruction are also linked with economic and political divisions. The political situation in many Asian countries has become volatile, and a sense of insecurity permeates particularly the minority groups.

Dramatic political and social situation

3.1.2 Politics needs, first of all, to become a purposeful activity which seeks the common good. The entire people of God is called to engage in such "politics", for the task of infusing the gospel and kingdom values of love and justice into the political, economic, cultural, and social world of Asia is an imperative of the gospel.

Participation and involvement are duties that flow from the secular implications of the gospel and the reign of God.

3.1.3 The involvement of the lay person in political activity confirms his rootedness in Christ, who called his community of disciples to be a leaven in the world and thus to labor for the common good. A Christian is a member of a God-people and of the wider community, the good of which he is called to promote, protect, and serve. To shut oneself totally away from the demands of the political transformation of Asia is, surely, in a sense, a denial of Christian identity.

3.1.4 Attitudes of apathy and indifference allow injustice to go unchecked and political powers to become masters rather than servants of the people. Evil is permitted to prevail simply because good men and women do nothing about it.

3.1.5 Hence, we have come to discover with joy that in all parts of Asia the laity are growing in political consciousness. Even in countries where the Church is a minority, they are gradually shedding centuries-old indifference. Protests, processions, vigils, and citizen committees organized for the cause of justice and the rights of the poor are the signs of this growing political awareness. The people of the Philippines who, in February of this year, were able to achieve a significant political transformation through active nonviolence inspired by faith in the Lord, have given us much to reflect upon.

The Christian laity are growing in their political awareness

3.1.6 The need of the hour in Asia is for competent and principled lay people to enter into the realm of party politics and, from within, influence the philosophies, programs, and activities of political parties and personalities for the common good in the light of the gospel. We commend the lay persons who already have contributed much to the area of public life.

3.1.7 In the past, the Church tended to limit itself mostly to the protection of its interests regarding religious freedom, the family, and schools. But now the Church is becoming involved in a wider range of issues pertaining to fundamental human rights and freedom, to labor and business, health, women, the arms race, the international order, and other issues of justice and peace that seriously affect the peoples of Asia and especially the poor and the downtrodden.

3.1.8 The response of the Church to the Asian reality has to be communitarian in character, if we hope to respond to the deeply entrenched and widespread network of political, economic, religious, social, and cultural injustices. Such a response will clearly indicate the presence of the creative and transforming power of the Spirit in the community of believers.

3.1.9 The phenomenon of religious revivalism and fundamentalism in various Asian countries is likewise a challenge. The positive aspect of religious revivalism is a challenge to the Christian toward a deeper renewal of his own faith. The negative aspect of the phenomenon, tending to religious dogmatism, fundamentalism, and intolerance in precept and practice, has even led to violence and serious conflicts.

3.1.10 The positive aspect is represented by the holistic view of reality. Asian religious cultures see human beings, society, and the whole universe as intimately related and interdependent. Fragmentation and division contradict this vision. In the light of the gospel, how does the Christian base the struggle for peace, justice, and wholeness in this holistic vision provided by the ancient religions of Asia? The negative aspect of religious fundamentalism challenges the Christian to witness to the radicalism of the gospel of love, even in the most provocative, intricate, and exasperating situations, and to be an instrument of unity and fellowship among various groups.

A dialogue of life with the believers of other religions

3.1.11 In every situation, the whole Church is called to a dialogue of life with fellow Christians of other churches, the billions of other religions, and the members of various social groups. Since the laity live in a more direct and day-to-day contact with people of other faiths, they are the ones most called to this living dialogue, especially regarding common problems which affect the life of the community.

3.1.12 Among such problems are: issues of fundamental rights, the rights of tribals and other minority groups, problems of political, social, economic, and religious development, and of justice and peace. Here, collaboration is necessary at the local, regional, and international level.

3.2 The youth of Asia

3.2.1 The youth of Asia are the mirror of Asia. Of the total population, 60% are between fifteen and twenty-four years of age. The life of the youth reflects Asia's manifold economic, political, cultural, religious, and educational problems.

3.2.2 One side of the picture of the life of the Asian youth is more visibly negative. Many are living under wretched conditions, unable because of poverty to liberate themselves from the bondage of ignorance and illiteracy, and are shackled to a life severly limited by inadequate skills and knowledge. They are also vulnerable to the temptations of materialism and consumerism; they become prey to various ideologies that claim to offer liberation from poverty and injustice. And because the doors of education are often closed to them, the sense of social belonging, already eroded by abject material conditions, is even more seriously weakened. Many among those who have had the benefits of education and find themselves unemployed or underemployed, or who see the inconsistencies between what schooling has taught them and what society practices and values, look for security and acceptance in the wrong place and among their often equally confused peers. Anxiety about the future, the apparent hopelessness of the present, alienation, and other pressures drive them to seek escape in destructive substitutes like drugs, alcoholism, suicide, vandalism, premarital sex, and delinquency.

3.2.3 There is also a positive side to the life of our Asian youth. We have discovered in our gathering that in the present struggles for social transformation in various parts of Asia, the youth are playing a substantial role. They are involved in awakening the consciousness of the people; organizing and mobilizing groups working for justice and peace; serving as community health workers, catechists, and leaders of Christian communities, organizers and members of pastoral teams, etc. They live their lives in witness to kingdom values; they stand out in contrast to those whose lives seem aimless, immature, and hedonistic. The idealism of youth, their energy, zeal, and determination, their commitment—these are some seeds of the kingdom within them. The Lord's call to be a leaven in the world resonates in a special way in the hearts of Asia's youth.

The situation of the young people of Asia

3.2.4 Full support and acceptance, trust, and confidence, presence, and availability on the part of other members of God's young people will surely empower the youth to become evangelizers, messengers, and instruments of God—not only among their peers, but also among their elders and in the wider society. On the other hand, nonacceptance and lack of support could lead to further alienation. Alienated from their families, from the wider society, and from the people of God, the youth would have no other option but rebellion or despair.

3.2.5 The youth of Asia are the Asia of today. The compulsive struggles for liberation in Asia are reflected in the pains of growth among the youth and in their deepest longings for a new world and a meaning for life. The people of God in Asia must become in a certain sense a "Church of the young", if it is to transform the "face of Asia, the continent of the young" (see Asian Bishops' Meeting, Manila, 1970).

3.3 The laity and the plight of Asian women

3.3.1 International media have highlighted how tourism and the entertainment industries have exploited, degraded, and dehumanized Asian women. However, this is but one aspect of the reality of Asian women today. Many are the injustices heaped upon them because of the traditional societies which discriminate against them, and because of the new economic and industrial situations. Dowry, forced marriages, wife-beating, and destruction of female fetuses weigh

Tragic situation of Asian women

heavily on them, driving many to desperation and even suicide. Modern industry exploits their work—for example, paying a paltry sum for their hard labor in quarries and on construction sites of local and multinational companies. There is discrimination against them in the employment policies, and as domestic workers they are also abused. In general, Asian society views women as inferior. Such are some of the tragic realities of Asian women that cry out for transformation.

3.3.2 On the other hand, there is a deep and genuine appreciation of women among Asians. A woman is considered the heart of the family. In times of crisis, she is the valiant one on whose shoulders others lean. The advancement and contributions that women have made in the professions—as doctors, lawyers, managers, accountants, political leaders, teachers, etc.—have been phenomenal, despite the obstacles placed in their path by tradition. In the Church, women contribute significantly in various ministries of teaching, healing, catechizing, organizing, etc. They serve as members of pastoral teams. In our assembly we have listened to them and have been made more aware of some fundamental facts and truths about the role of women in Asia.

3.3.3 A woman is an integral human person, no matter what race, class, tribe, or religion she belongs to. She is created in the image and likeness of God. To her too was extended the divine call of being responsible for the created world (Gen 1:27). The tragedy is that this image and likeness of God has been degraded and trampled underfoot and she is dominated in various ways. Therefore, women cry out to the Lord for liberation. We have heard this poignant cry from the women themselves, who have articulated here their deepest longings for dignity and freedom. They remind us that Mary is the Mother of God, that she, a woman, uniquely cooperated with Jesus so that the reign of the Father may come. It is, therefore, not just a human necessity but a gospel imperative that the feminine half of the world's population be recognized and their dignity restored, and that they be allowed to play their rightful role in the world and in the Church.

Women's aspirations for dignity and freedom

3.3.4 The laity thus have a special responsibility in their respective fields—be it in business, education, mass media, politics, or public service—to uphold and defend the dignity of women, and to change attitudes, policies, practices, and legislation that lead to the discrimination against and repression of women.

3.3.5 But recognition of woman's full personhood must equally be evident among the people of God, the Church. For the Church cannot be a sign of the kingdom and of the eschatological community if the gifts of the Spirit to women are not given due recognition, and if women do not share in the "freedom of the children of God".

They expect significant responsibilities in the ministries and decision-making processes of the Church.

3.3.6 The entire people of God would then become a credible sign of the dignity and freedom of women in society and in the world. The Church could then speak powerfully about the plight of Asian women and become their voice, with an authority unlike any other.

3.4 The laity and the family

3.4.1 Perhaps the greatest challenge to the Church in Asia is that posed by the Asian family. The Asian family is the cellular receptacle of all Asia's problems, poverty, repression, exploitation, and degradation, divisions, and conflicts. The family is directly affected by the religious, political, economic, social, and cultural problems of Asia, by the problems relating to women, health, work, business, education, etc.

3.4.2 But certain specific problems have been brought to our attention. We have reflected on them in the light of the gospel. For in the journey toward the reign of God, the Christian travels, not alone, but in community, and not only in a general community but in his own family.

3.4.3 The adverse conditions which Asian families have to face today are serious and many. Mothers and children at a tender age are forced to undertake hard labor or migrate to cities—often to alien countries—in search of employment. A hopeless struggle for survival benumbs the conscience, increases the number of unwed mothers and abandoned children, and causes rampant prostitution and abortion. A contraceptive mentality and population-control programs insensitive to moral and religious sensibilities have resulted in the systematic termination of pregnancies. As a result of such a situation, family life is disrupted seriously, and traditional family values are progressively undermined.

The adverse conditions of Asian families

3.4.4 But we continue to believe that the family as a social unit is a sacred and an important treasure. Most traditions and laws, beliefs, and practices are traceable to the family. Closely-knit family ties, filial piety, care and respect of the aged are among the deeply-rooted cultural values of Asia. Such cultural values and traditions are a source of strength for Asian families in deepening their call and providing the most favorable atmosphere for a life of love and communion.

3.4.5 Since grace builds on nature, the centrality of the sacrament of marriage for Christian families needs to be underlined. In many Asian countries, the Christian atmosphere also has resulted in a great number of vocations to consecrated life, the priesthood, and societies of apostolic life. Christian families have influenced their neighborhood to know and respect the values which Jesus proclaimed and have produced many lay persons who are true witnesses to the gospel in their work and professions.

3.4.6 As they listen to the gospel which calls them to accept their mission in the Church and in the world, the laity will find in the family the most important area for themselves to reflect on.

3.4.7 The first call to be a member of the Church comes normally in the family (see FC, nos. 15, 39, 49). Even before the call is heard in the parish, or the mind opens to the catechetical story of the call to growth and maturity in Christ, the child has already seen, heard, and experienced at home the reality of belonging to the people of God.

The Christian family 3.4.8 The Christian family is rightly referred to as the "domestic Church", where members assist one another toward a fullness of life in Christ through the ordinary circumstances and events of life. At home, in the family setting, in the daily events of living and giving, the lay person interiorizes culture as well as belief with an easy connaturality. In the little church of the family, as in the larger Church of the community, the members remain aware of the presence of God, seek to listen to his word in the Scriptures, and faithfully practice mutual forgiveness and sacrifice.

3.4.9 The values and attitudes necessary for evangelization of the Asian world are first practiced in the family. Love, justice, peace, truth, freedom, concern for the poor and the needy, faith in God, hope in his liberating goodness and power, responsibility and self-sacrifice and other gospel values are first learned by precept and example in the family. Here evangelization initially takes place and a "civilization of love" begins. Thus evangelized, the Asian family is enabled to evangelize, reach out to other families and communities, and together with them journey into the reign of God.

3.4.10 Certainly, the most direct and immediate task of the laity in the community of God is to make prosper within the family this double event, at the same time a grace, of evangelizing and being evangelized.

3.5 The laity in the world of education

3.5.1 Two important factors in the educational scene of Asia immediately strike us: the illiteracy of vast numbers of Asians and the high visibility and reputation of Catholic educational institutions, especially in non-Christian areas. These indeed urge us to reflect not only on the role of the laity, but also on the role of the entire Church in education.

3.5.2 Two of many negative observations are well known to us: that some Catholic schools seem to cater mostly to the middle class and to the rich and that they seem to support traditional structures and values, rather than act as vehicles of change. Such objections are constant reminders of our priorities for the poor and for transformation of society. They should encourage us to undertake regular evaluation, and we should not set these criticisms aside as simply invalid and uninformed.

3.5.3 How, indeed, can our schools reflect the Church's preferential option for the poor? This truly difficult question requires wisdom and evangelical courage. We do not claim to have the answers, but we do wish to make a number of observations.

Catholic schools and the preferential option for the poor

3.5.4 Undoubtedly, our schools in Asia have contributed significantly to the battle against ignorance and illiteracy and have prepared great numbers of people to take their place in society and to contribute to the common good through their professions. And here we acknowledge with deep gratitude the great contribution of the laity, who in the field of education greatly outnumber priests and religious sisters and brothers. The large number of women teachers in primary and secondary education may in a certain sense reflect the image of the Church as *Mater et Magistra*. We may rightly say that the laity in Asia play the major role in the essential task of facilitating the growth and maturity of the human person through formal education. Their role in the educational apostolate arises from their basic baptismal participation, especially in the character of Christ as prophet and servant.

3.5.5 For education in schools to become more effective as a vehicle of transformation in society, a true and proper vision and spirituality among teachers are needed. This vision requires that the task of teaching be viewed as a call from God to share in the teaching ministry of Jesus, who announced and taught about the kingdom, and that teaching is not simply the communication of knowledge but even more importantly the formation of values. From such a vision flows a spirituality involving sacrifice, other-directedness, concern, love, justice, and other gospel values. As in catechesis, the more effective is not the one who simply teaches, but the one who also witnesses (see EN).

3.5.6 The school has become the setting where it is possible for peoples of different faiths, races, backgrounds, social classes, and tribes to become a community. It is also where concern for the poor and the needy and the values necessary to transform the wider society into a true community are actually formed and shared. This kind of community will have to involve the collaboration of the teachers and the families. In a non-Christian environment, such a school community becomes a sign of the peace, justice, and love of God's reign.

3.5.7 We look beyond the formal school system and ask how the laity can carry out the ministry of teaching among out-of-school youth in urban and rural areas. This is not an easy task, yet we see its beginnings in literary programs, training in skills and leadership programs through non-formal education. This is particularly true of *The educational* the educational work that is taking place in basic ecclesial com- *work of basic* munities. Here again the laity play a major role. In both tasks, we *communities* see the need of innovative programs of education for the lay educators.

3.5.8 Some creative programs to prepare lay teachers for holistic teaching, such as Christian maturity formation seminars and colloquia on the ministry of teaching, are now being implemented in some Asian countries. We believe such formation will enable lay educators to become more effective in their response to the Lord's call to share in his ministry of teacher and servant.

3.6 The laity and mass media

3.6.1 This is the hour when the laity of Asia are called to evangelize their milieu through those most powerful instruments of mass media which modern technology has created. Pope Paul VI has drawn attention to "the growing role being assumed by the media and their influence on the transformation of mentalities and of society itself" (OA, no. 20).

3.6.2 Finance and the mass media determine to a very large extent the destinies of nations; in fact, finance uses the media to this end. Those in power are well aware of the potentialities of the mass media, which they manipulate to mold public opinion and to consolidate and perpetuate their positions. One test of the freedom prevalent in any society today is the degree of autonomy enjoyed by the mass media.

Mass media are 3.6.3 Today, the mass media in Asia are predominantly controlled *controlled by* by authoritarian governments or by a handful of economically and *authoritarian* politically powerful persons, while the vast majority of the Asian *governments* people are passive recipients. It has been noted that the impact of Church-supported media on the masses of Asia is minimal. While the consumer society exploits the mass media to further its materialistic ends, the church in Asia still lags behind in taking full advantage of these most powerful means of proclaiming the liberating word of God to the Asian peoples. Many of us are still not sufficiently acquainted with the idiom and impact of the media.

3.6.4 Still, we happily note the advances of media directly under the care of the Church or influenced by the Church through the laity. The establishment of mass-media centers in various parts of Asia, the efforts to educate Church leadership regarding the complexities and power of media, the training of personnel for this specific apostolate have made great strides. Many of the laity in the secular media are faithful to gospel values and are witnesses to these values—not only as individual Christians, but also in their professional lives where they exercise a positive influence on their peers and the recipients of their work. An admirable example of collaboration of the people of God—with the laity carrying most of the burden—is the crucial role that Radio Veritas has played in the struggle for truth, justice, and freedom.

3.6.5 The power of the media within a plurality of cultures is to be recognized and appreciated. Within such a situation the Asian church sees its task first of infusing gospel values, then of drawing out more explicitly "the seeds of the kingdom" found in diverse cultures and religions. Through the mass media, it thus may bring these values to bear upon all efforts at collaboration, unity, and fellowship among various peoples in view of the common good.

3.6.6 This vision will require of the people of God, and especially of its leadership, a supportive stance toward the systematic formation and training of the laity to assume even greater responsibilities in the media. This is a pastoral priority in the light of our Asian situation, where the people of God must reach out to millions struggling for social transformation, a struggle that requires an interfaith collaboration.

3.7 Laity in the world of work

3.7.1 When we turn our attention to the world of work, we come to recognize that through work of every kind we are participating in God's own ongoing process of re-creating and transforming our world. We are responding to the deep aspirations of vast masses of Asian people for liberation from sin and its consequences.

3.7.2 Nonetheless, we likewise recognize that these dreams and efforts for integral liberation are being shattered by complex, mutually reinforcing powers that are often beyond the control of workers: the dominance of transnational corporations and large local companies in traditional industries and their incursion into agribusiness, taking advantage of cheap labor or appropriating the land of small landowners; the banning of strikes and trade unions and so repressing legitimate protest; the exodus of rural workers into already overcrowded urban slums as the cities' cheap labor; the lack of supportive organizations among the vast majority of urban workers, small landowners, and landless peasants; long hours of work, harassment, job insecurity, and accident hazards; deterioration of health; unemploy-

Oppression and exploitation

ment and underemployment. Clearly, political, economic, and agricultural structures have made both urban and rural workers cogs of an anonymous productive machine, their work a dispensable commodity depending only on the law of supply and demand.

3.7.3 Reflecting upon this tragic situation, we recall the Church's rich social doctrine of work, the dignity and inherent worth of work, and the workers' fundamental rights and responsibilities. We do not intend to dwell on these at this time. The participation of the laity at our assembly has directed our attention to the spirituality of work, an area of reflection which has been largely neglected.

3.7.4 Work is often considered an obstacle to our life with God, as something worldly or secular with no religious meaning. Prayer and spirituality seem to begin only when work ends. A fundamental mission of the laity in the world of work is to recover the religious meaning of human work as an expression of human creativity and a participation in the work of the Creator. The task of transforming the present dehumanizing situation of work begins when the worker rises above the routines and monotony of day-to-day labor and questions the whole of life experience: Why work? What is the meaning of work? What is the meaning of life? These are the basic religious questions, expressing deep human aspirations for a happy life, liberation, and respect of the person.

3.7.5 Rooted in the Spirit of God, these aspirations cannot be stifled by any work system. So when workers struggle to create a work system more conducive to an authentic spiritual life, their efforts are, in the light of the gospel, really religious acts (see LE, nos. 24–27). This is especially so when these acts are consciously subsumed into the dynamic movement that makes work a participation in the healing, transforming, and redeeming activity of Jesus Christ, the Alpha and Omega of all endeavor.

3.7.6 It is necessary, therefore, that workers look at the activities which promote and defend their rights within the context of such a spirituality. Some of these activities are the formation of trade unions of agricultural associations, efforts to participate in decision-making processes, and mass action for cheaper agricultural fertilizers. The worker will find the meaning of life in such a spirituality of work.

3.7.7 In the light of the Church's preferential option for the poor, our attention is further directed to certain sectors of Asian workers: children forced to work endless hours in shops, restaurants, farms, etc.; young female workers coming from rural areas and often subjected to sexual harassment and inhuman working and living conditions; domestic workers in countries other than their own, who are exploited as cheap labor; migrants from villages to cities and other countries, who are uprooted and forced to struggle for survival under

Women and children in inhuman conditions

the most adverse conditions; vast numbers of Asian workers who remain unemployed or underemployed.

3.7.8 The whole Church has to listen with compassion to the problems of the poor and needy workers and to direct its pastoral concern and programs to their benefit. The cooperation of all Christians with other groups in society at the local, regional, and international levels is imperative so that present exploitation and oppressive work systems can be transformed.

3.8 Social responsibility in the world of business

3.8.1 Likewise, the transformation of the social structures of the work process is the mission not only of the workers but also of business people, government officials, managers, and policy makers. Cooperation among the different sectors of society is indispensable. This cooperation has to exist at national and global levels, and supposes that all sectors of society believe that the resources of this world belong to the entire human family and that social responsibility means stewardship of the goods of this world.

3.8.2 The countries of Asia have been following either a system of free enterprise or a system of centrally-controlled economic development. We realize that neither system exists in its pure or ideal form. Both systems, as they presently operate, have serious drawbacks which prevent people from consciously and creatively shaping the work situation. Free enterprise, or capitalism, proved its ability to organize labor for higher productivity and to unleash the modern technological imagination. Though it has considerably liberated the entrepreneurial and managerial classes, it has also degraded the working class to being a dispensable commodity. It has failed to recognize what Pope John Paul II has called the "principle of the priority of labor over capital" (LE, no. 12).

3.8.3 By contrast, centrally-planned economies, or socialism, have rightly stressed that it is the workers who create the economy, but they have mediated workers' control and solidarity exclusively through a centralized state. The workers are left with a new form of social domination, viz, the state. Thus neither capitalism nor socialism, despite their contributions, can provide a new model for the social structuring of the whole process of production.

3.8.4 The future, it would seem to us, lies in pioneering new forms of worker participation in industry—ranging from the renewal of the cooperative movement to worker cooperation in mixed or privately-held enterprises. This also means shaping an appropriate technology that prevents the concentration of power in the hands of a few, and supporting the use of technology in the service of labor

Technology at the service of workmen

and not the reverse. Such a model means developing small-scale technology that workers can own and control, at least as a cooperative.

3.8.5 In this context the laity belonging to the world of business hear the call of God to live out their faith according to gospel values and the needs of others. This involves a number of options in their businesses—from the simple exercise of the values of truth, justice, and love to their active participation in transforming the social structure of the whole process toward greater worker participation, more discerning consumer guidance, more responsible interventions by governments, and a more equitable society.

3.8.6 There is need for principles guiding the conduct of business, something like a code of ethics for business, to enable people in business to permeate their dealings with gospel values.

3.9 Laity and health services

3.9.1 At our assembly, the laity have communicated their concerns for the world of health. We thank the Lord for the marvelous advances in medicine, the product of human creativity and endeavor in the war against disease. But we are confronted every day with serious

The grave problems of modern medicine

problems rising from the application of modern medicine: the prohibitive cost of medical services, the overconcentration of medical health delivery systems in urban areas, the inadequacy of preventive medical services, to name only a few. More seriously, we are today witnessing the emergence of bioethical problems significant not only by their extent but also by their growing complexity. All these confont the entire Church, but more particularly the laity in medical services.

3.9.2 The most significant challenges are: abortion; negative attitudes toward Natural Family Planning; the extensive use of artificial contraception; confusion over moral norms on euthanasia; the high incidence of suicide, particularly among our youth; addiction to alcohol and drugs; and other moral issues arising from biomedical advances, particularly in genetics. The laity in the field of health services, physicians, nurses, and other medical personnel, in both Catholic and non-Catholic hospitals, have to live day in and day out with these bioethical issues. The entire Church is called upon to support them.

3.9.3 Beyond professional competence, they need to sharpen their understanding of the moral dimension of modern medicine and its practice. They should recognize the Lord calling them to bring the saving power of Christ that can transform the world of health care and make it wholesome.

3.9.4 They have expressed the need and desire for moral formation, so that they may discern what is morally right or wrong according to the gospel. A genuine moral formation of the laity in all the health services is imperative.

3.9.5 Our medical schools should not spare any effort to teach medical ethics. At the same time, Catholic physicians should be encouraged and assisted positively to become qualified bioethicists. Centers for bioethical studies should be given a high priority by our Catholic higher institutions of learning, particularly our schools of theology. Such centers can provide a network of competence that will facilitate the formation of the laity in the field of health services. Wherever in the health services such Catholic organizations exist, we need to show positive interest and support and provide guidance in the field of bioethics.

3.9.6 But even greater than the concern for the renewal of our traditional health institutions should be our concern for the great masses of the poor in rural areas who are very often deprived of the basic benefits of modern medicine due to their poverty and the lack of adequate medical services.

The great masses of poor in rural areas

3.9.7 The forgiving Christ is also the healing Christ who reached out to the poor and the marginalized to bring them the healing power of God. God's people, especially the laity in health services, must likewise reach out to farmers and workers, the landless, and the slumdwellers, so that through them the healing touch of God may be felt. This is why the resources of the Church in health services must be channeled to outreach programs that are community-based and community-oriented. It is with joy that we note the increasing number of churches in Asia which are responding to this serious need.

4.0 *Moving Ahead as Community*

4.0.1 The challenges of Asia are "the signs of the times" to be discerned by Christians and the Church of Asia. It is in the faith response we give these challenges that we will discern and discover the vocation and mission of the laity for the salvation of Asia.

4.1 Communion with Jesus

4.1.1 In order that we may discover our genuine and specific place in the multireligious cultural context of Asia, we need to rediscover Jesus Christ as the Liberator of Asia and his Church as the servant and instrument of that liberation.

4.1.2 The Spirit of the Lord is upon us and the thirst for liberation wells up from within us (see Lk 4:42).

4.1.3 Hence, the call today for us Asian Christians is to become a Church deeply committed to Jesus the Liberator. Such a commitment by all Christians will make the Church a communion of committed disciples—be they clergy or laity—working for the liberation of Asia. Such a communion with Jesus Christ and among ourselves is no alienation from the peoples or realities of Asia. On the contrary, our communion is strengthened when we become truly Asian churches, rooted among our peoples and in solidarity with them.

4.2 Communion of liberation

4.2.1 The communion of liberation is not lived in a static manner as a calm, composed Body of Christ in the sharing of all spiritual and material gifts among ourselves. Rather, it is lived within the dynamism of life in the Church and the dynamism of challenges from outside the Church.

4.2.2 This dynamism implies that we, within the Church and among ourselves, recognize all members of the Church as mature subjects and persons with dignity and freedom, with their gifts and powers as well as rights and responsibilities. Any defect in these basic attitudes will impair our dynamic communion and weaken our liberative thrust.

4.3 A messianic mission

4.3.1 The concrete manner of becoming effective agents of liberation is to recall and activate the spiritual characters and functions we possess by baptism as disciples of Christ. Jesus, who leads us forward on our journey to liberation, envisions the mission as priestly, prophetic, and royal. We share his vision and imbibe his character. We nourish ourselves for this journey with him by constantly hearing his word and recalling his memory through his sacraments within our churches. In this way, we are enabled to actualize the triple function conferred by baptism in relation to the realities we encounter on our journey.

A Church directed outwardly and toward the future

4.3.2 If we take our journey to liberation with due awareness and seriousness, then we cannot afford to be merely an inward-looking Church. We have to be outward- and forward-looking as we go along with him. In the past, we have directed our efforts in a way that has suited an inward-looking Church. We need now to rearrange our priorities and redirect our ecclesial energies to undertake our journey as an outward-looking Church.

4.4 Messianic functions

4.4.1 Following Christ as the messianic leader of our journey, we have to actualize our messianic functions.

4.4.2 The priestly function belongs to the whole people of God. The Asian realities themselves urgently demand that this priestly function be exercised by all of our Church. Our proper concern for the ministerial or ordained priesthood—either to improve the quality and number of priests or to meet the problems of formation—must not diminish or distract us from interest in and concern for the common priesthood of the faithful. This latter, though general in the sense of being shared by all Christians, is a real priesthood of life. It has its origins in Christ himself. The Christian disciple lives and participates by his day-to-day life in all the mysteries of redemption, viz, suffering, death, and resurrection. The ministerial priesthood has meaning and fullness only in relation to the common priesthood. Hence, the clergy have the obligation to live the common priesthood of all before enacting the sacrifice of the Eucharist sacramentally.

4.4.3 The prophetic function of the Church must not be limited to the teaching function of the hierarchy. It must be a witness and a service of the whole community to the saving truth of Christ and his Church. The sensus fidelium, or faith-instinct, of the whole people of God is a gift of the Spirit to all as a body. It demands that the leadership should not overlook the spirit and the prophecy of the believing community. Due listening to and consultation of the people of God to discern the spirit and wisdom of God in the people must be undertaken, especially in matters relating to their life in the world and consequent problems.

4.4.4 The royal function which is linked to the royal priesthood must be understood within the background of our human history as leading to the realization of God's reign. It cannot be seen merely as a basis for our leadership's guiding and governing. The laity too participate in their own way in the building up of the kingdom. Their actions within and outside the Church have a constructive value in the building up of the kingdom (see EN, no. 70). Such an understanding will provide new insights into the apostolate and ministry of the laity in the world.

4.5 Renewal of structures: communion, collegiality, coresponsibility

4.5.1 In our efforts to give a faith-response to the challenging call of Asian realities we are guided and strengthened in our convictions by the teaching of Vatican II. The Council called for a renewal of inner structures on the basis of collegiality, communion, and co-responsibility, and it recognized the values of subjectivity, and the maturity, dignity, and freedom of all the members of the Church. Concretely, it asked for a shift of emphasis so as to recognize the laity of our churches as full-fledged members, with their own gifts and charisms, their rights and duties.

The laity, members with full rights in the Church

4.5.2 The principles of communion, collegiality, and coresponsibility stressed by Vatican II demand that we reexamine our ecclesial structures with respect to their purpose and thrust and reorganize them to yield optimum benefit. The renewal of inner ecclesial structures does not consist only in strengthening and multiplying the existing parochial and diocesan organizations, nor in creating new ones. It consists in creating the right atmosphere of communion, collegiality, and coresponsibility for an active and fuller lay initiation, participation, and action.

4.6 Lay apostolate

4.6.1 Though our needs have become more challenging, some lay structures and their orientation remain unchanged and consequently unproductive. Especially with respect to lay apostolate groups and international organizations, whose inspiration and structures are given from outside, a reexamination is called for.

4.6.2 The lay apostolate of our churches still remains basically parish-oriented, inward-looking, and priest-directed. The need of our Asian context and the thrust of Vatican II to make the apostolate world-oriented or kingdom-oriented must be increasingly emphasized. The apostolate must involve more lay initiatives and the power of decision-making; and it must respond to the real needs of the people. The ordained leadership need not fear or be overconcerned about juridical problems in starting newer forms of lay apostolate or ministries relating to the contextual realities of their churches. Instead, they should encourage and promote more vigorous, world-oriented forms, initiated and directed by the laity themselves. Such initiatives will help the laity to mature, and consequently make the whole Church more effective and relevant in its mission to Asia.

4.7 Pastoral concerns

4.7.1 In the light of the above challenges and theological reflection we urge our local churches in Asia to undertake some pastoral actions, particularly with respect to the following.

The clergy-laity relationship

4.7.2 There is no one-sided renewal of clergy or laity. In a Church of communion we, clergy as well as laity, are mutually related and mutually conditioned. We feel the need for a basic change of mind and heart.

4.7.3 In a Church which is a communion that tries to liberate others from oppression and discrimination, collegiality and coresponsibility are urgent. We cannot afford to destroy our communion by words or acts of domination and discrimination. A magnanimous spirit of understanding and a recognition of the gifts of the other must be promoted. In this respect, the clergy leadership has a duty to make the initial moves to foster lay involvement and to recognize the emerging leadership of the laity.

4.7.4 Formation is not a molding of one by the other but a collaboration of persons in the Church with the Spirit of the Church, using appropriate structures. In light of the Asian challenges and theological reflection, three levels of formation appear as necessary:

Formation of the laity

4.7.5 A) General formation of all the Church, especially the laity. This entails an effort to conscientize all the faithful through preaching, teaching, catechesis, adult education, etc., about the new vision of Vatican II with respect to their vocation and mission in the Church and in the world.

4.7.6 B) Particular formation is needed for volunteers and selected leaders of our churches: from lay apostolate groups, parish and diocesan organizations, and special professional fields (work, education, health services, etc.). Seminars, weekend courses, or block courses can be the main forms of the formation programs. Bishops are already promoting this type of formation. However, in the euphoria about an awakening laity, we must avoid feeding these groups with minicourses of seminary theology, but rather give them courses suited to their lay context.

4.7.7 C) Ministerial formation is needed for those who enjoy the charisms for stable ecclesial service. The clergy, who have the responsibility to encourage, welcome, and help these charisms prosper for the benefit of Christian churches and their mission in the world, must offer assistance in accordance with what is needed. By reason of the lay character, formation should be done on the basis of the laity's own experience of the realities of the world. A secular context and a job-oriented formation must be encouraged.

4.7.8 D) The formation programs depend for their support on the local churches. While we are spending great sums of money to educate and form our clergy in large houses of formation and with well-organized programs, we cannot allow the formation of the laity, as particular groups or as lay ministries, to be neglected. The support of our sister churches from the West is appreciated. But the local churches must be encouraged to appreciate and support lay formation programs. Remuneration of lay persons for their stable services must respect the demands of justice and charity. Much could be improved in their programs of formation by an exchange of personnel and resources.

4.8 Lay spirituality

4.8.1 We have seen the complexities of challenges that the people of God face in Asia. We have reflected theologically on the vocation and mission of the laity and some pastoral concerns that flow from the theological vision. At our assembly the laity have asked us in many ways and different forms the age-old question of the rich young man in Scripture: "Teacher, what good things must I do to possess eternal life?" (Mt 19:16). While the words of Jesus were simple enough, his real demand required a radical following by the rich young man.

4.8.2 Discipleship, the following of Jesus—that is the simple answer to the eternal question. This "radicality of the gospel" is shown in the radicality of his own life. We wish now to communicate to you the reflections that the laity, religious, and priests have shared with us on lay spirituality.

4.8.3 Discipleship in Asia is rooted in the realities of Asia. Christian spirituality must be incarnated. It grows and matures in the midst of continuous tensions and struggles with the destructive powers of sin and its consequences, of conflict and injustice. Christian spirituality must also be Christocentric and inspired by the Spirit of Jesus, the Liberator. It is a "living in the Spirit" of Jesus (see Rom 8:1–17), urging us to be his disciples through a dynamic process of being incarnated into the realities of the times, as Jesus was, and of discerning in the Spirit those realities that lead to death and those that lead to life. Jesus was Spirit-led (see, e.g., Lk 4:1), and full of the Spirit (e.g., Lk 4:14); so too should be the Christian. Our spirituality is one of discerning the movement of the Spirit, who reenacts in us the mysteries of Jesus Christ in the contextual realities of daily living and struggling. Here is seen the value of the contemplative dimension, of Asian peoples who discern the movement of God in mundane events and activities. Such a prayerful attitude is immersed in life.

4.8.4 Intermingling with reality and inseparable from it, discipleship is lived in the community of the Church. Christian spirituality is ecclesial and communitarian. It emerges out of our incorporation into the Body, the people of God, realized and expressed in baptism and confirmation. Communion with Christ moves from an individual sharing in his suffering, death, and resurrection to the paschal mystery as lived concretely by the community—a community that is struggling against evil, suffering the pains and anguish of a people

Christian spirituality is ecclesial and communitarian

dying and reaching out for new life. Rootedness in Christ means communion with him and his people.

4.8.5 To be rooted in Christ and the community, Christian living and action must be based on the word of God. Christian spirituality is biblical. It is through the word of God that we meet Jesus. It is also the word of God that gathers us together. We need to listen to Christ as the Word, in the Scriptures and in the Church, but we need also to listen to the Word in persons and in events, in the ebb and flow of life; to listen to the poor and the needy and to reach out to them as Jesus did, for they are the least of his brethren. Here is where a preferential option for the poor, after the example of Jesus himself, demands a spirituality of incarnated "otherness", all that is meant by the simple words "love of neighbor".

4.8.6 Discipleship of Jesus, becoming a memory of him, is also based on the sacraments of the Church. Christian spirituality is sacramental. We have already mentioned baptism and confirmation as the gateway to Christian discipleship and Church membership. By these two sacraments, Christians are not only destined by Jesus to become his witnesses, but are sent by him on his mission. However, at the heart of the Church's sacramental life, and consequently of Christian spirituality, is the Eucharist, by which the paschal mystery of Jesus becomes sacramentally present in our life. Here is found the summit of the Church's sacramental economy and the source of the power and activity, for here Jesus himself becomes sacramentally present among us in his act of utter self-gift for the world.

4.8.7 The memory of Jesus brings the disciple to seek the reign of God (see LG, no. 31) in the world, to be poor, to thirst for justice, to trust completely in the Father as little children do, for of such is the kingdom of heaven. Seeking the kingdom that Jesus proclaimed is really to build it in the concrete experiences of the social, political, economic, religious, and cultural world of Asia. In Jesus, the reign of God began; he came that we might have life to the full. The struggle for fullness of life in Asia is a seeking of the kingdom. Discipleship then is not at all a withdrawal from the world, but an immersion into the wellspring of Asian reality so that it might have life. Communion, solidarity, compassion, justice, love are keynotes of a spirituality of discipleship. And since Jesus came to reconcile sinners with the Father, to remove divisions among people—that all may be one—this impulse from the Spirit of Jesus to be reconciled, to be one, is an essential ingredient of the spirituality of the people of God.

In the heart of Asian reality so that this may have life

4.8.8 Incarnational, Christocentric, biblical, sacramental, ecclesial, and communitarian, the spirituality of the people of God is a journey in the Spirit of Jesus into the kingdom of the Father; it is a journey of discipleship, of love and service, after the pattern of the dying and rising of Jesus himself. From the above, it is clear that fundamentally there is but one Christian spirituality, namely, that which is common to all disciples of Jesus in his Church, whether lay or clerical, priests, bishops, or religious. If a specific lay spirituality can be identified, it is in the sense that lay people are called to live their discipleship of Jesus and share in his mission according to their proper lay state in the Church. Stress must be laid here on the secular character of the lay vocation and mission. While through various charisms and ministries lay people are increasingly called today to share in the Church's inner life, this must not overshadow the specific character of their witness and action in the world. Lay people are sent by Jesus himself to infuse the gospel values into earthly realities and human society. The Christian witness and action must penetrate the various dimensions of their life—familial, social, professional, and political. Only then will they respond to their vocation and mission according to the Spirit of the gospel. To give such a response is what lay Christian spirituality is all about.

Practical suggestions   4.8.9 Some of the practical suggestions that we have heard in this assembly are the following: the deepening of our baptismal commitment, our incorporation and communion with Christ; growth in meaningful and inspiring ways of reading the Scriptures and of making the word of God the guiding and integrating norm of our daily life; exercising the mission of reconciliation out of a deep life of communion with God and with others; molding mind and heart toward a Christian-like sensitivity to the cries and sufferings of the poor in order to respond generously and courageously to their needs; joining these poor and those who struggle for a full life in committed solidarity; discovering forms of prayer transformative of values and attitudes and undivorced from life; integrating traditional practices and devotions from popular religiosity into a spirituality of involvement; becoming more deeply aware of the paschal mystery, the Cross and Resurrection of Christ as the basic paradigm of Christian life and of the struggle toward God's reign; the deepening of our appreciation of the sacraments as a participation in the memory of Jesus, becoming alive and active in the realities of our lives; assuming a discerning way of life.

4.8.10 Fullness of life, while being a gift from God, is then also a hazardous task for the people of God. It implies the challenging task of becoming involved in the transformation of Asian realities. The two dimensions, the divine and the human, though not identified with each other, involve each other. We thus reiterate our determination to exercise our service of the Word of God and of building up the community in such wise as will provide for our laity a more dynamic spirituality.

4.8.11 This will involve a deeper formation of the laity, but it will also require training the clergy for mutuality and service and team ministry. We are hopeful that there will then result a deeper integration of the priests' ministry and lay services for a better service of our churches to the peoples of Asia.

5.0 Conclusion

5.1 We now wish to conclude our sharing with you, dear brothers and sisters. We are thankful to the Spirit, who opened our eyes and led us in these days to share with one another, bishops, priests, religious, and laity, the anxieties and joys of Asia, its sufferings and its hopes (see GS, no. 1). Even more vividly than before, we realize that the path we all have to take as God's people is similar to the paschal mystery of Jesus, a journey to life through the cross in courage and hope. The following of Jesus is the following of him "whom they have pierced", the Alpha and Omega (see Jn 19:37; Zech 12:10; Rev 1:8) of all journeys undertaken in faith.

A journey toward life which must pass through the Cross

5.2 We believe that God, who promised us his kingdom, is with us in the midst of darkness. Within the paschal mystery the Cross of Jesus is both death as well as victory over death. He is saying to all of us: "It is I. Do not be afraid" (Jn 6:20).

5.3 As the laity, religious, priests, and our fellow bishops spoke to us at our assembly, it was as though the Risen Lord were speaking to us on the road to Emmaus, and we can only wonder: "Wasn't it like a fire burning in us when he talked to us on the road and explained the scriptures to us?" (Lk 24:32). Let our hearts remain warm and our spirits vibrant in the certainty that the Lord is walking with us as we move ahead grappling with the challenges of Asia.

5.4 Journeying in faith through this great continent of Asia and among its peoples, we repose our hope in Mary, who is for all of us Mother and guide on this journey. We commend to her the Church in Asia and ask her to be with us as she was with the first community of disciples (Acts 1:14).

May glory and honor be to Jesus Christ, the light of the East, the Sun that never sets.

May his kingdom come!

BUILDING AN OPEN CHURCH

Pastoral Letter
of the Japanese Bishops' Conference

To all the faithful of the Japanese church:

We thank you for having sent us the proposals for the themes of the National Convention for the Promotion of Evangelization; they are the result of zealous discussions by all of you.

For our part, as a conference of bishops, in the extraordinary assembly (December 9–12), after having prayed, we added our reflections upon the materials you sent us.

Reading the various proposals that reached us from each diocese, we had the impression that all of you treated the problem of evangelization seriously from the perspective of the specific situations in which you find yourselves. All these proposals are important, and are not to be underestimated for the evangelizing work of the Japanese church. Nonetheless, we have separated out and specified the basic problem, common to all the proposals presented, in the "separation" or isolation of the Church in the work of evangelization:

—the separation between faith and life as Catholics;

—the separation of the Church from Japanese society.

So then, as a bishops' conference about to undertake consideration of the problem of evangelization, we have chosen the following direction: to rethink faith with life as a starting point, and to rethink the substance of evangelization from the starting point of Japanese society.

To rethink the substance of evangelization starting from Japanese society

To this end, as the theme of the first national convention on evangelization, we have decided upon the following: Building an Open Church.

Our desire is not so much to attempt to adapt life to abstractly formulated principles of faith, but rather to renew our attitude toward

In view of the NICE (National Incentive Convention for Evangelization), held in the second half of 1987, the Japanese bishops asked their faithful for advice and suggestions. The Japanese laity, taking up the bishops' invitation, have worked out some 160 "proposals for discussion". After examining these proposals, the bishops sent to the faithful the letter which we are publishing here. What stands out especially in this letter is the invitation to "build an open Church", this being the condition needed for greater penetration into Japanese life and society. This letter has been translated from Italian by Lawrence Romani.

faith from the standpoint of attentive observation of Japanese life and society, so as then to give testimony about it.

This does not in any way mean the adopting of an opportunistic line or descending to compromises with the reality of Japanese society. Living the mystery of the Cross and the Resurrection in daily life constitutes the source of evangelization.

The mystery of the Cross and Resurrection is the source of evangelization

The three "pillars" into which we have divided the main theme look toward reeducation in view of evangelization with a starting point in real, everyday life.

During the less than one year that separates us from the national convention, we beg you to continue research, reflection, and activity within the guidelines of these themes.

4

EUROPE

THE CHURCH IN THE HOME

Conference of Cardinal Godfried Danneels, Archbishop of Malines-Brussels, Belgium

I would like to speak to you about the Church in the home, what we call the *domestic Church*. This is a term used by the Second Vatican Council, and a term much liked by Pope John Paul II. We need to study the many strong, close ties that bind the Church and the family together, making the family a microcosm of the Church, and a living icon of the mystery of the Church.

Let me tell you just one thing before I begin. It can happen that as we hear people speaking enthusiastically of the Church, or of the beauty of marriage and the family, some people may feel pain, because they are living with deeply wounded hearts, and it hurts them to contemplate other people's joy and enthusiasm. All I ask of them is this: humble your heart and don't think of yourself; let the Lord say what he has to say to you. At the end of this afternoon, I will talk about your pain, too. But first, let us look at the beauty of the family and the beauty of God.

To understand the family, we need the indwelling of the Holy Spirit, who teaches us all things and brings us to the full knowledge of the truth. So, let us be open to the Spirit. Let us keep silence in our hearts, let us purify our desires, let us bask in the light of God's free gift of love and the joy he gives to those he loves, and let us allow that love and joy to shine through us.

This spiritual conference was given for an association of Catholic families and was published in *Pastoralia*, the official publication of the Archdiocese of Malines-Brussels, in the June-July issue of 1986. In this transcript, the fresh and lively spoken style of the conference, which makes this document a marvelous tool for the work, study, and prayers of Christians, especially the family, has been reproduced as faithfully as possible in the translation by Mary E. Hamilton.

The Holy Trinity: Source and Model of the Church and the Family

It is impossible to explain the Church by means of sociological analogies or models drawn from secular society. The Church, as the Council says, is nothing but the Holy Trinity made present in history, before the very eyes of all the world, so that the Church flows naturally out of the Trinity, like a spring from its source. We can understand the Church only by seeing it in this way, through the eyes of faith, because it is both a visible and an invisible spiritual reality. It is God who allows himself to flow into the mold of time, into his own creation. The mystery of the family is exactly like this. In the Book of Genesis, God says: "Let us make man in our image and likeness". And he created them: man and woman. This means that there is something of God in the married couple; I might even call it the heart of God, that central spark of divinity that shines out from every man and woman who love each other. Because, on a human level, the family possesses the same qualities we see in the Holy Trinity.

First of all, the Trinity is One, but that does not preclude the existence of the three Persons: the Father, the Son, and the Holy Spirit. This unity in plurality can be found on the level of the family. The husband and wife are one: "Let no man separate what God has joined" (Mt 19:6). But at the same time, they are two different persons. That is to say, marriage does not fuse them into a single person. Each remains a distinct human being. Becoming one is not what love is; rather, this is the purpose of love. To have love, you need two persons—two bodies and two hearts. And if this plurality exists in the married couple as it does in God, one can recognize the image of God in their unity, their love, and their whole personalities. When a man and a woman commit themselves to one another in Christian marriage, one can speak of their likeness to the Trinity with even more certainty, and one can see in them, whoever they are, no matter whether they are educated or not, the image of God: Father, Son, and Holy Spirit.

Unity and plurality in the family

There is another way in which the family resembles the Trinity. The Father is the mystery of life, of creativity, of generosity, of self-giving, an unquenchable source of living water, of fatherhood and motherhood, of the energy, the irresistible flow of grace and beauty.

Notice that I do not say that these similarities are evident in the husband by himself or in the wife by herself. What I do say is that they both represent God the Father in his creativity. It is precisely because we are finite, limited men and women that we need a father and a mother to grasp the total image of what God can be in a person.

Husband and wife, sharers in the creativity of the Father

It is extremely important to reflect upon the married couple and feel that both husband and wife participate equally and simultaneously in the creativity of God the Father.

Then, there is the Son. In the Trinity, it is he through whom the light shines, he who lets the Father look through him at the world, who never gets in the way, who says Yes with total self-abandonment. This transparent quality, this openness, this opening of the self, are all to be found in the married couple: not just in the woman, but in the man as well. They are both, like the Son, transparent for God and for each other. A couple is distinctively and indelibly marked by this light that comes from the Son, by the Yes that the Son pronounced for all eternity, at the moment when he became man, on the Cross, and then in his Resurrection.

Finally, in God, there is the Spirit: he is the fire of love, life, and warmth, the kindling breath that wafts through the divine, igniting divinity's undying flame. Well, in the couple, the same kindling spirit dwells: it is mutual love and charity. The Spirit is also the Person of the Trinity who remembers: he keeps all things, he makes all things plain. As one of the Fathers of the Church said: the Father is the mouth (that is to say, the one who utters the word), the Son is the lips (that is to say, the Word that comes from the mouth of God); the Spirit is the kiss that joins the mouths and lips of both. This is perhaps the best image one can find to use when one speaks of God.

The Sacramental Life of the Married Couple and the Family

I would like you to take a look with me into the Church, where we find the sources of life that are the sacraments. The sacraments are sources of life for seven different situations. Let us see how the married couple and the family live by these sacraments.

Marriage

Let us begin with marriage, which is the first sacrament for husbands and wives. Christian marriage is nothing but divine love passing through human love. This divine love transforms the love between the man and the woman, without changing the nature of that love. This divine love is what makes them a Christian couple. It is God who overshadows the couple as he overshadowed Mary at the Annunciation, so that what is born of them is either literally or figuratively born of the Holy Spirit.

Now, what was born of Mary is of the Holy Spirit, but do we even dimly see that, beyond our poverty and our fallen nature, God dwells in us with his love and overshadows us with his Spirit? Do we believe that everything that is born of us comes from God?

Don't underestimate yourselves; don't founder in the morass of your interior poverty: look at the beauty of God's love within you, for this kind of beauty is what will save the world. This beauty has an irresistible attractiveness, more, indeed, than truth and goodness have, because the beautiful sums up what is true and what is good. When simple folk have been present at something that was presented intelligently, they always say: "It was beautiful". *The world will be saved by beauty*

Human love that is ennobled by Christ's love and by God's love always partakes of the virtues of the beloved. If we love someone, it is because he is handsome, kind, hard-working or generous. We love him for his good qualities. Human love is like this, it always starts in this way, but an entire married life cannot be based on these good qualities alone. What husband, after thirty or forty years of marriage, can still look like the athlete one sees on publicity posters? And what wife can still look like a cover girl after thirty, forty, or fifty years? If our love depends completely on the qualities of one partner or the other, it won't last. Christian love, God's love, does not work that way. It does not begin with the good qualities of the beloved, but rather, loves the other for what he is, just the way he is. If I were handsome and intelligent, kind, hard-working, and generous, just so that God would love me *right now*, he wouldn't love me, because I just don't have all these virtues. However, God loves us all, just the way we are. He accepts us as we are and says to us: "You don't need to be always standing on tiptoe, you'll give yourself a Charley-horse. Let me love you as you are. As far as I'm concerned, you couldn't be better. The first thing I'm going to do is accept you for what you are." Christian love, in marriage, is a divine love. I say to the one I love: "As far as I'm concerned, you can stay just the way you are. You can have the blues on Sunday afternoons in the winter when it's raining. On Monday mornings, you can feel like it's Monday morning. For me, you're what you are." *God loves us as we are*

I often say this, and sometimes, people who are listening to me reply: "If I say that to my husband, he's never going to change. He'll always be just like he is now. That's not much to look forward to!" Then I always say: "Ma'am, let's make a deal: you solemnly promise to accept your husband just as he is, for only three weeks; after three weeks are up, if he hasn't gotten any better, you write and let me know." I've never gotten any letters back—I don't know what happened. But what is true, absolutely true, is that there is nothing more unbearable than being loved for no reason at all. You can stand up under that for a few months, but finally, unconditional love breaks down all your defenses.

Couples also need a certain faith, a certain hope, a certain charity. On a merely human level, you have to have faith in your partner, because he can only give you little tokens of his love, and you have to guess that there's a great love behind all those little tokens.

Let's take a few examples:

—I have a husband who works from morning until night; is it because he loves me or because he wants a promotion? Well, you'd better believe it's because he loves you.

—My wife is an excellent hostess: she knows how to entertain, she's a good housekeeper. Is it because she loves me or because she's obsessed with cleaning? You'd better believe it's because she loves you. Even if there *is* another possible explanation.

The Holy Family

I shall end these reflections on marriage as the source of life with something that will astonish you: it's the Holy Family. Nobody ever talks about them. We tend to think they were a family that wasn't quite normal. If Saint Joseph ever said anything, the gospels don't record it. Now, Joseph is an extremely modern man: he got over his doubts about what was most precious to him, Mary's love. Does she love me? In spite of this fundamental doubt, in spite of this testing, Joseph believed. I freely admit that the gospels tell us nothing about the psychology of Joseph and Mary. All the same, we can imagine a little how transparent they were, the beauty of their relationship, their mutual respect, their respect for each other's bodies, the faith they had that conquered all their doubts, in Mary and Joseph's family. Let's not hesitate to pray to the Holy Family. Let's not be afraid to ask for the grace to be Josephs and Marys, because I think that there, we have a mystery we'll never solve. At the Last Judgment, when we finally get to heaven, we'll be flabbergasted when we see why God wanted to be born into a family and how he managed to live in a family.

Baptism

Baptism is where life and birth in the Church begin. The family has a baptismal character: it actualizes life, it gives life. To carry life within oneself, in either a literal or a figurative sense, to be father and mother, is first of all to experience profoundly the coming and growth of a child.

The expectation of the child as a new Advent

God gives most families the gift of a child. To nearly every family, God gives two, three, four . . . times a kind of Advent, a time of expectation. Every time he does this, God gives us an opportunity to live this experience of waiting that is made up of silence, of turning inward, of warmth, of patience. That's what Advent is all about.

Make the years when children are being born into your families real Advents. That's what Advent is: carrying life inside you and knowing joy, joyous waiting. Of course, there are, unfortunately, families that don't have children. Even priests and nuns can have this kind of Advent, too, as they give people life by being their spiritual fathers and mothers. In fact, there is a spiritual fatherhood and motherhood that is perhaps even more important than physical fatherhood and motherhood. Physical fatherhood and motherhood are just a first step. The child has to be born again, into adult life. In every family, and even when there are already children, there are still more times of waiting: because we have to let our sons and daughters become what the Lord created them to be; that is out of our hands and can really cause us a lot of worry. But what an enormous blessing it is to have a son or daughter and watch that child grow! The family is a place where there is continuous life and growth.

You know, the greatest gift we can give anyone is the gift of life! The Church and our society will grow old, without joy and consolation, without life, the day we do away with the possibility of giving life. You have your conscience, and God respects that conscience, but he is asking me to tell you today: please, if a baby is asking to be born, don't say No, because giving that baby life is the source of all kinds of happiness, of youth, of strength. In addition, let us give thanks for the gift of life that we ourselves have received and the gift of life that it is in our power to give, because that is the greatest gift God has ever given us.

Confirmation

The family is also a place of growth, of growing up into adult life. The sacrament of the Spirit, who is life within the family, is the gift of the Holy Spirit that we receive at Confirmation. There is a kind of confirmation for the family as the Spirit causes the couple's and their sons' and daughters' humanness and happiness to grow. There is a Pentecost just for the family. All families have only to ask, to be given the grace of the Upper Room. It is the Spirit of God, the Holy Spirit, who enters into the family and teaches them. Of course teaching presupposes pedagogic and psychological techniques, but the Christian family believes that, through everything the family does for its children, the Spirit achieves the growth that brings to maturity the children who are born into the family. And when can I be certain that the Spirit of God is at work? He can work in a clear and irrefutable way, at momentous events in family life; he can also work very quietly, over many years, very gently.

The so-called "Baptism in the Spirit" occurs as the Holy Spirit comes into the family. God is free to give it whenever he chooses, in his own rhythm, but we must believe that the family has to enter into the Upper Room. All we need to do to receive the Spirit into our families is to do what Mary and the apostles did in the Upper Room: pray.

To receive the Spirit in the family

Now, God assures us that if we pray, if we truly enter into the Upper Room, Pentecost will come, quietly, gradually, or suddenly. It is for God to determine how it will come, for it is he who knows us best. Some people move slowly; then, the Spirit comes upon them slowly. Others are more impulsive, and for them the Spirit can descend with a rush of wings, irresistibly. God is like a dove. What does a dove do when it flies down? Have you ever seen a pigeon or a dove fly down in the summer? Just before it lands, it flutters its wings a little, as if to say, "I mustn't damage the ground", and it lands very lightly. I think the Holy Spirit does exactly the same thing: he comes down, but before he does, he hovers above us for a moment so that he won't hurt us. He respects our feelings and makes his landing according to the condition of the landing-strip.

How do you know when the Spirit is present? He is always present, because we have been baptized. I think, however, that there are special signs of his presence that we can recognize.

The experience of Jesus' living presence

—The Spirit comes when we understand the Scriptures, that is, when we happen to remember a sentence from the Scriptures and say to ourselves: "The Lord said that for my benefit."

—The Spirit is within us if we begin to experience the living Christ. He is there, in front of me. I speak to him. I'd never talk to a picture of my father or my mother, but I do talk to *them*. If you never say a word to Jesus, he becomes only a photograph. When you're in the kitchen and you hear something dropped into your mailbox, none of you would call out "Thanks, Postman!" But when we open the door for the postman, we say thank you. The living Christ is with us when we speak to him and call him by his name, Jesus.

—The Spirit has come, and he does come, on the day when we begin to discover our special gift, our charism within the family or the Church. There are some very simple charisms. When somebody is always in a good humor, he possesses a charism. There are charisms of prayer, charisms of love, of consolation, charisms of husbands toward their wives, of fathers and mothers toward their children, but there is also the charism of consolation children have for their fathers and mothers.

Confession and absolution

The other day, I heard quite an extraordinary bit of testimony.

There was a single girl, aged twenty-seven, who literally had gone all over the world looking for some meaning for her life. She happened to spend a few days with a family of very simple people. She told them that she had been searching for a long time, and had not yet found what she was looking for. No convent suited her. She could not find a guru she felt comfortable with. The lady of the house said something to her I wouldn't have dared say, myself: "Honey, you've been wasting your time. You've been everywhere, and you've come up empty. Go make your confession and go to Communion, and come back home." Well, she did it. And now she says: "Only then did I understand that every false step I had made was because of one thing: I wanted to be myself and stay myself, in charge of my life; I wanted to *make myself* into a spiritual person, *make* my own vocation, *make* my own spiritual life. This woman changed me when she said to me: 'Give yourself, abandon yourself, be obedient, do something you didn't deliberately choose to do now. It's me that's telling you this'."

This testimony struck me, and I can't keep from talking about it. The family is also the place where we are pardoned; in it, there is an attitude of perpetual confession. What do we have to do to make it a place of pardon? We have to live in God's presence, in the presence of his love and mercy; there has to be a place somewhere in our family life where we can open our hearts to Christ on the Cross. Devotions to the Sacred Heart have gone out of style in families today, but no family can become a "domestic Church" if there is no place in their family life for hearts open to Jesus and his mercy, hearts open to the kindness and forgiveness flowing from his pierced side.

In our family life, we need times when we all place ourselves before the heart of Christ, and times when we all know for sure that the Lord has forgiven all of us.

Nothing is more joyful than a family who have all received and given God's forgiveness. To live out merciful love in the family means to live mutual forgiveness in deed as well as in word. We have to accept each other's failings and limitations, and the little everyday trials we all undergo, and we have to forgive things that aren't really sins. For example: He's never on time for meals—she always starts cooking too late—she doesn't understand my business—we are always running out of things when all the stores have closed—her ideas on educating children don't agree with mine—we can't agree on how to raise our children. Mutual forgiveness is important, just as it is important to forgive children. Parents have to

To live mutual forgiveness, accepting the limits and defects of others

imitate God, and God is the only one who does all three of these
things: he makes his own laws; he gives everyone the strength to
obey those laws; and finally, he forgives those who don't obey.

To make laws, to give strength to obey, to pardon the disobedient:
these are God's ways. If a government says, "I order you to pay
your taxes, I even give you the money to pay them with, and if you
don't pay them, I forgive you", that government will fall. God is
the only one who does not collapse when he makes laws, makes
people capable of obeying those laws, and then forgives them when
they don't. In bringing up children, we have to imitate God. We
must make rules. We have been too timid about being fathers and
mothers. It's too easy to say: Oh, I don't know what to do any
more. We have to try to teach our children to obey rules, but we
also have to help them obey and forgive them when they don't.
What would you say about a father who wanted to teach his kid to
swim, took the child to the swimming pool and the kid says: "I'm
not going in the water." "Well, O.K., dear, you just relax. I'm going
to swim, myself—you can watch me, and you'll learn right away
by just watching." That child will never learn to swim. You have
to grab him, put him into the water, jump in yourself, and teach
him how to swim.

It is also important to teach children to forgive each other. We
ought to have "forgiveness days" in our families; for example at
New Year's, or Easter, or Holy Thursday. We also ought to forgive
each other in church, when we go to Mass together. A house that
is full of forgiveness is always a home full of joy. Maybe part of our
depression comes from our never bothering to work at forgiving
each other.

Along the same line, we are invited to keep Lent together as a
family, and join in family spiritual exercises; spiritual training always
ought to be a family affair. It's no good when each individual goes
off into his own private corner. We also have to do penance we can
really feel physically. Not so many intellectual penances. We need
to do penance, even at mealtimes. Do we really have to have high
tea every Sunday morning? However, if it makes you surly, by all
means have your high tea, because God doesn't want us to be miserable when we are fasting. But I'm not sure that everybody all over
the world would be unhappy with plain bread and butter. And even
children can understand that and feel sorry for children who may be
starving.

Another beneficial method of spiritual training is: don't anticipate
feasts. For example, what ruins Santa Claus is that he always comes
into the department stores in September or thereabouts. What wrecks
Christmas is putting up Christmas trees at the end of November or

the beginning of December. What spoils Easter is gobbling candy eggs in the middle of Passion Week. It's business that makes us hurry the feasts. In my own life, I start celebrating too soon when the good Sisters make me chocolate Easter eggs on Wednesday in Holy Week; then, I'm done for. I have nothing left to rejoice about on Easter. I'm already stuffed with sugar and chocolate. Thus, we are invited to prepare joyfully for feasts, but not to celebrate them ahead of time.

How can we translate our desire for forgiveness into action?

I suggest ten practical ideas for a family who want to practice forgiveness on a regular basis:

Ten practical proposals for a method of forgiveness in the family

1. Learn to accept ourselves joyfully, just as we are.

2. Remember that we have received more than we lack; be thankful rather than complaining.

3. Accept others as they are, beginning with those closest to us: our spouse, our parents, our brothers and sisters, our neighbors, our family.

4. Say nice things about others, and say them loud enough for others to hear.

5. Never compare ourselves with others, because that kind of comparison leads only to pride or despair; it never makes us happy.

6. Live sincerely, without being afraid to call good things good and bad things bad.

7. Resolve conflicts by dialogue, not by force. Bottling up our anger inside ourselves only makes us permanently depressed. Not telling people to their faces how we feel leads to talking about them behind their backs, or at best, to futile complaining. It is better to have a real dialogue and get it all out into the open.

8. In this dialogue, start with what you agree on and leave what divides you until the end.

9. Take the first step in resolving a disagreement before evening comes; "The sun must not go down on your wrath" (Eph 4:26).

10. Be convinced that being able to forgive is better than being right.

The Eucharist

Just as, in the Church, there is growth and development toward adulthood through Confirmation, so in the family, there is a kind of growing and maturing. As in the Church there is forgiveness in the Sacrament of Penance and Reconciliation, there is in the family a type of continually self-renewing forgiveness. As in the Church there is the Eucharist, so in the family there is what I would call "the Mass in miniature". In the Mass, there are three features: we listen at length to the Word of God; then we offer the Father his Son, the perfect sacrifice; and finally, we are present at his banquet, partaking of the Body and Blood of Jesus. So, in the family, we have times of listening, times for sacrifice and surrender of our wills, and at last, times of banqueting.

Times of Listening

The family is a place for listening to the word of God. In every family, there ought to be plenty of time for listening in prayer, but also for listening to one another, because religious values are slowly and almost imperceptibly taught and absorbed in the family. To teach these values, there have to be witnesses who live in the family. I don't think parents have to give lectures. They are called on to be witnesses as much by being silent as by speaking. And I would say that evangelization is not the unique task of fathers and mothers: the children, too, teach the gospel to their parents.

In some families, there are children who convert their parents to God and to Christ.

To be a witness, to tell about the life of Jesus, the story of God among his people, one should begin when the children are very young. I don't think I'll be much mistaken if I say that all the great religious attitudes of listening, of prayer, of the sense of what is sacred, of respect, of kindling love, are learned between infancy and the age of five or six.

To transmit God's ways　　Thus, it is right at the beginning of life that the Faith and the gospel are passed on, especially by how we act. There is a way of picking up a baby that lets the baby know how much God loves his children. There is another way of picking up a baby that does nothing but let the baby know how far away God is. Passing on God's ways of acting: that's what evangelization is. Don't be afraid to tell children, even the smallest ones, exactly what the Bible and the Gospels say, even if it does happen that later on, the child understands that Adam and Eve were not Mr. Adam and Mrs. Eve, but that the story should be read on a symbolic level. Even if later on he has to learn that some things are symbolic, tell him the Bible stories just as they are written in the Bible, because the child has a right to his dreams, even to his religious dreams. Don't worry about the day when somebody will tell him that the Holy Spirit is not a bird and that God the Father is not an old man with a beard. He will understand that when the time comes. But start by reading him things just as they are written. I don't hide the fact that I believed in Santa Claus until I was nine or ten years old. I was the oldest of six children. My father used to say, "If I tell him something, he will tell all the other children, and so, I can't tell him that there isn't a Santa Claus." Thus, I was kept in my ignorance for quite a few years. But my childlike faith did not keep me from feeling the kindness of my parents and the goodness of God. There have been times—I hardly dare admit this—when I have thought that if I now as a Cardinal wear some of the things Saint Nicholas wore, such as a mitre and a pectoral cross, it may be because I believed in Santa Claus when I was a child!

So I say, you can't start too young. Those who can't talk about things they haven't done themselves are beyond help. However, I do believe that vivid religious impressions *are* stamped on a child at that age. I still remember, when I was very little, and my mama was doing her shopping, she would pass by the church that was located in the middle of the village. Sometimes she would go in and sit down, and I would kneel, in the back pew. She prayed; as for me, I didn't understand any of it, except that "This is serious", because Mama was serious. That is the way I got the impression, that has lasted the rest of my life, of the greatness of God, of sacredness, of silence. That is the sort of thing that forms a child's religious sense.

Then, at the age of ten or fifteen, begins the time of learning patience. Parents and grandparents go through a lot when they see their older children or their younger children not growing up the same way they did, abandoning the values they themselves hold dear.

After the joyful time of his preaching in Galilee, Jesus started on his way to Jerusalem. These pains are like those of giving birth all over again. What can you do? There's nothing to do: except, don't get discouraged, don't despair. Say to God: "Lord, I did my best to bring him up properly when he was little, now it is time for you to work with him, because if I can plant a seed, I cannot make it grow. But I believe, and I surrender myself to your power that is much stronger than anything else. By your Word and by your Spirit, take care of him."

If your children are fifteen or sixteen years old, or older, you can also put them in contact with other witnesses. When a real witness is visiting your area, never fail to invite your young people to go with you to hear him. I am thinking of Mother Teresa, Helder Camara, Brother Roger of Taizé, a man like Daniel Ange. Go to hear them with your older children. This may be a moment that will be a blessing to them throughout their lives. They will have seen men and women who are totally consecrated to God.

To encounter authentic witnesses

What is important, too, is to help them to make the acquaintance of young saints. I realize that Rome is not very keen on canonizing children and young people, because it is said that they have not suffered enough. How could they be heroic? This is poor reasoning, because there are some children who are extremely holy. A few months ago, Daniel Ange published a book entitled: *Witnesses of the*

Future. Read it. It is a collection of stories of the saintly lives of about twenty children and young people. Young people will be converted by other young people, as workmen are converted by other workmen, as families are converted by other families, and as priests are converted by other priests. So put them in contact with youthful saints.

The time of incomprehension How can you get the strength to withstand this very difficult time, when your children are between the ages of twelve, thirteen, eighteen, twenty, twenty-five? By drawing your strength once again from the sacrament of marriage. Because it is God who is the real father of this child. "Lord, without me he couldn't have been born. But he is yours, I received him from you. Now, it is your turn to look after your child!" We make all too little use of the source of energy God gives us day after day in the sacrament of marriage.

We can also draw strength from the prayers of the Church, of the priests, and of religious, contemplatives who pray every day throughout all the world for families and young people. Atop hills and mountains all over the world, contemplative monasteries and convents, and the whole Church as well, stand like Moses with hands raised to pray for those who fight down in the valley. The prayer of the Church—which is the prayer of the Bride—God finds irresistible.

To change this painful time of estrangement into one of confidence, we can also take our pattern from Mary, because she was the first to pass through the winter of not understanding: "Son, why have you done this to us?" Mary possesses in her innermost being a strength of serenity, of tranquillity, of calm joy in the midst of suffering. Her faith is without limit: "Let it be done to me as you say." So go to her if you too find yourself in difficulties that seem insurmountable. Above all, don't feel guilty. Don't be too quick to say: "It's my fault." Sure, it's always a little bit our fault, but I don't believe our faults are very interesting to God. What interests him is our faith. When somebody comes to us with complete trust and says to us: "You can do something for me", what he says arouses more energy in us than a long wail over all his faults would. God says the same thing to us: "Your sins are not of interest to me. What I'm waiting for is your trust, your faith in my providence."

Times for Sacrifice

Gradually, throughout our lives, God prepares us to surrender ourselves, our lives, our joys, and our sorrows—to commit ourselves into his hands as Jesus commended his spirit into the Father's hands on the Cross, and as he gives himself every day on the altar in the

Eucharist. He is there, stretching forth his hands, looking toward the Father on high in the heavens, offering himself through the prayer of the Church.

In this surrender, there is also adoration. To adore is to expose one's whole self, body and soul, to the light and warmth of God. It is to stand before God, before the Blessed Sacrament in the monstrance, before the consecrated Bread. Not saying anything, not doing anything, as one says nothing and does nothing when one lies in the sunshine. One is simply there, and one comes back refreshed. Adoration in the family! I can't hide from you a secret wish of mine: *Adoration as* I wish that in every Christian home where it would be sufficiently *a family* safe to do so, the Blessed Sacrament could be reserved, in a separate, carefully protected place. But I cannot grant this permission, because the Church says No. This is painful for me, but I obey. I know there are dangers: danger of lack of respect, especially the danger of making some families a privileged class, as formerly happened in the private chapels of castles inhabited by lords and ladies. But I still keep, deep in my heart, this desire; probably it will never go away. The presence of the Blessed Sacrament completely changes the character of a house. You can get used to it, perhaps a bit too used to it. But all I can do is say: pray with me that the Pope will change his mind!

Times of Banqueting

The Eucharist is also a meal. I am thinking of mealtimes in families. Here, we are in serious trouble. We get together around the table very infrequently. And instead of being a time of joy, mealtime is often a time of uneasy silence. Our families have lost the sense of banqueting. Of course, we don't all have time to prepare elaborate dinners. We bring in caterers, especially for special occasions; I can understand that. But a meal that we have not prepared ourselves just is not very memorable. It is a passing thing. Our dining rooms have turned into snack-bars. We rush in and out of the dining room like the wind; we don't eat, we get nutrition; that's something altogether different. And especially, we hardly ever all sit down at the table to *All together* eat together. Where is the Last Supper Jesus took with his disciples? *at table* What has become of Maundy Thursday?

I know a rather vigorous mother who says: "My children are all grown; they are eighteen, twenty, and twenty-two years old. Every Sunday, I absolutely require them to be at the dinner table from noon to two in the afternoon. All of them, even the ones that are engaged to be married. They are not allowed to see their fiancées until after two o'clock. No matter what, on Sundays from twelve to two, they have to be here. And even now, they do it." I think she's right. It is not a good idea to break the family circle at Sunday dinner.

The Eucharist is the Sunday Mass. Often, parents ask me: "What should we do about our babies and small children as far as the Sunday Mass is concerned? Give us your advice." I think you can require your children to go to Mass with you, as long as you take them with you on your vacations. If they spend their vacations with you, at the seashore or elsewhere, I believe they ought to attend their Sunday Mass with you.

It can happen that at age sixteen or seventeen, you can no longer insist that they go to Mass with you. One must exercise prudence. But in twenty years, when they reach forty, your children will probably say to you: "What impressed me about you was, not your liberal views, but your silence, something I never understood. You've been hiding something from me!"

I know it isn't easy, and I also know the Church should make a greater effort to bring in families and make them welcome, with their children and babies, as they are doing at Erpent nowadays. When a child squeals or cries in the middle of a sermon, it's annoying to everyone.

The Mass for the family

There's nothing more painful for a mother than to have to take her shrieking, weeping child in her arms and go out of the church because the child is disturbing the congregation. There is only one solution to this problem: have Masses for families with small children. There doesn't have to be anything very special about these Masses. Sometimes, only slight accommodations will be enough.

—The first thing to do is to have the priest say: "Brothers and Sisters, this is a Mass for families with small children: prepare yourselves, they're going to cry. And now, in the name of the Father, and of the Son, and of the Holy Spirit."

—Another idea: where there are not too many children present, the ones that are three, four, and five years old and older, can be invited to sit around the altar. They will participate, each in his own way: they will also play and get into fights, but you must warn everyone and announce this before the Mass begins.

—Before Communion, the priest can say to the parents, when there are not too many children present: "Come, with your children." The priests or the extraordinary ministers who are going to give the people Communion can lay their hands on the heads of the little ones who are too young to receive Communion, and then immediately communicate the parents.

It is very important to personalize this contact with the very small children. Nothing is more frustrating than the sight, at Communion-time, of fathers or mothers either hiding two- or three-year-olds behind their backs or yanking the children around trying to make them be still and not make too much noise. Instead of making them stay behind you, guide them along in front of you so that the priest can at least make a little sign of the Cross on their foreheads before he gives you Communion. There are a great many things we can do about family meals, the Mass, the Eucharist, and adoration.

The anointing of the sick

The Church is a place of healing, through the Sacrament of the Sick; the family is likewise a place of healing. The curative power of love—married love, parental love, love of children—is for healing each family member's wounds. Our families have to be places where this healing can be accomplished. The first way of healing, the easiest, is encouragement. As a father, as a husband, as a mother, as a wife, exercise your ministry of encouragement; we never encourage other people enough. Let's not forget that small children and young people also have a ministry of encouragement toward their parents. I am thinking of their spontaneity, their admirable sense of equanimity and joy, even in the midst of the most difficult situations. When a family is in mourning, everyone suffers and weeps, except the child. After the funeral of a neighbor, people often serve a light meal. This meal starts off very sadly, and then the children come in, and everything comes to life again. Because we do not honor the dead by weeping for them forever. We honor them, on the contrary, by perpetuating the life we received from them, the life that lives on in us.

Be encouraging to your school-age children, whether they attend primary or secondary school. Give them support when they come home from school each day, because it is very hard to be a Christian child at school. There are some pint-sized martyrs, six and seven years old, in the schools. An example: I heard the other day about a teacher who asked her pupils, at the beginning of the school year: "Which ones of you here go to Mass?" Out of a class of fifteen, three children raised their hands. Well, for the duration of the school year, those children suffered the nearest thing to persecution little children are capable of dishing out. Yes, indeed, you can be sure we have little martyrs! It is even more serious, and even harder on the adolescents in high school. So, when the children get home from school, encourage them and practice your ministry of consolation and support to them, because they need it. Antagonism, ridicule, and sarcasm are often extremely painful, and religion and faith are such sensitive matters! Care, too, for your children's system of values. They hear quite enough contradictory "truths". How do you go about caring for the value system in a very young child, or even an older child?

To encourage your children

You tell the truth. Heal their memories, that is, show them concepts that are beautiful to think about, to counter all the pornographic, violent images to which they are subjected. Their memories are totally inundated with ignoble things. Further, care for their hearts by loving them, and above all, exercise this healing with the charism you have received as fathers and mothers in families, because you have a special grace of consolation.

Our families are also places of healing when they are willing to take in, within reasonable limits, the "wounded birds" who roam the streets: the handicapped, refugees, young runaways of fifteen, sixteen, and seventeen whose faces show that no one loves them. Let them spend a few hours in your home, don't make a fuss over them, but let them sit down at your table, play games you enjoy as a family. Open your doors. Let them come in, because our families who believe in Christ and want to spread his Good News are places of healing for them.

Let's not forget about healing the elderly. I know that at present, due to the cramped dimensions of modern apartments and our hectic lives, it is rather difficult for us to keep our grandparents at home with us. In many cases, I can understand that. But Christmas, New Year's, or Easter ought to be a minimum number of times when we *must* bring them home and entertain them, or at least take them a few little delicacies. I think we have to exercise healing ministry toward them, because the aged are undergoing sufferings heretofore unheard-of. Why? Because forty or fifty years ago, people just didn't live long enough to get old. We get very old, and our loneliness lasts ten or fifteen years longer.

The family,
a place of healing
and welcome

One Belgian family had everything they needed to be happy: four healthy children, a good job for the husband. One day, these people got a telephone call from a nurse, a cousin of theirs who worked in a maternity ward. She told them, "There is a little handicapped baby here, with serious birth defects; he's only three days old. His mother is unable to care for him. We don't think this baby is going to die. We will eventually find him a place in an orphanage or a home. But couldn't you take him?" They took him, they even adopted him; he has become their fifth child. They say that there has never been so much love in their home until these last few years. The handicapped child's presence completely transformed the whole family. But I said to myself, and I expect I said to them as well: "Aren't you afraid that in ten or twenty years, when you have not a handicapped baby but a handicapped adult, that you may get discouraged? A small handicapped baby is just as cute as other babies! But when he's grown up, and in a wheelchair, he won't be cute any more." Here is what they said to me: "My Lord God has given us the grace to take him

now, while he is small, and God will give us the grace to keep him
when he is twenty, because God does not change." That made a big
impression on me.

I would like to end this little chapter on Anointing of the Sick in
the Church and healing in the family by telling you that I suspect—and
I hope it is true—that Christian families will become modern "Courts
of Miracles".

In the Middle Ages, the destitute, the lame, and the blind used to
gather in the squares outside the churches, or in the courtyards,
which came to be called "Courts of Miracles" because of all the sick
people who came there to pray to be cured. There, they were given
minimal care and a bit of food. Well, I think there are modern "Courts
of Miracles": they are families. In the family, one finds warmth,
sincere concern, enlightenment, and encouragement for all who are
crippled or handicapped either in soul or in body. If anyone asks me
what the Christian family is, I would say that it is primarily a place
of healing.

I AM THE RESURRECTION
AND THE LIFE

The Pastoral Letter of Cardinal Franko Kuharic, Archbishop of Zagreb

The Last Things and Man

The Resurrection of Jesus is also the revelation of the absolute future
of man. The gaze of God stretches from eternity (Sir 39:20).

Taking into account what the apostle Paul says, it is clear that the
Resurrection of Jesus is an event that has an importance for each one
of us. Precisely this event illuminates our entire existence; in it is
also revealed the meaning of our life and our future stamped by
eternity. The Resurrection represents a certain future toward which

The pastoral letter of Cardinal Kuharic is dedicated to the "Last Things", a classical
theme of Christian doctrine which has been neglected today. This was for us an
additional reason for giving a voice to an Eastern European bishop. The letter was
written in 1986 and published in the official bulletin of the diocese of Zagreb. It has
been translated by Robert and Veronica Royal.

the Church is moving in her path through history. The people of God in the Old Testament were led across the desert out of the slavery of Egypt to the possession of the promised land. The Church—the people of God in the New Testament—goes through tribulations in this world and the trials of time, toward her culmination in the heavenly glory.

In the risen Jesus Christ lies the beginning of a supernatural world and, beyond the future world, a new earth and a new heaven. Long ago, the prophet announced the word of God: "For behold, I create new heavens and a new earth . . . be glad and rejoice for ever in that which I create" (Is 65:17–18). The invitation is offered to every man to enter into this future.

This is the fundamental truth of the revelation of God to man. Therefore, we are trying to think about the truths that concern the last things about man in the light of the Resurrection of Jesus, according to the Credo of the Church. This is all the more necessary in a time when precisely these truths are decisively rejected. There are many who believe in God in their own way, but they do not believe in the life beyond the grave; they reject the great truths of the hereafter. On the other hand, although people living in a materialistic climate have distanced themselves from belief in eternal life, nonetheless the desire to come into contact with the hereafter reawakens in man. Because of this, spiritualist seances have become more frequent; these seances are sought out and paid for at a high price; black magic is not at all absent from the contemporary and civilized world. Many people, even young people, have been trapped by curiosity about various occult phenomena. Even Satanic cults exist in the countries that pride themselves on having achieved the highest level of civilization. When one loses the true faith, the superstitions flourish!

Anxiety about the life to come fosters spiritualism

All this leads us to meditate seriously on what the Faith reveals to us about the grand mysteries of human immortality. It is extremely important and speaks to every human being, even if he does not admit it or has doubts. It is a case of a great, holy, and moving reality; it concerns, in fact, the revelation of God. The book of Wisdom says: "It is hard enough for us to work out what is on earth, laborious to know what lives within our reach; who, then, can discover what is in the heavens? And who could ever have known your will, had you not given Wisdom and sent your Holy Spirit from above?" (Wis 9:16–17).

The faith of the Church is in fact trust in a God who reveals himself. The revelation is a great historical occurrence. It is the manifestation of God and the manifestation of man. These two are inseparable. "The most intimate truth which this revelation gives us about

God and the salvation of man shines forth in Christ, who is himself both the mediator and the sum total of revelation" (DV, no. 2).

The faith of the Church has its own certainty in divine truthfulness. The Resurrection of Jesus is the seal on the entire revelation of God. Even our faith in the last things is based on the word of God. "For our appeal"—writes the apostle Paul to the church of the Thessalonians—"does not spring from error or uncleanness, nor is it made with guile; but just as we have been approved by God to be entrusted with the gospel, so we speak, not to please men, but to please God, who tests our hearts" (1 Th 2:3–4).

Jesus' resurrection is the mark of God's entire revelation

It Was Decided That Man Must Die

Divine revelation manifests to us the depth of the mystery of death. From the beginning, it has been the sin of man that has caused death. This is the mystery of the Faith. Death is a fact. And life is its opposite. Life and death exclude one another in turn. Life is a mystery, and death is a mystery, because man himself is a great mystery. Has not contemporary man lost his respect for this mystery? Today's man is so consumed by his work, his standard of living, his science and technology, his economics and politics, his amusements and his worries, that he is in danger of losing himself in the very flow of time. Contemporary man, being too proud of his power and his ability to know, has perhaps lost his sense of the important questions. He discovers the secret of the atom. He dabbles, irresponsibly, in experiments with the secrets of life, he holds in his hands the tremendous and marvelous, deadly and life-giving energies of the cosmos. Because of this, perhaps, he thinks no other secrets exist. He thinks that there is nothing important outside temporal and bodily reality. He has lost his humility toward eternal realities. Man finds himself in danger of denying his very self, if he excludes from his consciousness the mystery of his own humanity.

Man has lost humility with regard to earthly realities

The great thinkers of humanity never took up such a frivolous attitude toward the mystery of man.

There are other realities far from human consciousness, and thus man is not able to see into their depths. What is life itself? The life of an amoeba, of a flower, of a hundred-year-old oak, the life of a fish in the ocean, and of a bird in the air, the life of the entire animal kingdom. Life! Can chemistry alone give us an explanation of it? Can man alone give life to the inanimate elements of matter?

All this is similar to the question: Will man be able to infuse thought, consciousness, freedom, and conscience into his electronic computer? Is there not an abyss between inert matter and life? Is there not an unbridgeable chasm between man and his computer? There are abysses that only the Creator can cross. If for living beings with whom man comes in contact death, whether natural or violent, represents the end of a biochemical process of life, is it also the same for man?

It is certain that every man is subject to death. This is inevitable and unchangeable. All men are subject to death, however powerful, strong, rich, or proud they may be.

The daily news speaks of death. Our proud century is full of death, even more than past centuries. There are hundreds of men killed in wars, revolutions, revolts, violence, and other incidents. Perhaps all this has made man insensitive to the mystery of death. When contemporary civilization accepts, within its own conscience, without any remorse and "in accordance with the Law" that hundreds of millions of human beings are deprived of life in their mothers' very wombs, is not this a sign that contemporary man is about to extinguish his own sensibility of the sacred mystery of life?

Man's life and death

What is the life of man? What is the death of man? Certainly it is a reality that goes beyond all the phenomena of life and death in the vegetable and animal kingdoms. Man is above all this. On account of this, the life of man is incomparably superior to animal or vegetable life. And the mystery of his death surpasses without comparison the deaths of all other living beings.

However, many people attempt to convince the human race that man is only a body, and even if they try to impose their convictions on us as a scientific conquest, nonetheless these affirmations cannot change the essence of the human being. Each person possesses an indestructible spiritual nucleus: his conscience. This unique being—man—cannot be reduced to his corporality alone. These unique beings also possess a spiritual component that cannot be reached by the mere bodily ego, that is conscious and reflective, alive and life-giving, immortal and free. In this spiritual nucleus, in this spiritual profundity, unfolds the conscious life and the life of knowledge of man, the life of the conscience and of decisions, of love and hate, of good and evil. In this depth, the choosing of options and final decisions takes place: the acceptance or rejection of God.

On account of this, the chemical process can only reach the corporality of the human being, and can never undermine his spiritual reality. The entire divine revelation confirms this. If it were not thus, could Jesus on the Cross say this to the good thief: "Verily I say to you: today you will be with me in paradise" (Lk 23:43).

In this regard, the Second Vatican Council confesses the permanent faith of the Church: "When [man] recognizes in himself a spiritual and immortal soul, he is not being led astray by false imaginings that are due to merely physical or social causes. On the contrary, he grasps what is profoundly true in this matter" (GS, 14).

The desire for immortality is profoundly and permanently rooted in the human heart. The entire history of civilization and of human culture attests to it. A significant expression of it is the cult of the dead in all civilizations. To deny the immortality of man means to deny his final destiny, his meaning and his dignity.

The desire for immortality is profoundly rooted in the human heart

"Happy the Dead Who up to Now Have Died in the Lord"

When in the light of the Faith, we meditate on death, then it seems something different from how it is thought of by others who do not have hope (1 Th 4:13). The redemptive death of Jesus on the Cross, being the supreme act of love, has taken the sting out of death (1 Cor 15:55). In the same way, our death in Jesus Christ, too, can be a definite and supreme act of love for our life. With the redemption, Jesus Christ consecrated our whole life. If we accept his redemption, Jesus consecrates our death as well.

On account of this, the apostle Paul wrote to the Romans: ". . . because if we live, we live through the Lord; if we die we die in the Lord. Therefore whether we live, or whether we die, we are the Lord's" (Rom 14:8). We who are believers ought best to think about our death. While we see the suffering dying in their beds, we have to see Jesus in them, who in their agony makes present his generous love that burns for the salvation of the world. United with Christ, those who are dying become participants in redemptive love. This love increases the holiness of the Church; sinners are led to conversion, and the extent of good in the world increases.

If with faith and with love we incorporate ourselves consciously in the agony of Jesus on the Cross, then we will certainly be included in the glory of his Resurrection. This is the revelation of God. "If we are in fact deeply rooted in him, by a death similar to his, we will also be deeply rooted in him by a similar Resurrection" (Rom 6:5). "If therefore we die with Christ we believe that we will live also with him . . ." (Rom 6:8).

The apostle Paul also writes to the Thessalonians: "For since we believe that Jesus died and rose again, even so, through Jesus, God will bring with him those who have fallen asleep" (1 Th 4:14).

Baptism has united us with Jesus through its newness of life and through a holy death. This union with Jesus the redeemer has been explained to us by revelation. The apostle Paul writes to the Romans: "Do you not know that we are all baptized in Jesus Christ? That all of us that are baptized in Jesus Christ are also baptized into his death? Therefore, we have also been buried with him in his death through

Baptism unites us to Christ through a newness of life and through a holy death

baptism, so that as Christ was raised from the dead through the glory of the Father, so also we may walk in a new life" (Rom 6:3–4).

Thus the death of man is not the end of his life: it is not the eternal destruction of his being; it is not his annihilation. Rather, death is one of the most serious and moving moments of human life: the transition into a new reality, into another mode of living. Everyone dies alone. This experience remains incommunicable. The reawakening of the self in the other world fills the soul with an inexpressible surprise. How strong the recognition must be: Now I exist in eternity! In what eternity? It is one of the most important questions of our entire existence. The response to this question depends on our choice in the life of this world.

THE CATHOLIC FAITH IN
A MARXIST STATE

Pastoral Letter of the Catholic Bishops of the German Democratic Republic

Brethren:

Our pastoral work ought to be dedicated to helping believers lead the life of the Spirit by doing the work of Christ. Every Christian is called, as the whole Church is called, to witness to the truth of Christ before men and before all the world. Further, the Church is to infuse the spirit of Christ into the world with the help of the testimony her members give by their own lives and by their efforts to conform more and more to God's will. Only then will the Church fulfill her mission to be "a city set on a hill" and "the salt of the earth".

To help believers to identify their mission on earth and accomplish it as fully as possible, we should start by carefully studying the social environment in which we live. Is there a chance for us to make our presence felt as Christians within the institutions that characterize

As the title indicates, this letter presents the situation that presently confronts believers in the German Democratic Republic. Catholics, placed at a disadvantage by Marxist propaganda, need to be careful to avoid being lured into collaboration with it. The letter, published in the *Frankfurter Allgemeine Zeitung*, October 24, 1986, was translated into English by Mary E. Hamilton.

socialist society and its way of looking at the world? Or should we, because we are Christians, steadfastly remain "in the world but not of it" and, by so living, keep a clear conscience? These are questions many of our members ask, as we ourselves do, as pastors and spiritual guides. We should like, by means of this letter, to invite you to reflect upon the pastoral problems tied in with our Church's existence in a socialist state. The goal of the explanations we are about to give is to guide and direct pastoral action. We ask you to continue to analyze the questions raised here, through pastoral conferences and discussions among priests.

Let us first consider the various aspects of social environment, before discussing possible results of our pastoral work.

I. The Present Situation of the Catholic Church in East Germany

It will be difficult to summarize our Church's situation in East Germany in a few sentences. We shall therefore have to confine ourselves to those aspects that principally concern the direction of souls.

1. Ideology's ambitions

Few words are needed to illustrate the difficulties our pastoral efforts encounter in our country. Among the problems that have always existed, most striking is the challenge offered the Faith by the wave of secularization sweeping, not just over East Germany, but over other countries as well. A radically atheist mentality pervades both the world and our daily lives. Practical materialism, of the kind that stifles belief in God or makes belief in God impossible, insinuates itself into people's consciousness as a novel and up-to-date way to lead one's life.

But there is also another challenge flung in the face of the Church, from the fact that Marxism's materialistic view of the world is the dominant ideology in our country. Undeniably, this ideology makes pastoral work harder, although it gives toughminded and concerned men an opportunity to think deeply about the Faith and to try to find a way of deepening personal religious convictions. Pastoral problems arise from Marxism's set purpose of influencing the whole social context. For clearly, our Church does not exist in a society merely tainted with secularism (as is the case in almost all other Western countries), but rather more in a society that, in conformity with Marxist-Leninist tenets, must take on an altogether different meaning: that is, socialism; and beyond socialism, full-blown Communism. All elements in life are pointed toward this end and influ-

Ideological materialism, a challenge for the Church

enced by it. How far has it succeeded by now? We can skip that for the present. But we must keep in mind that in principle, there has been a large-scale attempt to structure society around an all-embracing ideological concept. This has considerable consequences in all aspects of human life: work and leisure, the family, education, science and culture, the private life of individuals and social interaction: all these have become legitimate ideological battlegrounds. In this sense, the state is not just a single neutral factor, but an ideological force. The socialist state insists on its citizens' adherence to its values and on their conscious support of social "progress".

2. Society as an area of conflict

In our pastoral activity, we are dealing with the future of people who have never lived under a social system other than the socialist state and its particular institutions. This is especially true of our children and young adults. Believers, like other citizens, accept this situation as a fact of life. On the one hand, they feel they ought to pay special attention to the relationships between the state and society. They have carved out a niche for themselves that is most important for their professional and public lives, and they are trying to protect it. On the other hand, they endure serious social pressures precisely because of their Christian principles, tensions that disturb both their family life and their jobs, stresses that can make them either bitter or resigned to the situation. Thus, some see the bottom line only as how to obtain exit visas to get themselves and their families out of East Germany. Areas where these conflicts occur are the school systems, professional training programs, and economic and administrative bureaucracies in the fields of education, defense, and military service, where the decisions believers make according to their consciences decidedly do not correspond to what society expects.

Many believers have been trying valiantly to defend themselves against society's unjustified incursions into questions of conscience. Others have adopted a spirit of compromise; this, we think, is a dangerous thing to do. Still others are simply puzzled, or they just muddle through, without trying to arrive at any definite rules for their conduct toward the state and society. It is often quite difficult for a pastor to give advice or concrete suggestions to a person under this sort of pressure. But we have a duty to point out to all believers the way that will allow them to live here as Christians without going against their consciences. That means, as it has always meant, that we must articulate our Church's positions clearly, holding views that will be compatible with the Christian Faith. It also takes no little courage to give new hope to the many people who have given up

Some of the faithful reach disquieting compromises

trying, and to think through every possible way of marking our social milieu with the spirit of Christ.

3. The ideological character of the educational system

An important area of conflict for Christian believers and their children is that of the socialist educational system. The ideological makeup of the schools, where attendance is compulsory for all, including Christian students, is openly admitted. The dialectic behind this rationale has already been explained in Section 2, above. Both curriculum and content to be taught in schools and other educative establishments are determined by the Marxist-Leninist philosophy and system of values.

This is equally true of what the schools teach about religion and Christianity.

The SED (Unified Socialist Party), the ruling party in this country, categorically and unequivocally rejects religion as a false idea. Religion is judged to be a fallacious representation of nature and society within human consciousness, standing in total contradiction to scientific data. (Cf. *Matérialisme dialectique et historique: traité d'études fondamentales de marxisme-léninisme* [Berlin, 1984], p. 409. All subsequent references in this letter are from this book.)

In any ideological confrontation, the continuity of Marxist-Leninist criticism is strictly preserved, as is evident from an examination of the volume just mentioned. All educational institutions strive to awaken the scientific consciousness in young people.

These institutions must not only promote learning about Marxist-Leninist theory, but they must also induce personal acceptance of this philosophy. The Schools Act of 1979 requires teachers to give their pupils a Communist education, one that is oriented toward atheism. Certainly, however, a few Marxist teachers can be found who would soften this judgment against religion slightly.

In our country, not only do inquiries concerning man in art and literature contribute to this softening-up process, but religions and churches are also gaining influence over world events. We ought to pay close attention to these tentative efforts even if they do not look very significant on a day-to-day basis in the ordinary educational and cultural life.

4. An attempt to integrate churches and individual Christians into the political system

Current party efforts of a social nature, in an attempt to raise East Germany a step above the level of ideological confrontation, sometimes tend to contradict the fixed ideological objectives of the Party itself as it searches for an effective way to unite Marxists and Christians politically and morally.

Their agenda include enlisting both the churches and individual Christians in the struggle for the building and reinforcement of a socialist society; promoting peaceful relations controlled by the party and the state; and preserving social progress. This is why they declare that atheistic, Marxist-Leninist education, including its criticism of religion, is secondary in importance to the proletariat's struggle against the bourgeoisie for the establishment of socialism and Communism.

Without departing ideologically from its position on scientific atheism, and without making concessions to religious faith, the Communist movement's pragmatic political philosophy turns toward creating and strengthening a firm alliance of all those in the working class and even with people in religious work (note, for example, that the Communists' cooperation with believers to bring about an advanced socialist society is a fundamental principle of strategic value to the SED [pp. 37 and 413]). It is not so much a struggle against religion that is primary, but the establishment of a classless society. Thus we read: "Contrary to bourgeois materialism and bourgeois atheism, Marxist-Leninist doctrine does not advocate a struggle against religion as the root of all social evils. Rather, it offers as a basic principle that the abolition of capitalism and the building of a Communist society together open the way to a way of life that advances human dignity and removes exploitation and oppression, replacing them with liberty and social justice" (see especially p. 413).

For us Christians, it is a paradox that the criteria of a new society and a new kind of human being can be blended into a philosophical materialism stamped with the seal of Marxism. In this frame of reference, Christian values, and in a general way, human values, are defined in a new fashion; or, more exactly, these values are completely transformed.

What Marxist-Leninists suggest is that this collaboration they hope for between believers and atheists can actually be effected.

Christians are discriminated against in research and in professional life

In cases where a required world-view cannot be accepted by Christians as a whole, for example in the case of educating children to hate enemies of the class struggle, difficulties start to crop up. This is how it happens that Christians must constantly encounter and undergo discrimination in education and professional life, including all attendant disadvantages, and also how it comes about that they are forced to become conscientious objectors in the matter of military service or even military training. This conclusion is valid yesterday, today, and at all times, even if it should happen that redress can be obtained, or wrongs can be proved to have originated in the arbitrary behavior of isolated individuals. Religious party-politics today and the direction the state is taking obviously reflect the tension between an ideological concept of religion and the way the churches are really treated. In spite of the independence and self-determination granted to churches in ecclesiastical matters, churches must submit to collective social programs, renouncing, by that very act, their own right to exist.

Nevertheless, even if the churches' right to exist is disputed, it does not follow that they therefore are socially useless or indeed a detriment. One cannot really speak, then, of any kind of alliance or association between church and state. For this reason, it is understandable that the key question right now, as far as the position of Catholics and Protestants is concerned, is apparently not an ideological one, but the practical dilemma of being stuck with working for and defending the state and its socialist society under orders given by the SED. This also explains the campaign on the part of the CDU[1] to get Christian lay people, and, if possible, priests as well, to cooperate in party-politics. This tendency is just as evident in the idea of *Jugendweihe* (Consecration of Youth). In the jargon of Communist education, *Jugendweihe* represents one stage in a vast scheme for instilling into the younger generation a vision of a world dedicated to atheist culture. This is why we reject, and will continue to reject, *Jugendweihe*. Now, we understand perfectly that, in practice, it is interpreted simply as a solemn promise to the socialist state, and that its ideological dimension remains concealed. This in turn reinforces the erroneous opinion that *Jugendweihe* is only a civil ritual that has nothing to do with the Faith. This is nothing but a smoke-screen that creates just one more worry for believers, who already are under a great deal of pressure.

The Jugendweihe *as a living atheistic culture*

In the matter of religious politics, the state has still other strong-arm tactics up its sleeve, in addition to its gradual attempt to involve the Church and individual Christians in building and promoting a socialist society by means of discriminatory treatment of churches, church dignitaries, and ordinary Christians.

The Church will likewise need to note that administrative measures to reduce her sphere of influence, and ordinances formulated to discipline the Church must never be thought of as things that cannot happen.

Long experience has taught us these things, giving us a realistic attitude about the Church. The articles of the 1949 Constitution of

---

[1] Christian Democratic Union, a satellite movement of the SED. [Not to be confused with the CDU (Conservative) Party of the Federal Republic of Germany.—Tr.]

the German Democratic Republic concerning the churches and religious communities, and the amendments of April 1968 are sufficient proof. Now, in more recent times, the state's territorial institutions have grown in independence, so that notable variations in local application have come to be expected in the concrete manifestations of state religious politics.

II. *Conclusions*
for the Church's Pastoral Activity

Consistent with her nature and her own definition of what she is, the Church cannot react in a merely political manner to the situation described here. She has to answer in a pastoral way, and her answer will assuredly have a political impact.

The Church exists for mankind, as the Lord ordained her to exist, regardless of the social conditions under which men live.

Among the incontrovertible facts that proceed from this premise, the following seem to us to warrant special emphasis.

1. The Church's concept of herself

The Church has her own definition of what she is, her own identity. This comes from Jesus Christ, who wills to come into the world through his Church, to lead the world to give itself voluntarily to the will of God the Father. In this sanctification of the world, the Church serves only at her Master's pleasure. She cannot, and must not, on the pretext of extenuating circumstances, appropriate to herself the right to construct her own justification, either of her existence or of any of her works, nor, naturally, of the state or of any party owing allegiance to a state.

Similarly, the Church cannot cast away the indestructible chain that binds her to her own independence in her relations with the socialist state. This is why it is hard to exaggerate the value of the separation of Church and state. Certainly it is imperative that we avoid giving the impression that the Church is subservient to the state or to some political party. We know how even the apparent subservience of religious authority can seem to serve interests that are none of its affair. This sort of impression could cause the most serious harm imaginable to the Church's autonomy and credibility. In this regard, it is proper to call attention to the particular importance of our Church's keeping inviolate her bond of union with the universal Church, the Pope, and the College of Bishops of the universal Church. We are not a national church, but the universal Catholic Church within a country. We must always return to this idea for

We are the Catholic Church present in one nation

the image of ourselves that we show the world. If every member of the Church abstains from all political activity in the strict sense, it permits the Church to preserve her independence and freedom. The Church's function finds its fullest meaning in work for the unity of the people of God. For priests, the care of souls often clashes with the social and political conduct of believers toward other men. The one who has souls entrusted to his care must put himself in a position where he will be believable and persuasive to all, whence he can give his people an orientation drawn from the gospel to guide their public and professional dealings. We ought not to enter into everyday social and political involvements except in the name of the Lord (compare David's behavior: 1 Sam 17:45); if we act otherwise, we can become the playthings of foreign interests. This means, in concrete terms, that priests, deacons, spokesmen for church organizations, administrators of charitable institutions, and everyone else, must staunchly resist the tendency, so warmly encouraged by the CDU and other similar groups, to join in the party's political and social activities. This does not mean that the Church or her representatives should be prohibited from approaching the civil authorities on a concrete problem. But it should be clear that, if she chooses to take such action, the Church should stick to her own mission and not let herself be swept into projects that have nothing to do with her apostolate; for example, propaganda activities. The directives church authorities issue on relationships between the Church and agencies of the state, as well as on the relationships between the Church and political and social organizations, are grounded in this system of priorities.

2. Putting the situation into a realistic perspective

We have to remember that our position is not so unusual as we may sometimes think. This is immediately evident from a quick study of what is happening in the Church in other countries and on other continents. Since the apostles' time, the Church has survived in many different political and cultural climates, not all of which were always congenial to Christians. It should not upset us unduly that our Christian Faith today may find itself sorely tried, nor that the state does not, in its dominant ideology, consider us one of society's most promising avenues. The apostle Paul's observation is addressed to us as much as it was to the early Church of Rome: "Do not conform yourselves to this age but be transformed by the renewal of your mind, so that you may judge what is God's will, what is good, pleasing and perfect" (Rom 12:2). In this sense, Christianity and its distinctive world-view are, as they have always been, two sides of the same coin.

Even the political and social realities are subjected to God's power

Moreover, we must not forget that God rules over the "socialist" system, permitting it to exist just as he does the "capitalist" or any other social system in the world. We do not believe in historical determinism. Political and social realities are, indeed, subject to God's power; he can deal with them as he sees fit. This view of the Faith can be analyzed as a concept that borders on the religious. In this connection, the first commandment, "You shall not have other gods besides me", has long had a political meaning completely apart from any idea of "myth". Thus, our Faith does not judge social realities to be secondary in importance. They also must be "sanctified" according to God's will; they too must be filled with the spirit of Christ. This rule is equally valid in a social scheme that has ambitions global enough to extend into every area of human life, and that tries to make its atheist philosophy politically interchangeable with its truth-claims.

The Christian Faith, then, allows us to weigh the realities that characterize the state and society, and to accept them as part of the testing and proving-ground for Christians. We don't want to over-dramatize the situation, nor to glorify it out of all proportion. A sound realism will prevent us from thinking that the label stuck to the outside of the box always tells what is inside. Do we think every sporting event we win is a victory for socialism? Is every good harvest only the mathematically predictable outcome of socialist production methods? We may certainly admit that we get a kick out of sports, and that the agricultural policies employed by members of the farming cooperatives (LPG) assure the populace of a good harvest. In our pastoral community, everything depends on a natural perception of reality, and reality only manifests itself as it is influenced by the spirit of Christ. Christ and the witness of his life on earth do give an effective answer to one of this society's questions.

3. Potentialities and limitations of social activity

Paying strict attention to social realities can help us in a concrete way in our examination of how far we can go, and how far we ought to go, in social involvement. In this matter, we must distinguish between the Church as an institution and each Christian's involvement through his personal initiative.

As far as the institutional Church is concerned, it is important to recall the message of the Second Vatican Council: "The Church, by reason of her role and competence, is not identified with any political community, nor bound by ties to any political system" (GS, no. 76). To the Church and her clergy, that means: the Church must remain the Church, and not turn into an extension of state or social interests (cf. Part II, 1). Further, it should be clear that the Church partakes of the needs and cares of mankind. This is why the Church has the right and the duty to take positions on today's important questions; it goes without saying that these will be public stands. In words and actions, she will bear prophetic witness to God's truth and mercy.

Dialogue between the state and the Church on matters of common interest, within the boundaries of both parties' responsibilities, is not outside the realm of possibility. For example, this dialogue might be about the problem of stabilizing marriage and the family, about the generation gap and how to close it, about the value of life for the unborn; it could extend to the problem of how the Church and the Christian religion are presented in textbooks and study manuals used in schools.

As for the ordinary Christian's responsibilities, first he must be aware of his calling to cooperate with people of different opinions in matters touching the good of individuals, and in the broader area of matters of common or general interest to society as a whole; at the same time, he ought, if possible, to live and act in a way that shows he fully belongs to God and is not ashamed to confess it. Our Yes to the world and its needs must be centered in our Yes to God. For the Christian, there can be no participation in projects and institutions whose Marxist shape and thrust has been repeatedly and insistently demonstrated. This is especially true of membership in the SED. Nor, for the Christian, can there be any social "sharing" that would tend to require him to hide his Christian Faith or pull away from his roots by changing his personal convictions. In the Bishops' Pastoral Letter on "Christian Education" (1974), the following rules were enunciated:

Our Yes to the world must remain united to our Yes to God

"The Christian cannot cooperate
—in situations and activities that would entail the necessity of his leaving the Church;
—in circumstances that would result in his separating himself from Church and parish life;
—in cases where he would have to hold opinions contrary to the Faith and his conscience;
—in cases where some action is required that is contrary to the love of one's neighbor and is conducive to feelings of hatred toward others."

Furthermore, we should examine particular cases to see how the Christian's involvement becomes possible and necessary in various aspects of social life. We, as spiritual fathers, must act in such a way that individual Christians consciously and courageously place themselves in work where their human and Christian talents are sought after. This will not always occur without tension; but insofar as we are Christians, we need not, we must not hide our Faith. Helping our neighbors, caring for the sick and the handicapped, creating a good atmosphere in business or in groups, showing solidarity with people who are being neglected or oppressed, working together of parents with the schools or kindergartens, and participating in sports or cultural activities that give pleasure to others are several areas in which Christians can give themselves free rein and from which they ought not to let themselves be excluded. In this connection, we, as spiritual fathers, must consult with believers to find out how, under present conditions, social service and Christian witness can be shown in public. When these concrete conclusions come out of conversations with individuals and groups, it is not just religious principles that need to be discussed, but also, for example, individual taste, inward sincerity and outward credibility, and personal conduct that does not give other members of the Christian community an excuse to opt out.

From this point of view, decisions clearly thought out beforehand take on greater meaning. Experience teaches us that such decisions make one's way of living easier in the long run. The man who procrastinates over a long period finds himself acting without having made a free decision and has to content himself with uncertain compromises; he is running the risk of becoming lax on a more or less long-term basis, and is likely to go wrong on essential points besides. Further, a free and unpressured decision is also appreciated and respected by the unbelievers who surround us; it may be that they even secretly long to see us make such decisions.

It is the duty of all Catholics to know how much their Faith and the gospel mean to their work for a just, humane, and peaceful world; all Catholics have a duty to know how to put their Faith and the gospel into practice. In the Christian's home and workplace, his Faith ought always to have some influence over his environment. We immediately think of concrete examples of fields of action such as conscientiousness on the job, making the best use of leisure time, ethical responsibility in business undertakings, protection of the lives of the unborn, concern for the welfare of children, resolution of conflicts in marriage or at work, and education for peace among nations. Thus, the public's attitude toward the Church's charitable works is one of appreciation of this apostolate as socially meaningful involvement. However, we must not rest on the laurels of this institutional witness alone. Christians, whose Faith molds their entire lives, also need to play a positive role as leaven in every society, including ours [in East Germany]. We firmly support and encourage this kind of commitment. For the Christian involved in this way, there is no need to join any group, party, or organization whatsoever. But we must not leave our commitment for the Church to carry out for us.

The Christian's faith must penetrate the surrounding environment

The Christian Faith, growing in this world so that God's kingdom may come on earth as in heaven, gives us a firm foundation and a quiet mind; we might almost say it gives us serenity. Truly, the Christian Faith does not brood over injuries; there is no limit to its endurance. Such a faith will triumph by the strength of its radiance alone, because anyone can see that Christians like living in an atmosphere where people are peace-loving, humane, and honest. This Christian "world service" can be accomplished by everyone who holds to this Faith. Perhaps our society survives more because of this quiet commitment on the part of Christians than we even suppose.

4. Spiritual help for Christians living in the world

An important duty for us as spiritual directors is to cast light, by our preaching and spiritual dialogues, into every area in which the members of our community live and move, the way Jesus did in the gospels. Believers need tangible help to put them on the right road, and give them proper guidance so they can fulfill their mission here on earth in the most effective way. When it is a question of ensuring human rights and keeping the representatives of particular agencies of the state or of society from violating those rights, this task is not so easily accomplished. It is even more important to suggest positive options so that people can let the voids in their lives become filled with Christ's spirit. We need to show believers not just the risks, but also the opportunities that are open to those who would follow Christ even into our deserts of atheism. For example, for a Christian working in a supervisory capacity, we could show him that his relationships with his colleagues and subordinates, and with people he meets in business are part and parcel of his Faith. We could reveal to him that whatever efforts he makes to introduce a quality of humanity into his sphere of influence, either to show solidarity with others or to place obstacles in the way of those who cause human suffering, all this is like the service rendered by a deacon, and just such service has always kept Christ's Church alive and will continue to keep that Church alive. Also, we could show this Christian supervisor that his own hard work, in any place where order and a sense of responsibility are lacking, has quite a bit to do with the sanctification of the world and the perpetuation of Christian hope.

Our pastoral work must not take human beings away from real life in this world in order to allow them to concentrate on knowing God. We have to learn to teach Christians to appreciate the mystical value of "the daily round, the common task", because everyday life in this world, which seems abandoned by God, surely provides a

"An everyday mysticism"

genuine chance to meet God face to face. This cannot happen without a deepening of our spiritual lives; it cannot happen without prayer, sacrificial giving, and self-denial; and above all, it cannot happen until we are able to open ourselves spiritually to families and to groups, learning together to care for each other. On this point we are supported by the conciliar documents and the documents of the pastoral synod, all of which impel us to work for these goals.

5. Actions the Church should take on behalf of dissidents

We, the bishops and priests, have a duty to act as protectors of individuals who suffer hardships for reasons of conscience occasioned by their religious beliefs. Unfortunately, we are still learning that the Christian or clerical "designation" creates an obstacle to getting a suitable education or management post in a trade or public service. Above all else, it is the bishops' constant duty to remind the civil authorities that Christians want to continue to live, work, and act in this country. However, Christians do not want to have a particular world-view forced upon them by a dictatorship that drafts them, under the banner of socialism, to build a religionless, atheist society. As Christians, we are not waiting for the pillars that hold up the State House to be reset in the mortar of Christianity. But we hope to be able to live together in that house with all other citizens, receiving equal rights and respect. It is the duty of the civil authorities to translate this just expectation into a tangible reality, at all levels, including that of education and professional life. We, the bishops, judge that a government claiming to uphold a uniform standard for the well-being of all citizens cannot, in the long run, bear the responsibility for having cut off an important segment of the population from responsible jobs and initiatives which are in everyone's best interests, simply because of their choice of religion. We hope that this opinion will gain some ground with the state in the future.

6. The community of all Christians

Finally, we should be aware of the significance of the Christian community. Protestant and Catholic Christians are, from the standpoint of their world-view, all of a piece. The differences between the Protestant and Catholic churches, in ritual and theological interpretation, have not been fully resolved. But they and we are together nowadays, and they are very much on our side whenever it is a question of determining how the Church ought to act and what road she ought to take on her journey of faith. But because ecumenism's faith in mankind binds us together more than it separates us, this faith should be identified by a spirit of mutual love and concern for all people, in contrast to an atheistic ideology and a materialism operating artificially. So, let us offer our parishes and families something that will truly help them, the mission of announcing the Good News of Christ. As soon as we have done that, we too shall become bishops called to encourage open and fraternal dialogue between the Protestant and Catholic communities.

Beloved Brothers!

Regarded in a different light, the situation of the community to whom the first Epistle of Peter is addressed was comparable to the one in which we find ourselves at the moment. The author is writing to a community that lives, as a minority, in an environment that has gone from scorn to open hostility toward Christians. There is only subtle persecution, but there are plots against the community, disagreements, even some discrimination, and all these occur both publicly and privately. Now, what does the author suggest these Christians do?

"Though the pagans may slander you as troublemakers, conduct yourselves blamelessly among them. By observing your good works they may give glory to God on the day of visitation" (1 Pet 2:12). "Rather, become holy yourselves in every aspect of your conduct, after the likeness of the holy One who called you . . ." (1:15). "Live as free men, but do not use your freedom as a cloak for vice. In a word, live as servants of God" (2:16). "Should anyone ask you the reason for this hope of yours, be ever ready to reply . . ." (3:15). But the author further insists: "Do not be surprised, beloved, that a trial by fire is occurring in your midst. It is a test for you, but it should not catch you off guard. Rejoice instead, in the measure that you share Christ's sufferings. When his glory is revealed, you will rejoice exultantly" (4:12–13).

"Your conduct among the pagans should be blameless"

Would we, as bishops of today, have the ability to write our people such a pastoral letter as this one? It is worthwhile to read Peter's epistle, study it from this angle, and use it for our people's spiritual benefit.

We appreciate your faithful spiritual service, with all our hearts. We pray that God will give you the strength and confidence you need to accomplish the pastoral duty we share together, and we greet you in the unity of Christ's love.

THE CHURCH'S MISSION

Conference by Cardinal Giacomo Biffi, Archbishop of Bologna

Preface

It is not easy to consider a concept so frequently used in Christianity as that of *mission*, seeking to be faithful to perennial truth without being obvious and repetitive.

This is the task that we propose for ourselves, and though arduous, it is useful and worthwhile: precisely the most well-known ideas— which are usually the most important ones—run the risk either of being trivialized or of being subjected to awkward attempts at rejuvenation through introducing elements foreign to the genuine perspective of revelation.

Let us take as point of departure the "roots" or foundations of the mission, that is, the one who carries it out, and that for which it is intended, in order better to understand a few thematic consequences, which seem to me to merit attention, among which are the comparison between the baptismal priesthood and the ministerial priesthood and the correct use of the notions "layman" and "the laity".

I am obliged to advise that this is the reflection of a bishop; that is, one who long ago studied a little, has had the opportunity to forget a lot, and, when nonetheless he succeeds in the work of reflection, does so while immersed in the daily labors of the pastoral life. Thus, this treatise will have neither the completeness nor the formal rigor of a professional theologian's: which, in some aspects, can also be considered a good thing.

I. *The Foundations of the Mission*

Indicating the foundations means answering this fundamental question: where does mission originate?

We refer here to the Church's mission in itself, without specifying for now if we mean the mission of the whole Church, or of the individual men who constitute the Church. Or perhaps it is better

This conference, important as much for its theme as for its manner of treatment, was held at the Second International Convention of Movements in Rome, February 3, 1987. Translated from the Italian by Joseph Illo.

to say that our reflections are valid for all the members that it will
be possible to consider further on.

The word *Church* in our concept of the *Church's mission* indicates
that, even if we refer to individuals, they are always seen as belonging
to the *total Christ*, that is, they are seen as members of the Church.

Obviously, our meditation is born and develops within the "Sacred
Doctrine", that is, within the vision of things that proceeds from
the act of faith: it is a discourse between believers who want to
understand more deeply the reality that has been revealed to them,
and with which they have entered into a communion of life.

1. The theological foundation

The Church's mission has one theological foundation, which means
one root that reaches to the life of God itself.

The mission has its roots in the very life of God

The ineffable and eternal act with which the Father communicates
to the Son the totality of the divine being acquires by a free decision
a new relation with creation: it is therefore a giving that is radically
inscribed in the absolute mystery of the uncreated nature, but which
also overflows, so to speak, beyond the infinity of God and reaches
the world. And so he who was generated before any dawn is sent
to us and is born as a man in time. "God has so loved the world as
to give his only-begotten Son" (Jn 3:16).

Jesus of Nazareth, the Son of God, crucified and resurrected, is
thus the first subject of the mission, from which every mission on
earth derives power and meaning. He is "the apostle" par excellence
(cf. Heb 3:1), he whom the Father "has sent" (cf., e.g., Mt 10:40;
Mk 9:37; Lk 9:48; Jn passim).

The mission of Jesus, clothing itself in humanity, extends itself to
and abides in those who are precisely for this reason called "apostles";
"As the Father has sent me, so I send you" (Jn 20:21).

The Lord confirms this "transmission" by the pouring out of the
Holy Spirit. The mission of the Spirit on the part of the Risen One
is the secret and the cause of every authentic participation in the
redemptive mission of Christ: "As the Father has sent me, so also I
send you. . . . Receive the Holy Spirit: To whomever you will
forgive their sins they will be forgiven" (Jn 20:21–23).

The Church, the community of the saved, is sent into the world
of the Risen One, who is the principle of the pentecostal pouring
out upon the Church (see Acts 2). The disciples must "remain" ("You
will remain in the city") until they will be "reclothed by the power
from on high" (Lk 24:49); after the coming of the Paraclete they will
leave and go to all the peoples. The mission of the Spirit connects
Christ to the Church and ensures that the apostolic impetus of the

Head runs through and pervades all of the ecclesial body. With Pentecost, the Church emerges from the "closed doors" and throws herself into the mission.

2. The anthropological foundation

Mission finds a second foundation in the new man himself. This means: mission pours out from the life of faith and from the life of charity. It is plain that we are dealing always with a "supernatural anthropology".

A. The structure itself of the act of faith brings with it a tendency to illuminate the one who stands beside us.

The knowledge of faith demands propagation

Every knowledge, and especially the knowledge of faith, is a light that desires to be spread. Only the "darkness"—that is, unbelief and spiritual stupor—prevents it, closes it in, tries to suffocate it. Instead, he who has been reached by the "true light which enlightens every man" (Jn 1:15) is made, in his turn, a source of enlightenment to others.

Through believing, we come to know that God "wills that all men be saved and come to a knowledge of the truth" (1 Tim 2:4); that "one alone is God and one alone the mediator between God and men, the man Jesus Christ, who gave himself in redemption for all" (1 Tim 2:5); "that there is no other name given to men under the heavens by which they can be saved" (Acts 4:12), other than the name of Jesus of Nazareth, crucified and risen.

It is therefore clear that, as much from its nature as from its content, the Faith intrinsically needs to proclaim and evangelize itself.

Indeed Saint Paul rigorously posited the connection between the desire for universal salvation of the "Lord of all, rich in mercy toward all who call upon him" (Rom 10:12) and the urgency of mission: "Whoever will invoke the name of the Lord will be saved. But how will they be able to believe, without having heard about it? And how will they be able to hear about it without one who proclaims it? And how will they be able to proclaim it without being first sent forth?" (Rom 10:13–15).

He who has been overtaken by the gospel must become a herald of the gospel

He whom the gospel has truly penetrated must certainly make himself a proclaimer of the gospel, which should be his ecclesial station. "From faith to faith" (Rom 1:17), to insert in this discourse a word of Paul's, which in fact in itself is not very clear.

B. Charity, then—in which the new vitality of a disciple of the Lord naturally issues forth and expresses itself—is like the flame that continually strives to propagate its own fire.

Love is born in us because we have been penetrated by the love of the Father: "We love, because he has loved us first" (1 Jn 4:19).

Especially manifesting and incarnating itself in the love of Christ, divine love forms in us the need to love each other: "As I have loved you, so also must you love each other" (Jn 14:34). "The love of Christ spurs us on from the thought that one has died for all" (2 Cor 5:14).

This love is turned toward the Father, toward Christ, toward our brothers in faith, but also toward all other men, because "neighbor" is he whom I, in loving him, make as such (see Lk 10:29–37). From this we have the farewell wishes of Paul: "May the Lord make you increase and abound in the love between you, and toward everyone" (1 Th 3:12).

Every love—but more than any other, the one that "was poured into our hearts by the Holy Spirit, who was given to us" (Rom 5:5)—desires true good for others, bestows on others its own richness, reaches out to assimilate the others to it, and joins with them in a single living unity.

Now, the true good of men is the possession of "Eternal Life"; that is, the true good is that they should come to know the only true God and he who was sent, Jesus Christ (cf. Jn 17:3). Our most substantial richness is our participation in the divine nature, which is conferred upon us by sanctifying grace (cf. 2 Pet 1:4). The fullest and most authentic way to unite ourselves to others is when we and they grow in the likeness of the Son of God, and are, in the fullest way possible, brought into him, and therefore into the life of the Church.

As is clear, the life of charity—which is the life proper to redeemed man—carries with it our responsibility fully to conquer and transform all men by the love of the Father, which is revealed in the crucified and risen Lord Jesus.

3. The psychological foundation

The mission also has a psychological foundation, of which contemporary Christianity does not seem to be very aware. Even so, this foundation remains essential and indispensable, and providentially, the magisterium of John Paul II has recently revived it explicitly (cf. the talk in Loreto, no. 4).

Naturally, we're talking about the "psychology of the believer", continually supported and nourished by the act of faith. It is the psychology of the "new man", precisely the one who possesses the "mentality" of Christ (the *nous* of Christ, of which Saint Paul speaks to us in 1 Cor 2:16).

Evangelization—as the task of individual believers and of the community—emerges on the psychological level and is nourished by the awareness of an imbalance: the imbalance between the great richness that was communicated to us in Christ with the baptismal life and the great spiritual poverty that afflicts those who have not yet been penetrated and transformed by the salvation of the Redeemer.

If this imbalance is no longer felt, one could still have the "dialogue", the "confrontation", the attempt to make harmony between the gospel and the extra-Christian culture, but the will to evangelize will fatally decline. If a Christian—in virtue of a certain "worldly optimism" and of a certain "ecclesial pessimism"—persuades himself that there is no great difference between the state of one who is in the Church and lives his life fully in her, and the state of one who is outside the Church or in some way is not essentially enriched by the gift of grace, he will not have any psychologically tenable motivation for his decision to proclaim the gospel and to adopt it, because men would give themselves in an open and conscious way to Christ anyway.

On the ontological level, there is a vast difference; this imbalance is inscribed into the reality of things: we must constantly keep this fact in mind.

To have clear ideas about "things as they are" is therefore the first requirement in order that a desire and a concern for evangelization might spring up in the soul of a disciple of Christ. This clarity is exactly that "consciousness of the truth", without which every missionary task little by little loses its meaning and becomes worthless.

"The consciousness of truth"

The problem of the need to evangelize can be complicated and obscured by the theological problem of the possibility of salvation offered to all men. These are, however, two different questions: evangelization is our concern, as well as that of the Holy Spirit, and we cannot evade this responsibility by hiding behind a theology that would relieve us of this duty; the salvation of all men, on the other hand, is a "concern of God", who—independently of our conjectures—will know well how to find opportune means lest anyone be lost through geographical, historical, or sociological reasons alone.

It can even be said that one of the ways in which God realizes his will of universal salvation is precisely to arouse and nourish in believers the passion for evangelization for the good of all men. It can also be said that our "mercy" toward the "alienated" objectively seeks to manifest itself within the mission more than within theological suggestions given to God.

In any case, we are obliged to proclaim Christ, so that every man—who is a free and rational creature—may know the name and the face of him who is the creator of his salvation, and so that in the life of the Church man may be able to join and conform himself to the Creator completely.

This psychological principle, it should be noted, springs from the awareness of the very nature of evangelization.

The mission of the Church has at its origins a "revelation"; that is, a communication of a truth. It is not, therefore, something purely pragmatic—as are commercial or scientific projects, in which only a few determined guidelines are proposed—but it is primarily the pouring forth of a light; a light that without doubt must become the principle of a new life and even of a new being in him whom it has reached, but which primarily is and must be light, that is, the attainment of truth.

An ecclesial mission in the world, unconvinced of the obligation to offer truth to those who do not yet possess it, would be a contemptible ideological initiative aimed at dominating men in some aspect and at leading them arbitrarily to be what we want. The evangelical mission, however, proceeds from the desire of both evangelized and evangelizers to be ever more completely overcome, dominated, and profoundly transformed by the light of truth, which, with the coming among us of the Word of God, has finally vanquished the oppressive night of our history.

4. Ideological opposition to the "consciousness of truth"

The "consciousness of truth" of Christians—that is, the certitude that they should have of having been overcome by the merciful light of God and of being therefore themselves the "light of the world" (cf. Mt 5:14) and being trustees of a salvific knowledge—this is today sometimes the object of sarcasm and reproof. The idea of the absolute, primary, sacred, and salvific value of truth is ridiculed in our contemporary culture and is greatly weakened even in the Christian mind.

Paradoxically, we have even gone as far as to hold the reaffirmation of all the truths of faith to be contrary to the spirit of the Second Vatican Council. Thus, we want to define proponents of the perennial certainties as *integralist* or *pre-conciliar*, almost as if, among the intentions of the Council, there had been a sort of spiritual suicide of the Church, "pillar and bulwark of truth" (1 Tim 3:15), and a repudiation on the part of the Church of her most intimate nature.

We live in a society that seems to privilege doubt. According to some, doubt is the sign of a free and open mind, while certitude implies narrowness, dogmatism, intolerance, and a mind closed to any dialogue. Unfortunately, even Christians, demonstrating a notable lack of critical capacity, sometimes let themselves be infected by these opinions, and so the "consciousness of truth" ends up being obscured from their sight and their sense of mission grows feeble.

A few simple reflections on this account would be useful.

A. Certitude is in itself a positive quality of the intelligence, not a defect: when a student answers a question correctly and without hesitation, he deserves a better grade than another who is unsure of his answer. Naturally, this applies to a true knowledge, for erroneous knowledge is not really knowledge at all.

Doubt, on the other hand, is an imperfection of knowledge, of which there is no reason to brag; it is an unhealthy state from which man, who was made for the truth, must always try to escape.

Certainty, it is obvious, does not have anything to do with ostentation, which is the unjustified defense of opinions without foundation; and doubt, in its turn, does not have anything to do with the right and praiseworthy effort to explore new dimensions and new implications of what we already know.

B. Even if, on the psychological level, it can seem otherwise, inquiry, dialogue, and the very desire to communicate with others are possible only by virtue of the presence in the mind of a group of initial certainties: without a minimum number of certainties, every intellectual life and every relation would end up being unfeasible.

C. On the existential level, then, it is not difficult to realize, with a little consideration, that those who accuse others of having certitude and almost castigate them for it always have convictions themselves that they retain as indisputable. And so we realize that we are not dealing so much with the reasoned criticism of certainties as with an antipathy and intolerance toward the certainties of others.

D. Christian certainties have a greater possibility of being spiritual values and not pure ostentation, if the one who invites them into his soul perceives them and strives to possess them not as his own ideas, but as a full and personal communion with the great certitude of the Church, to which they were imparted by the Spirit of Truth; a certitude that remains the inalienable patrimony of the Lord's spouse throughout the centuries of her history.

While "worldly" certainties are often acts of individualism, or, at best, adherence to systems of thought that have been recently formulated and are linked to a specific culture, the true Christian certainties possess a *catholic* character, that is, they are universal. That is to say, they possess one of the characteristics proper to truth.

E. Naturally, we need to guard against presenting our personal convictions, or the particular convictions of our social, ideological, and ecclesiastical groups, or the ideas current and prevalent in a specific setting and historical period, as "the consciousness of truth" of Christ's Church. Also, in connection with the truth, we need to be careful never to mix, in the sanctuary of our consciences, the one and living God with the multitude of dead and deadly idols, or even with the meaningless little idols of our whims and our questionable preferences.

In summary

We can now try to put together what we have discussed so far concerning the foundations of mission, rethinking it synthetically in the light of the existence of the renewed man "in Christ".

In general, the fundamental norm of Christian morality consists of emulating the life of the Son of God made man: "He who says that he lives in Christ must live the same way that he lived" (1 Jn 2:6). Therefore, even the "mission" of Christ becomes the mission of Christians.

More profoundly, the "consciousness of truth" in the Church is, in essence, the self-knowledge of the whole Christ: the Church knows herself, knows herself to be the "body" of the Lord Jesus, and all the skeptical clouds of the worldly culture cannot obscure this clarity.

The skeptic fog breaks against the Lord Jesus

And as she knows herself to be the body of Christ, she knows that the whole of humanity is called to become the body of Christ, and is therefore destined to be transformed into her own reality as the Lord's Spouse.

The life of faith and charity, through which we participate in that warm splendor with which the Word of God permeates the humanity it has assumed, renders us with him the light and love of the world. The "holy nation"—created and formed by the redemptive mission of the Only-Begotten of the Father—is joined to Christ through his being sent for the salvation of the world.

This is an aspect of the mystery of the "New Eve", celebrated by the Fathers. Originating from Christ, the "New Adam" through his mission and his sacrifice, the Church joins herself to him, to his mission and to his sacrifice, and with him becomes the co-principle in the propagation of new life in the world.

II. *The Subject and the Receiver*

The first subject of the mission, and the one from whom it proceeds, is the Lord Jesus, as has been said repeatedly. Rightly, therefore, does the Epistle to the Hebrews ascribe to him the title of "Apostle" par excellence (see Heb 3:1).

The receiver of the mission, the one to whom it is directed, who is "taken on", so to speak, is the world. "God . . . sent his son into the world, so that the world might be saved by him (Jn 3:17). The term *world* here means *humanity*, which, created by God and contaminated by the Fall, is waiting for salvation. This waiting might be unconscious, but is always real, because it originates from the most intimate fibers of man's nature.

The Church, the fruit and subject of the mission

Renewed humanity, which means the Church, is the fruit of this mission: Christ "gave himself for us, to save us from every iniquity and to create a pure people that now belong to him" (Titus 2:14). But this people, even as it is the fruit, is also the subject: to the degree that it is reached and touched by the mission of Christ, it actively participates in that mission.

What we have briefly described here concerning the subject and receiver deserves a closer consideration.

A. This participation in Christ's mission is by all the Church and by all the individual members of the Church. Even as the subject of the mission, however, the Church always lives and works according to her inherent nature, which is that of being a gathering that originates from the apostolic charism through the power of the Risen One's Spirit, that is, from the fabric of the missions that have come specifically from the mission of the Twelve. It was primarily to the apostles that Christ said: "As the Father has sent me, so also I send you" (Jn 20:21), and: "Go out into all the world and preach the gospel to every creature" (Mk 16:14–15).

There are two elements that must remain both actively meaningful and in balance for a proper understanding and exercising of the Church's mission. On the one hand, we recognize that regeneration as such unites man to the mission of the Church, in which he participates by virtue of his baptism. Without baptism there would be a general need for subsequent sendings. On the other hand, we forcefully affirm that the Christian is sent out to evangelize and to save the world not as an isolated individual, but as a member of the "Holy Nation"; and so he lives, works, and spreads the faith in harmony with the Church, according to her own structure, which regulates the existence, action, and mission of the Church, and therefore in full, respectful, and obedient communion with the apostolic charism, which presides over the whole life of the Church, assigns its various ministries, makes valid and harmonizes the multitude of charisms.

Essentially, this means accepting, without alteration, the sacramental design according to which the Church was established, that is to say, not mitigating the formative function of the sacrament of orders and at the same time fully accepting the inherent missionary character that is immanent in the sacrament of baptism.

B. The "receiver" of the mission, whom we have described as the one in the "world" who is "taken up", also deserves consideration.

To whom must we bring truth and grace, for whom were we made at once benefactors and stewards by the coming among us of the Word of God? Where is the "world" that is waiting for our mission?

Each of us carries within himself a "world" to be evangelized. There are whole areas of our concept of reality, our psychology, and our behavior that are not yet fully and integrally Christian, and that are waiting to be permeated by the light and power of the gospel.

This first evangelization is important, and remains in the foreground because the true effectiveness of a Christian missionary depends on the degree of his actual "conversion" and on his internal reception of the kingdom of God.

Furthermore, it can be said that every fellow Christian needs to be helped to persevere and grow in the life of redemption. This help is offered not only by the knowledge of the word of God, by the celebration of the divine mysteries and by the active responsibility of charity, but also by every type of social life that is in harmony with the Christian ideal. From this notion we see what makes up "Christianity"; that is, the complex of institutions, common usages, and habitual actions that support the Christianization of souls.

In conclusion, the mission of all Christians should be directed toward all men who have not come to know Jesus as their Savior and Lord, whether because they have lost sight of Christian truths or have never had them.

III. *Participation in the Priesthood of Christ*

To deepen and clarify our consideration of the Church's mission and the relation between the sacrament of baptism and the sacrament of orders, as they are understood as distinct and complementary sources of life and apostolate in the Church, we should now reconsider the truth of our participation in Christ's priesthood.

1. Christ the Lord, Priest and "Servant"

When the Epistle to the Hebrews calls Jesus "the apostle and high priest of the faith which we profess" (Heb 3:1), firmly uniting, as we see, the two offices, even so much as to put them under a single article, it serves to demonstrate that the notion of priesthood is organically linked to that of mission and is almost another facet of the same reality.

For an understanding of the priesthood we have to start from Christ. He is "the priest that was needed: Holy, innocent, without stain, apart from sinners and exalted above the heavens" (Heb 7:26), "mediator of a new covenant" (Heb 9:15), "who offered himself once for all" (see Heb 9:28).

And, in offering himself, he presented himself as one who wanted to be our servant: "He has come . . . to serve and to give his own life in redemption for many" (Mk 10:45); "I stand among you as one who serves" (Lk 22:27).

It is, however, a serving not only of sacrifice, but also of guidance and of leadership: Jesus is the Master and the Head in all the essential events of the small community gathered about him: in prayer, at the Last Supper and the Eucharistic rite, and in normative decisions.

As with every other element of the richness of Christ, so too his universal priesthood and his function as shepherd of the people of God is transmitted to the body of the Church. In him, therefore, we find the source, the model, and the fullness of the priestly dignity of Christians and of the ministry itself of the apostolic charism.

Historical note on the word "priest" It would be useful to consider the development that sacerdotal terminology has undergone in Christian usage.

In the New Testament, *priest* is used to signify both Christ and the *holy nation*.

Very early in the Church, however, this term began to apply to ordained ministers. This is a usage that began at the end of the second century and came into full use by the end of the third, with Hippolytus and Cyprian. This transfer of meanings happened especially under the influence of Old Testament typology, which was the tendency to read the institutions of ancient Israel as figures of the new reality of the Church (a process which was already beginning in the Letter of Clement, 1 Cor 43–44).

Although the more ancient usage did not disappear—Augustine still taught that for Christians *omnes sunt sacerdotes, quoniam membra sunt unius sacerdotis* [all are priests, because all are members of one single priest] (*De civitate Dei* 20, 6)—the more recent usage prevailed and became the standard. We find indications of the priesthood of the faithful in only a few passages in the first Epistle of Peter and in the Apocalypse, which obviously continued to be known and commented upon.

For example, St. Ambrose spoke in this way to the neophytes: "What is the people itself if not a priestly people? To whom was it said: You are the chosen race, the royal priesthood, the holy people, as the Apostle Peter affirmed? Each of you is anointed for the priesthood, is anointed for the kingdom, but we mean a spiritual kingdom and a spiritual priesthood" (*De Sacramentis* IV, 1:3; see also *De Mysteriis* 6, 30). This is, I think, the only text of his that can be cited.

After the Second Vatican Council, the two usages have co-existed, and are both employed purposefully and frequently. Because of this, there is a risk of confusion and incorrect transpositions, a risk present today as it has never been before.

The document *Lumen Gentium* carefully provides the basis for a clarification, in a statement that will never lose its force. "Though they differ essentially and not only in degree, the common priesthood of the faithful and the ministerial or hierarchical priesthood are nonetheless ordered one to another; each in its proper way shares in the one priesthood of Christ" (LG, no. 10).

We have already emphasized how these two priesthoods are related to the one priesthood of Christ; now we should go further in order to understand the essential difference in their contents.

2. The baptismal priesthood

A priesthood, as privilege of the whole Church, is spoken of in one passage from the first Epistle of Peter and in three passages from the Apocalypse. These passages use expressions that derive from Ex 19:6, where it says that Israel is a "kingdom of priests" (Hebrew) or a "royal priesthood" (Septuagint) and a "holy nation". The first Epistle of Peter uses the Septuagint version, while the Apocalypse uses the Hebrew text.

"Setting yourselves close to him, the living rock . . . you too will be used as living stones for the building of a spiritual house, for a holy priesthood, to offer spiritual sacrifices pleasing to God, through Jesus Christ. . . . You are the chosen race, the royal priesthood, the holy nation, the people that God has won over so that it may proclaim his wonder . . ." (1 Pet 2:4–10).

"To him who loves us and has freed us from our sins with his blood, who has made of us a kingdom of priests for his God and Father, to him the glory and power for ever and ever. Amen" (Rev 1:5–6).

". . . You have redeemed for God with your blood men from every tribe, tongue, people, and nation and have made of them for our God a kingdom of priests and they will reign over Earth" (Rev 5:9–10).

"They will be priests of God and of Christ and will reign with him for a thousand years" (Rev 20:6).

We will limit ourselves to a few observations.

A. The doctrine contained in these passages is an extension of the content of Exodus: having entered into the covenant with God, the people of Israel possess a unique and distinct dignity that puts them in a very special relation with their Creator and ally. This dignity distinguishes them from all the other peoples and assigns them a sacred function of mediation in their dealings with the whole world: "You will be for me my own possession, because all the earth is mine! You will be for me a kingdom of priests and a holy nation" (Ex 19:5–6).

Isaiah 61:6 contains an echo of this theme: "You will be called priests of the Lord, you will be named ministers of your God", where, in accordance with the post-exilic perspective, the passage refers to the Israel of the rebirth and of the everlasting covenant; and in 2 Maccabees 2:17: "God has saved his people and has bestowed on all the inheritance kingdom, priesthood, and sanctification."

It is to be noted that these teachings do not raise any contradictions or structural problems with the existence of the levitical priesthood, which is present and recognized in the Hebrew world: evidently we are dealing with two realities on different planes, which therefore run no danger of interference.

The priesthood is a prerogative of the new people of God

B. The innovation of the New Testament is that the sacerdotal privilege has been claimed by the New Israel, which means by the people of the New Covenant, who have been consecrated by the blood of Christ.

Setting themselves close to him, the living rock, believers become "living rocks" of the "spiritual house" and can be called a "royal priesthood" (cf. 1 Pet 2:4–10). He who "has freed us from our sins with his blood" has made of us "a kingdom of priests for his God and Father" (Rev 1:5–6), redeeming us out of "every tribe, tongue, people, and nation" (Rev 5:9).

C. It is clear that the "priesthood" spoken of is not a function to be exercised individually within the Christian community, but a privilege of the people of God as such. It is the Church, the "Holy Nation", that is to be invested with priestly dignity, by virtue of its bond and its conformity to the one Priest of the New Covenant.

Certainly it is a dignity that is inherent in baptized individuals, not as individuals per se, but rather, as members of the "Whole Christ".

It is, so to speak, a "universal priesthood", through which the Church offers God not only her own praise, gratitude, and adoration, but that of all creation; she prays for all men, offers the sacrifice that can sanctify, and gives new life to the entire human family.

Because of its priestly function, the people of God is also called to extend Christ's salvific mediation to all peoples, proclaiming to everyone the truth that illuminates and frees, and making of itself the universal sacrament of salvation.

Clearly, here lies the origin—the "ecclesial foundation"—of the mission with which the "chosen race", called to renew and to reconsecrate the earth, has been entrusted.

On the other hand, it does not seem that this universal priesthood could properly be considered the foundation of particular ministries—

ordained, instituted, or de facto—within the Christian community, if it were not for the fact that only he who is integrally taken into the Church, the priestly body, is enabled to exercise a ministry in the Church.

3. The ordained ministry

The so-called "ordained priesthood" fits into the organization of the ministries, but it is quite a different entity.

Within the body of Christ, where everyone holds the highest and unsurpassable dignity of the royal priesthood, the Spirit distributes the ecclesial tasks, that is, the various ministries and different charisms, according to that vision of the "different members", which Saint Paul described in his Epistles (see 1 Cor 12:4–30; Rom 12:3–8; Eph 4:11–16).

The apostolic charism-ministry (which is transmitted by the power of the sacrament of orders) presides over the life of the Church, as it wells up and spreads out, through the exercise of the magisterium, of the sacramental power and of the authority to govern, from which the whole life and the whole mission of the Church comes to life and is regulated.

Also, the apostolic charism-ministry precedes all the different ministries, ordained, instituted, or de facto. More than commendations, they are services; more than honorary citations, they are duties; more than appreciative gestures to the person, they are enrichments to the community. The true dignity of the Christian comes from belonging to an ecclesial body (and therefore from the baptized priesthood); true honor is being counted among consecrated people; true personal worth is given by the intensity of faith, hope, and charity.

Observations

On this note, a few extravagant notions can be put into perspective and a few clarifications pointed out.

A. "Ministry" is an important and deciding element in the life of the Church, provided that it is put at the true service of the "mission". It is not enough to multiply and enlarge ministries: it is also really necessary to benefit the desire and urge to evangelize humanity, and to renew the world with the energy of the Spirit, which should come from the whole people of God.

B. On the other hand, no effort to evangelize or to renew the Christian community can be considered authentic, unless it has an integral relation with the apostolic ministry.

From baptism originates every spiritual impulse in the Church;

but none can survive and develop correctly unless it is in submissive and sincere communion with the episcopal ministry and, in particular, with the ministry of Peter.

C. We must rediscover certain basic truths, which, precisely because of their fundamentality, risk fading slightly in the Church's consciousness, distracted as it is by other concerns.

The highest title of our dignity is membership in the flock of Christ

The highest title of our dignity comes from our being numbered among God's flock. This is our blessing, the cause of our nobility, the foundation of our hope.

The privileges of any other function (hierarchical, ministerial, charismatic) are not comparable to the ontologic richness, the salvific value, and the eschatological promises that come to us from our condition as the Lord's sheep.

Everyone in the Church is, above all else, a dweller in the sheepfold of Christ. Everyone, from the pope to the newly baptized, possesses the true source of greatness, not so much from being entrusted with this or that task in the Christian community, as from being of the "little flock", which need not fear, because it has pleased the Father to give it the kingdom (see Lk 12:32).

There is, therefore, an essential equality among all believers, more relevant and ultimate than any other designation in the Church, and this equality is the condition of their truly believing: only in believing may one enter among the sheep of Christ (Jn 10:26).

This is also the primary source of our joy. We had strayed like sheep without a shepherd, but the Lord had compassion on us, on our abandonment (Mk 6:34), on our weariness (Mt 9:36), and gathered us together. And we have returned to the shepherd and guardian of our souls (1 Pet 2:25), and we have a very close intimacy with him.

He who offered his life for us (Jn 10:15), knows us (Jn 10:14) and calls us one by one by name (Jn 10:3). He walks among us, and we follow him because we know his voice (Jn 10:4).

IV. *The Lay State and the Laity*

Our reflections on the participation in Christ's priesthood help us to shed a little light on the ideas of the "lay state" and the "layman". And this too will be a valuable contribution toward our understanding, in its true colors, the "Church's mission".

1. The lay state

We often hear the lay state praised as a basic aspect of the Church which we should rediscover and improve.

It is an argument that is acceptable and compelling inasmuch as it says that the inner make-up of all creatures—and especially man—should be respected: these creatures are already "true", good, and meaningful in themselves, without the need of dressing them up with additional values and designations.

This argument is acceptable and compelling inasmuch as it discourages us from "clericalizing" things and people, and invites us, rather, to understand and appreciate them for what they are. We need to guard ourselves from supernaturalism that is extrinsic and juxtaposed that fears being not sufficiently Christian unless it attaches labels savoring of religious or outright clerical reminiscences to certain objects.

But the glorification of the lay state becomes pure nonsense when it seeks to convince us that to understand creation completely we should ignore, even if only methodologically, a consideration of God or of Christ, or that things have a full value and a complete meaning independent of God or Christ.

All things take their reference from God, and we can grasp their correct and inherent significance only through their essential and intrinsic religious dimension. And, in fact, all things—and especially men—are inherently connected to Christ, in whom they are conceived from the beginning, and in whom all things—and especially men—find their archetype and their perfect model.

Above all, insisting on the lay nature of the people of God can be extremely ambiguous: we risk forgetting or losing sight of the wonderful teaching of Revelation about our common royal priesthood and our state as the "chosen race" and "holy nation". Since we have been baptized, we are a race of consecrated ones, and by virtue of our consecration we are the "people that God has gained", so that we may be, so to speak, the "priest for all peoples", and so that we may tirelessly bring the whole human family to salvation.

In a certain sense we can say that, in the order of things planned and realized by the Father, the "lay" state does not exist: it does not exist in the Church, because in the Church everything is sacred and everyone is a promoter of the cult of the true God; and it does not exist in creation, because everything is already "Christian" from the beginning and seeks to bring its initial likeness and belonging to Christ to a logical perfection in the life of Christ.

2. The layman

Emphasizing the concept of the layman can also be an occasion for theological obscurities, if by layman we mean the believer who is not a part of the ordained ministry (a concept that already appeared in Clement of Rome: "The layman is bound to lay precepts" (1 Cor 40:5).

The emphasis placed on the layman is explained as a reaction to the unilateral and improper idea that at one time the function of "clerics" was made so important as to give the impression that the Church identified itself with the ordained ministries, such that the others seemed to be, so to speak, only objects of the Church's consideration and almost "clients" of the institution.

However, we must not react with a diametrically opposed outburst, but with a better understanding of the truth of the matter.

From a concept of the layman which would be, because of its own unique content, purely negative—a correct and substantial theological and spiritual doctrine about the nature and role of the layman can be developed only with difficulty.

A sacrament of "not being a priest" does not exist, nor does one of "not having been ordained"; the sacraments of baptism and of confirmation exist, and they bring the specific grace needed to exist in every legitimate manner.

Whatever true, good, or beautiful thing we want to obtain with the "promotion of the laity", we can and must receive from the power of baptism and the "priestly kingdom" of which revelation speaks to us.

More than from the generic and negative consideration of the laity, a real spiritual and ethical heritage, a specific bestowal upon the Church, can be obtained from reflecting upon the diversity of ministries, from charisms, from existential tasks, from understanding the proper graces connected with individual states of life, and from intelligently and sympathetically receiving the gifts of light and divine power found in all genuine movements that the Holy Spirit is causing to spring up in the Church.

PART THREE

THE LIFE OF THE CHURCH

I

AFRICA

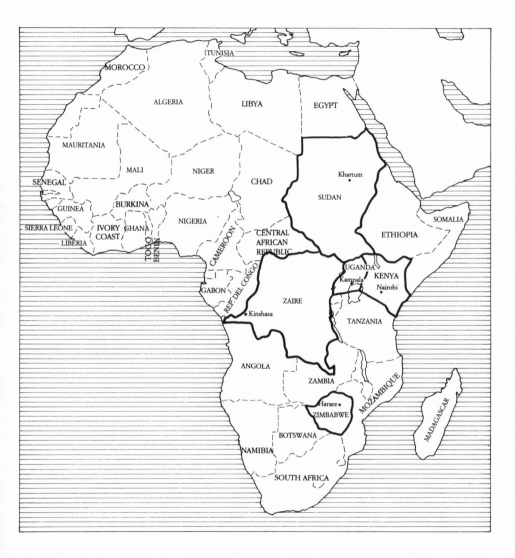

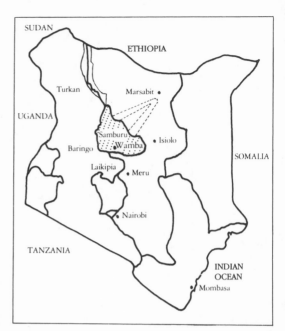

Kenya:
The north of the country is settled by
the Samburu tribe, a nomadic people

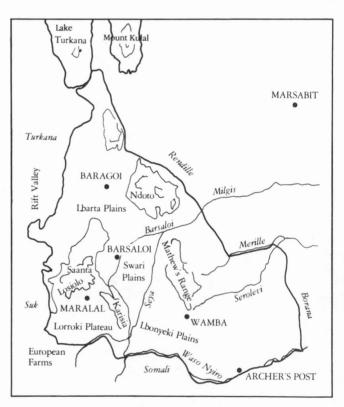

The Marsabit District:
The hospital directed
by Dr. Prandoni was established
in central Wamba

TWENTY YEARS OF HOPE

The Hospital of Wamba in Kenya

by
Fortunato Fasana

In the North of Kenya, there is a vast region inhabited by the Samburu, a tribe of nomadic shepherds of Nilo-Hamitic origin. The *The Samburu,* Samburu, around 75,000 individuals, prefer to be called *Lookop*, *formerly nomads,* "they who possess the earth", in order to signify their nomadic *in the north* wanderings in Africa throughout centuries. Their land, the savanna, *of Kenya* is a kingdom of sweat, wind, thorns, sand, and rocks baked by the sun. In this environment, they watch over their herds—cows, goats, camels—in a continuous cattle-drive, a perennial search for well and pasture. Civilization has scarcely touched them, and, like all nomadic and pastoral peoples, the flock is their sole wealth, their principal worry. The lance and knife are the arms that defend their flocks from the raids of neighboring tribes and the attacks of ferocious animals. Rains fall in the spring and autumn, but frequently rainfall (an average of 14 inches a year) is scarce and water shortages result. Pestilence is frequent among the animals, as are malnutrition and hunger among the population.

The Samburu live in huts of leaves and mud, in a society ruled by their elders. They eat berries and the blood of their cows, obtained by bleeding the cows from their jugular veins and mixing the blood with milk. When the weather is favorable, their diet includes a mush made from corn they cultivate near their huts.

In 1986, the twenty-year anniversary of the hospital in Wamba was celebrated in Kenya and Italy. Wamba is a small village in the district of Marsabit in the northern region of Kenya and is inhabited by the Samburu people. Founded by the initiatives of the Missionaries of the Consolation and by the Bishop of Marsabit, the hospital has been directed all these years by Doctor Silvio Prandoni, former collaborator of Doctor Fortunato Fasana. Fasana has passed his life in missionary hospitals, prepared the plans for the first construction in Wamba, and often has taken the place of Doctor Prandoni as director of the hospital. Dr. Fasana has contributed this testimony about what his friend Prandoni and the hospital have meant to the Samburu and to the group called the Friends of Wamba. This article was translated from the Italian by Robert and Veronica Royal.

In 1966, the Fathers of the Consolation decided to found a mission at Wamba, on the invitation of the Council of the elder Samburu. To this end, the Samburu moved a group of their huts and made available a large plot of land.

In those years, I was directing the hospital in Nyeri, and I had the good fortune to be the colleague and collaborator of Doctor Silvio Prandoni of Legnano. He took his degree in medicine in Milan, and after two years in orthopedic practice and plastic surgery he came to Kenya as a lay medical missionary.

Doctor Prandoni remained with me almost a year, and since then I have been linked with him by a fraternal friendship and by a great esteem for his extraordinary moral gifts and professional capacity. *The hospital* In 1969, Prandoni finished erecting the hospital in Wamba. In one *work begins* of his letters, he wrote: "I am completely isolated from the world, lost in the desolate savanna under a scorching sun—so many elephants, leopards, rhinoceros, lions, and snakes. In the hospital (twenty beds), there are many difficulties. There is no sink, not a single chair, the language is difficult, and the Sisters don't understand it; the witch doctor is my rival. I work with confidence, and in time I hope to give to those poor people a passable hospital. I cannot hurry—in Africa time does not count. I feel the need to do something for them because no one takes an interest in them."

The growth of the hospital and of its services, which took place in order to meet the needs of a growing number of patients, meant an increasing financial burden and great efforts and sacrifices as well. The plans for the hospital had to be studied with particular care, keeping in mind the mentality of the patients, the functionality and efficiency of the work, and the clinics, which had to be modified and adapted to local necessity. For construction materials, for building forms, and for equipment and supplies of every kind, today as in the past, it is necessary to depend on Nairobi, an eleven-hour distance by land rover. Tiberio Mandelli, a volunteer first in Rho and now seventeen years in Wamba, has been the director of operations, the head laborer, electrician, plumber, carpenter, welder, and chief of transportation. In the last three years, he has been helped by Gerard, a Canadian volunteer, who looks after the vehicles and goes to Nairobi one or more times per week to buy necessities or transport medical teams.

In 1969, the hospital had forty beds; in 1971, more than sixty; in 1974, one hundred, with special wings for the men, the women, and the children, a laboratory, a radiological department, and an emergency room. In 1979, the emergency room was completed with rooms for eye doctors and dentists, and a new radiology section.

The large waiting room handles an average of three hundred patients per day.

Other areas indispensable to the functioning of the hospital were also built: a kitchen, a laundry room, a steam generator, shops, an office, a carpenter's shop, and a central pharmacy. In 1977, a doctors' residence was completed for the doctors working temporarily in Wamba. Today the hospital has two hundred and ten beds, including an isolation ward for the children, given the recurrent epidemics of measles and scarlet fever, and the numerous cases of meningitis, encephalitis, and tuberculosis. As Doctor Prandoni writes, "The hospital has become a focal point and a stimulus for our population." The construction of these buildings has given years of work to local laborers, who have progressed from being mere manual laborers to being expert bricklayers. The nursing school opened in 1970 and, *The school* recognized by the government, provides about twenty new graduates *for nurses* every year. Among the graduates, residents of the district are hired by the hospital itself, and the others find employment in the dispensaries and government hospitals in the rest of Kenya.

In 1976, Friends of Wamba, a volunteer support network for the hospital, was formed, which consists of one hundred doctors, technicians, and collaborators. Carlo Treccani, the secretary, runs this group and also directs all of its initiatives. Teams of oculists, guided by Professors Vannini, Galeazzi, Musini, and Rama, have created the Opthalmic Center—still unique in Kenya—where even corneal transplants are being done. At the same time, professors from Italy and from other countries and hospitals with a complete range of specialties offer their services to Wamba for various lengths of time. Specialized workers regularly spend their vacations in Wamba, engaged in the finishing touches to the hospital and its plant. The foundation called "A Leader for the Samburu" sponsors young, deserving students, enabling them to attend specialized schools, thus obtaining technicians and laborers qualified for the hospital and the other facilities in the district.

In 1984, the drought that had plagued the Sahel region for years *The drought* also reached the district of the Samburu in the North of Kenya. In *of 1984* that year, there was no rain at all, and in 1985 the rain was still very sparse with the consequent loss of 80% of the livestock. There were numerous victims, even among the human population, especially among the young and the old. Long lines of the Samburu, walking skeletons covered with rags, stood in front of the dispensary waiting for the half-kilo allotment of corn flour that lasted them three days. The vehicles of the hospital and of the mission left in the morning loaded with sacks of flour to distribute in the villages and returned in the evening loaded with Samburu who no longer had the strength to come to the hospital.

Hunger and malnutrition aggravated diseases such as malaria and tuberculosis and stimulated growth of epidemics. Even today, the population continues to feel profoundly the consequences of that tragic period. The Friends of Wamba organized a hunger foundation that continues daily to provide meals to the thousand children who gravitate to the mission; the Foundation gives subsidies to the heads of families, creating possibilities for them to work; it also buys animals for them, to restore their livestock destroyed by the drought. Even now, however, it is still not rare for the Samburu to present themselves to the doctor and say simply: "I am fine and I don't need your medicines, but I am hungry and I come to you because you can give me something to eat."

Giorgio Torelli wrote at the end of his visit: "When one arrives at a place like Wamba, one wants to stay and ask: give me something to do." The tasks for the future will be many. A department of *Tasks for* physiotherapy and rehabilitation has been completed that stands *the future of* alongside the center for the handicapped currently being erected and *the Samburu* run by an institute of Indian Sisters.

A new maternity wing and the addition to the pediatric department are on the drawingboard for the future. Doctor Prandoni, even though he has been working twelve hours a day for years, still needs a colleague who would remain permanently, full-time at his side, and also an experienced physiotherapist. Man needs man.

The patients continue to come, more and more, from all the districts of North Kenya, from Uganda, Ethiopia, and Somalia. And for many of them, Wamba means the last hope.

The following statistics recap eighteen years of work in Wamba: 13,000 cured, 60,000 outpatient visits, 7,200 operations performed (1,900 eye operations), 25,000 radiological tests, 40,000 laboratory tests—an average of 1,200 patients treated annually. Last year Prandoni wrote to the Friends of Wamba: "Years pass and leave their marks not only on our faces but also around us: the hospital is a marvelous accomplishment. At times perhaps we have erred, but the essential spirit that animated us animates us still. Our spirits, too, have grown with the years, gaining in serenity and devotion. We will continue thus; there is still much to do together in order that the hospital may become the concrete sign of our friendship."

TO SEE CONTEMPLATING:

A Comboni Missionary in the Sudan

by
Fidel Gonzalez

I have been in the Sudan to give three series of the spiritual exercises to missionaries at El Abide and Khartoum. I went to the Sudan with enthusiasm and with the spirit of a pilgrim who is going to visit places sanctified by *martyrs*, the witness-disciples of Christ. My visit helped me to understand situations of the past as well as things read and studied in missionary history and to taste—so to speak—a little of that living history. As for those who deny their own history or forget it—we need only cite the thoughts of the philosopher George Santayana—that these people are condemned to repeating their history or reliving it. My voyages to the Sudan have become to me a living memory.

I arrived in Khartoum on April 24, the anniversary of my baptism and also my name day. I was immediately struck by a world that was for me both new and different from the Africa I had known: the tremendous heat (113°F), the people, the dust, the flat and immense city. I went about the nice part of the city, then through the poor neighborhoods. My eyes were wide open to what was around me, and I listened attentively to the fathers, who, out of extreme kindness, had accompanied me and helped me to understand so different a world. I went with the fathers to celebrate Mass at two centers on the outskirts of Khartoum. I visited two other centers on the outskirts of El Obeid, where I saw a destitution and poverty the likes of which I had never seen in the Africa I had known before that moment.

A destitution and poverty never before seen in Africa

At El Obeid, I also came into contact with the work of the missionaries there. Here I was able to participate in an annual pastoral

In April–May 1986, Father Fidel Gonzalez, professor of Church history at the Urban University of Rome, was invited to give the spiritual exercises to the missionary brothers of the Sudan. There, he could see the poverty, the disease, and the sacrifices of the Sudanese and the missionaries, but also he was able to contemplate "a persevering and faithful presence, filled with hope". This article was translated from Italian by Robert and Veronica Royal.

gathering of the diocese. I made a visit to Omdurman, that place of so many sad memories for missionaries who were prisoners of the Mahdia from 1882 to 1898.

The Hard Mission

1. Of all the missions that I visited in Africa—Senegal, Togo, Benin, Ghana, Zaire, Uganda, Malawi, Zambia, Kenya, and Egypt— Malawi, the Sudan, seems to me without doubt the most difficult and needy. Difficult because of the climate: a suffocating and unnerving heat. I think about my weeks spent at El Obeid, in which the thermometer was constantly around 113°F in the shade, and I understand what it means to be a missionary now, as in the times of the earlier Comboni. I think of the voyages and the enormous distances: the journey from Darfur (El-Fasher) to El Obeid takes five days by land rover, from Babanusa to El Obeid three days, and so forth.

Notwithstanding all this, the priests and sisters came to the exercises. To travel in the desert on roads of infernal sand, in terrible heat, with drinking water long since become warm; sleeping at times on the edge of the road . . . I believe you have to live it to understand it! And then one is also better able to understand the writings of the early missionaries and their long desert crossings. I think of the missionaries like the Spaniard Father Parlade and his companion, who worked in Damazin, five days by truck from Khartoum. In that mission they had no vehicles, they traveled only by merchant trucks, with days full of sun and dust: to visit the villages took hours and hours on the truck, and hours of walking on foot, at times eight or ten hours, sleeping along the streets and in the huts, eating whatever one found. And this is the life of the greater part of the missionaries, both men and women, who live in El Obeid and Khartoum.

A Poor Mission

2. It is a poor mission, poor from the sociological point of view. It is not really poverty, but rather dark and sad destitution: in these villages everything is in short supply, especially on the outskirts of the cities, even the three large cities of Khartoum (Khartoum, Khartoum north, and Omduman), which are linked together by bridges on the White and Blue Niles. These are places where a bucket of water costs a dollar, and perhaps more. The climate is full of dust, sweat, and heat, while water is scarce.

A dollar for one pail of water

3. In the midst of these people, I have seen missionaries who work with a poverty of means and yet with incredible possibilities: a little house like the others lived in by the poor people is rented and trans-

formed into a "Christian Center". Most of the time, the government does not permit the purchase of land. Nonetheless, in these places are born, in much poverty and much hope, Christian centers in the midst of a pagan or Islamic world. There are missionaries like those of Damazin in the diocese of Khartoum (larger than Illinois in terms of territory), or Babanusa, where the priests live in rented huts, without water, light, or the least amenities. The Combonian sisters of Babanusa live, sleep, and eat in a little house not more than fifteen feet square, in the midst of a courtyard that serves as a school, catechumenate, resting place, kitchen, and everything else. . . .

4. There is the poverty of the missionary, who lives solely in hope and uncertainty and at risk of being sent away from one moment to the next. To get around, even to visit the Christian center of a parish outside his own location, requires a permit from the police. Even if this permission is normally given, the situation is nevertheless precarious. The Church has become poor in this way, because it has no power other than that of the Holy Spirit.

5. But I have also read of various reasons for urgency in missionary activity here, in these places.

a. The arrival of the Southern Blacks into North Sudan must be considered salvific: little by little, it is bringing about a transformation of a monolithically Islamic society, from the cultural, social, and anthropological point of view.

This society is becoming more and more a mixed society. Who knows if the Lord might not have his plan here and that the proclamation of Christianity in Islamic societies may not occur by means of the Blacks, i.e., the most looked-down-upon members of society, and those called slaves by their former masters? It would be a unique occurrence in the modern history of Christianity, an occurrence similar to what happened at the beginnings of Christianity, when the first disciples, coming from a colony, although nonetheless citizens in the true sense of the word, evangelized imperial Rome. . . . Today, something similar could happen in the Sudan.

—The fact that this emigration is moving toward the North and the large cities is in line with a common phenomenon today in all the so-called Third World. This will give rise to new societies, different from the traditional ones.

—Therefore, I think, from the point of view of the missionary vocation, it is a high priority to meet the needs of these thousands of people (in Khartoum there are already a half-million and perhaps even more) through an integral evangelization: evangelical preaching, but also social and cultural activity. The methodology of the "catechumen clubs" has struck me. These clubs are run by the Comboni missionaries at locations throughout Khartoum. One Father

The catechumen clubs

Sergi, for example, conducts a meeting from four to ten each evening attended by about a thousand young people who are learning the catechism as well as how to read and write. . . . The catechumen clubs are a meeting place for diverse tribal groups, and also a place where catechism classes take place; these prepare the young people for their meeting with Christ in the Church. These clubs are run, in part, by the young people themselves, who at times must come five or ten miles on foot to these evening meetings after work.

Another sociological fact is that culture is created in the cities, that is, it is the city that extends itself to the underlying *pagus* (villages), and not the other way around. Someone who becomes a Christian in the city does not lose his identification with the faith easily. Therefore, I think it is possible that the ancient phenomenon may repeat itself partly today, the phenomenon of the evangelization of "pagans" (i.e., those in the villages) on the part of the "city dwellers", as in the time of the Roman Empire.

Arabic, furthermore, is becoming the *lingua franca* of these people as the *Koine* Greek was in ancient Rome.

b. The presence of the missionaries among the Moslems is an authentic missionary presence. A missionary is not measured by the works that he achieves or by immediate results, but only by the intensity of his life and the missionary witness that he gives. It is a matter of a persevering and faithful presence, full of hope. History belongs to God, not to man.

A Mission of Hope

c. Still, consider that the missionary presence among the Moslems, and the presence of the Church in the scholastic field as well, ought to be lived and with this aim! It is a service to a poor people who have many needs. Social assistance, work in the hospitals, etc., is necessary. Perhaps it will be necessary to make an authentic discernment about the way to make more visible certain presences and works from the Christian point of view. And in this sense a discernment is necessary. But to say that this presence is not missionary would be a great error and a lack of Christian perspective.

Christianity comes alive when it is converted into a cultural reality

d. Christianity comes alive when it is transferred into a cultural reality. Only then does it enter into the life of man, without fragmentation or losses. Unfortunately, in many places in today's Africa, Christianity is not a cultural reality. It does not touch the lives of the people (cf. the letter of the Ugandan bishops, Lent 1981). And this is because we have believed, at times, that Christianity was solely a "ritual fact" (sacraments), and ritual facts do not last, nor do they affect history. I believe that, in this sense, schools ought to become a way for producing a Christian culture, even if they have to begin from only a human basis. The school in the middle of a Moslem neighborhood is a privileged means that the Lord puts in our hands to carry forward this mission, which is of extraordinary urgency in Africa today. At times we become a bit myopic in our missionary activity, because we do not stop to "contemplate" history, to understand what the Lord is telling us.

History does not unfold haphazardly. In the Christian conception of history, God is the Lord, and we are called to act so that history will become the story of salvation. If the Lord began the missionary history a hundred years ago in the Sudan, it was not by mere chance. It was a duty, a moment of grace, a specific gift to carry forward this dialogue of salvation. We cannot deny our history, or disengage ourselves from it: that would be to separate ourselves from our original charism.

A visit to Sudan helped me "to see contemplating" and to praise the work of the missionaries there. And it also helped me better to understand the history and the very identity of the missions.

THE FINAL GIFT OF A WHITE MAN

The Testimony of Father Giuseppe Ambrosoli in Uganda

by
Lorenzo Gaiga

February 7, 1987, was a tragic day for the Kalongo mission in Northeast Uganda, a region inhabited by the Acholi people. At this mission, there had arisen a famous hospital and an obstetric school, which was the pride of the entire country.

The European missionaries, doctors, and sisters were allowed seven minutes to present themselves to the governing military authorities and to listen to the military chief's brief, blunt, and unchangeable order to leave: "You have twenty-four hours to leave with your sick, and all that you can carry with you. You can go to Lira." For some minutes, none of them could say a word. Some stood looking at the syringes that were still in their hands, some were nervously shuffling the clinical papers, which they did not even have time to put down, and some looked at one another with fear.

You have 24 hours to get out

Twenty-four hours to dismantle a hospital of 330 beds and a mission as large as an entire country. . . .

Kalongo had been a fixed point in the difficult medical situation in Uganda, which for more than 15 years has endured a civil war and the most profound anguish and which has already seen hundreds of thousands of innocent victims. Sick people came to the Kalongo mission not only from nearby nations, but even from India, in order to undergo complicated operations. With great success, the hospital

Father Giuseppe Ambrosoli has been known in all of Eastern Africa as the "great doctor", "God's physician". He expanded the Kalongo hospital and founded various associated dispensaries, as well as the famous schools of nursing and obstetrics. Every day, streams of people arrived at his home, and he strove to cure them both physically and spiritually. And yet, in the final days of his life, Father Ambrosoli had to see the sun set on his work. In repeated encounters between the army and guerrillas, the priests, doctors, and nurses had to evacuate the Kalongo hospital within 24 hours. It was February 7, 1987. A month and a half later, on March 27, 1987, Father Ambrosoli died from kidney failure. To the human eye, he appeared defeated, but his sacrifice, pleasing to the Lord, will not fail to bear fruit for the Ugandan church. This article was translated by Robert and Veronica Royal.

at Kolongo also took care of numerous lepers in their own homes. And yet the hospital at Kalongo was born in humility, like all the works of God.

The Beginnings of the Hospital

In January 1934, several Comboni missionaries set out on the nearly impassable paths of the Acholi tribe, under the banner of humility, poverty, stubbornness, in search of a place to found a mission. They were called "God's desperate ones" because, after having selected the site and built the first huts, the great rains came and transformed the whole area into an immense pond with no exit. Naturally, they did not lose spirit, and with a great force of will, challenging the mosquitoes, the snakes, every imaginable insect, they built an embankment which allowed them to communicate with the rest of the world. Why so much labor? Why not go to a more accessible place? It was obvious: there were so many people in this place who had never heard the gospel, and there were also so many bodies that were waiting for a good Samaritan. In fact, Christ, for whom the missionaries had not hesitated to give their lives, is a body, too—the body of a sick person, a leper, a handicapped person, a cripple. Thus it was that in 1943, Sister Eletta Mantiero improvised her "little hospital", something between a hut and an emergency room. Appetite comes with eating, and in 1949 she was transferred to a large regular dispensary, to which was added a maternity wing. The fame of the Kalongo hospital spread throughout all of northern Uganda, so much so that it was necessary to organize a transportation service for the sick.

Christ is also the body of the sick

The Arrival of Father Giuseppe

During the decade 1952–1962, 8,061 Ugandan citizens were born in the maternity wing in Kalongo. Every year approximately 1,000 surgical operations are performed, an incredible and tenacious labor, sustained by the compassion and collaboration of benefactors and other hospital operations outside of Uganda. Volunteer doctors were not slow to arrive, lending years of service to this forgotten area of Africa. The soul of Kalongo was, without doubt, Father Giuseppe Ambrosoli, the head doctor. Always smiling, he heroically made himself available to others, and he always displayed decisively superior intelligence. After having graduated from Milan in medicine and surgery, Father Ambrosoli went to England to specialize in tropical diseases. He had already decided to leave Italy to bring medical treatment to the neediest of the earth, our brothers in the Third

World. But how? The fogs of London were a light for him. In fact, there he reestablished acquaintance with the Comboni missionaries; he lived alongside of them, thought highly of them, and understood that he could become one of them: a doctor of souls and of bodies. "God is love, there is a neighbor who suffers, and I am his servant", he wrote.

There is a neighbor who is suffering and I am his servant

To become a missionary in the full sense of the word, Giuseppe had to leave behind a large and prosperous family business, which produced candy and honey. He never hesitated. He was fascinated by the poor, and they seemed to him more worthy of attention than

candy and honey. He chose the poor with all the enthusiasm of a twenty-eight-year-old, and, in September 1941 he entered the Comboni novitiate of Gozzano (Novara), in order to prepare his soul and his heart for the great African adventure.

When, on December 17, 1955, he prostrated himself before the bishop of Milan for his priestly ordination, those present in the church saw that he had holes in the soles of his shoes. His mother shuddered, but she was not surprised because she knew what kind of son he was; his brothers burst out laughing when they noticed that even his suit was patched in several places.

The Distressing Suffering of the People

Father Giuseppe's thirty-two years in Africa were an epic deserving more than the few lines of this article. He was a missionary on the new frontiers of sorrow, of hope first and then of despair, of peoples whose wounds drip blood. The force of always saying yes to everyone, with a smile on his face and with the gentleness of a great lord who finds himself at ease even with the most humble of suppliants, comes easily to him from his habit of making his medical instruments a means of prayer.

The strength to say yes to everyone

In the last few years, he had lived with war and threats. Just recently, he wrote, "The future, humanly speaking, seems very dark. Even more disturbing is the great suffering of the people. In these clashes, how many children and old people fall ill and die from lack of medical assistance! For us, there is nothing else to do, praying that God will illuminate hearts in order that a solution may be found to the political and economic problems of the country." Therefore, Father Giuseppe stayed close to his people.

Thirty-four vehicles, in part provided by the army, and fifteen hundred people, both soldiers and civilians, some on foot and some on the running boards, left Kalongo at three in the afternoon on Friday, February 13, 1987.

Father Ambrosoli was bothered by his kidneys and by the overwork and stress of those days. Nevertheless, he took heart and encouraged others. "While the two-kilometer-long convoy was moving"—writes one witness—"we saw a column of black smoke rise behind us: the food stores we had gathered together with many sacrifices were being burned along with the warehouses: they were also burning the medical supplies, everything that we had gotten together over so many years. . . . The army that was drawing back wanted to leave nothing to the enemy guerrillas. The automobiles with the missionaries, the sisters, the medical personnel, and the sick were interspersed with the military trucks. If there wasn't an ambush, it was because in the column there were missionaries for whom the Acholi have great respect and love."

Another witness recounts: "After ten hours of forced march, under a hot sun, we arrived at Patongo, another mission around twenty miles from Kalongo. We hoped to be able to stop briefly, to quench our thirst, but we were not allowed to stop. Father Ambrosoli began to feel the lack of water more than others because of his kidney problem but he gave no sign of any worry. Every now and then, the soldiers would shoot to frighten away any potential attackers. A soldier was accidentally killed by one of his comrades; at the very same time, a woman was giving birth to a baby girl. Life and death alternated during this journey, which took almost twenty-one hours to cover only 75 miles!"

Even though his own health worried the other doctors, Father Ambrosoli dragged himself around at great labor among the sick, who had been made as comfortable as possible at the mission. When *We must begin* he was asked to return to Italy for treatment, he replied: "No, we *again without* have to begin again without losing our spirit. Uganda still has need *losing heart* of doctors and of qualified nurses. I must continue with their training . . . and all the sick. . . . No, no! Now is not the time to go away."

His disease, meanwhile, despite treatment, quickly became much worse. Nonetheless, Father Giuseppe remained in the breach up until the last, untiring, infusing courage in anyone who was overcome by the gravity of the moment, always ready to give himself to whoever had need of him.

Then came the sudden collapse, unexpected for a doctor like him. Father Giuseppe smiled for the last time, went to bed and said: "God's will be done." These were his last words spoken aloud, and then, murmuring the Our Father, he died. He wanted to be buried in the mission of Lira, as he had asked his associates. Father Giuseppe is a new witness of fidelity to the missionary vocation: the final gift of a white man.

THEY ARE STILL HERE;
THEY HAVE NOT GONE AWAY

Letters from a Convent of
Poor Clares in Zimbabwe

THE AFRICANS ARE THE BEST THING
THAT GOD HAS ON THE EARTH
by
Sister Maria Rachele Muguerza

Marondera, Zimbabwe
March 10, 1985

Today, March 10th, the third Sunday after our arrival in this land, we send you these few lines from a dreamy locality, Mutare, which I will call "paradise", to allow you to share in the moving missionary experience we have lived during these first three weeks.

First of all, I would say that the Africans are the most beautiful people God has created on the earth, and that Africa is the most beautiful place, notwithstanding the serious problems which afflict the people on every side, convinced, as we are, that "beyond evil there is good".

On the first day, we went to Victoria Falls, where the famous Zambezi cascades are located. The second day was even more beauti- *Our first* ful: it was our first encounter with real, true Africans. We were at *encounter with* the Sacred Heart Mission, where twenty-five years ago there were *the Africans* only a few huts, like those we saw throughout the journey, but today

On the 18th of January 1985, at the request of his Excellency, Patrick Fani Chakaipa, Archbishop of Harare, five Poor Clares from the convent of San Domingo Soria in Spain arrived in Zimbabwe. Their purpose was to make a foundation of cloistered nuns in Marondera, 42 miles from Harare, the capital of the country.

The Sisters have been warmly welcomed, and the community has been quickly absorbed into the life of the Church and the society of Zimbabwe. These letters of the Poor Clares, authentic fioretti of Saint Francis, bear witness to the spirit with which the foundation was begun. The first letter dates from March 1985, immediately after their arrival in Africa; the others were written in 1986.

These letters have been translated by Father Dismas Gannon, O.C.S.O., and Brother Dominique Nelson, O.C.S.O.

there are various schools with about fifteen hundred students and twenty-five teachers.

Father José Alberto, of Saragossa, a man whose complexion is almost as dark as the natives', showed us the beautiful and spacious church, delightfully cool despite the scorching sun outside. The church is circular and, properly African, it has, as its sole ornament for the Tabernacle, a tiger skin like those used exclusively by the great chiefs.

Then in much haste we set out for Hwange to visit, on the next day, all the missions of the district. Our good guide, Bishop Ignazio Prieto, accompanied by the missionary who lives with him, Father José Maria Garcia, came to pick us up very early that morning.

We went to visit the mission of Santa Maria, where the Bishop had begun his apostolic work in Zimbabwe. It is located on the peak of a hill, from which a beautiful panorama can be enjoyed, but below, reflected off those sandy, rocky slopes, the rising sun makes one sweat.

From Hwange we set out for Dete. First of all, we visited a mission with five hundred Christians. The church is dedicated to Saint Francis Xavier, and, with much pride, Father José Culebras showed us a relic of that saint.

Opposite his poor and tiny house, there are many flowers, and the missionary told us that some time before, in the dead of night, a herd of thirty-two elephants appeared like a whirlwind. Not knowing what to do, he began blowing a whistle to frighten them. But a little while later, other elephants appeared. You can still see the trees uprooted by these corpulent visitors.

Father José Culebras has a house for the elderly with sixteen guests. They greeted us and made us aware, with their vigorous handshakes, that they were very happy. Nearby is the novitiate of the Sisters of Calvary. All are very kind, and one of them is Spanish.

A little further on, on the other side of the street, there is the diocesan seminary and the house of the Marist Brothers; the seminary is like a self-contained city in the forest, where the formation of the young Africans takes place; some buildings serve as dormitories, others as refectories, and then there are the classrooms. . . .

To care for all these young people, Brother Ricardo, a Spaniard from Valencia, keeps two hundred cows in an open pasture. On the day before his wedding, his fiancée said to him: "I want to become a nun, a Poor Clare." Then he in turn thought: then I will become a missionary. Now he has been here for several years, sustained no doubt by the prayers and penance of the woman who had been his fiancée. Don't you think that is lovely? Now, he is happy to have the Poor Clares in his mission territory.

Close by, there is the house of formation for the Sisters of Calvary. *A genuine*
We were their guests; all are Africans. The postulants and candidates *African welcome*
plied us with many questions about our contemplative life. They are
hospitable and fraternal as only the Africans know how to be.

We spent the first Sunday of Lent in the mission of Jotcholo, where
Father José Luis Ruis de Agreda works with two Spanish Sisters:
Sister Blanca from Madrid and Sister Carmela from Burgos. The
Mass was celebrated by Father Mark, an African priest, in the poor
and tiny village church. This was an unforgettable experience for us:
without haste, with long chants marked by the rhythm of the drum,
while all danced and affectionately exchanged the kiss of peace with
their melodious *Sali Bonana yeevo*. And then everyone's hands raised
at the Our Father, and all those surprised children who were looking
at us! Unforgettable!

In the afternoon we were at Bulawayo, the second capital of the
country. We stayed for two days in this beautiful city, and were the
guests of the Franciscan Sisters of the Divine Maternity. As at Victoria
Falls and Hwange, our father Saint Francis offered us hospitality, in
the person of two of his daughters. They have beautiful convents
and welcomed us with true affection and exquisite courtesy. The
Lord will know how to reward them.

From there we set out for Harare. And finally the dawn of the
28th arrived. Father Pascual and Father Tomas came at 8:00 A.M. to
take us to Marondera, where our little monastery would arise. We
were very excited. Something within us impelled us, and something *Divine strength;*
inspired fear. The strength came from God. The fear was human, *human fear*
that is, fear of the unknown.

Behold Marondera, with its gigantic trees, its flowers, its land,
the green of its meadows. Beautiful Marondera! We greeted that
land, we gave thanks to God, we prayed, we sang, and we wept.

Our property extends to a little lake, its waters so clear that you
can see right to the bottom. There is so much to be done. The
beginning will be hard, as always; but perhaps this will be a stimulus
for us. The brother of Sister Teresa Maria, Angelo, our architect,
who accompanied us on this trip, will spend a few days with Father
Tomas and Father Sean to complete the project, to stake out the
land, and to prepare whatever is necessary.

We continued on for another thirty-two kilometers, all the way
to Macheke, where the Sisters of the Most Precious Blood welcomed
us warmly. We shall stay with them during these first months, learning their work, their songs, their dance, and their customs. They
want us to feel at home. There are ten Sisters, eight African Sisters
and two German; eight candidates are already close to postulancy
along with another eight native girls.

Our first San Damiano in Zimbabwe will be very simple and humble. It will have a corrugated roof, and the floor will be of cement. Even so, it will be expensive because all the materials are imported and difficult to find locally. For the present this has us a little anxious, but still, we are confident in Our Lord. He knows what we need and he will provide for us.

MOTHER EARTH'S CARING CHILDREN
by
Sister Teresa Maria Vallejo

Harare, Zimbabwe
March 1986

We feel renewed by the visit of Don Carmelo Jiminez and Don Ladis, the most beautiful Christmas gift possible (I don't know if it was Soria that flew all the way to Zimbabwe or Zimbabwe that flew all the way to Soria). Happiness, joy, homesickness, encouragement, a new boost. . . . Our feelings were all jumbled up! It's wonderful to realize how much we can love those who are far away, and at the same time the people who are so near. These were happy days that brought to a close our first African Christmas. A thousand thanks for your letters, your gifts, your affection, for everything! . . .

About mid-January we began work on the enclosure wall which, with a team of ten workers, was completed in two weeks. Really, our convent wall is a simple wire fence that will very soon be covered by a flowering wall-creeper; in this way it will look like a proper boundary wall. . . .

For now, Graham's little house remains within the enclosure. He is an employee at the Franciscan house, and has three children: Magi, aged five; Esther, aged three; and David, barely a year. They come to meet us with the other children of the neighborhood, greatly delighting us every time we go into the garden. Or else they call us from the windows: "Sita, sita, kiss Mwari . . .", which in their language means: "Sister, Sister, let me kiss the Crucifix. . . ."

Sister, Sister, let me kiss the Crucifix

The first word that little David learned was: sita; he capers about behind us on his little bare feet, his two white teeth sparkling. Sometimes, Magi, his elder sister, carries him on her shoulders, behaving just like a grown child. Rosi will be more or less six and she is already a little imp, but alert, and she acts like a little mama to everyone. She teaches us phrases in Shona, and she, in turn, very quickly learns them in Spanish. Ennor already goes to school and knows how to speak English. Will some of them one day be our postulants?

By February we had already begun our work with the hosts, which we supply to about a third of the diocese of Harare: five churches and communities. Two Sisters are engaged in this work morning and afternoon. We change jobs each week; in this way we can put all our talents to their best use.

For example, in the kitchen, it is interesting to see and taste the recipes each one invents to take utmost advantage of the scraps left over from the hosts. With these we can make some little buns for breakfast, some surprise sweetbreads; then there are the others like béchamel sauce and meat stew. Fortunately, we are only seven at table, we Sisters and Kenneth. Even though the cooking is simple, not all succeed equally well.

Kenneth is our helper in the garden. He is young, diligent and clever. Thanks to him, we do not find ourselves lost in the grass which grows with such unbelievable rapidity. Every morning he begins work at 6:30, after having traveled for four miles.

He has built us a henhouse of stakes and straw that looks like a hut. At Christmas, we received a rooster and a hen as gifts. We could not bring ourselves to kill them, and so we decided to keep them, thinking of future eggs and baby chicks. The fable of the dairy maid! Yes, but just the other way around! The beautiful cock served us well for the feast of Saint Joseph and half of the octave. . . .

The hen has already begun laying eggs! What a feast we had for our very own first egg! We ate it fried . . . the only way to divide it among us all. Now there are sixteen hens, because Father José Garcia, a missionary from Hwange, has given us a gift of fifteen more. They began to lay eggs immediately.

Father José's visit has been a blessing. He had to come to Harare, and so took advantage of the occasion to give us a hand. He has organized the whole garden with its nurseries, its vegetables, flowers, and fruit trees. He has taught us how to prune, how to prepare the fertilizer. In short, he has given us all the necessary instructions. He has lived in Zimbabwe for many years and knows the land very well.

On the feast of Saint Joseph, his patron, Father José celebrated Mass with Father Agustin, who was celebrating his silver jubilee. Also present was Sister Cecilia, from Navarre, of the Congregation of the Daughters of Calvary, of which Congregation she has been superior general for many years. We were all very deeply moved. Saint Joseph continues to spoil us.

It seems that there is a snake hidden in the garden, among the cacti. Kenneth has seen it and told us about it. We must get used to

Serpent in the garden

visits of this kind. On Good Friday evening, into the house came a little grass snake—not poisonous—which we killed very easily.

Some beautiful lattice work with crocuses, besides protecting us, is very decorative and begins to give the house the air of a monastery. We have also begun the arrangement of the choir. We are studying how to remodel it, since for the moment there is no question of any new construction. I think we will end up deciding hastily, because the cost of living is rising at a dizzying pace.

The rains this year have been superabundant, so much so that our little garden went almost completely to ruin. We were able to save only three tomato plants, and numerous insects attacked the beans and cabbages. Now that it is raining less, it looks like the plants are beginning to recover. The lettuce and beets are very lovely. We have harvested a large sack of potatoes, and we now impatiently await the harvest of the peanuts, which will be a novelty for us. Perhaps in all there will be four pounds! That's not bad for our first attempt. Thanks to Father José's instructions, some improvement has been seen.

We have never been so dependent on our sister Mother Earth!

AFRICA, THE FERTILE!
by
Sister Maria Rachele Muguerza

Harare, Zimbabwe
June 1986

To the rhythmic music of the tom-toms filling the esplanade in front of the parish hall, the children and their parents come streaming. With curiosity depicted on their faces, they are prepared to spend several pleasant hours.

This puts me in mind of the pilgrimages we had in our village when I was a child. The festive climate is the same, but here there is more sun, more color, more flowers.

The jacaranda trees, about ten to fifteen meters high, command one's attention. From their bald, dry branches, bluish florets blossom. In just a few days you no longer see trees covered with greenery; rather, they are completely blue and lilac. What breath-taking beauty! In this season, these are the trees which make the landscape so attractive. Everywhere climbing plants are growing, many of whose names I do not know. Now they are all in full bloom.

But now let's go to the feast, or pilgrimage, or "fiesta", if you wish. Today all the parishioners are transformed into sellers and *Parish Fiesta* buyers. There they are with their friendly faces, ready to do business. All the proceeds will go for the parish expenses: furnishings, improvements, etc.

Each one contributes what he can: vegetables, fruit, potatoes; little trees ready to plant, flowers, hens, rabbits, sweets, cakes, used clothing, used and reused shoes, sweet-cakes made of flour and corn; used books. A little bit of everything . . . the most curious and strange things! Then there is the food section: little salads, sausages, cutlets, chicken that is roasted right there in a corner, a gift from a parishioner who has a butcher's shop. There are fresh drinks, tea, even ice cream. . . . As good parishioners, we contribute our own cooked grains, and cookies decorated with faces so inviting that they all sell immediately.

Since we still don't have our enclosure wall (the workers have yet to finish with it) we decided, after dinner—our noon meal—to pass beyond the fence separating us from the festivities being celebrated right on the esplanade directly in front of our convent! Here we are!

The following Sunday, when the administration announced the amount collected, we answered with a burst of applause. We far surpassed the collection of the preceding year. This is one way of keeping the Faith alive: reciprocal help given in a genial manner. We feel like one big family which comes together each Sunday to share the same Faith.

Some time ago, on returning from his vacation, Father Jesus Barrios of Segovia stopped in to see us. He works among the Tonga, whom, naturally, he adores. All the missionaries have a weakness, *All the* almost a passion for their people. These Africans have something *missionaries have a weakness* that manages to bewitch and steal their hearts in such an irresistible *for their people* way.

Speaking of "stealing", I will tell you something that happened to us a few days ago. Someone stole our chickens. Yes, sir! They were "good thieves" though, since they left us with half of them. We had felt sure of our fence, but one fine day, upon rising, we saw the hens fluttering outside the hen-coop. What's happening? It had already happened! Someone had taken flight together with the linen and clothesline. As if someone could resolve their difficulties with our coifs! One day or other we will see someone wearing them, for with regard to the style of dress here, anything goes.

Two days later, some sisters in the active ministry who live near us said to us: "Today they took ours. . . ." Another fourteen hens. The women who came to hear of the fact brought us one-and-a-half dozen eggs to "compensate" for the loss.

Thanks be to God, the rains have begun. (I am not speaking now of the animals and other little creatures that become "sociable" at this time of year.)

Each week, we must regularly take tablets against malaria, otherwise we run the risk of catching it. The heat and the water make the plants grow as though they were under a spell. Even dry sticks blossom. One afternoon, in the garden, now at the height of its growth, we were surprised to see that even the stakes supporting the tomatoes were sprouting with myriad little green "eyes". Africa, the Fertile!

As I said at the beginning, there are still many, many things to be done, and, though they are small and simple, they require much time and money. I wish to thank you once again for the generous gifts that are arriving. Thanks to everyone, sincerely, thank you! With St. Paul, we say to you from our heart: "Each time we think of you we give thanks to the Lord, and each time we pray for you we do so with joy." We are sure that God will most generously pay you back, as only he knows how to do.

FEAST OF SAINT CLARE
by
Sister Maria Rachele Muguerza

Harare, Zimbabwe
August 1986

August 11th dawned, a beautiful day! We were at the beginning of the warm season, although here at Harare the heat is not excessive. Brother Sun likes to be an early riser, and at 6:00 A.M., he was already shining brightly in the clear sky, caressing with a golden smile the thousand little flowers that were awakening, joyfully shrugging off the cool of the night.

Our hearts also awakened happily, and merrily sang with all creatures the "praises" of the Lord, in honor of Saint Clare, our mother. The canticle of the three young men, "Heaven and earth, sun and moon bless the Lord . . . to him be glory and honor forever", resounded in our church today with universal echoes, in union of spirit with all the Poor Clares in the world, and we feel close to so many sisters with whom we have lived and who today sing with so much joy in heaven.

The Mass was concelebrated by three Franciscan priests. Several friends were present, and we venerated the relic of our mother [Saint Clare]. Then we called everyone together in the parlor to have some tea. Congratulations, songs, dances, and even a dance from Seville, or something of the kind, that Sister Maria Rosario played on the guitar and Father Eamon graciously danced. He is a very happy friar who always seeks to make others happy. He lives in Marondera and cares for their five postulants, who will very soon become novices.

We closed the happy reunion with the canticle of Brother Sun and Sister Moon, which Father Eugenio accompanied in such a masterful way on the guitar. A couple of our friends presented us with an abundance of food for our feast: meat, sweets, and even a bottle of wine.

On the following day, the feast continued in Harare and . . . in our convent. What a welcomed gift from Saint Clare, a young girl, twenty-three years old, came to experience our life for a week with us. It seems as though she has a vocation and has decided to enter the convent. Blessed be the Lord for this first experience that has blossomed in our community! There are other girls who are also interested. A joyous hope that gladdens our hearts, obliging us in a certain sense always to live out our vocation in its radical intensity.

Our first postulant

The work in choir is finished, and the result is lovely. We are pleased, and others are also content because they see that we are like a family, and this makes them happy.

The family that had been living in our garden has begun to build their new little house beside our enclosure wall. It is worth seeing David, the youngest, begin to run when he sees us, and, panting, with much emotion, cries out: "Sita . . . sita!" When we take him in our arms, he looks toward his mama, as if to say: "They are still here . . . they have not gone away!"

Kenneth is working as quickly as he can to complete the enclosure wall around our property. He wants to finish before the rains begin. The garden is in full growth and our incipient harvests are arriving, complemented by the gifts of our neighbors and friends, who bring vegetables, fruit, and even a little sack of peanuts. In this wonderful sharing, God manifests his love.

Harare is still living in days of intense preparation for the great political reunion that will take place during the first week of September. More than one hundred representatives from 101 nations are expected. The city is in one big frenzy: bustling about are the workers who are laying out the streets and gardens and erecting the gigantic field tents that will allow them to welcome so many visitors with their legendary graciousness and goodness. I'm sure you have seen news of this from television programs, and can also get some estimate of how much has taken place here within a few days.

And now some news of our relations with other African convents. There is one priest to assist all the Poor Clares, Father Liam McDermott, who resides in South Africa. He welcomed us, and later we received from him various circulars inviting the abbesses and the delegates from English-speaking convents (Southeast Africa) to a reunion whose scope was to study the possibility of constructing, if not precisely a federation, something similar, for greater contact and reciprocal help.

Contacts with African convents

In 1972, a federation was created, formed by the convents of Madagascar, Malawi, Uganda, Zaire, Zambia, and the Central Republic of Africa. It was dissolved a few years later because of the difficulties encountered: language, distance, costs, times, etc. . . .

In 1981, a delegate from the Holy See visited all the African monasteries and drew up a report for the Sacred Congregation of Religious. As a result, in 1984, Father Liam, O.F.M., was named to assist the African convents. In 1985, the time seemed ripe for a new attempt at a union to strengthen our common growth.

Last year, there was a reunion of the various delegates at Bukoba, in Tanzania. The twenty of them set up study groups based on the themes of the agenda. Priority was given to formation, according to the following general policy lines:

—A formative program for each monastery, problems, solution, and reciprocal help.

—Formation in prayer, Franciscan contemplative life, liturgical life, and community life.

—Formation of those in charge of formation.

They also spoke on the enclosure in its African context, and on other themes that arose in the course of the meetings: selection of candidates, time of probation, African culture, the horarium, etc. . . .

When the topic of the possibility of a federation was discussed, it was clear that the opportune moment had still not arrived, since there continue to be the same difficulties encountered in the 70s. So we thought about forming an association. The statutes that were drawn up were then sent to Rome for approval. We elected a coordinator, Mother Clare, abbess of Lilongwe, and two councilors. The new association is called the St. Clare Association of Bikira Maria, and we celebrate its inception on the feast of the eighth of December.

St. Clare Association

And now some news of the "outside". Our parish community is preparing with real enthusiasm for the confirmation of forty young people, which will take place on the first Sunday of September. The whole community feels itself responsible, and there are extraordinary catechetics, meetings, and rehearsals. It is very beautiful to see how everyone is working to prepare for the event.

With joy and united in the love of God, your sisters from Zimbabwe embrace you, for all the manifestations of generosity you have shown to us.

2

AMERICA

The state of Paraná in southern Brazil. In the north of Paraná is
Londrina, the city where Father Victor Groppelli, from Crema in
Lombardy, lives and works.

MY FAITH IS STRONG

The Brazilian Laity's Commitment to the Church

by
Vitor Groppelli

When Abraham left his homeland for a destination known only to God, he did not have a cultural past to hang onto. Ahead of him, the future that God had promised opened wide. His strength lay in his having faith even though there was no history on which to base it. But when I left for Brazil fifteen years ago, I had roots in a vocation firmly planted in the history of the people of God, a people that had already extended all the fullness of its missionary strength over five continents. And ahead of me lay the future of a Church whose purpose was to live out this mission. I was the final link (and I still am) in a long chain of arms open to the gospel. Within me and beside me walked the church of Italy. Moreover, I was a diocesan priest. Indeed, as recently as thirty years ago, being a missionary had been the exclusive preserve of congregations and institutes of religious. The miraculous touch of the Holy Spirit that was to invade dioceses in Italy, raising up missionary vocations among clergy and laity alike, came later.

What Brazil Is Really Like

Coming to grips with what Brazil is really like has not been dull. Being whisked suddenly from one level of civilization to another has caused serious adjustment problems on the psychological level, but not on the level of faith. When I arrived in Brazil, I had no doubts about my vocation, but I felt quite keenly how weak I was. I was too much the Italian to be able to rise quickly above the religious and social culture-shock that immediately confronted me. Brazil is

I felt all my weakness

Father Vitor Groppelli, from Crema in Lombardy, has been in Brazil since 1972. After having worked for four years in a parish in North Parana, he was called by the bishop of Londrina to be vicar-general and coordinator for diocesan pastoral work. Presently, he is both rector of the seminary and pastor at Londrina, a city of 450,000 inhabitants in the northern part of Paraná. This article was translated by Mary E. Hamilton.

a nation of many races and cultures, expressing this pluralism on the religious plane as well. It is true that according to the Registry Office, the majority of the population would call itself Catholic, but once you begin to grasp what is really going on, things get rather complex. During the hundred years of missionary activity within its borders, this country has experienced slavery and tyranny for its Indians and descendants of slaves from Africa, colonialism, and European and Asiatic immigration. This explains Brazil's variety of religious expressions. In fact, here there still exists animism, the spiritualism of A. Kardec, Buddhism, Islam, Umbanda, traditional Protestantism, and many sects, both Christian and exotic. All this flows into a syncretism that creates a severe problem for the Italian evangelist, who has only a very approximate notion of the cultural and religious climate of Brazil.

Many in Europe imagine the Brazilian as black, Indian, and of mixed blood. They do not realize that the successive waves of immigration built large communities and cities where for a hundred years and more people have spoken German, Italian (their own dialects), Polish, Japanese, Spanish, and so on. This pluralism translates into a cultural richness that surely will make a strong impact upon the future and that reinforces the statement that there is more than one Brazil. However, the people are united by one national language— Portuguese—that is as much the tongue of illiterates as it is of those who are highly educated. This fact alone, in a country twenty-seven times as large as Italy, seems almost incredible.

The contrast between a little town like Crema and North Parana (a state in southern Brazil) was really striking. My new life seemed like an adventure in a joint Christian experience with the coffee and sugarcane plantation workers. There was the shock of the poverty, the exploitation, and the limitations to what one person could do. *People hunger for God and for justice* The people are hungry for God and for justice. There is hardly any difficulty in bringing God to them through the sacraments. The people are good and full of understanding. Every evening, you will find them gathered around the priest in a school or chapel. Their faces show the fatigue of a long day of hunger and hard work, but they know that the word of God will strengthen them. These meetings happen at whatever times they can during the year, since the communities are numerous and scattered. Great distances and the lack of priests are a real challenge. My first parish was larger than the diocese I came from, and it had only three priests. However, there is impressive fervor. Besides normal pastoral work, weekend meetings for youth take place. In this way, more than a thousand young people participate in spiritual exercises each year. This is really their first direct encounter with Christ, and, perhaps, the last opportunity they will have.

The seventies were a time of military repression that tolerated only traditional evangelization. But the Church was already committed to identifying with the new dynamic of the base ecclesial community. It was slow work, too, on account of the lack of priests. The average now is one priest for every 9,639 persons, but this statistic does not tell the whole story. There also must be taken into account population distribution, large ethnic groups, internal migrations, and the exodus from the rural areas to the cities.

Social unrest, increasing with the passage of time, has forced the Church to take a courageous stand on behalf of the poorest of the poor. Any unifying effort to bridge the gap between missionary work and what it can reasonably expect to accomplish extends pastoral work in six different directions that gradually merge into one, namely, the bringing together of all levels of society. In a country very rich in natural resources, yet having a very poor population, the Brazilian church is practically the only voice that speaks in defense of the dirt-poor and the marginalized victims on the fringe of Brazilian society.

Ever since I came to Brazil, I have been in a position to watch the growth of the laity's commitment. For eleven years I have been working in the middle of a diocese of some 700,000 souls, cared for by sixteen diocesan priests (of whom eight are from abroad and eight are native Brazilians), and about ten religious (the majority of whom are foreigners). This scarcity of clergy has fostered the laity's growth. Today there are about a thousand lay people who work as catechists, as ministers to the community and to the sick, as ministers of the word, and as extraordinary ministers at the Eucharist. They work with no thought of personal recognition and with a generosity that is moving to behold. They can be found anywhere and everywhere in the field, wherever there is pastoral work to be done.

The shortage of priests has fostered the growth of the laity

A Good People

The Brazilians are a fundamentally good people. In spite of the consequences of poverty and the insecurity that comes from an inflated economy, in spite of fighting over land rights and the arrogant and autocratic attitude of the large landowners, their hearts are open and generous. They have an impressive sense of hospitality and of wanting to make people feel welcome. They can always find time to entertain a visitor with sincere thoughtfulness. Even in poor families, there is always room for an orphan or a baby abandoned by its parents.

Men and women sitting or lying on the sidewalks holding out begging-bowls or caps to beg alms from passers-by are a sad and frequent sight. Usually, it is also the very poor who stop to say a kind word to these beggars or to give them what little money they can. A group of lay-people in the city where I live goes each evening through the downtown streets where the "tramps" spend their nights. They give them hot food and whatever medical supplies they can get; they take the sick to the hospital and collect women with babies to take them to the public shelter.

It was lay people who started a vocational-technical school that now assists four hundred of the fifty thousand or more needy youths in this city.

Recently I said the funeral Mass for a lady who had been bedridden for over ten years. For two days, an uninterrupted line of people from every social class filed by her body. One of the humblest of these mourners went up to her family to tell them: "How many times I have been able to feed my family, thanks to her." This is the kind of gratitude that comes from the poor, from those who no longer have a government that will look after them, but who still are always ready to offer a helping hand to anyone in need.

Among the serious scars, such as drug abuse and male and female prostitution, that mar all classes of society, the one that appears most frequently is alcoholism. The drunk is, at times, an amusing character, but he frequently destroys the peace in the family atmosphere. Loved ones have organized themselves spontaneously into associations. Some young people I know have started the "Christ Loves You" movement to help alcoholics recover and to give assistance to their families. Twice a week, more than 150 people meet in a hall at the cathedral to release their tensions by talking over their problems with one another and to compare notes on their individual difficulties and the attempts they have made to reach sobriety. Sudden miracles do not happen, but love, understanding, and friendship come in time to be, if anything, very useful in conquering different types of dependencies.

The people's faith   The people's faith is touchingly pure. As this faith is demonstrated in various circumstances, it seems at times naïve and at other times full of courage. When the three-year-old daughter of one of the laymen who works with me died while I was away, a priest-friend of mine went to comfort him. The man said to him, "Father, I can't mourn for her. This is the first time the Lord ever gave me anything that was really and truly mine. So, even though it breaks my heart, I cannot deny him my daughter, for he gives me such peace!"

I met a lady who on Sundays when the weather was good made a trip of almost twenty-five miles to participate in the 7 A.M. Mass.

Another friend, too, whose young wife died of a cerebral hemorrhage at the age of twenty-seven, leaving him with their four sons, said to me: "Don't worry about me. My faith is strong. You know how much we loved each other, but I think I can say without fear of being misunderstood that like Saint Paul, it is now no longer I who live, but Christ who lives in me."

How can I ever forget those coffee-plantation laborers who, after an exhausting and poorly paid workday, still found the strength to meet at the chapel for worship and the study of the gospel? One of them said once: "Father, our kids may not have enough to eat, we may be paid badly or mistreated, but God never lets us down. We feel his presence in our midst. He enables us to withstand and overcome anything."

A Brazilian priest who works in Amazonia related this episode to me. Someone advised him that a little old lady wanted to receive the sacraments before she died. The problem was distance. The priest changed his usual itinerary of pastoral visitation so that he could visit the community, which was spread out through the forest and along the rivers. After a week's journey by boat and several hours on foot, he reached the sick woman's cottage. The old lady was lying doubled-up with pain. When she saw the priest, her face lit up. With the little strength she had left, she managed to raise herself in the bed and murmur in a weak voice: "Thank you, Father. I was sure the Lord wouldn't let me die without receiving Holy Communion." The missionary priest celebrated Mass in the little house and anointed the lady with the oil of the sick. As she received Holy Communion, the sick woman could not keep from weeping. She died saying over and over, "Thank you, Lord." Her face wore an angelic smile, and with this smile, she went to meet her friend the Lord. Once more, the Bible was right: the just shall live by faith.

The people have a special thoughtfulness toward priests. On his birthday, they all want to give the priest a hug and a small gift: *Love for the priest* handkerchiefs, socks, shorts, shirts, and so on. Once each year, the priest receives practically a whole new wardrobe. But the thoughtfulness does not end with just that. In one parish, a priest was starting to have a breakdown and was beginning to show signs of illness. Groups of parishioners formed secretly to pray for him before the Tabernacle, to pray for God to give strength to the unfortunate man. If some people gossiped, the prayers won out. The priest got over the crisis and resumed his apostolic labors with enthusiasm. He was amazed when a lay minister in the community said to him: "You have been magnificent. You've done it. You deserve our congratulations." Only then did he realize that his recovery had not come entirely through his own efforts.

Even a superficial acquaintance with these good people will reveal their love for the Bible, our Lady, and the saints. Thanks to the revival of catechetical instruction, every family in the community is sure to have a copy of God's word in the home. Besides, there are Bible courses and Bible study groups. The people want to know as much as possible about the Bible. This insatiable thirst for biblical knowledge has transformed the life of the Church in Brazil. A great debt of gratitude is owed to the movements for renewal that have found the land a fertile ground, well-adapted to the development of a new vitality. In families, the Bible has stopped being just something attractive to place on a table: it is a fountain of life, light, and strength. In communities without priests, responsible men take it upon themselves to gain a certain competence in biblical studies so as to be able to clarify and resolve ordinary problems and to inject some hope into the people's harsh daily life. The same Protestant sects that have always used the Bible as a weapon against Catholics are now forced to admit that times have changed.

In my first parish, for four years, I had a group of young people who met every Wednesday at five o'clock in the morning to study the Bible and the documents of Vatican II. Where I work now, about sixty persons take the parish theology course, while some of the lay-people have enrolled in theological studies in the major seminary, with good results.

Devotion to our Lady   Our Lady is as close to the Brazilian as his own mother is. Her name is on everyone's lips and in everyone's heart. Around her, there have grown up thousands of devotions, some of them at times slightly bizarre, but always filled with a profound love. It is undeniable that devotion to Mary Most Holy has had the happy result of checking the advance of Protestantism, especially that of the most radical sects that, through ignorance or impudence, treat our Lord's Mother with scant respect. Every project undertaken in her name is successful: pilgrimages, novenas, rosary devotions, processions, vows. The people, in their simplicity, find in her not only protection, but also a role model to help them find the strength to bear the heavy cross of a life of deprivation.

I could write a book about the Brazilians' devotion to the saints. These devotions, innumerable and colorful, are not always quite orthodox. I rather think what they need is just a good housecleaning. Things are getting better slowly as people begin to see the centrality of Christ and the strength that comes from his Resurrection. The liturgical renewal has favored this process, although at first it caused some confusion when so many statues and altars to saints were removed.

Conclusion

I have taken care to speak only of positive things. I have done this on purpose. Still, the negative aspects are not absent. What will the future of the Brazilian church be like? If she can conserve her flourishing and enthusiastic lay people, one may predict great things. But these lay people are presently functioning only on a local level. Perhaps they are not yet mature enough to confront the whole of society and its enormous problems. Our lay people are the backbone of the cultural, political, and economic life of the nation. Not one Christian among them is capable of expressing, on a national level, how to change the status quo that is so unjust and so costly. In this one country with a population of 130,000,000, where there are 36,000,000 needy youths and twenty percent of the total population live in the most dire poverty while all the power and wealth are concentrated in the hands of a tiny minority, the Church simply cannot limit herself to bringing lay people together in small, isolated communities.

The laity must confront social problems

Perhaps the laity is totally dependent on the hierarchy in the field of social justice. Fortunately, the National Conference of Bishops seems to me to be both aware and courageous in taking positions on issues and situations where there is injustice. But the Council really needs to think about educating Christian leaders for the future. This great country cannot be saved by brotherhood campaigns and public protests, but rather by preparing Christians to be competent and capable, ready to assume their role as leaders in the present-day life of their country.

BREATHING IN UNISON WITH
THE UNIVERSAL CHURCH

An Experience of Missionary Activity in Ecuador

by
Cirillo Tascaroli

It is no exaggeration to say that the missionary is, by definition, the special envoy, the messenger of the word. He is always ready to go wherever situations of absolute necessity or emergency occur, where the kingdom of God has not yet taken root, or where it is still in a phase of slow, youthful growth.

After working hard for many years in the heart of Africa (in southern Sudan, to be exact), and after having been expelled, I dedicated an equal number of years to missionary activity in Europe in the field of social communication. After a dialogue with my Superiors, the kind of dialogue that does not always admit of alternatives, I was invited to change continents. To the friends who asked me or, more exactly, who "asked themselves", whether my Latin American destination would not be a useless dissipation of energy, I have answered with firm conviction: "Where God wants us, there is the terrain on which we must cast the seed of the word and of grace." After all, God always gives us much more than the little that we give him.

In this way, after a long African and European trajectory, I arrived six years ago in Ecuador, one of the smallest nations of the Latin American continent, but not for that reason any less worthy or less open to renewed missionary activity.

My mission in Quito
My mission was not to be realized in the spiritually and socially underdeveloped province of Esmeraldas, where my confreres had energetically sacrificed themselves for more than thirty years; rather, it was to be in the capital of the country itself: Quito. The work would be that of support for their missionary activity, with the help

Father Cirillo Tescaroli, a Combonian Father, has been in Quito, Ecuador, for the past six years. His task has been the reawakening of the missionary conscience of the Catholics of the country. The enterprise, which initially appeared extremely difficult, now promises to bear good fruit. Translated by Father M. Dismas Gannon, O.C.S.O., and Brother M. Dominique Savio Nelson, O.C.S.O.

of the so-called "group media": a new missionary review, *Iglesia Sin Fronteras*; an even more recent publishing company, Editorial Sin Fronteras; and various radio programs. A rather vast sphere of work, and bristling with difficulties, and not only from the economic point of view, if we take into account the general situation. There was also a lack of literary stimuli, a different production pace among the printers, etc.

Faced with this panorama into which I had to fit my multi-media activities, there is need to ponder and thoroughly assimilate number 368 of the Puebla Document:

> The time has finally arrived for Latin America to intensify its mutual services between the individual churches and to be carried beyond its own borders: *ad gentes*. Undoubtedly we ourselves need missionaries; *but we must give from our poverty*. On the other hand, our church can offer something both original and important: her sensitivity for salvation and liberty, the wealth of her indigenous religious devotion, the experience of the base ecclesial communities, the flowering of her ministries, her hope, and the joy of her faith. We have already taken into account the missionary endeavors that can be further developed and must be propagated.

Number 369 of the same document adds by way of completion:

> We cannot neglect to express our gratitude for the generous assistance which comes to us from the universal Church and from our sister churches, praying that they will continue to help us especially in the formation of indigenous workers. In this way we will see ourselves increasingly encouraged to take on such a universal commitment, and we will have a greater capacity to respond to the proper service of our particular church.

No lengthy explanation is needed to plumb this concept of apostolic dynamism. In human institutions, to give gratuitously almost always means to lose, but the gospel teaches us that to give freely for the sake of the kingdom is not to lose, but to gain.

But it is not easy to convince the faithful—to say nothing of the priests and religious—of a Church born of the generous activity of foreign missionaries, that if they wish to resolve their internal problems, they must open themselves to outside influence, to the strengthening spirit of the universal Church. This is especially true in Latin America, where the scarcity of clergy is deeply felt, and, in no few cases, despaired of.

I confess that this "uneasiness", as they prefer to call it here, still manifests itself whenever we present missionary problems of the Church in the world, but years of slow, steady effort have succeeded in sapping its vigor. For example, we have an apostolic vicariate like Esmeraldas, where, in a population of more than 300,000, there is a majority of blacks; within a few decades we have seen numerous vocations to women's religious orders spring up; there is even the instance of a black religious going to work in Uganda, while the other young black sisters are being prepared for missionary life *ad gentes*. Hence we begin to say: "The finger of God is here."

What has been done by the missionary activity of the national corps under the aegis of the Pontifical Missionary Work, with the cooperation of some institutes, and supported by the missionary press along with other means of missionary communications, is to

The first fruits are already at hand

impart a new rhythm to the individual churches. The first fruits are already at hand, and, God willing, the full harvest will manifest itself in the coming decades.

A missionary review must be concerned with forming the consciences of the people of God to be more sensitive to their responsibility in relation to the universal Church. Likewise, it must be concerned with cultivating an apostolic spirit among the youth, which will urge them to consecrate their lives to the missionary ideal.

Despite the insufficient means at our disposal and the various difficulties that frequently arise, we can see that with God's help we have already made good progress, though much remains to be done.

Editorial Sin Fronteras, where I presently work, has, within the short span of six years, succeeded in producing a goodly range of missionary publications: more than thirty brief biographies of apostles of the gospel, serialized articles of personal religious experiences, missionary liturgy, meditation booklets, etc.

No less noteworthy have been the commitments made in the field

The audiovisuals

of audiovisuals, which especially benefit radio programs, religious communities, schools, catechists, base ecclesial communities, etc.

For example, the radio program "El Nazareno", which presents the life of Jesus in twenty audiocassettes of ninety minutes each, covering a period of thirty hours, has become the war horse of radio and school.

For about three years, from the time the National Catholic Radio of Ecuador began functioning, I dedicated most of my time to the preparation of five radio programs per day, of a biblical, informative, and missionary nature. Many of these programs were retransmitted from other broadcasting stations of Ecuador, and from other Latin American countries, such as Peru and Costa Rica.

Perhaps never as in these most recent years has Latin America begun to breathe, with profound and regular rhythm, the universality of the Church. And all this, thanks to the new perspectives delineated by the Council, which have had a great influence on the episcopacies of various countries, on religious congregations, the local clergy, the laity, and other ecclesial groups. For these reasons we can look to the future with much hope.

THE UNIVERSITY: ITS PLACE IN EVANGELIZATION AND HUMAN ADVANCEMENT

The Catholic University of Villarica in Paraguay

by
José Felix Gonzales

Toward the end of the 60s, the *Movimento Cursillos de Cristianidad* made its appearance in Paraguay. It proposed, by way of personal conversion and the emergence of leaders called "pillars", the Christian transformation of the ambience of life and, consequently, a change of structures.

Many of us had passed through the experience of the Cursillos de Cristianidad; some of us had already been a part of the Catholic Action Movement or other ecclesial movements; but others had not had any former experience of membership in a Christian group. The impact of the Cursillo movement was significant, the more so because it coincided with a critical moment in almost all phases of the secular apostolate.

The Catholic University was affected by this movement in a unique way, mainly because the movement sought out people of rank to influence the culture, and so considered the University a privileged field of action.

In 1976, the first Organic Pastoral Plan (Piano di Pastorale Organica, P.P.O.) of the Church in Paraguay materialized as the fruit of a long process. It generated its own special dynamism and gave impetus to the formation of *cadres* of the Church, with an emphasis

The first Organic Pastoral Plan

The title "The University: Its Place in Evangelization and Human Advancement" is redundant. In reality, every Catholic university should favor both human and Christian growth. However, it is often difficult to see the forest for the trees. In this testimony, José Felix Gonzales recounts how, by way of solidarity with the ecclesial movement "Cursillos de Christianidad", teachers and students of the Catholic University of Villarica, Paraguay, have experienced in their lives the truth of this affirmation. Since then, their witness has become both active and fecund. This article has been translated by Father Dismas Gannon, O.C.S.O., and Brother Dominique Nelson, O.C.S.O.

on the lay sector. In 1978, the Diocese of Villarica became the first
diocese in the country to formulate a P.P.O. for the laity.

"The ways of the Lord are unfathomable", and chance does not
enter into his designs. So we considered it providential that all of us
who were part of the Diocesan Team for the Laity in the years
1977–1984 and who had taken part in the direction of the Cursillos
de Cristianidad Movement were made part of the teaching and governing group of the Catholic University. With the help of numerous
professors, richly motivated by a dynamic of their Christian life, this
circumstance made possible an ecclesial experience of pastoral activity
in the Catholic University, called *Christian Experience*.

"Christian Experience": An Example of a Pastoral University

From the time of the founding of the Catholic University in Villarica
in 1961, the theology classes for the first three years of graduate
study (economics and business, jurisprudence, and philosophy) had
exclusively been taught by priests. However, beginning in 1975,
laymen were incorporated into the theology faculty in order to fill
vacant positions. As a consequence, the theology classes underwent
a transformation, becoming primarily an introduction to an experience of Christian living.

A systematic program on "Christian Experience"

Because we were not theologians and because of the more concrete
orientation that we wanted to give the material, we laymen who
were teaching theology proposed a change in the name of this instruction to "Christian Experience", not realizing that in so doing we
were greatly increasing the responsibility of the teacher. Thus developed a systematic program on "Christian Experience" for the separate
courses, based on an outline proposed by our bishop.

In this way, the program succeeded in bringing the university
students closer to an awareness of the problems of the community
and to the exercise of Christian charity by "work in action" in its
two-fold dimension: (a) social help (for example, hospital, prison,
orphanage, and social pastoral concerns); and (b) social amelioration
(clinical analysis and health education in the outlying schools, with
formation courses for families).

As a synthesis of this and other analogous experiences, we gradually
discovered that the identity of the Pastoral University had to be that
of an institution of higher formation permeated by a sense of Christian
responsibility in a rural context.

When, in 1986, the Bishops' Conference of Paraguay brought out
the document on pastoral activity, "The Mission of Our Catholic
University in the Evangelization of Culture", it was a cause of great
satisfaction and a stimulus to further action for all of us who were

taking part in this initiative of "Christian Experience". In fact, we discovered in this document the principal lines of our work set down as directives with which the church in Paraguay defined the future role of the Catholic University in our country.

From this group and their document there emerged "a global vision of the Catholic University in Villarica" as "a specific service for the Church in the rural context in which it works".

Within this concept of a service–University, the Regional Health Services Project was born.

A Contribution to Health and Education in Paraguay

In 1978, through its attempt to respond to the needs of the rural community in which it works, the Catholic University of Villarica formulated the Regional Health Services Project (P.R.S.S.), which, like the Organic Pastoral Plan of the Church in Paraguay, "represents an original model because, basing itself on the success or failure of the services rendered to the people, it directs research and initiates new courses of higher formation". This project covers the entire region of Villarica, Caazapa, Caaguazu, Alto Parana and Canindeyu: a vast territory with a population of a million people (one-third of the entire country).

An ambitious project   Judged by many to be overly ambitious, this project will encounter the obstacles and difficulties of all great undertakings. These will be accentuated by the fact that it is a private project, in a poor country, in an "interior region" of the country, far from the decision-making centers. To this we must add the most formidable obstacle of all, created by the radical inversion of the classic plan of university behavior. What the Regional Project has done is put service foremost, followed by research and then by teaching, and has finalized this orientation by instituting a program for the formation of professionals destined to work in these services once they get under way.

Thus it was that, in the 80s, the Pedagogical Unit emerged with a dynamism and an activity that was wholly unusual:

In Coronel Oviedo, twenty-seven miles from Villarica, the Unit created graduate courses in pedagogy, agriculture, and veterinary science within the Institute of Rural Communication and Agricultural Science of the P.R.S.S.; and the service P.A.P.A. (Project to Help the Little Farmer) was born.

In Caaguazu, fifty-four miles from Villarica, a probative entrance course was initiated with the intention of promoting entrance to the University by the youth of the city and its outlying districts.

In the city Presidente Stroessner, 144 miles from Villarica, courses in economics and commerce, pharmacy, jurisprudence and technology were founded along with a probative entrance course.

In Villarica, graduate courses will begin in chemistry and pharmacy, as well as a course in nursing and obstetrics, and a graduate course in medicine (this last is still awaiting recognition from the government). All of this centers on the Regional Health Services Project, and these courses were derived from the previously existing ones.

The Voluntary Medical Assistance Units   As many as 110 U.V.A.S. (Voluntary Medical Assistance Units) were created throughout the region, in villages with fewer than 2,000 inhabitants, which were otherwise deprived of medical services.

With all this expansion, an original structure, unfinished, was created in our country: a pedagogical unit with the juridical structure of a university, with satellite centers in four cities of the country, with ten faculties, and with an overall plan of services for the entire region. "Ask and it shall be given to you, knock and it shall be opened to you."

We have need of a hospital to which we can refer the ill from the areas serviced by the U.V.A.S., where students can take medical and paramedical courses, and for the removal of one of the major impediments to the government's recognition of the faculty of medicine. Because of these needs, we have done everything in our power for this work. Many national and international doors have been opened to us. Members of the association Impresari Cristiani and of other German Catholic institutions, as well as those of other nationalities, have responded to our request for help.

The result was that, in 1985, we were able to centralize all the university services on the new campus, which was constructed on about 48 acres of land, situated two and a half miles from the center of Villarica and donated by the bishop to the University. This transfer, however, did cause much opposition from some of the students, parents, and members of the community, who did not understand the reasons behind it.

Five wings were constructed on the campus, including a chapel and the hospital complex. As an initial gift for the hospital, we received both instruments and equipment.

This "gargantuan and titanic effort", as it was termed by one foreign delegation, familiar with the difficulties encountered in constructing works of this nature in a poor country, has been responsible for the value of the estate belonging to the Catholic University of Villarica appreciating some 6,000 percent over the period of five years from 1982 to 1986.

In May of 1984, two Italian priests and one Paraguayan layman from the Communion and Liberation Movement visited the University for the first time. The Board of Directors' dialogue with them centered on two themes: the history of "Christian Experience" and the "Regional Health Services Project" (P.R.S.S.); they, for their part, impressed on us that the history of Europe could be synthesized in two facts: her old cathedrals and her universities.

Help from the Communion and Liberation Movement (CL)

That evening's dialogue continued and, working intensely, we reached the formulation of a project in collaboration with the Voluntary Association of the International Service of Casena (A.V.S.I.), which already exists in other Latin American countries.

To this agreement, the recognition of the faculty of medicine by the national government was added in November 1986, after innumerable requests on our part. The project, born in collaboration with the Catholic University of Villarica, was made possible with the help of both human and material resources and, above all, with strong missionary motives, something which is all-important to us.

The friends of the A.V.S.I., through an international cooperation which is fully integrated with our Regional Health Services Project, will see to the providing of five doctors and the construction of five fully-equipped hospital wings within six years.

Nothing is lost in the economy of grace   When seen through the eyes of the man of faith, our efforts and our work are never lost. The Lord knows how to transform and distribute our efforts in a way that benefits and bestows grace on the whole community.

If the sorrows and sacrifices—especially of those who first labored in this work of faith and love—were many, the satisfactions received from having sought to discover God's plan for each of us, have also been many. In this place, where the Lord has called us to collaborate with his creative work, let us be aware that any great and good work is born in sorrow, and let us recall that "The seed must die in order to give birth to the tree, which, in turn, will bear its fruit."

THE SEEDS OF RESURRECTION
AT MARIANO MELGAR

A Missionary Community among the
Pueblos Jovenes of Lima

by
Emanuela Gardich

"I wish to welcome you as a mark of gratitude to the Lord. Gratitude because you can be with us, because the Lord gives you the possibility of being part of a sister church. Come with the wealth of a church that has formed you and come with the desire to immerse yourself in a young church."

With these words, His Excellency Bishop Schmitz, Auxiliary Bishop of Lima, welcomed us upon our arrival, during our first Eucharistic celebration together on Peruvian soil. Our hearts, too, felt gratitude together with many other sentiments. We were conscious of having arrived in a country with great needs. It seemed as though we had always loved these millions of brothers who have neither the bread of the word nor that of the Eucharist, and who lack even bread for their daily subsistence. Each one of us wanted to offer himself and his potentials, so as to be broken along with the Bread of Life. At the same time, we were aware of being in a world of discovering, of listening, of loving. We knew that, just as they were giving their testimony of having been overtaken and touched by Christ and in him, by the God of Love, we had simultaneously received the wonders wrought by the Spirit in the midst of the little ones. We felt called to give, to announce, and to receive; to let

A country with great needs

The missionary community of Villaregia di Contarina in the province of Rivigo was founded by a priest, Fr. Luigi Prandin, and by Miss Maria Luigia Corona. It was canonically erected in the diocese of Chioggia in 1981, and it is divided into four nuclei: consecrated men, consecrated women, consecrated within the family, and consecrated couples.

At present, the community numbers 130 members, and, besides being in Venice, Sardinia, and Brazil, is also in Peru. Emanuela Gardich's graphic account of the experience of the community in Lima, Peru, has been translated by Father Dismas Gannon, O.C.S.O., and Brother Dominique Nelson, O.C.S.O.

ourselves be converted to the purity of the gospel by our poorer brothers, the beloved of the Father. With fear and hope, we began a new adventure of the reciprocity of love, of a trinitarian relationship with the Peruvian people.

With this attitude of communion, we accepted the invitation of Cardinal Landazuri to go and work at the crowded outskirts of Lima, where the situation of misery is indescribable.

In this capital, which lies at the foot of the Andes and looks out over the Pacific Ocean, a most sensational population explosion has taken place. From 2,000,000 in 1960, the population grew to 6,000,000 in 1980, and today, it is believed to be much higher. People continue to arrive from the Sierra and from the jungle in search of work, frightened by terrorists of Sendero Luminoso or by the violence of the police themselves, who kill every suspect, either in jail or in the midst of the people. Families set up house on sand hills where everything is unsightly and covered with dust, where there is neither water nor electricity, where even a hint of minimal infrastructure is lacking. They protect themselves with four mats that constitute their house. In a few square feet on the bare, humid, dirty, sandy ground, five to ten persons live, without hygienic provisions, in promiscuity, and in a sea of growing problems. These hovels, known in Spanish as *choza*, cover vast areas like a cloak. Every free space is taken up by the poor and by misery. These settlements are called *pueblos jovenes*. Certain areas were "invaded" ten to twenty years ago, but the conditions in which men, women, and children are found are always subhuman. Regarding the *pueblos jovenes*, there is the struggle for life, the hope that does not want to die. Even when the future seems dim, there is the will to build a more human existence, to organize socially, to gather families together.

6,000 peublos jovenes

In Lima, more than 6,000 *pueblos jovenes* have been counted, spread about every little valley, on arid hills, in every direction throughout the city, so much so that this capital, once flourishing and rich in gold, now seems like one immense *pueblo joven*.

So many people are either unemployed or underemployed. The streets of the city are filled with poor open markets and hawkers: men, women, and children who seek to sell off whatever they can in the hope of earning bread for survival.

Many feed on the fodder prepared for animals, made up of scraps of ground fish. It is cheaper than rice or bread, but extremely dangerous for one's health.

For those without work there is no medical assistance available. Most people cannot go to the doctor, even in a case of grave necessity, for they can pay neither for the doctor nor for the medicine. For the poor, to become ill means to die.

And from the religious point of view, they are very backward. There is no help, e.g., from social services; they lack priests, they lack proper structures. For those six to eight million inhabitants, the diocese provides only 200 diocesan priests. But what little germ of faith is present in these poor people turns into hope driven toward the God of Life. Here is a church that wishes to be born and seeks help.

In our littleness, we feel we have been sent from our church to this sister church, in order to walk with this suffering portion of the people of God, toward that God who has vanquished death.

When, with Bishop Schmitz, we looked into the various possibilities of our integration and pastoral work, our criterion of choice was the existence of a minimal structure which would allow us to begin: a small house. Our attention fell on Mariano Melgar, a *pueblo joven* which had built a church, with the work and sacrifices of fourteen years, but still has no priest. Mariano Melgar is in the poorest area.

Our first contact with these simple people was rich with human kindness and the presence of the Spirit. About sixty adults and young people assembled, representatives from the native *pueblo* of Mariano *Mariano Melgar* Melgar and from other neighboring *pueblos jovenes*, to seek with us and with the bishop the most just way to begin a journey together. When Bishop Schmitz asked us how we would support ourselves financially, some of the fathers and mothers of families stood up to say, in their simple, transparent language, that just as they, though poor, do not allow their children to die, so neither would they allow their missionaries to die. They declared themselves ready to share their last crust of bread with us. We were also moved: that we should desire to depend entirely on Divine Providence was a strong sign. And so we are here, here to live with our brothers, to build a church with them. And we are experiencing the extent to which so harsh a poverty destroys poetry.

Because of an unfortunate crossing of air currents, Lima lies in a large basin where, despite a humidity of more than 90 percent, there is no precipitation. It has not rained here for seventy years. The sand on which the thousands of hovels are situated is a receptacle for every kind of filth and disease. Typhoid, dysentery, and hepatitis are very common. Diarrhea claims many victims, especially among the infants. Passing among the shacks, one can easily see emaciated pretty little faces, with clear signs of dehydration, forewarnings of a premature and unjust end. So many babies are extremely dirty. They live, play, and pass their whole day on the humid sand, with no kind of hygiene whatsoever. Many of these little creatures suffer eight bouts of diarrhea per year, and their resulting debilitation is intense. Often, they must resort to *flebo* [blood-letting] in order to sustain them and to avoid irreparable dehydration. Too many children die. Many times, even the vaccine given them against TB or polio or other diseases, instead of fostering the formation of antibodies, brings about disease in those weakened bodies which are in no condition to fight off even the few and almost impotent bacilli injected with the vaccine.

Our medical records show that seventy percent of the women who give birth do so without any assistance at the time and without any medical follow-up. The consequences for the mother and child are often very grave, if not fatal. Many women are crippled by the trauma of giving birth.

The woman's situation
The situation of women, and consequently of the family, is most pathetic. The families are often formed along the lines of natural unions (living together) begun when the man is seventeen and the woman is fifteen. These unions are easily destroyed by separation, whether caused by military service or by the necessity of working outside the city. The woman remains without education, passing from being a servant to her parents and brothers to being a slave to her husband. Influenced by a strongly macho mentality, the man can command and decide any question whatsoever. He often leaves all the responsibility of raising the family to the wife, who, in order to feed the children, is reduced to prostitution.

Families are divided. Many men try to avoid problems by throwing themselves into alcoholism, leaving their wives and children in despair. This lack of serenity, of family unity, destroys the emotional balance of the youth and of the population in general.

The percentage of unwed mothers and women with children abandoned by their husbands is very high. Organic diseases, coupled with undernourishment and the lack of hygiene, are complicated by emotional diseases.

Anxiety, constant preoccupation, and a life which is no more than survival are manifested in insanity, exhaustion, and stupor. Some statistics say that forty percent of the illnesses here are either mental disorders or are psychosomatic. Pain and sacrifice kills man. There is such a thing as psychological death.

In this context, it is to these brothers we wish to announce Christ, the New Man, and Mary, the Mother of God and the Mother of
Initiative for human advancement
humanity. We feel that every initiative toward the advancement of women smoothes the way to the Virgin Mother. Every step toward a more humane life renders present the New Man. Therefore, we confidently supplement the work of proclamation and evangelization with some initiatives for human advancement.

The parish has at its disposal a small wooden house situated directly in front of the missionaries' house, which serves as an *atelier*, a little tailor's shop, for a group of mothers who prepare, at a cheaper price than can be found at the store, school uniforms for the children of the *pueblo*. Besides being a service and a saving for the families, and bringing in a little earnings for these women who are working, it becomes an opportunity to meet others and of formation toward a Christian and human growth. Selected articles of clothing, collected by Italian youth in their respective fields of work, or in their parishes, furnish concrete help for immediate necessities and material for the dress-making and sewing school for many girls, future mothers.

The presence of the consecrated missionaries in the midst of so much sorrow and pain, itself becomes a sign and hope disfigured by misery. Magi's encounter with Maria Rojas, a mother with tuber-   *Maria Rojas*
culosis, is an example of how love is the tangible, distinctive response to the person:

> On Wednesday of Holy Week a woman approached me to ask for information on the school uniforms for her children. I answered her questions, and then I noticed that she wanted to say something else. I listened to her pitiful story.
>
> For several years she has been afflicted with TB. At times she has been at the point of death. Of her eight children, six live with her, while the oldest ones are in the grandmother's district. She gave as the reason for the absence of these two sons that they were taking the wrong path. Of the children at home, only the smallest ones come close to her; the others, as well as her husband, fear the contagion. This woman, who felt rejected by everyone and was without work, was bordering on despair. She repeated often: "Mother, I want to go far away, I don't know where, but I want to go far away, because here, no one wants me. Everyone rejects me. I have always been faithful to my husband. I have done nothing evil. I am afraid."
>
> I entreated her to rely on the help of others. I told her that the Church is like a family. It seemed to me that these words opened her heart. Until that moment she had never smiled. Mirrored on her face was a despondency that could only come from her having been brutalized by suffering. Now she began to relax her countenance; she told me that for so many years she had not thought about God, because she was too preoccupied with her children and she was always working; but her difficult situation and the impossibility of working now had caused her to begin reflecting. Slowly, she once again began thinking about God. She wanted to draw close to the parish. While at first she said: "No one wants me, I want to go far away", now she was able to hope: "I am sure that God will not reject me. Even if I have committed the greatest evil, forgetting about him, I am sure he will not forget me." She went away a little uplifted, her face sweetened with a smile, for her outlook had been changed.

The sad story of Maria Rojas unfortunately is not unique, for it reflects the abandonment in which many women are living. The confidence that arises within these bitter stories, the friendship that love knows how to beget and win are seeds of the Resurrection. Our condition, the Church with the poor and among the poor, will not be able to resolve social problems on an international level, but it will have the power to evangelize the poor by rendering them the blessed of the kingdom, and giving to us the full experience of the mercy and faithfulness of our God.

Seeds of solidarity   The flowers of solidarity that are blossoming in the Parroquia de la Trinidad (Trinity Parish)—the name of the parish erected by the cardinal on our arrival, a parish embracing about 80,000 persons—testify to this, and they are able to give to the hope of this people a countenance, a name: The Living Christ.

Dora and Raffael, two young people who frequent our community, she a nurse and he a paramedic, are willing, in their free time, to take care of a small parochial medical post for the poorest of the poor, who otherwise would never receive such care. Even if their service does not solve vast problems, it is at least a hand stretched out to the suffering. Already, twenty large cases of assorted medicine have arrived from Italy, thus creating a bond of love which truly makes us sister churches.

Magnolia is a young wife who chose to begin her marriage by going to live at Ricardo Palma, a *pueblo* without water or light, on the top of a hill. There, by bringing Christians together under a tent which she sets up from time to time, she is fostering another young community.

William and Maura live with the bare minimum. He prepares sweets, and she sells them. They have three children, the youngest of whom is handicapped. Generously, they dedicate all their free time to the nascent Christian community.

We believe that under the guidance of these simple men and women, who give their little, a miracle will take place. These hills are going to be snatched from the desert, foot by foot, and transformed into a country of men, into the promised land for the people whom God has saved.

3

ASIA

South Korea, a country in rapid economic development. For its part the Catholic Church in Korea is young, vibrant, and growing.

"WE ASK THE WHOLE CHRISTIAN WORLD FOR ITS PRAYERS"

The Religious Life of a Parish in Seoul

by
Piero Gheddo

I think I have traveled the world enough to say, without fear of being mistaken, that there is no church today that is as alive, young, growing, and full of enthusiasm and hope, as is the church in South Korea. With two million Catholics out of a total population of around 42 million, it receives 100,000 adult converts each year and shows a remarkable increase of priestly and religious vocations. I have visited the two seminaries, in Seoul and Kwangju, and several novitiates for men and women. Owing to problems of space everywhere, hundreds of boys and girls are forced to give up vocations for lack of teachers and structures. Cardinal Kim, the Archbishop of Seoul, like other bishops I interviewed, is worried by this chaotic growth that is so difficult to follow. Kim says, "We are like a baby who grows too quickly. The Holy Spirit sends many converts, many vocations, many new initiatives in every area of evangelization and human promotion. How can we give everyone a profound Christian formation?"

I think that this young church, born of the blood of 10,000 martyrs between 1784 and 1886, has much to teach us. This first of all: that in a country undergoing rapid economic development the Faith is lived with enthusiasm and with an exemplary lay missionary commitment.

A young Church born from the blood of 10,000 martyrs

In this brief testimony of a trip across the country and through the South Korean church, I would like to recount my experience in a parish located on the outskirts of the Korean capital, Seoul. Among

South Korea is increasingly gaining world attention. The political situation is tense, but the true economic miracle in Asia is Korea more than Japan. For its part, the Korean Catholic church is young, alive, and growing. The intense religious life in the Kuro 3-Deng parish is a good example of the Church's situation throughout the country. This article was translated by Robert and Veronica Royal.

its ten million inhabitants, more than a quarter of South Korea's Catholics (600,000 out of a total of two million) live in the city. The parish, Kuro 3-Deng, is dedicated to Saint Francis de Sales and is located in a working-class neighborhood, among factories, markets, schools, and playing fields, which, in a very modern city like Seoul, are found everywhere. The pastor is a Salesian, Father Paul Kim Bo Rok, and he is assisted by a Spanish Salesian, Father Joseph Blanco, and several Salesian nuns. The parish includes exactly 9,537 baptized Catholics out of a population of about 150,000.

"Our parish, like many others here in Seoul", Father Paul tells me, "has one problem that takes precedence over all the others: how to receive into the Church and form in the Christian life the 600 to 700 adult converts yearly. In Seoul, new parishes are being created (there are already more than sixty), but they are not enough because the Christian population is increasing very fast, perhaps too fast. But how can you send away those seeking baptism? Since the visit of the Pope to Korea in May of 1984, the number of those seeking instruction and baptism has increased even more."

In his parish, I ask, how does he keep track of these hundreds of catechumens who are baptized each year?

The laity carry out religious instruction

He replies that there are only two priests and four nuns. The lay people do the real work of religious instruction. In the parish, there are eight courses of catechesis, at various hours for different kinds of people, as well as very active church movements. The priests only supervise this activity, while the sisters are directly involved in catechesis and visiting families of parishioners and catechumens. Furthermore, there are numerous other courses at the diocesan and city levels, to which they send persons with special needs, e.g., university professors, doctors, professionals, etc.

The Kuro 3-Deng parish, like others I visited in various Korean cities, is a forge in constant activity: from early morning until late night, it is difficult to find an empty hall, or a room not being used. An impressive number of people come to the parish in any given day for prayer, for instruction, and for a thousand other reasons. All or nearly all this activity is run by lay people. The Korean church has a long tradition that is relevant, because in the beginning it was founded by lay people and, then, during almost a century of persecution, it survived through the work of lay confraternities, forerunners of the current church movements.

"The Korean church", Father Paul tells me, "is centered on the parish. We have few religious and few activities outside the parishes. But within the parish is a variety of initiatives and movements. In Japan, you feel the influence of the religious more; here among us, the church is founded on the laity."

"I have heard it said, however," I respond, "that it is a church which is still very clerical; the priest commands and the others obey."

"That is partly true. There is a very strong Confucian tradition here; offices and hierarchies are respected in the family, in society, and in the Church. Therefore, we have a hierarchical and clerical Church on the one hand, and on the other a laity that does everything. We are changing the mentality and style of ecclesial life little by little as religious instruction of the laity grows."

"Which movements do you have in the parish?" I ask.

"Almost all the movements that exist in Korea, quite a number, each with its special charism, spirituality, and style of apostolate. All of them, however, are centered on helping parish growth. In some countries, I know, there are tensions between the parishes and the movements. Here, in general, the bishops themselves have advised formation of committed laymen through the movements. The organization is at the parish level, even if the centers of action and formation are regional or national.

"The story of Korean church movements is extremely interesting and should be better known as a significant example of the integration of institution and charisms. The national movements are numerous: Legion of Mary, cursillo, charismatics, Focolare, Better World, Marriage Encounter, Young Christian Workers, Happy Family Movement, Blue Army, and so forth. The fundamental characteristic of all these movements is the formation of a missionary faith, committed to the service of the Church and society. The mission comes from a strong identity with and practice of the Faith. From this stem the eighty percent Sunday Mass attendances, the exceptional generosity toward the priests and the Church ($15.00 usually offered for a Mass and an average of $.25 per person in the weekly parish collections), and the missionary sense and commitment to Church and parish activities."

So many Church movements and so well integrated

"We hold two celebrations for adult baptisms every year in our parish", Father Paul Kim Bo Rok tells me. "Each time, more than 300 people are baptized, following a year or more of instruction. And I have to admit that the lay people complete the work of evangelization, not only the catechesis, but the visits to the families, the administrative work of the parish, home prayers, contact with those who live far away, and so forth."

"How are the lay people organized in the parish?"

"I have about seven or eight hundred directly involved in parish activities, but many more available if I need to ask for something. Like most Koreans, my parishioners work eleven or twelve hours per day, with only one day of rest out of every fifteen, and around ten days of vacation per year. This is the normal work load in industry, offices, and public services. The average Korean salaried worker labors fifty-four hours a week, while in the U.S. you work fewer than forty hours. My parish is organized into various lay movements. Let us take, as an example, the most widespread movement, the *The Legion* Legion of Mary, which originated in Ireland and was brought to *of Mary* Korea in 1953 by Irish missionaries. Today, it is virtually a national Catholic group. In my parish, there are twenty leaders for adults and eight for young people. Each leader has from twenty to thirty members, who meet once a week for an hour and a half. They recite the Rosary, do some spiritual reading, each member reports on his work, each one assumes tasks for the following week, a private collection is made, and a sermon by one of the movement's lay people is heard. The Legion of Mary has a very strict rule that the Koreans accept: for them obedience, according to the Confucian spirit, is an important virtue. When they have carried out the tasks assigned to them by the Manual and by the movement, their consciences are clear."

"But isn't there a danger of mere formalism?"

"Certainly, that danger exists, but it is the whole culture of the Korean people that is set up in this way. Christianity is the principal force creating a personal conscience, personal liberty."

"What commitments do the members of the Legion of Mary take on?"

"Above all, a commitment to Christian life as persons and as families. Then, the missionary commitment, that is, to bring into contact with the Church their friends, relatives, acquaintances, and so forth. If we have 600 to 700 adult baptisms each year in the parish, it is because of these lay people, who speak openly of Jesus Christ, visit families, organize activities in various settings including the workplace, distribute flyers and invitations, etc. The Koreans have a profound religious spirit, and are seeking answers to their problems. Traditional religions, such as Buddhism and Shamanism, have no answers to give; they are not historically incarnated. It is inevitable that the Koreans become Christians, Catholic and Protestant, since they feel this deep religious inspiration."

"Do you have other parish movements?"

"Yes. The Cursillo movement, charismatics, Focolare, Blue Army, Young Christian Workers, and the movement for a Better World. Each one engages a number of laymen in the service of the parish, each through different functions and special charisms. The charismatics, for example, are those who attract non-Christians by their way of praying; they create prayer groups everywhere, stimulating joy, friendship, and interest in the Church. Every group commits itself either to outside missionary activities or to parish duties, not only inside the parish, but outside it as well. For example, visiting Christian families: if someone does not come to church or go to confession at least for Christmas and Easter, we go to his home to find out if he has any problems."

"How do you find out if someone does not come to confession?"

"Well, here in Korea there is an ancient tradition that everyone accepts, so that when you enter the Church, you accept the Church in its entirety, even the traditions. This is the Korean spirit: either enter and accept, or do not enter. To become a Christian is certainly an act of faith, but also it means to enter a group, to pay your share, to respect the rules. If one does not accept or, subsequently, rejects something, he does not protest: he simply leaves. But he remains and is Christian; for example, he comes to Sunday Mass, even at great inconvenience. And he confesses twice a year at least. At the beginning of every year, everyone receives little sheets of paper with their code numbers, the number registered in the parish of their baptism. When one of the faithful goes to confession, he gives one of these little sheets to the priest, which do not bear individual names, only the code numbers. The priest delivers them to the person responsible for the records, who marks those who have been to confession, who send their children to catechism classes, who pay the levied amount for the church and its activities, etc. At the end of the year, they add up accounts. Those who have not confessed (or not paid their share) are visited by the nuns or by some lay person, to find out about the situation and to ask if they still wish to remain Christian."

He who enters the Church accepts it in full

"What if you go to confession outside the parish?"

"It does not matter, you still give the priest the little sheet, and he sends it to the right parish. Confession sheets have the name and address of the parish printed on them."

"So to become a Catholic requires a strong spirit of sacrifice and of solidarity", I comment.

"In the Protestant churches it is even worse. They are much more demanding than we are. We try to create a spirit of liberty and personal conscience. While we recognize the danger of formalism, we have begun to notice the opposite danger is growing, i.e., secularization, and practical materialism in life, which distances people from the religious spirit. South Korea has undergone a prodigious economic development. The poverty and destitution of thirty years ago have completely disappeared. Now, abundance and wealth are a constant temptation. Up until now, church attendance and conversions have not diminished in intensity. But we think that the prime danger, even for us, is practical materialism, the atheism of a life completely dedicated to earthly goods. We must react with a more profound, more personal Christian formation, with convictions of adult conscience. Our church is in a difficult moment, particularly because it is overwhelmed by these waves of conversions, new Christians who need time, attention, formation. We ask the whole Christian world for at least the help of its prayers."

UNDERSTANDING WITH YOUR VERY SKIN

Fifteen Years of Missionary Experience in Japan

by
Pino Cazzaniga

1974, the year of my definitive departure for Japan, was also the year of the Synod of Bishops, who met in Rome to discuss the problems of evangelization. The following year Paul VI masterfully gathered together the results of the discussion in his apostolic exhortation *Evangelii Nuntiandi*, which may be considered the Magna Carta of evangelization for the world of today.

The influence of that document in the transformation of the ecclesial mentality here in Japan is noteworthy. The demands of inculturation are now recognized without hesitation; but in those days I was not in the condition of spirit necessary to study that document calmly and at the level of theoretical reflection.

In those days, I was realizing the inculturation process in a concrete way, paying the cost in person, as were many other recently arrived missionaries. And that was all to the good, because, as the Japanese proverb says, "the truly important thing is not understanding with your head, but understanding with your very skin." The process began with a not at all pleasant experience: the inability to speak the Japanese language. It took me six or seven years of effort to arrive at a passable competence in the language, but that was only one of the barriers, and not the worst. Only now, after almost fifteen years of life there, have I begun to understand how much the Japanese are different from us. The effort of inculturation was difficult, but also abundantly worthwhile. When I met the Japanese for the first time, I found them polite, but also distant and cold. When I said "hello" to them, even though it was temporarily in Italian, they were flustered

The language and cultural barrier

Father Pino Cazzaniga, a missionary of Pime, has lived in Japan for fifteen years, eight of which have been spent in the outskirts of Tokyo. According to his testimony, after a period of suffering, adaptation, and listening, the Japanese church has arrived at the time for a harvest. Toward this end, the Japanese bishops have called the first national conference for evangelization. This article was translated by Robert and Veronica Royal.

and even disturbed. Their ability to adapt had made them capable enough in the use of syllogistic reasoning, but only in the technical and scientific fields. When they entered into the sphere of the spiritual, or religious, life, they preferred intuition and personal contact. For them, abstract thought was more an obstacle than a means of communication. Once the wall of cultural separation had been eliminated, at least as much as was possible, the very persons of the missionaries became the vehicles of evangelization. Even the conciliar problematic simplified itself, because, almost without noticing it, we were meeting in the context of concrete daily life. For example, it is still very moving for me to remember the profound friendship, both at a religious level and at a human level, that I have had with several Protestants and Buddhists.

In the pastoral letter on the fundamental outline of the church in Japan issued by the Episcopal Conference in June 1984, non-Christians are happily designated as "those who do not yet sit around the table of the Lord". There are many of these, more than ninety-nine percent of a population of almost 120 million. Catholics barely amount to 400,000. An insignificant minority then? Yes, if you judge according to mere numbers; no, if you put this in a sacramental perspective. Certainly, in Tokyo you do not see a church and a cross in every neighborhood, as is the case in South Korea's capital, Seoul. The church in Japan is a church in the desert, but a desert where everywhere oases of salvation are now well established. The approximately 500 missionary priests and 450 native priests in Japan are, above all else, signs of the convocation of a community that, little by little, is becoming missionary. This makes it possible to follow the Gospel parable of the king who sends his servants to call all the suffering and poor to the banquet of life.

"Those who still do not sit around the table of the Lord"

In Tokyo: The Neighborhood of Fuchu

After an experience of missionary work in the "provinces", I came to the neighborhood of Fuchu (200,000 inhabitants) in Tokyo, where, earlier, the Pime had constructed a community center and a church. In a short time, there gathered together there a community of 150 Christians living in the area. This group included intellectuals and professionals, but, in general, consisted of simple people, not without their own problems, anxieties, and weaknesses. From Monday through Friday, the church was not often visited because the men are deeply involved in their work, so much so that it is common for children not to see their fathers for an entire week at a time. The women are involved in the education of the children and in taking care of the home. The boys are regimented in an educational system that at times hardly allows them time to breathe, even on Sunday. Notwithstanding all this, in that community the force of the gospel began to work. Fuchu is known because the prisons of the capital are located there. The superior of our community was invited to be a spiritual director to the prisoners who requested it. There was no flood of conversions, but hope grew in that place, which is considered to be the tomb of every hope. For the Japanese, losing your reputation is one of the greatest disgraces, and one cannot redeem oneself except by suicide. Poor, weak, and unhappy prisoners discovered the value of the human being in prison, and then they discovered the courage to swim against the current outside of prison.

There is also the problem of old people, which is grave in the large cities of Japan. When I left Fuchu, the *obaasan* (the grandmothers) gave me a little going-away dinner, where smiles and happiness were the most pleasant part of the meal. Prior to the creation of this community, those dear persons did not even know one another and had to lead their lives in solitude—supported well enough according to the standard of their culture—but, nonetheless, frustrated and troubled. The phenomenon of loneliness is becoming more widespread among many types of people, even young people. Absorbed by the frenetic and dehumanizing rhythm of the efforts required during the work day, many are unhappy even on the days of rest. On Sunday morning, the atmosphere of our little church contrasts greatly with that of a Shinto temple in the city not far away. The temple is sadly deserted, even if it retains its natural majesty; our church is a little bit noisy, but is filled with serenity. The bread of the word and the Eucharist that the *gaijin* (foreign) priests distribute becomes the element of cohesion and of spiritual experience. Even some non-Christians, desiring prayer, ask to be able to attend.

The problem of isolation

And the children? To be able to read a newspaper, it is necessary to study hard for at least nine years. The ideograms offer a marvelous service when they are well-known, but they are demanding masters while you are in the learning phase. Nonetheless, in Japan there is no illiteracy. In every subject, the system of education is carefully and minutely programmed, and is effective for the acquisition of ideas—including ideas that are somewhat negative for the development of the person. It appears that this programmatic rigidity and lack of true humanistic ends contributes to the frequent truancy from lessons that, for about a decade, has been becoming more widespread in the middle and high schools.

Thanks to the efforts of my co-worker, Father Alberto di Bello, and to the help of several Christian mothers, we have set up a "Sunday School". Our school is set up so that the children create an atmosphere of friendship, where they are able to develop the first shoots of the

"Sunday School"

life of feeling and the spirit. The mothers, almost all non-Christians, enthusiastically pitch in. Thus, one can even organize summer camps.

Our church is not exceptional in these various activities of evangelization and pre-evangelization. Similar centers of spirituality are found throughout Japan. If we take into account the activities of our Protestant brothers, the panorama of the Christian presence in this country is very wide.

An Open Church

"As for the task of evangelizing our country, the fundamental problem at the base of all the others lies in the separation between faith and life, and between church and society." Thus the declaration of the Episcopal Conference in the document with which it enunciated the theme of the N.I.C.E.

Beyond the statement itself, which is linked to the well-formulated teaching of Paul VI in *Evangelii Nuntiandi*, the genesis of this episcopal document is enlightening. It was not a pastoral letter worked out by the episcopal body separately from the rest of the Church. The bishops based their work on 160 discussion "projects", the fruit of a debate which took place in all the dioceses, and at all levels. The lay Japanese Catholics, through experiencing this dialogue, in which they showed a level of maturity higher than anyone might have expected, learned the meaning of an ecclesiology of communion. The "listening sessions" were particularly significant. These were held both at diocesan and regional levels. The bishops were always present, but deliberately did not take initiative in speaking. In a certain sense, the "teachers" became "learners", which had a noteworthy pedagogical effect. The faithful were educated in taking an active role, and distanced themselves little by little from their attitude of too passive obedience, an attitude favored by a clerical ecclesiology and by the Confucian cultural tradition. Thanks to this spontaneous contribution of the laity, who live in various sectors of society, the bishops are in a position to see the full panorama, and, consequently, to choose priorities and directions. "It is necessary", one reads in the document, "to rethink the Faith beginning from life experience and to rethink the mode of evangelization starting from the Japanese social reality of today." Up to now, the starting point had been abstract doctrine, formulated, for the most part, in Western cultures. One tried to adapt life to the doctrine. The gospel thus appeared as something extraneous to the Japanese cultural milieu and not a part of everyday life. Now there has been a change of mentality. Father Okada, director of the Pastoral Mission Institute, does not hesitate to call it a Copernican revolution in the pastoral practice of the church in Japan.

With the bishops' declaration, the movement of dialogue has not come to an end. A second phase has begun, which has led to a national convention in November. The *entire* Japanese church is learning to become a *missionary* church for the *whole* society.

For several years, Monsignor Peter Shirayanagi, Archbishop of Tokyo, has not missed any occasion to remind everyone that this is a propitious time for evangelization in Japan. There are two reasons for this situation. First of all, there is no other nation in the world, including those of the Christian West, that enjoys the degree of liberty of religious expression that Japan has. Further, one notices that spiritual hunger is more and more marked in vast strata of the population.

A recent study (January 1987) carried out by *Asahi Shimbun* (the most widely distributed and authoritative daily newspaper in Tokyo) asked the following question: "What do you give preference to, the satisfaction of your material needs or your spiritual needs?" Eighty percent of the people interviewed chose spiritual requirements.

In Japan, religious sects have undergone a "boom" because they present themselves as an answer to the existential anxiety of today. The Christian Church must accept the challenge, in obedience to its Lord, and owing to its love toward all its brothers. It is not a case of selling Christianity cheap, but of returning to imitating Jesus, who ministered to the sufferings of all. The Japanese church has decided to make this attitude its own, as it enters its new path of evangelization.

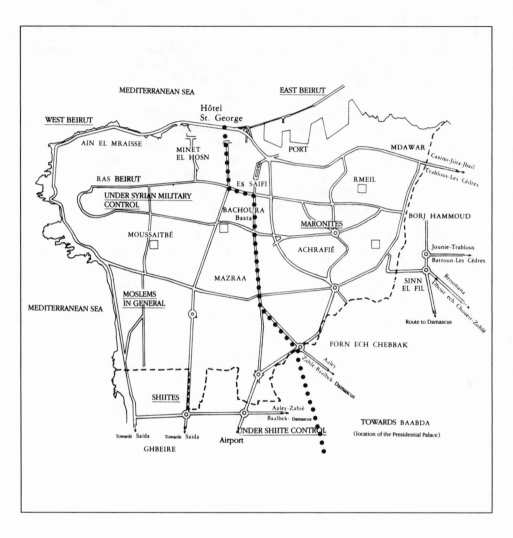

Beruit, Lebanon's bloody capital, is divided into Syrian, Shiite, and Maronite zones. Father Labaky's choral group has crossed over these unmarked boundaries to sing of peace in the midst of war.

LEBANON'S CHILDREN OF HOPE

by
Father Mansour Labaky

War is nothing but death, death to towns, villages, households, countrysides, souls, and bodies. War is the death of all the rights of man.

I've said so before, and I'll say it again: "Anything that by definition is nothing but destruction cannot safeguard anything, especially not life."

Now, life is a gift of God, his most beautiful and most precious gift. And life comes before everything else, because life is made of love.

When children are thrust without warning into horror, when they learn the dreadful power of hatred before they even know what it means to exist, when their love and gentleness are yanked out of them by the roots, what else can we do, we who know what it was like to receive a heritage of love, what else can we do but hold these children close to our hearts and try to help them to hear again the marvelous rhythm of a heart that still beats, will always beat, for them alone? What else can we do but wrap them in tenderness, the tenderness of God, who gives each of his children a soul, even in the midst of hatred. What else can we do but help them to grasp the fact that it is not God who intended this war, but man's folly, and that the only way to stop it is not to fall into the abyss of that folly, of that death, but to be, oneself, a God-bearer: that is, a bearer of peace and tender love.

After the massacre in my parish, in January 1976, I founded the Orphanage of Our Lady of Joy for war-orphans from all over Lebanon. Most of these children had watched their parents die in agony.

In 1976, Father Mansour Labaky founded the "Little Singers of Lebanon", a choir of children who have frequently traveled across the country seeking to quiet the noise of arms with their songs of love. 1986 was the tenth anniversary of the choir's foundation, but Father Labaky had no time for celebrations. As the account here published reveals, on the contrary, he was busy giving new life and a new initiative to help the children because "our situation is so desperate that only a miracle can save us. And the children are the only ones who can obtain this miracle." This article was translated from the French by Mary E. Hamilton.

I won't go on about their traumas, their blank stares and their nightmares, nor their need to have someone there to cradle them, their need for quiet and safety—in the face of such despair, sermons are ridiculous—I didn't have to reacquaint these children with love, and with the forgiveness that comes from trust. No, not one of my children wants revenge. They know that to seek revenge would be to cause other innocent people to suffer; that would be putting them through the same horrid fate, and there would be no end to it. They want to try to clamp the ends of this hellish chain, not add more links to it.

Not one of my children seeks vengeance

Step by step, following Jesus in the manger, Jesus on the flight into Egypt, Jesus on the Cross with all the crucified children of the world, then Jesus risen from the dead, they rediscovered the Light and said Yes to all the values taught in the Gospels. These children, who have been so deeply and so inhumanly hurt in heart and body, know exactly what we mean when we talk about the rights of man. They are the best possible ambassadors for these rights, for life and for tenderness. To get the message across, they had to sing it, with their children's voices as pure as brooks in springtime, their children's firm belief that does nothing by halves, their tragic experience of a ruined childhood. With them, with this handful of orphans who wanted nothing but to love and be loved, I started the first small group in the choir we called "The Little Singers of Lebanon".

Our first concert was at the Palais de la Culture, in the Christian Zone, then in the Moslem Zone: we sang on Lebanese television, on Radio Lebanon, and at the Unesco Building, where the audience, mainly Moslem, sang along with the chorus of one of our songs:

From the Christian area to the Moslem area

> Teach me thy love, my God.
> If I have hurt anyone, teach me to ask forgiveness.
> If anyone has hurt me, teach me to forgive.

And in December 1981, to close the Year of Hope, we gave a Recital of Hope with 350 Little Singers, both orphans and non-orphans of all faiths; it had an immense impact, especially on young people.

We sing about love, peace, and forgiveness. We sing about these things because we live these things. And believe me, nobody can live them and sing of them better than children. One has only to look into their eyes, shining with faith, and see their smiles, fresher than a dawn in May.

When we gave the Recital of Hope, a little girl was interviewed by Lebanese television. They asked her what she felt when she was singing. She replied: "I feel like my faith, my love, and my hope are getting bigger and bigger, and I love sharing this faith, this love, and this hope with everybody in the whole world, especially with the ones who are suffering."

With the help of these children, we want to spread prayer throughout Lebanon. Our situation is so precarious that only a miracle can save us. And the children are capable of obtaining this miracle. We want the adults to stop destroying what keeps the children together. All the children of the world are alike. They know nothing of hate. If you give them a little love, they forgive anything. In spite of their wounds, they grow and develop in marvelous ways. The reason for it is that they are professionals at hoping. Not for nothing did God call on us to be like them.

With my orphans and my parishioners, I also started Kilo Day. *Kilo Day* On the great feasts throughout the year, everyone brings at least a pound or two of something: food, clothing, books, toys, medical supplies, and so on. One year, my children surprised me by bringing their Lenten self-denial offerings: two pounds of pennies for "other children poorer than we are". Another year, they gave sacrificially to the children in Poland, and to the little children in Africa, "the ones that are *really* hungry". Thus, we are harvesting something of inestimable value, something that is irreplaceable: not just alms one gives to quiet one's conscience, but acceptance into our own hearts and lives, for all our brothers, of no matter what race or creed, to share our daily bread.

At present, with the devaluation of our currency, we must share everything, every day. I have begun the "By the Grace of God" project, which consists of making sure that the children of the refugees who come to school with empty stomachs have at least a sandwich for breakfast. Holy Wisdom School at Jdeidet, where I am principal, participates in this program. We have quite a few children of refugees among our students, but nobody knows who gives and receives. Gifts are placed in the school hall and given out immediately, along with the gifts from the parish, to those who are most in need. In this way, we continue to live our faith in sharing without regard to creed; we share not just food, but our availability to others, everyday love and caring, the love of the Gospels that teaches that because God is our Father, all men are our brothers.

I have just enlarged my choir by bringing in some students from Holy Wisdom School. All these children, and I mean *all* of them, *At school after* frequently come to school after having spent the night in an air-raid *having passed the* shelter, which means they have spent the night in fear and the sort *night in shelters* of feeling of helplessness that can lead to rebelliousness if one is not otherwise directly, intimately, profoundly close to God. And one cannot be close to God if one is not close to one's brothers. When we share in the way we do, we think no more of destruction, or of revenge, but of sowing love with overflowing hands.

Six thousand years of history, two thousand years of Christianity, and a thousand years of different religions living together are not going to be blotted out by twelve years of war—as long as we live our Faith, as long as we pass this Faith on to our children by planting it in their souls with love and with hope. And our children do hope. The more the bombs rain down from the sky, the more the children sing and the more they pray. Because when one has been nourished by love, when one can feel that love in others and make others feel it too, no matter what happens, no matter what sufferings must be borne, we cannot despair.

Only the kind of tenderness drawn from the heart of God can give life back to these children who have been wounded by hate.

"ONE CANNOT THROW AWAY A HUMAN PATRIMONY"

René Péchard and the Children of Mekong

by
Elisabeth Tingry

"Even though they chose to be free, they are still behind barbed wire." Hanging over the barrier that surrounds the Phanat Nikom Camp, René Péchard, seventy-five years old, tries to make contact with the Vietnamese children who can be heard playing behind the corrugated sheet-metal fence that separates them from the outside world. A small boy climbs up onto an overhanging tree-branch. He left Saigon six months ago, by sea. He is one of the surviving boat-people. His parents could not go with him. He is all alone. For him, there is no such thing as a future, and he is not yet fifteen years old. René Péchard knows thousands of stories like that.

To help children in that kind of trouble, he founded the "Children of the Mekong" Association in 1975.

René Péchard has lived in Indo-China for thirty years: ten years in Viet Nam, twenty in Laos. He has seen the suffering undergone by numberless children, both those who are refugees and those who simply have been abandoned. He, however, could not find it in his heart to leave them to their fate.

In 1956, René Péchard arrived in Laos, having spent seven years in Viet-Minh prisons.

Being a dentist, he set up housekeeping in Vientiane, opened an office, and hired two teenagers, whom he soon registered in the Xieng-Khouang School so that they could continue their studies. The following Christmas, he went to see them at school.

A dentist's office at Vientiane

"It was such a miserable place", he remembers, "that I resolved to plan a real Christmas for them the next year." Noting the chill

René Péchard is a seventy-five-year-old French dentist who has spent thirty years of his life in Indo-China. Tireless in his efforts to aid the needy when he was in Laos, he did not diminish his activity on their behalf when he was forced to return to France. He became father of many "Children of the Mekong", who are now, thanks to him, dentists, engineers, accountants, etc. This article was translated by Mary E. Hamilton.

357

Viet Nam, Laos, Thailand, Cambodia: countries of the Mekong known in the West for a series of struggles that troubled the consciences of everyone. René Péchard went beyond a facile expression of concern and dedicated himself to helping alleviate the sufferings of these people.

at Xieng-Khouang (elevation, 6,000 feet), he looked for—and found—blankets.

With a few friends, he started the "Association of Friends of St. Joseph's Boarding School", that tried to solicit sponsors in France who would pay for the poor children's schooling. The French responded magnificently. Gradually, the Association extended its sponsorships to include other students, in addition to the boarders at St. Joseph's School. But the secret got out. At the end of the sixties, when the French troops left Laos, the French consul called René Péchard in: "What you are doing for the Laotian children is all very well, but you ought to be thinking of French children." Five hundred Eurasian children had been left fatherless by the French retreat.

René Péchard proceeded to find homes in France for 195 of the Eurasian children.

The rest, he simply took in himself. He opened three orphanages: one for babies, one for grade-school children, and one for adolescents. At the same time, he found sponsors to pay for these children's education. Between 1964 and 1975, he found 701 sponsors.

In 1975, the Pathet-Lao Laotian Communist Party won in the election. That was the year René Péchard was getting ready to take a trip to France to visit the Paris Association and the young people who had been sent to study in Paris. On this trip, he went by way of Thailand. There, he met the first boat-people fleeing Viet Nam and the first Cambodians fleeing the Khmer-Rouge.

Touched by their plight, he resolved to help them. But when he got to Paris, he was warned that the Pathet-Lao planned to arrest him if he went back to Vientiane, on the grounds of "kidnapping Laotian children".

Faced with the impossibility of going back, René Péchard determined to remain in France and continue his work from there for all the Mekong children, be they Vietnamese, Laotian, Cambodian, or whatever; all of them were destitute.

Return to France in 1975

René Péchard set out to find more sponsors for children in the camps, leaving it to the clergy and religious to determine which families were the poorest, and to give these families the few hundred francs that would permit them to buy the bare necessities of life.

In France, he opened an orphanage for abandoned adolescents. As far as possible, he placed them with families, believing that children develop most fully within the family structure. He personally guided and supervised their studies until graduation.

His work is a real response to misery. To be content just to hand out money is only a short-term solution to the problem. The truly effective way to deal with this problem is to extend a helping hand to the child or teenager until he can walk by himself, until he can take care of himself, until he is capable of living a life of his own.

In this way, René Péchard has "followed" 2,005 children of the Mekong. These children are now dentists, engineers, business executives, teachers, chefs, mechanics. . . .

René Péchard does not limit himself to refugees. He runs, in addition, development programs in Thailand, a soup kitchen for impoverished children in the northeast part of Thailand, where there have been serious famine conditions, and schooling for children from the Bangkok slums, to keep them from turning to prostitution or drugs. He also supports orphanages like the one in Sra Keow, which needs medical supplies, clothing, and so on.

I saw their misery

What makes René Péchard work so hard for Asiatic children at a time when most people care only for leisure? "I have seen their poverty", he says. "These children are bright and talented. To forget about them would be to sacrifice a priceless human resource."

René Péchard never took time to get married, but he has been granted fatherhood far beyond what an ordinary man can hope for: fatherhood as the Church describes and encourages it in *Familiaris consortio*. René Péchard has lived fatherhood beyond its widest definition.

4

EASTERN EUROPE

THE MILLENNIUM OF THE "BAPTISM" OF THE RUSSIAN PEOPLE

A Round-Table Discussion of the Situation of the Church in Russia

Question: From what perspective can we celebrate the millennium of the "baptism" of the Russian people, and what can each of us do in this regard?

First Answer: It seems to me that the millennium of the "baptism" of the Russian people is going to be celebrated without too much official fanfare. Nevertheless, the celebration will revive whatever is organically most authentic and profound in the Russian ecclesial tradition. To develop that tradition and take advantage of it, we need to know it as profoundly as possible; we need to steep ourselves and the people around us in this tradition. But acting in this way will result in our running up against many obstacles placed either by the secular authority or, unfortunately, by the ecclesiastical authority.

But it is absolutely vital that we find a middle road, a golden mean between the obscurantist atheism of the official propaganda on the one hand, and the obsequious attitude toward the state by the ecclesiastical hierarchy on the other.

It is not enough to know that "we have been baptized in Christ"; we must also know that "with him we have been repeatedly clothed" throughout the course of our history. It would be a crime against our past to reduce it all to ceremonial folderol, to empty boasting. *A sober and honest judgment on our experience* The best thing we can do in view of the millennium is to attempt a profound, sober, and honest judgment on our experience.

Certainly this "baptism" is going to be seen first of all as a meta-historical event, an event of our "sacred history". And if we presume

In the USSR, the reflections of the Christian community, in particular the Orthodox, are concentrated on preparing for the celebration of the millennium of the "baptism" of the nation, which takes place in July 1988. Beyond the official commemorations, the faithful aim at rediscovering and deepening their Christian tradition. These considerations emerge from a round-table discussion which took place in the autumn of 1986 among a number of Orthodox intellectuals. The discussions have been published in *Archiv Samizdata*, no. 5911. This article has been translated from Italian by Father Dismas Gannon, O.C.S.O., and Brother Dominique Nelson, O.C.S.O.

to be truly the people chosen by God (this concept is also found in a thinker who is as far removed from a narrow nationalistic position as V. Solovyov), this is by no means the same thing as saying that we are exempt from sin. We must never forget the history of the people of Israel.

Moreover, in this case, we also have a major responsibility for our sins. The present-day "Babylonian captivity" is an eloquent proof of this: because in an epoch far removed from our own, the Church, in order to please the state, failed in her vocation as light of the world, and thus planted the seed that has so sprouted.

What we truly need is not a smug sense of national self-satisfaction, but a profound and sincere consciousness of national repentance, which is born of the repentance of each member of the Orthodox Church. What we need to do is "forget the past and reach out toward the future" (Phil 3:13), to seek redemption and rebirth not in the traditional forms of the past, but in the glory of Christ who is to come.

We have no choice but to pose the problem of a creative attitude toward our Christian vocation in this radical way, and, perhaps, for the Orthodox Church, the problem is so urgent as to pose the alternative "either creativity or death".

We must continue to seek for this creativity without fear of making mistakes, treasuring both our own experience and the experience of the West. Finally, we need to measure ourselves by the sweeping vision of the universal Church. Not by chance is the spirit of Christianity that of God who has made himself "all things to all men".

Nor should we forget that immediately after the millennium of the "baptism" of the Russian people another anniversary draws near: the second millennium of Christianity. This does not mean that we must downplay the national aspect of our celebration; quite the contrary, we must preserve it, and enhance it by highlighting its better aspects and making it flow back into the patrimony of the universal Christian spirituality—in the last analysis, into the patrimony of the kingdom of God which is to come: "The kings of the earth will bring to him their treasures" (Rev 21:24).

Second Answer: The possibility cannot be excluded, unfortunately (and we may need to learn, in the event, humbly to accept this), that because of the offenses against God's law by the Russian people, the millennium of this "baptism" will be celebrated by the hierarchy's dining on caviar and vodka; by official society it will not be celebrated at all; by the authorities it will be celebrated with a torrent of atheistic propaganda, and by the laity . . . each one as he can. We must resign ourselves to the idea that a scandalous "celebration" of this kind is extremely possible, and that it could become an historical fact, quoted

later in all the textbooks. However, we must not forget that the
crucifixion of the Son of God was also a scandal and a catastrophe
in the eyes of his contemporaries. We Christians do not hide the fact
that our religion, our Faith, our hope is founded on what appears
to be folly, a scandal, a catastrophe; on the unjust and scandalous
death of him who is the Savior of the world, on his iniquitous
condemnation. And therefore, even in evil, even in the ruin of whole
civilizations, we always discern the seeds of good, and we know that
Jesus Christ is with us; he is our leader and we are his soldiers. These
are important and demanding words, but we are not free to act as
though nothing had ever happened, given that we consider ourselves
Christians. And "blessed are they who wash their robes: they will
have a share in the tree of life and they will be able to enter through
the gates of the city" (Rev 22:14).

Our Faith is based on what appears to be folly

Third Answer: If, with God's help, we set out on the path of life
lived in the freedom of faith, we will move toward the approaching
millennium of the "baptism" of the Russian people in a manner
worthy of the event. Each of us can bring his own contribution,
since each one possesses a talent to invest for the glory of God, secure
in the knowledge that he can make use of it for the benefit of the
Church, and based on the possibility that he can choose to work in
the field he so desires. The only thing that matters is that this desire
be truly sincere and constructive.

Again, even if there has been a strong falling-off of our religious
reawakening over the past five years, I have the assurance that it is
precisely in these years that work has been done, hidden but indispensable, for critically understanding our basic experience in a new
way. This situation has led us to a greater care, sobriety, and maturity.
The result of this work will undoubtedly be judged by the ardor
with which the new generation will seek Christ, and we, rendered
wise by experience, must help them to avoid our errors. To some,
the present situation appears almost desperate, but I would not be
inclined to abandon myself to discouragement since it takes but a
little yeast to leaven the dough, and the grain necessary to knead it
has already been winnowed of many weeds.

Only a little yeast to leaven the dough

As the blessed Fr. Joann di Kronstadt said at the beginning of this
century, "Russia revolts, suffers, and is tormented in God's rejection,
but Divine Providence will not abandon Russia, not even in this sad
and ruinous situation." Also, having left Golgotha behind, we can
look ahead full of hope, and contribute creatively to the building up
of Christianity with humility, diligence, and indefatigability, without
scepticism and thoughtlessness, since we have properly perceived
that the Lord has not, and will not, abandon us.

FOR HAVING "CORRUPTED" CHILDREN AND YOUTH

The Trial of Fr. Josif Svidnicky

In the center of Novosibirsk (population 2,000,000) at no. 2 Prospekt Mira, there is a little chapel which, with the permission of the government authorities, has been open for about two years. It is the church and the See of the Catholics of that region. Of these, there are, counting only those practicing their Faith, more than 1,000. They are predominantly German, Polish, Lithuanian, Latvian, and Ukrainian. Here, on December 19, 1984, at 9:00 A.M., Fr. Josif Svidnicky, the founder of the parish, was celebrating Holy Mass. Suddenly seven men in civilian clothes burst in; they approached the altar, interrupted the celebration and arrested Fr. Josif. It was only six days before Christmas. Fr. Josif was thrown into jail in Novosibirsk, which at that time held more than 5,000 prisoners (although it was built to hold only 1,000). There is no heating in the jail and in January of 1985 the temperature outside fell to 50 degrees below zero. It was impossible to send help, clothing, or food to him, for, besides the obstacles placed by the prison authorities, there were the difficulties created by the other detainees, the common criminals.

Who is this forty-seven-year-old priest, so brutally torn away from the altar? Today his name is very well known, not only in the Soviet Union, but also abroad. Born in Podolia, near Zhmerinka, he had, since 1959, studied and worked in Riga, and then, soon after military service, studied construction engineering in Leningrad for five years. Almost immediately he began thinking about the priesthood. He repeatedly asked to be admitted to the seminary of Riga, without however wresting this permission from the government authorities. Consequently, as a self-taught person he prepared himself for the priesthood. At last, by now ready to become a priest, for five years

On April 2, 1987, Fr. Josif Svidnicky, a Catholic priest who had been arrested at the end of 1984 and condemned to three years in prison, was released. An indefatigable apostle, Fr. Josif was arrested for having attempted to carry out authorized pastoral activity in a church rigidly repressed within the limits of the celebration of the liturgy. The testimonies which we report, through the kind permission of the *Archivi di Russia Cristiana*, refer to the apostolate and the trial of Fr. Josif. This article has been translated by Father Dismas Gannon, O.C.S.O., and Brother Dominique Nelson, O.C.S.O.

(from 1967 to 1971) he persistently asked the government authorities for permission to be ordained. All in vain.

So it was decided to take a risky step: a bishop would ordain him clandestinely. Thus began a most difficult period for the young priest. From 1971 to 1975 the authorities prohibited him from exercising his priestly ministry. Only on January 10, 1975, did he obtain permission to leave Riga to go to Zhitomir in the Ukraine to develop his pastoral work as a chaplain. Here he remained exactly one year, from January 20, 1975, to January 20, 1976.

Clandestine ordination

During this year in Zhitomir he drew attention to himself by his industry and contacts with the youth who flocked around him in great numbers. Because of his work and the popularity he enjoyed among the Catholics of the city, the authorities prohibited him from continuing to exercise his priestly ministry. For six months, he worked as a watchman, but in the autumn of 1976, he decided to go to Kazakhstan to exercise his priestly ministry there. Passing through Kirgiz, he had a talk with Bishop Köller in Frunze, who advised him to go to Tadzhikistan, to Dushanbe, the capital of the Republic. Here, in fact, the Catholic community of Germans, deported from the Volga in the 30s, had met for 40 years in a cemetery and had fought to build a church and to have a priest.

When Fr. Josif Svidnicky arrived among them they told him that precisely on that day they had completed a novena to our Lady that she might send them a priest. He stayed. On December 24, 1976, at 7:00 P.M., he celebrated his first Mass in Dushanbe, in a private house. Two years later, he built a rather large church, of 3,000 square feet, in the city. The year after that, in 1979, he built a second, smaller church, south of Dushanbe, in the region of Kurgan Tyube.

The first Mass in a private house

Besides that, he also served in four private centers of worship, one of which had its own little chapel (this was in the country of the Vakhsh). The Catholic community in Dushanbe was becoming increasingly consolidated: for Easter of 1979, in Dushanbe, 1,200 people went to confession, in Kurgan Tyube 500, and in Vakhsh 400. Fr. Josif, indifferent to lassitude or fatigue, incessantly dedicated his energies to his faithful. On Sundays in Dushanbe, the first Mass was at 7:30, the second at 10:00. Then, after a journey of around 60 miles south, at 2:00 P.M. he celebrated Mass at Kurgan Tyube; then, after another 13 miles, and at 5:00 P.M., he celebrated Mass at Vakhsh.

Fr. Josif's intense religious activity worried the government authorities. Thus, at the end of May 1983 he was forbidden to celebrate religious functions anywhere in the territory of the Republic of Tadzhikistan. And so these three regions once more remain without a priest. The only concession the authorities allow is that, once every two months, for a period of ten days, the faithful may bring in a priest from Latvia, 3,750 miles away, to satisfy their religious needs. In such circumstances, the Catholics from the area celebrate their religious functions by themselves. They read texts of homilies already written. They lay the sacred vestments and the missal on the altar. Nothing, however, can substitute for the sacramental life, without which there is no religious life.

Meanwhile, mindful of the firmness of purpose and zeal of the first apostles and ministers of the Faith, and having been banished from Tadzhikistan, Fr. Josif went to Novosibirsk, because the Catholics of the area, especially the Germans, had obtained permission to have a chapel and a parish set up there. He bought a very modest house, 30 by 36 feet and hardly 10 feet high. He restored it with his own hands and began his pastoral work. At one time there was a large Polish parish there, and again in the 20s a splendid Catholic Church dominated the city. Later it was demolished. Today the pastoral work had to begin again from scratch. (Fr. Josif's pastoral care was expanded over an ever wider area until it finally extended as far away as the inhabitants of Siberia.) Every Sunday he celebrated two Masses in his Siberian chapel in Novosibirsk. Immediately after the second Mass, which was the solemn one, he left, about noon, by air, to Tomsk, where he celebrated two Masses three times a month. Here, also, at one time, there had been a splendid parish with a church built in 1805 and dedicated to the Immaculate Conception. Today it is used as a planetarium.

Fr. Josif knew neither lassitude nor fatigue, but the government authorities were watching him attentively. A little before Easter of 1984 some unknown people (but who does not know them?) robbed him of all his sacred possessions: a chalice, vestments, a missal, and other liturgical texts. Only his soutane was left to him. Thoughtful friends helped him replace his lost possessions. A little before Christmas of that same year, 1984, the criminals were no longer unknown; they were official representatives of the secret police and they arrested him and locked him up in jail.

Arrested by the secret police   It very quickly became known that the only Catholic priest working in the Russian Socialist Republic east of the Urals had been arrested. Preparations for the trial were begun. Fr. Josif had no chance of defending himself or of making contacts with his friends and the faithful. He began a hunger strike. According to some well informed insiders, he was fed artificially for forty days, but of his own will he drank only water. On April 10 in the court house of the regional tribunal on Pisarey street the trial against him was begun. He was brought to the court house in the company of another detainee, a common criminal who had killed his wife.

The trial, nevertheless, was postponed for a month since, almost as if by accident, there were some Catholics among the spectators, and the authorities wanted to have a sure and reliable public before them. The trial was resumed on May 11 and was concluded on May 17. Fr. Josif was indicted on the basis of articles 190 and 191 of the penal code of the USSR. The charge was that he had derided the Soviet flag, corrupted children and youth by spreading religious propaganda, and lent religious books and money to a certain Ljudmila Petrovna Gerasimouk (a resident of Novosibirsk at 66 Studenceskaja Street). This woman was in fact, a well-known *agent provocateur* in the service of the secret police. Because it was precisely she who, originally from Kiev, had already appeared several times in the capacity of a witness for the prosecution in former trials against priests and other of the faithful. This time she was used against Fr. Josif Svidnicky.

The priest did not have the privilege of being assisted by a lawyer or a counsel for the defense. Tat'jana Ivanovna Anfirova, public defender, had actually sought to defend him on the first day of the trial but, surprisingly, on the second day he was not present in the court, the reason being that at just this moment, the authorities had granted him a vacation to spend time at a hot springs health spa, a favor he had been waiting for for several years. The court astutely granted him this leave of absence so that he could not function as a counsel for the defense.

There was also a certain Alina Zuraska of Zhitomir who was brought in against Fr. Josif. It was she who, in 1983 had been interrogated in the capacity of a witness for the prosecution against Sof'ja Beljak, whose dramatic story deserves special attention.[1] The authorities sought to use her against both Fr. Josif and Sof'ja Beljak, but her presence in the court definitely weakened the case of the prosecution since she has, despite her youth, a very strong personality, and she has now become a symbol for the Catholics of the Soviet Union.

Two other persons, young Germans whose names we do not know, were also called to testify against Fr. Josif. They entered the hall and, with much gravity, turned to the priest and said in German: "Praised be Jesus Christ". Then they knelt before the accused and asked him for his blessing. That ended their testimony at the trial.

On May 17, 1985, the regional court of Novosibirsk condemned Fr. Josif Svidnicky to three years in prison. The accused welcomed

Condemned to 3 years in prison

---

[1] Sof'ja Beljak, born in 1954, a Catholic of Zhitomir, was condemned on October 10, 1983, to five years in the labor camps and five years imprisonment for having collaborated with Fr. Svidnicky to create a young Catholic community in Zhitomir. She is presently in labor camp no. 3-4 of Barashevo in Mordovia, where her health is in very serious condition.

the sentence with tranquillity but not without some homesickness. For in fact, just a little while before this, the authorities had allowed workers to build a church on the exact spot where his little chapel had been previously. But Fr. Josif did not lack consolation even at this dramatic moment: at the end of the tribunal about 500 people had assembled, an unheard-of event for Novosibirsk. Not only Catholics were there but also Orthodox and Baptists. One of the Orthodox said in a rather loud voice as Fr. Josif passed in front of him, "Fr. Josif, we are all with you." And it is true. Many of the people of Novosibirsk today are heart and soul with Fr. Josif. Even the prison guard whose duty it is to keep personal watch over him, says: "Officially, he is a detainee, but one day, I would like my son to be like him."

For fifteen years Fr. Josif exercised his priestly ministry in Latvia, in the Ukraine, in Kirgiz and in Novosibirsk, in private houses and in churches, in order to announce the gospel. Today he carries out his apostolate through his suffering in prison no. 1 in Novosibirsk.

"HOW BEAUTIFUL IT IS FOR US TO BE HERE"

Letters of Lithuanian Catholics from the Labor Camps

Gintautas Iesmantas, a journalist and poet, was sentenced in December 1980 to six years in labor camps and five years in prison for having published poems and articles in the underground publications known as *Samizdat*. He wrote the following from prison.

"For five years now, your prayers and concern for my welfare have accompanied me along the road of suffering. They have given me the strength and assurance that my sacrifice has not been dissipated in the darkness of anonymity, that there are people who have my fate at heart, people whom I do not even know. Now that I am in prison, I have the opportunity to thank you for the inestimable moral support you have given me by your letters expressing concern for my welfare, and by the warmth of your hearts and souls that have reached me as far away as the snowy expanse of the Urals, notwithstanding all the interposed obstacles. Often, your letters do not even succeed in reaching me. Still, I have sensed their existence. That helped me to live, and to lose neither the Faith nor hope, not even for an instant. For me, they were the voices of my home, so dear and precious in these isolated places.

Your letters have helped me not to lose faith and hope

"In the last six months I have been in Camp no. 36 . . . with me there was Fr. Alphonse,[1] always active, serene, full of faith and hope. I am happy that destiny brought us together. He is a man with a wonderful spiritual strength, a keen mind, and a great openness. I

Lithuania is a Soviet Republic with a strong Catholic presence (it is calculated that 80% of the inhabitants of the country adhere to Catholicism). The review *Cronaca della Chiesa cattolica in Lituania* is the voice of the Lithuanian Catholic movement, and it is determined to make known the violations of religious rights and the struggle for the Lithuanians' cultural and religious identity. The heading "Our prisoners" (under which we carried some extract passages from fascicule no. 78 of April 1986), carries letters and testimonies from the places of suffering. This article was translated by Father Dismas Gannon, O.C.S.O., and Brother Dominique Nelson, O.C.S.O.

[1] Fr. Alphonse Svarinskas, condemned to ten years of confinement for his missionary and pastoral activity in Lithuania, is in Camp no. 36 in the region of Perm, where many political and religious dissidents are detained.

will never be able to forget him. When we encounter men of such caliber, to live becomes easier, and we understand how it is possible to endure all the way to the end with a firm spirit and ready for anything, carrying one's own cross. . . ."

Podcer'e, 14 April 1986
Gintautas Iesmantas

Address in prison:
169715 Komi ASSR
Vuktylskij r-n, pos. Podcer'e,
ul Sovetskaja 1

On February 14, 1986, Fr. Tamkevicius, one of the leaders of the Catholic movement, who was condemned in 1983 to ten years' imprisonment, succeeded in sending a letter from the labor camps:

". . . Thanks to all for everything. I wish to remind you of the words of St. John Chrysostom: 'Give bread and receive eternal life. Give a garment and receive the garment of immortality. Give temporal goods and receive eternal goods. You receive more than you give.'

The Bible, my most precious gift
"The most precious gift for me has been the sacred Scriptures. During free periods, I read and meditate in my heart on the words of our Lord. When I am freed, I will have a million things to do and a million preoccupations. I have not succeeded in deepening and plumbing the depths of things. God has brought me to the Urals and has so arranged things that I must remain at length in order to hear the Lord's word better and taste the Lord's bread in a more concrete manner. The three apostles, after having tasted the proximity of God, cried out: 'How beautiful it is for us to be here!' In whatever place we find ourselves, whether in freedom or in prison, at the altar or in the kitchen washing dishes, the presence of God comforts us and cheers us. Remember me in your prayers to God, so that his presence may become more and more the reality of my life.

". . . There is absolutely nothing new in my daily life. The hammering on a length of rail calls me to work every morning. It is my Nazareth. . . . I am seeking to be introduced to the solemn spirit of Lent. How time flies! Sometimes I am seized by fear: 'Lord, do not let these days that follow one another so quickly be empty; let them serve in some way the growth of the kingdom of God'. . . ."

Fr. Sigitas Tamkevicius

The last to write is Jadviga Bieliauskiene, a teacher, condemned to four years in the labor camps and three years in prison for having taught her pupils to live according to the Christian vision of life and for having gathered signatures for a petition in favor of religious liberty:

"I have been very ill, I have had three relapses. But this sacrifice is a sign of confirmation. My soul has been inundated with clear light, as I have never before experienced it. This light has accompanied me, and accompanies me continually, illuminating the way toward an ever more profound awareness and lucidity in adversity or perhaps a preparation for the sacrifice of death. If it should happen in this way, be happy and pray the Lord that this humble sacrifice which I offer to him, even though it is so unworthy and hesitant, may guard the salvation of our children, of our youth from despair, from alcoholism, and from the crises that tear the family and our entire society to pieces. . . .

"The gift of faith helps each one to regard suffering as a source necessary for purification.

"I understand that suffering is fecund only when we accept it with humility; only then does it open the eyes of our soul. The desire to draw our dear ones out of evil allows us to confront suffering and to accept it with joy for their salvation; then we grow in the love and freedom that extinguishes all fear. 'In love there is no fear' says the Apostle when speaking about charity (1 Jn 4:18). How many unhappy souls leave this world without ever being open to love! What sadness! I pray every day that they may reawaken at least at the hour of death, because they will be awakened by the God of mercy. . . .

Suffering is fertile ground when accepted with humility

"Greetings to all, to each one of you. . . .

"Beloved, I am always with you at the feet of Christ in the Eucharist."

Jadviga Bieliauskiene

IN SLOVAKIA
THE CHURCH IS ONE

An Interview with
Bishop John Chrysostom Korec
of Bratislava

Question: Your Excellency, how do you judge these thirty-five years
of your episcopal life, so different from those bishops who can
live in normal conditions?

Answer: Not only my life, but also the lives of so many others have
been radically different from what we projected in our youth.
In 1939 I entered the Society of Jesus and there it all began. My
life has been special, just as special as has been that of the great
bishop Voktassak who in his old age was, as the Gospel says,
"girded by others". Life has prepared great surprises for many
laymen and priests, as for the whole Church and the Slovak
people. In Bohemia the situation was different, but even there
the Church suffered a great deal. We have chosen neither the
moment in which to be born, nor the place, nor the historical
situation. The important thing is what we do in that situation
and how we respond to our task. For us Christians the security
that God knows everything and accompanies us is very important. When did Thomas More reach the height of his mission?
Was it when he was the king's chancellor or when he was a
prisoner? And Saint John Chrysostom, when did he serve the
Church, God, and the people better? When he was a patriarch

On the 24th of August 1986 the bishop of Bratislava, John Chrysostom Korec,
celebrated thirty-five years of episcopal consecration, of which eight years were spent
in prison. Korec, sixty-two years old, has lived for years adapting himself to works
of every kind. In his interview (the first granted to journalists), Korec gives a panoramic
view of the religious renaissance which is taking place in Slovakia, and which is
expressed in the increase of communities of study and of prayer, in both the university
and worker's surroundings.

Other expressions of this renaissance are the pilgrimages, to which Korec alludes:
Levoča, Šaštín, Velehrad, Trnava have become centers for a growing number of
pilgrims.

This article has been translated by Father Dismas Gannon, O.C.S.O., and Brother
Dominique Nelson, O.C.S.O.

or when he was in exile? Both always carried out their mission wherever they found themselves.

According to the Gospel, the apostle had always to bear witness with his word and his life before tribunals, the king, and the pagans. Neither the faithful nor the priests have been promised an easy life. "Blessed are they who have believed", and this is also valid for the years of witness rendered to Christ even among false accusations and in prisons. According to the Acts of the Apostles, Paul and Silas "prayed and sang hymns to God" while in prison, and the head of the prison and "all his household" were converted and asked to be baptized. Saint Paul was a great saint both at the moment of glory and in the moment of ignominy: although he was persecuted he was never overwhelmed, and even in very painful situations he always remained cheerful!

An easy life has not been promised

The cross is part of the life of a Christian and firstly, that of the priest. In faith, love, and hope destiny is never hostile.

Q. How do you view the past years?

A. I never cease giving thanks to God for I never gave way to despair. And then why did we in Slovakia not have to give a witness of our gratitude for the gift of the Faith which we received eleven hundred years ago and a witness of love for the welfare of the people by means of a more arduous life? Yes, my life has been harsh, especially those twenty-four years lived as a laborer under rain and snow. . . . But neither the study of philosophy or theology nor the preparation for preaching or lecturing could have made me understand the meaning of fidelity to God as he has made me experience it in the fatigue of remaining faithful to him in the circumstances of life.

It was as if everything was against me, but the crucified and resurrected Lord, together with the Spirit of truth and power, were ardently present in everything. I have never desired (nor do I today desire) to live a different life from that which I have lived. I never envied my classmates, the career of some of my friends, their power to make themselves appreciated, their capacity to enter into other spheres. Even today I pray for all of them, for they can appear before God with their hands overflowing with good works. Along the road I have traveled I found many thorns, many dangerous moments, but also much peace and much joy. I give thanks to God for never allowing me to lose the taste for life, the taste for new life.

I do not have many merits. All is God's goodness and mercy. Goodness because he gives us life, talent, stamina, faithfulness, love for our brothers. . . . Saint Paul has written: "If I am who

I am it is by the grace of God." And all is mercy because all of us have been saved by the Cross of Christ in baptism, and we are continually saved by the forgiveness of the Father. Which of us can say he has no need of this? Who can boast before God? What a great responsibility! We must call to mind all omissions as we always do at the beginning of every Mass. God alone is great, heroic, majestic. If there is any good in us it is by his grace. I am most grateful to God for, the more time passes, the more this awareness grows in me.

Q. Fr. Korec, you are isolated from the other bishops of the world. In this situation, how do you live the catholicity of the Church?

A. My exterior isolation is indeed great, but not my interior isolation. Unity with the Church is lived primarily with the faculty of reasoning and with the heart in fidelity and love. Thus, during our time in prison we are united to the faithful, to the priests, to the bishop, and to the successor of Peter. It is true our information on the life of the Church is reduced to the minimum, but what we have is sufficient for us to love the Church more and more and to gain courage. The Church is one, holy, catholic, and apostolic. Vincent de Paul, Thérèse of Lisieux, all who have given their lives for their brothers, Maximilian Kolbe, Leo the Great, John Paul II. . . . All have lived or are living for the Church. Certainly, the Church has to confront difficulties and criticisms. The first, difficulties, are conquered with firmness of purpose; the second, criticisms, with the evidence of our life. The Church is continually being purified. Note well with what enthusiasm, with what truth and courage she announces the gospel to a world which has lost all good sense. The Church defends the person, the family, the people by developing and applying the directives of the Council.

Unity with the Church in fidelity and love

Even though she is attacked and criticized on both the left and the right, even though she is continually persecuted, the Church carries out her proper mission filled with confidence.

Q. For you, who is the Holy Father?

A. Every day we give thanks to the Lord for the gift that the Holy Father is for the entire Church. We admire his personality, his talent, his capacity to endure, his creativity, his faith, and his love. He offers himself to everyone, and he is very close to us Slovaks. He remembers us on every occasion. The Church needs such men. She needs the *rock* of witness of the Faith and of charity, of messengers of peace. Also, the contemporary world, which has been destroyed by violence and hatred, needs such a *rock*.

Three days after the attempt on his life, he recited the Angelus together with the whole world, and he forgave the man who tried to assassinate him, going to see him in jail. There are those who criticized him, but for us this is just one more reason for loving him. In our situation he is the rock on which unity is built and when we hear his voice it seems to us that we are a single family together with the whole world. We feel part of the universal Church.

Each prayer and each experience of the Church encourages us. We are grateful for every word of truth uttered in whatever part of the world, and we are delighted in the knowledge that in Austria, in Germany or in France, there is someone to defend us. We stand firm leaning against the rock who today bears the name of John Paul II.

Q. The Czechoslovakian Communist Party is seeking to divide the Church into a legal church and a clandestine church. You were clandestinely ordained a bishop thirty-five years ago. How do you judge this power play?

A. Yes, speaking about the "clandestine Church", they brand us with this label, but no one is asked why among us there exist priests and bishops cut off from the pastoral life, for whom it is forbidden to approach the altar in order to publicly celebrate the Holy Mass. No one is asked why there is no "clandestine Church" in Austria, France, or Chile.

As far as I am concerned I have never made distinctions, nor have I ever divided the Church into clandestine and legal. *In Slovakia the church is one*, just as the priesthood of Christ is one. Priests can either be faithful to him or unfaithful. Many priests in the exercise of their mission are true examples of the apostolic life, and they guide the faithful toward salvation in a difficult situation like ours, and for this reason the Church is profoundly grateful to them.

And the unfaithful? The priest must examine his own conscience, questioning himself on what he truly loves and on the way in which he bears witness.

The priests of Slovakia are deeply loved by their people, who consider them true fathers. It is rare that people leave the faith because of an unfaithful priest, just as the apostles did not leave, even having had among them Judas, who had struggled for the poor (as those priests who follow liberation theology do today), but then he sold Jesus Christ for thirty pieces of silver.

The priests in Slovakia are deeply loved

The priests who cannot perform their liturgical actions in public are priests in all respects and in this way also the religious. Each one can consecrate his own life to the Lord, and it is not important if this takes place publicly or in private. No one can prevent it. Both in Slovakia and in Bohemia there are laymen who have given themselves totally to the Church. They are a precious gift for all of us, and we are grateful to God for them. Many priests, religious, and laymen—both consecrated and non-consecrated—contribute to the building up of the Church by means of an intense pastoral work, thanks to which the Holy Spirit has revivified our communities and our missionary spirit. All have the obligation to be light, salt, and yeast. Without living the life of the Church we can only become sectarians. The truth is one, and we ought to give witness to it, and it is the truth of the Gospel, in the way the Church who is our guide and master announces it and interprets it.

We can not proclaim our own truth or give directives which are at variance with those of the Magisterium, because the Church is built on the foundation of the apostles and of Peter. The apostles are the bishops, Peter is the bishop of Rome. Every Christian is united to them in the service to the truth. He who wishes to be "independent" cuts himself off from the Church. Despite the difficulties we encounter in our pastoral work we cannot renounce unity. The Bible alone is not sufficient. There must be a just interpretation, the sacraments, teaching, and guidance are necessary.

Q. We often hear of the problems that exist among the priests. How do you think the priests in our country should act?

A. The priest is always and everywhere a priest of Christ. Sacred Scripture, and especially Saint Paul, describe for us the indispensable characteristics of a priest. If we discuss these things too much it means that we are losing contact with revelation, because in it (revelation) the essence and the mission of the priest are clearly explained.

In any case, first of all, the priest has to be rooted in Christ with his mind, with his heart, and with all his being. Then, he must be anchored to the Church by way of unity with his bishop. His fidelity to Christ must be based on his fidelity to the Church. These are the foundations. And then there must be meditation, study, generosity, charity, humility, availability, courage, confidence in God. . . .

If someone refused to accept celibacy it is better that he should not become a priest. He will spare himself and the faithful many problems. Fortunately this is not a problem among us and there are many young men who are asking to become priests.

Q. Last year we took part in the pilgrimages to Levoča, Šaštín, Velehrad, Trnava. . . . And we could see a real religious fervor among the young. Is this phenomenon due to motives of a psychological, political, or a social nature, or to a more profound process?

A. The reawakening of religious life in both Slovakia and Bohemia is first of all the work of the Holy Spirit who dispenses his gifts generously. The first of these gifts is a living Faith which reveals God's presence. Often the gifts of the Spirit are surprising, they are a miracle. What we have seen taking place in our country for some years now is like a miracle, that is, a work desired and built by God: thousands of young people, but also adults and old people, seeking God with a surprising persistence, and they find him, encountering Christ in the Church.

When they encounter him, the Faith which is born in them is animated by love and can be suffocated by nothing and by no one. We are living a new Pentecost. People seek, they build and live community with much creativity and much courage. They are continually more numerous, those who gather around priests, monks, and laymen, encouraged and sustained by the Church. They meditate on the words of the Holy Father and of the Gospel; daily they celebrate the Eucharist together; they read, study, desire to know and understand the truth of the Faith, the history of the Church, and the experience of the contemporary Church; they spend their vacations together living in the love of a Christian community, bearing witness to those who are in a situation of enquiry and they support one another.

We are living a new Pentecost

All of this cannot be born solely from human elements. It is, rather, an expression of the divine mercy toward the people, an expression of a gift of the Holy Spirit which we certainly have not merited. Nevertheless, there exists an economy of salvation based on the communion of saints, therefore no one has suffered in vain: not the families, or the children in school, or the priests in prison, or the bishops.

Q. Not only in our country, but also on the international level, we can see that people are permeated with a certain torpor, a scepticism, and the loss of all confidence. In this situation, what contribution can the Church make to the world and to the Slovak people? And in this context how do you judge the action of Charta '77 and that of the Committee for the Defense of Citizens unjustly persecuted (VONS)?

A. Historians and sociologists seek to give an interpretation to these phenomena. . . . We know the situation well. In our clandestine literature I have read many upsetting testimonies. However, all this has little to do with a Christian outlook, with a Christian attitude, for we can only live in hope. One who despairs can bring to light negative phenomena by his writings. But why be satisfied with this alone? It is not sufficient to read these analyses. Go among our youth, speak with them, go skiing together, make the Stations of the Cross or a night adoration with them, or go mountain climbing with them. There you will see what hope is. There, there is no room for scepticism. Hope is a treasure for the Church and the Church is the *columna veritatis*, "the pillar of truth". She knows how to face up to problems, she knows where she is going. She does not base her Faith on man, but on God, and so she never falls into scepticism and despair. It is not theory that gives her strength but a life of prayer, of the word, of sacraments, of communion with the Redeemer. Hope, rendered more lively by faith and by love, is the fundamental reality of the Christian life.

A mother has no time for scepticism

It is not a matter of abstract terms. Look at a mother of a family: she has no time for scepticism; she loves her children and gives her all to them. Or, take the example of a young man who wishes to become a priest: there is no room for scepticism because he wishes to live for God and for his brothers, and he is full of enthusiasm, of interest, of zeal. And look at the people who put themselves at the service of the sick: in the name of Christ they seek to save the lives of other men, and they do everything so that the lives of the sick may be more tolerable.

This is the Church. Look at Mother Teresa: the work of her daughters is enkindling the world. Look at the missionaries (many are Slovaks); their life is guided by love, by faith, and not by scepticism. And last of all, look at the Holy Father: in the course of one single apostolic journey he is able to give about ten or so discourses as well as speaking and listening to all whom he meets, and in such a world he gives courage to us all.

We have not fallen, and we have no intention of becoming fixated exclusively on the evil and barrenness of life. We know that these things exist and that they are part of our experience, but we also know what life is like according to the Gospel and how problems are going to be faced in its light. The Church knows how to face life, even where she is in the minority, as in Japan or in India, where she has developed a splendid network of solidarity and charity for the poorest of the poor. The Church is a sign of the creativity and vitality of the gospel. She lives not only within the walls of the church: the faithful, in fact, go forth from the church to flow into the streets of the cities to work, live, bear witness. People are well aware of this, even those who live in countries in which the Church suffers persecution. Even non-Christians regard the Church with respect.

We are filled with joy when reading the newspapers from India, in which for a century a powerful personality like that of John Paul II had not been seen. Not with triumphalism, but with gratitude because the Church is living and vivifying.

Our people love the Church. She conceived us and has allowed our people to continue to live throughout the ages. She has spoken to us in our own language, she has built schools and universities. Priests have guided our people, they have given them literature and culture. The more famous names of our history, the Jesuit Benedikt Sölosi, Ián Baltazár Magin, Bernolák, Hollý Moyzes, Radlinský, were priests. Our writers and our poets have been educated by the Church and by men of faith, Janko, Silan, Sládkovic, Vaianský, Hviezdoslav.

Who can surpass this spiritual wealth; who can silence it? We have a great task: to make known to the youth that the Slovak people exist because the Church exists. Who can alter past history? *Stat Crux, dum solvitur mundus*, which can be roughly translated in this context: The Cross is the axis on which the world turns. Our generation is responsible for the survival of the people. If we will live our faith, God will not abandon us.

Our country, these mountains, these rivers, these valleys, these fields, these villages, these cities—this is the body whose soul is the people, who thinks, has a memory, a conscience, morals, its own creativity, its own culture. Our task is to take care of this soul which belongs, by means of the Church, to God. The motherland, if she has a healthy soul, has the responsibility to blossom and bear fruit.

It is not only we who are working for the life of our country; others also, men of great integrity, are suffering in order to defend the rights and dignity of man, and to save both liberty and justice. We hold them in high esteem, and we collaborate with them. Our perspective goes beyond purely human grounds. We have always had high esteem and admiration for the members of Charta '77 and of VONS, and we likewise esteem and admire all those who cooperate in defending man and his dignity.

Others are suffering for the rights and dignity of man

Q. Czechoslovakia is governed by men who do not conceal their intention of suppressing the Church. From the human point of view the battle is unequal. On what do you base your hope that the Czech and Slovak people will not lose the Faith?

A. All that is corporeal is also mortal. As persons, we men die. Also, people will exist until the "new heavens and the new earth" will begin. But a people is a value worth defending, guarding, and allowing to grow. The survival of a people does not depend solely on its greatness and power. In fact, even great and powerful peoples have vanished from the stage of history when they have lost their spiritual identity, when they disintegrated on the moral level.

Our people live not only from the bread which the fields bring forth, but also from the word of God which the Church has given them. The people know why they are living. This consciousness has been experienced with the rosary beads in their hands, it is expressed in proverbs and songs. The whole culture of our people has trumpeted this truth. In this Mystery, which is called Christ, people are born and have lived. In this Mystery they have entered into eternal glory. Our people have lived from faith. The Tartars and the Turks came, but the people succeeded in defending their own existence and their proper identity. The anti-religious enlightened thinker has not found room among our people. And even today the people resist the anti-religious and atheistic culture. We are not pugnacious, and it is true, we are weak. Often our faith is superficial, and often we are indifferent, but only a few are openly God's enemies.

The Church has suffered severe losses: all our tools for evangelization have been taken away. There are no longer any periodicals, publishing houses, book stores, associations, seminaries, or religious orders. Both Bibles and catechisms are lacking. The entire educational system, from nursery-school to university, the press, the radio, the television, the theatre, and literature, all openly fight against the Church. We have returned to the Middle Ages; we reproduce books by copying them by hand. We strive to meet and help one another and we try to live out our faith. How? Levoča, Velehrad . . . have shown us.

The Slovaks feel the presence of the Mystery

How is all this possible? The Slovaks feel the presence of the Mystery, they experience him in the course of their entire life. A Slovak is well aware that today he may possess something but tomorrow he could lose it all. He knows that everything in life is a gift, and the gift can be taken away from one moment to the next. Ask one of us how he is doing, and he will answer you: "I thank God for my health!" His answer expresses the awareness that health does not belong to him, that it is fragile and that it is a gift which presupposes a Giver, before whom he stands in a posture of humility.

If our people know how to preserve this humility, this awareness of the Giver, they will stay alive. For a people like the Slovaks it is not easy to throw out one's own Christianity. It would be like throwing out the spinal column from one's own body. The whole history of our nation, all its culture, its creativity in literature or in the plastic arts; its churches on the hill, its crocuses along the road, in the fields, in the forests, on the mountains; its popular songs, all speak of God and his Son. An atheist can not easily live among such a people. Nor will he ever succeed in reversing all this. We know cases of persons who, after having denied the existence of God throughout their lives could no longer oppose grace, and at the end they called for the priest. We have cases in which atheists, communists, high dignitaries, ask for a religious funeral at the end. We have many young men who, even though coming from atheist families, find the way of salvation. One atheist writer has said: "I can imagine a dying person with the Bible in his hands, but I find it impossible to imagine him with *Das Kapital*." I believe in the goodness of God. I am convinced that for both the Slovak and Czech people there is the possibility of living the Faith within the Church. Indeed if we will be true Catholics, the family of our brothers in the Faith will grow. The people who, up to now no longer have illusions, seeing our testimony of life, will unite themselves with us.

For us the battle is not unequal. If God is with us who can be against us? I am certain, and life is reaffirming me in this, that what is impossible to men is possible to God and to men who place their trust in him. We are sure of being loved by God. He has called us here and in baptism we have become his chosen people. I cannot believe he has called us here to bring us to shame. . . . But we can not boast, or recklessly put our trust in, or wait in fear for, future events.

Yes, we need to have confidence, but this must be joined to a boundless courage, and we must do everything that is possible to us. Slovakia today is overrun with courage, faithfulness, and missionary zeal. The people are conquering fear and confidence in God is growing. One day we shall all stand before God. What on earth do we want to save if we should lose our soul and with it eternal happiness?

Many are beginning to be conscious that there are no reasons for fear. A people without fear is a strong people. Our faithful *There are no reasons for fear* are prepared to work, to sacrifice themselves, to bear witness, to meet one another, to transcribe texts and distribute them, and all that in profound unity with the Church and with the successor of Peter.

Faith is a value for our citizens and they are ready to sacrifice their career and a higher salary rather than renounce it. For them life without faith has no value. For them it is clear that man has a conscience by means of which he seeks to resolve the problem of death and of the meaning of life.

At times he seems to be able to do almost nothing for the Faith and for the Church, but it is always possible to do something. It is sufficient to just look around. The important thing is not to remain alone, the harvest is great. First of all, one must remain firm in the Faith and aspire toward heaven, conscious of having on our part right, truth and justice. The Church has been living with our people for 1,100 years. Our great poet Janko Silan wrote: "Our work is one which does not degrade, which does not remain isolated on the peaks of the mountains, which does not let itself be surprised by the struggle. Our strength is truth. Those men who renounce their rights are not strong." And Jesus in the Gospel says to us: "Holy Father, keep those you have given me true to your name, so that they may be one like us. . . . So that I may share my joy with them to the full" (Jn 17:11–13).

Jesus' words both encourage and strengthen us. We are his and he protects us. We are weak and fragile, but we are overflowing with confidence because in the struggle for the Faith it is God who has the last word.

5

THE MAN OF THE YEAR

"TO LOVE SOMEONE IS TO SHOW HIM HIS BEAUTY":

Jean Vanier and *"L'Arche"*

by
Corinne Vallery Masson

It was with Raphaël and Philippe that I first began to learn. When I took them out of the asylum, I really felt I was, or imagined myself to be, a kind of savior. In a way, they were mine; they were part of my projects. Of course, when I started *L'Arche*, I thought I was creating a Christian community. I was to find out that forming a Christian community was not Raphaël's and Philippe's main concern. They needed friendship and security, someone to take a real interest in them, someone to listen to what they needed and wanted, someone to hear what they had to say. I was to learn that *L'Arche* was not just my own project, but Raphaël's and Philippe's as well.

Jean Vanier, founder of *L'Arche*, a network of small, sheltered communities built for the mentally handicapped, had no idea, in 1964, that his project would experience such remarkable growth: the first community was started at Trosly Breuil near Compiègne, France, when Jean Vanier decided to make a home for Raphaël and Philippe, and to live there with them; today, there are more than eighty of these communities that are home to about three thousand persons in twenty different countries. As a place where people live together, *L'Arche* is first of all a place for listening and for loving. Its ultimate identity is not to be sought merely in structures; it is built simply on love for the handicapped person, who calls out for what lies deep in the human spirit, and awakens that something; that is, the heart, and within the heart, whatever points to the mystery of God's presence in the hearts of the poorest of the poor.

This article's title serves to introduce a model of faith whose spiritual gifts have demonstrated the inexhaustible creativity and newness of the Christian Faith. For 1986–87, we have chosen Jean Vanier, a Canadian professor who has helped the whole world to see the beauty of weakness, the strength of fragility. "God chose those whom the world considers absurd to shame the wise", as Saint Paul wrote (1 Cor 1:27). Vanier has proved that this statement is still true today, in this article, translated from the French by Mary E. Hamilton.

Jean Vanier's special calling cannot be adequately defined by reciting the simple succession of events in a life that did not thrust him into direct contact with—or make him particularly sensitive to—the person with a mental disability. He himself says that he would have been able to arrive at the same vocation by living among other sorts of people: young drug-addicts, the sick, the elderly, immigrants or refugees, the impoverished inhabitants of the shantytowns of the third world, or the homeless. Instead, it was a matter of an inward drawing that slowly intensified over a long period, taking many twists and turns along the way, a calling that found its first response in his early contacts with the mentally handicapped. In a recent television interview, a journalist asked Jean Vanier why he had not entered the priesthood; he answered that the priesthood "was not what he had been chosen for". Jean Vanier's story is thus a witness to his opening of himself, his allowing himself to wait upon God and to listen carefully as the call he had chosen to follow revealed

A mysterious call that arises from misery

itself: "I feel in a mysterious way that there is a silent cry that comes out of utter wretchedness, out of mute tears; and in the depths of my being I hear that cry . . . a still, small voice. . . . Life has meaning in direct proportion to the amount of love I put into it." For Jean Vanier, as for Saint Vincent de Paul, it is the poor who teach us: for the hundreds of young people who learn about *L'Arche* each year, the poor open the way to interior healing and freedom. In this sense, for the Church, the meaning of *L'Arche* and the Faith and Light project goes far beyond the handicapped people who benefit from these efforts. *L'Arche* is, in fact, a deeply human apostolate, not just a social work devoted to the outcast of society, but a work that is spiritually rooted in the mystery of the Eucharist and founded upon the poor man as he himself constitutes a sacrament of the presence of God.

How Jean Vanier Started L'Arche and the Faith and Light Project

Jean Vanier was born in Geneva, Switzerland, in 1928, the son of General Georges Vanier, a former Governor-General of Canada, and his wife, Pauline. As one of five children, he spent his early years mainly in England. At the age of thirteen-and-a-half, he enrolled in the Royal Naval College at Dartmouth (Great Britain). Some years later, he was a naval officer on the English battleship *Vanguard*, and subsequently on Canada's only aircraft carrier, *The Magnificent*. He resigned from the Royal Canadian Navy in 1950, and began his long search that led him some time later to live near Paris in a lay community for students, the *Eau vive* [Living Water] Community, under the direction of Father Thomas Philippe, O.P. Two years later, Jean

Vanier provided spiritual leadership for that community. The fact that he was a layman posed a problem, and the consequent misunderstandings came to an end four years later when the community broke up.

This experience left an indelible mark on Jean Vanier, who was then preparing for the priesthood in the diocese of Quebec. He decided not to finish his final year of seminary, and he went to live alone for a while at the Trappist Monastery of Bellefontaine, moving after this to a small, isolated hermitage in Normandy, and finally to Fatima, where he stayed for two years. In 1962, he successfully defended his thesis on Aristotle's *Ethics* at the Institut Catholique in Paris, after which he joined the faculty of Saint Michael's College at the University of Toronto.

In 1963, Father Thomas Philippe was appointed Almoner of an institution for the mentally handicapped, called "Val fleuri", at Trosly Breuil, where Jean Vanier would arrive one year later, at Father Philippe's invitation. This was a turning-point for Jean. He bought a cottage as soon as he got there and brought Raphaël and Philippe to live with him, knowing that by so doing he was taking a step from which there was no turning back. The cottage was christened "*L'Arche*" [The Ark]: this was on August 4, 1964.

With Raphaël and Philippe

In 1965, the director of Val fleuri resigned, together with most of the staff. Jean Vanier was asked to take over the directorship. He immediately found himself plunged into the chaotic world of thirty handicapped men, a world of depression and violence. One by one, people arrived to offer a helping hand, never in great numbers, but just enough people to fill the need. Mealtimes became occasions of celebration, and the day's activities were punctuated with times for prayer. *L'Arche* became a family for those who had no families, a welcoming place, full of faith and joy.

Jean Vanier organized pilgrimages every year to different Marian shrines. With Marie-Hélène Mathieu's help, a way was found to invite the relatives and friends of the handicapped to join these pilgrimages and to add an international scope to the movement. Thus was born "Foi et lumière" (The Faith and Light Project), as a result of the 1971 pilgrimage that, after three years of planning, brought twelve thousand persons to Lourdes; four thousand of them were mentally handicapped.

This was a gigantic outpouring of joy. During the five-day pilgrimage, groups were formed: persons living in the same areas, who wanted to keep up the friendships and contacts they had made while on the pilgrimage. Faith and Light was to undergo a remarkable growth in membership, at the amazing rate of fifteen percent per year. Today, there are more than seven hundred communities of about thirty members each, in some forty countries. Its members gather at frequent intervals in an atmosphere of cordial fellowship and prayer. Faith and Light is a support group for parents and relatives, an opportunity for many young people to get involved in helping the handicapped, and a chance for handicapped persons to find real joy.

Jean Vanier does not like to be called a spiritual director. Besides, the designation hardly fits him, in view of the fact that his purpose is not to dispense knowledge to students in love with learning. Because he lets himself be led by the faltering appeal of the poor, he hardly knows where he is coming from or where he is going.

His story and the story of *L'Arche* and Faith and Light are stories of the work of the Holy Spirit, in the sense of the Holy Spirit's working through man without man's knowing it. Thus, people's encounters with Jean Vanier and his communities are not marked by reactions of excessive enthusiasm or transports of excitement: those who have become instruments and servants do not make a big thing out of what they are doing. These men and women are on the move, in the valley of the shadow of the mystery of human suffering, and yet also at the gate of the mystery of joy. They do not let the visitor seek security by fixing his attention on them, as opposed to "those people" they are caring for. As Jean Vanier says, "Don't be surprised if you find that the ideal *L'Arche* community does not exist. Each community is made up of people who are struggling, hoping, and growing." And truly, these people are not advocating anything; they listen more than they speak: they have developed the simplicity of those who are used to being poor. It will not do to compose a hagiography on Jean Vanier. That would be doing him a disservice, and, moreover, it would prevent people from discerning what dwells within him, what can always spring up anew in many different forms, and what tells us, through everything he stands for, that the poor are our spiritual teachers: "*L'Arche* would die if we did not walk among those who are wounded; if we ceased to look upon them as prophets, calling us to repentance; if we no longer saw in their weakness the presence of the eternal God." The poor extend the mystery of the Incarnation into our own day. If anyone listens to them and serves them, he will come face to face with the mystery of God and will be transfigured by it. This is the message Jean Vanier has for the world. When he was asked to preach a retreat in the diocese of Toronto in 1968, he inspired the Faith and Sharing movement, which regularly organizes retreats all across Canada and the United States. Jean Vanier certainly knows how to touch the heart, for his words come from his daily experiences, lived among handicapped persons in the light of the gospel.

L'Arche and Faith and Light, work of the Holy Spirit

The Cry of the Handicapped

Each mentally handicapped person suffers from his own physiological deficiency. Generally, he has poor manual dexterity as well as diminished intellectual capacity. Even if, with the aid of special education, the capabilities he does have can be as fully developed as possible (*L'Arche* combines its work with that of doctors, psychiatrists, and psychologists), there is little likelihood of a cure or even a great improvement. But the greatest pain for the mentally handicapped person is not to be recognized or loved for the person he is, the pain of being shut out of our world. Each such person has a permanent feeling of having been a disappointment to his parents and his close relatives, a feeling that he is an undesirable, a bad person. He does not blame his family for this, but, rather, bears alone the weight of a profound guilt, a keen anguish that often leads him to self-destructive behavior. His whole being is a cry: Am I worth anything? Can anyone love me? Is my life worth anything to anybody else? Mixed with this need for human relationships, recognition, and love, is a despair of ever being accepted. A great deal of anger, anxiety, and frustration builds up in this way, when the mentally handicapped person can never find enough acceptance, enough people to make him feel welcome and to have confidence in him (as a community can do), so that he can be allowed to win his freedom from this broken self-image and believe in his own special gifts. His life is arrested at an extremely fragile stage, and, for those who know how to appreciate it, seems a threshold of promise. Here the weakest ones have a tremendous hold on those who reach out to them to awaken their capacity for commitment and heartfelt participation in human relationships.

L'Arche's spirituality is very concrete, based on the person-to-person relationship of people living in the same community; it is a relationship that integrates emotion and sensitivity. Its secret is that God is hidden within this fragility that can act with such power to open the heart of anyone who is willing to let himself be touched. *God hidden in weakness* This is why *L'Arche* is all for the human being as a privileged place where God reveals himself. The handicapped person reaches right into our hearts, and whatever relationship we have with him determines how sensitive we can be. When two people are one in heart, it releases the capacity of both persons to grow, that is, their respective abilities to accept suffering that culminate in sharing their unique gifts and personalities in a real bond, and, for the handicapped person, a new sense of self-worth, as he discovers that he is loved and that he is worthy of being loved. "To love someone", Jean Vanier writes, "is not primarily to do something for him; it is to reveal his beauty;

it is to have faith in him; it is to be glad he is alive. That is why the principal characteristic of *L'Arche* and Faith and Light communities is to be welcoming places; it is to say to the handicapped person: We believe in you, you are important, and we are happy to have you around. You have a place of your own."

The cry of the handicapped person places him in a unique state of poverty and makes him very receptive to God's grace. The poor man of the gospel is he who cries out in his insecurity: he is the one who waits upon God. Jesus can reveal to him things that cannot be given to the wise and the intelligent, the "rich men", those who have knowledge and power. Those who live and work at *L'Arche* are moved by the particular sensitivity handicapped people demonstrate, their way of living, their trust in the gospel, and their openness to grace. "God chose those whom the world considers absurd to shame the wise; he singled out the weak to shame the strong. He chose the world's lowborn and despised . . ." (1 Cor 1:27–28a). Jesus does not use the complicated words of the intelligentsia. His is a simple language, the language of love, of tenderness and pardon.

A New Type of Community, "with" and Not "for" the Poor

It is not, however, necessary to idealize the poor. The mentally handicapped are far from being saints. Within them, there exists a world of shadows, anger, and hate. They can have bouts with violent behavior and depression. But they also have a huge capacity for asking, receiving, and forgiving.

The cry of the poor can be disturbing

Those who live and work at *L'Arche* cannot but be cognizant of the significance and seriousness of their commitment. The cry of the poor can make one a bit crazy. Sometimes, it is unbearable: it demands too much. The person trying to help the poor may discover within himself an unsuspected tendency toward aggressiveness, toward wanting to hurt or even toward hurting someone weaker than himself. Experience has shown that for many, the beginning of their time in the community is a time of wonder: the cry of tenderness coming from the handicapped person reveals something very deep in their own hearts. But little by little these helpers discover that love is not a matter of mere emotion or sentiment. Loving another person is knowing how to answer when he calls, helping him in his quest for inner freedom, knowing how to get through to him and giving him a sense of security.

Very soon, the helper discovers the obligations and responsibilities of love. By assuming these, he learns to accept his own limitations, his own scars, his own mental blocks, his own violent impulses. Experiencing his own weakness and inner poverty leads him to pay attention to his own cry. He will have come to *L'Arche* to serve the poor, and now he experiences poverty in himself, as he finds himself incapable of bearing the burden he had hoped would be a loyal and generous gift of his whole self. If the helper survives this crisis, he will come out of it freed from his timidity and fully accepting his own poverty. He will be helped in this liberation by the handicapped, who never asked him to play the role he was trying to play at first. If he has good support—and each helper is bolstered by the priest and an elder of the community—this moment of truth will become for him a new discovery of the Faith, of the good news of the gospel that is not for the man who serves the poor, but for the poor themselves. "He hath put down the mighty from their seat: and hath exalted the humble and meek . . ." (Lk 1:52). In this way, the ones who bind themselves to the poor find out what community is, and how this bond begins at the level of their mutual fragility. The handicapped, through their sadness or their poverty in things of the mind, find their human dignity in the message of the gospel. As for the helpers, they find themselves called upon to forsake many of their former human values in order to unite themselves with the handicapped, and through this renunciation, they necessarily become rooted in the same gospel message.

L'Arche, however, is not founded on words. Its primary objective is not to teach anything at all. Further, the handicapped cannot be reached by logic, or even by the idea one wants to use to help them live. The community is founded on the body in the sense that to get to the heart one has to work through actions related to sensory stimuli: eating, touching, looking into one another's eyes, having parties, dancing.

So, daily living at *L'Arche* is very simple. Helpers are not called there to do great things: their life is made up of getting up and going to bed, sharing chores, meals, and feasts, working in the shop or garden, and so forth. Conversations with the mentally handicapped cannot be held on a very high level. A log is kept of daily happenings: games, jokes, and laughter. Days come and go, sometimes interrupted by crises. But at *L'Arche*, any occasion can be cause for rejoicing, for celebrating, for dancing. The key word is personal availability, an availability the handicapped need almost constantly. And the community's main activity is to celebrate being available to one another, throughout all of life's daily tasks, at prayer times, and at daily Mass.

Presence is the keyword

It is a question of creating a family atmosphere, where freedom of self-expression allows everyone to have a feeling of belonging to a community devoid of exclusivity and judgmentalism. Of course, this family life makes no attempt to exclude suffering, which is ever-present and familiar. But the attention, respect, and welcome to the one who is having a crisis ensure that this suffering is never pushed aside or belittled.

Structures within L'Arche

From the time he created L'Arche, Jean Vanier has paid particular attention to procedures. He knows that structure is indispensable if L'Arche is to survive beyond the life of its founder. Because the accent is on daily living, the community must rethink itself in terms of permanence. Its organizational structure is circular rather than vertical, with responsibilities changing regularly. Priority is never given to structure, but to the needs of persons. In this system, the one who must exercise authority is never isolated but finds himself and his authority surrounded and supervised by yet another structure. L'Arche communities are recognized by the legal authorities and are integrated into the social systems of the countries where they are located, under the same regulations that govern other institutions for the handicapped. Thus, many of the communities receive grants or subsidies for their work. On the other hand, they are flexible when local administrations are concerned about the possibility of not applying quite so conservatively all the strict rules and regulations of social policies—especially as far as wages, benefits, or working hours are concerned. In fact, employment at L'Arche represents the choice of a state of life, and those who work there immediately give up any idea of advancement or promotion.

As for its place in the structure of the Church, L'Arche is attached to the Pontifical Council for the Laity, in spite of the denominational pluralism it embraces. Monsignor Peter Sutton, a bishop from Canada, as been specially designated to care for the Catholic members of L'Arche communities.

A Call for Dedication to Peace and Ecumenical Work

Ecumenism at L'Arche

L'Arche accepts people on the basis of their cry and their special needs. Thus, communities in England, Scotland, America, Switzerland, and Australia have been called upon to receive persons from different Christian traditions. Experiences in ecumenism at L'Arche in England have been marked by suffering and by trial and error because most of the helpers are Catholics, while most of the people accepted are Anglicans. It took several years to study all the ramifications of such a situation and to determine what L'Arche's duty was to help handicapped persons to find a place within their own traditions, to make contact with their own priests or pastors. And since *L'Arche* makes no attempt to be a church in itself, it has to operate on the level where those churches were operating in their own particular situations. Thus, for example, it has to cope with the impossibility of intercommunion in its ecumenical communities. But when people live together on a day-to-day basis, sharing both joys and sorrows, this impossibility of receiving Communion together at the same altar is really painful. Many *L'Arche* and Faith and Light communities have lived through this heart-rending situation.

Little by little, however, *L'Arche* has found its vocation to unity. For many young people throughout the world, the churches' lack of unity is a scandal that seriously affects their faith. It is hard for them to believe in a message that still must leave them separated from one another. *L'Arche* and Faith and Light try to show that men and women who have been baptized into Christ and believe in his name, can love one another in spite of differences. However, the pain of division is all the more acute in these communities because the handicapped are unable to understand it and to accept its consequences.

L'Arche works for unity in a still larger sense, because some communities contain not only Christians, but Moslems and Hindus as well. It is true that today barriers have arisen between religions, and some countries are refusing to accept Christian missionaries. But even these countries can sometimes accept men and women who are ready to work with the mentally handicapped, building homes for them where Christians, Moslems, and Hindus can learn to live as brothers and accept the poorest of the poor. There is no question of adopting any kind of syncretism; the idea is to encourage each person to be faithful to the tradition of his own faith. These men and women, helpers and handicapped alike, learn to live and pray together because they all believe in God. In this way, the 1986 meeting at Assisi, at the invitation of Pope John Paul II, was a confirmation for *L'Arche*, as more and more the profound unity which binds all men and women on the earth was discovered. For *L'Arche*, the different religions, far from separating us, can unite us when we look to the source and when we concentrate on the poorest of the poor.

The various religions can be united

Both *L'Arche* and Faith and Light came into being almost by accident, without any prearranged plan. Both have grown steadily, like the seed planted in good ground. Both were founded on a spirituality of acceptance—acceptance of the weak and vulnerable, the sorrowful, the suffering, and the lonely.

Today's world makes people more and more fragile. Many people are alienated. The family, the parish, and the town are, if not destroyed, at least fragmented. People are fighting for survival or status, and they are losing their sense of belonging. The community as a body in which each member has a rightful place is tending to disappear.

To rediscover a sense of belonging

L'Arche and Faith and Light call upon people to rediscover a sense of belonging, a sense of family, a sense of all humanity as one body, by inviting them to create a community centered on those who can't make it on their own, around people who are weak and easily hurt. This acceptance of others in need implies accepting the whole person, inasmuch as he is a human being who has to find, not only meaning for his life, but also his human dignity; he must see how much he can grow, on both the human and the spiritual levels. *L'Arche* communities have thus succeeded in gathering together, around the mentally handicapped, those who are celibate and those who live in families—clergy, religious, and lay people—all with the most widely differing personalities, each one having his own place and his own personal commitment.

Young people these days are too often in despair, feeling powerless in the face of all the evil that is in the world, the dangers of modern warfare, and the dehumanizing influence of technology. They have lost confidence in themselves, and sometimes seek escape in all sorts of stimuli. *L'Arche* and Faith and Light are a means whereby they may be enabled to develop their capacity to love in a very simple manner, by helping them to enter into relationships with the poor and humble and thereby to discover the bond that unites them by belonging to a community together. If they do this, they will find once more that faith does have meaning, that unity in Christ is a reality that lives, celebrates, and bears fruit.

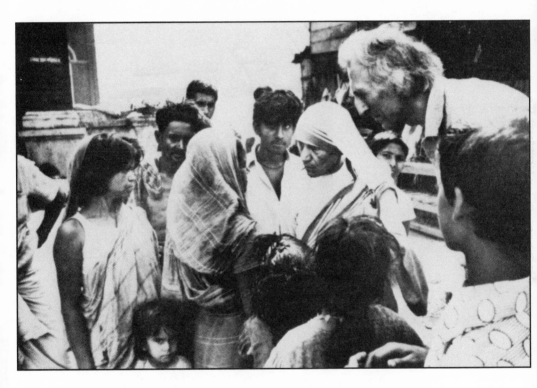

BIBLIOGRAPHY

Bill Clarke. *Un Pari pour la Joie*. Montreal: Ed. Bellarmin, 1975. 155 pages.

Jean Vanier. *Be Not Afraid*. Mahwah, N.J.: Paulist Press, 1975. 160 pages.

――――. *The Challenge of L'arche*. New York: Harper & Row, 1982. 286 pages.

————. *Followers of Jesus*. Dublin: Gill & Macmillan, n.d.

————. *I Meet Jesus: He Tells Me "I Love You"*. Mahwah, N.J.: Paulist Press, 1982. 208 pages.

————. *I Walk with Jesus*. Mahwah, N.J.: Paulist Press, 1986. 208 pages.

————. *Man and Woman He Made Them*. Mahwah, N.J.: Paulist Press, 1985.

————. *Tears of Silence*. Denville, N.J.: Dimension Books, n.d.

ABBREVIATIONS

AA   *Apostolicam actuositatem* (Decree on the apostolate of the laity). November 18, 1965.

AAS   *Acta Apostolicae Sedis* (Acts of the Holy See).

AG   *Ad gentes divinitus* (Decree on the Church's missionary activity). December 7, 1965.

AH   Saint Irenaeus. *Adversus haereses*.

DH   *Dignitatis humanae* (Declaration on religious liberty). December 7, 1965.

DS   H. Denzinger and A. Schonmetzer. *Enchiridion symbolorum definitionum et declarationum de rebus fidei et morum*. Barcelona-Freiburg-Rome, 1979.

DV   *Dei Verbum* (Dogmatic constitution on divine revelation). November 18, 1965.

EN   *Evangelii Nuntiandi* (Apostolic letter of Pope Paul VI on evangelization in the modern world). 1975.

FC   *Familiaris consortio* (Apostolic letter of Pope John Paul II on the role of the Christian family in the modern world). 1981.

GS   *Gaudium et spes* (The pastoral constitution on the Church in the modern world). December 7, 1965.

LE   *Laborem exercens* (Encyclical letter of John Paul II to commemorate the ninetieth anniversary of *Rerum novarum*). September 14, 1981.

LG   *Lumen Gentium* (Dogmatic constitution on the Church). November 21, 1964.

MC   *Marialis cultus* (Apostolic exhortation of Paul VI on the cult of the Blessed Virgin Mary). February 11, 1974.

MD   *Mediator Dei* (Encyclical letter of Pope Pius XII on the sacred liturgy). November 20, 1947.

NA   *Nostra aetate* (Declaration on the Church's relations with non-Christian religions). October 28, 1965.

OA   *Octogesima adveniens* (Apostolic letter of Paul VI on the eightieth anniversary of *Rerum novarum*). May 15, 1971.

OE   *Orientalium Ecclesiarum* (Decree on the Catholic Eastern Churches). November 21, 1964.

PC   *Perfectae caritatis* (Decree on the up-to-date renewal of religious life). October 28, 1965.

PD   Puebla Document. General Conference of Latin American Bishops. 1979.

PG   J. G. Migne, *Patrologia Cursus Completus*, Series Graeca.

PL   J. G. Migne. *Patrologia Cursus Completus*, Series Latina.

RH   *Redemptor Hominis* (Encyclical letter of John Paul II on the Redeemer of man). March 4, 1979.

SC   *Sacrosanctum concilium* (Constitution on the sacred liturgy). December 4, 1963.

UR   *Unitatis redintegratio* (Decree on ecumenism). November 21, 1964.